CHINA'S POWER GRAB
AND
EXPANDING CLAIMS

Projecting Influence & Control Throughout Asia

Rachel A. Winston, Ph.D.
&
Ishika Sachdeva

LIZARD PUBLISHING

Copyright © 2021 by Lizard Publishing

All rights reserved. No part of this book may be reproduced, stored, or transmitted by any means. In accordance with U.S. Copyright law, the scanning, uploading, and electronic sharing of any part of this book without the permission of the publisher constitutes unlawful piracy and theft of the author's intellectual property. Prior written permission must be obtained. Inquiries concerning the reproduction of any material from this book must be submitted to Lizard Publishing.

Lizard Publishing ®

7700 Irvine Center Drive, Suite 800

Irvine, CA 92618-3047

www.lizard-publishing.com

Our mental process is fueled by three tenets:
- Ignite the hunger to learn and the passion for making a difference
- Illuminate the expanse of knowledge by sharing cutting edge thinking
- Innovate to create a world that may only exist in our dreams

Maps and Illustrations by graphic designer, Abiyy Suryowibisono

Book design by Michelle Tahan and Obinna Chinemerem Ozuo

Typeface: Garamond

Book Website: southchinaseabook.com

First Edition: January 2021

Both authors are available for speaking events.

ISBN: 978-1946432087 (paperback), 978-1946432094 (hardback), 978-1946432100 (ebook)

LCCN: 2020917699

This book was published in the U.S.A. Lizard Publishing is a premium quality provider of educational reference, career guidance, and motivational publications/merchandise for global learners, educators, and stakeholders in education.

This book is dedicated to Malka Mirvis who never witnessed the realization of her dreams.

and

This book is also dedicated to Robert A. Helmer, Bobbie Werner-Hansen, Rinku Sachdeva, and Serge Sachdeva whose ceaseless support and undying devotion have made the creation of this incessant voyage of discovery a possibility.

Acknowledgments

"If I see so far, it is because I stand on the shoulders of giants."
– Isaac Newton

There is never enough room to acknowledge every person who contributed to an individual's perspective, assisted in the development of a person's knowledge base, or taught indelible lessons that last a lifetime. In this book, we gratefully acknowledge our family, friends, colleagues, and professors.

We would also like to thank our fellow students we have met along the way from whom we have learned from their perspective and wisdom.

Isaac Newton once said, "If I see so far, it is because I stand on the shoulders of giants." A few of those giants in our lives whose shoulders have lifted us higher and helped teach us invaluable lessons include: Bill Hayton, Dr. John E. Mearsheimer, Dr. John E. Roueche, Dr. David A. Waugh, Serge Sachdeva, Rinku Sachdeva, Michael Okaisabor, Julianne Alfe, Sameer Ghai, Abiyy Suryowibisono, Dr. Matthew Baum, Dr. Robert T. Whipple, Chenoa Craver, Dr. Janice Marshall, Dr. Linda Lebile, Dr. George Boggs, Dr. Juan Garcia, Dr. Patricia Levine, Dr. Annesa Cheek, Dr. Leslie Coward, Dr. David Hinds, Dr. Mia Leggett, Dr. Karla Canto, Dr. Melinda Lemke, Dr. Cat Jones, Dr. Dana Sendziol, Dr. Jeffrey Holmes, Dr. Kay McClenney, Dr. Norvell Northcutt, Dr. Robin Court, Dr. Maxwell McCombs, Shamlal and Janky Sachdeva, Usha and Padmesh Paul, Shivin Sachdeva, Ruby and Jugel Sachdeva, Pooja and Atul Ghai, Arti and Bikka Ghai, Mala Bakshi, Madhuri and Kunal Paul, Rupal Paul, Rhea Sachdeva, and Rebecca Smith.

Meet the Authors

Rachel A. Winston, Ph.D.

As a retired university professor, former Academic Senate President, Full-Time Faculty Member of the Year, elected statewide leader, and winner of the McFarland Literary Achievement Award, Dr. Winston continues to write and publish on key educational, societal, and international issues. She taught at UCLA, Chapman University, Embry Riddle Aeronautical University, Cal State Fullerton and holds graduate degrees from Harvard University, the University of Chicago, the University of Texas at Austin, George Washington University, Claremont Graduate University, Pepperdine University, Cal State Fullerton, and CSUDH.

Ishika Sachdeva

Ishika Sachdeva is a championship debater and public speaker who has channeled her passion for international issues to sharing insights with others in platforms such as Google Classroom. She has traveled around the world to seek out wisdom from scholars and laypeople. As a prospective student of political economy and international relations at the University of California, Berkeley, Ishika has committed her globally-connected journey to investigate topics, explore human rights, and educate in every capacity possible.

Foreword

"China's Power Grab and Expanding Claims" is the second in a series of serious glimpses into the heart of China - a heart that has hardened into the autocratic power of the Chinese Communist Party (CCP). As the authors contend, nothing happens in China without the sanction of the CCP and that includes the activities of the everyday lives of all who reside within the borders of China, including those who do business there. The implication is clear: do not cross swords with the CCP. You will lose. This book tells the story of the century - the unraveling of the world's progressive sanctuary for the human species. Heretofore untold in this clear and visual way are Beijing's unsettling implications, even for the near term. Easy to read, each point is made succinctly and clearly, inviting one to develop a clearer understanding of the probabilities for a hospitable future.

The first book in the series, "Raging Waters in the South China Sea", took a close look at developments in this vitally and increasingly important part of the world. In the South China Sea, honor for rules of conduct, such as they are, should be a matter of priority and morality - and should be mutually respected. This is not the case presently, and perhaps never was fully respected by many of the regional countries, each having a competitive interest in the wealth of the waters and the land beneath. However, as a newly powerful nation, China, with overwhelming resources both economically and militarily, dwarfs the capacities of its neighbors to wage war or to otherwise protect their lawful areas of jurisdiction. "Raging Waters" addresses the many givens and contradictions about relationships between nations of the South China Sea.

China's rapacious reach, as the authors inform in their new book, is far from being limited to the South China Sea. "China's Power Grab and Expanding Claims" expounds on Beijing's reach, encompassing Asia and, as such, impacting the entire globe as each state considers intra-national and extra-national strategic implications. This second book takes on China's aims for Asian dominance, regional hegemony, and infusion worldwide through its strategic and focused capture of sovereignty, be it a port, an island, an enclave, a military base, or other presence on the soil of another sovereign nation.

Beijing has taken a whole-of-world approach, as reported, with calculated intent to commit victims inside and outside of its states and 'autonomous regions' to capitulate. In some instances, as in the historical nationalities of China, it is an outright loss of identity and enslavement. In others, as in "development aid", the proof may be found in the fine print in the legal documents to which they often unwittingly agreed. Parading initially as a generous contribution to a nation's economic health and prosperity, the trap closes. Sadly, in some instances, bribery, corruption of leaders, and unrelenting insistence on repayment of development loans on time, and in full, lead to unbelievably disastrous consequences. In my experience, development aid, nation to nation, or loans through international financial institutions, rarely, if ever, implied or resulted in loss of assets, resources, or sovereignty. This awakening dilemma and more is the contribution Winston and Sachdeva make in their second book.

Dr. David Waugh, United Nations, Retired

Table of Contents

1. China's Brand of Global Diplomacy — 1

1. The Chinese Dream: Change in the World Order — 2
2. The Howl of the 'Wolf Warriors': Aggressive Twitter Strategy and Raging Battle with Words — 10
3. Salami Slicing with 'Chinese Characteristics': Inch-by-Inch, Stealthily Taking Control of the Planet — 22
4. Chasing Tigers and Flies While Hunting Down Foxes: The CCP's Scrutiny, Harassment, and Elimination — 28
5. The Fortune 500's Kowtow to China: Kneeling in Submission to China — 34
6. Nibbling Away: Gobbling Up Each Tasty Bite of Asia Around its Perimeter — 40

2. Propaganda, Control, and Digital Surveillance — 48

1. No Place to Hide with China's 5G Network: Tracking, Scanning, Lurking, Watching, Punishing — 50
2. China's Surveillance: China's Networks – Who Are They Watching? — 56
3. China's Global Digital Pandemic: Dual Power Digital Weaponry – The Great Firewall and The Great Cannon — 62
4. Social Credit Rating & China's Surveillance State: Dystopian Social Acceptance – Obey or Face Consequences — 66

3. Quest to Silence Devout Practitioners — 74

1. What is Religious Persecution, Harassment, Torture? Freedom of Religion Stripped as People are Imprisoned — 76
2. China's Church Demolitions: Remodeling Buildings, Cultures, and Social Norms — 82

3. The Persecution of the Falun Gong: China's 'Unprecedented Persecution' — 90

4. Cleansing of Oppositional Thought: CCP Institutes "Control Measures" Demanding Members to be "Unyielding Marxist Atheists" — 98

4. Imprisonment and Torture of the Uyghurs — 106

1. Disclaimer and Trigger Warning — 108
2. The Uyghurs of Xinjiang Province: Background on China's Muslim Minority Group — 110
3. Defining Moment: How the 2009 Uyghur Massacre Changed Xinjiang — 116
4. Uyghur Internment Camps: The Imprisonment of the Uyghurs in Concentration Camps — 120
5. The International Response to China's Persecution of the Uyghurs: Human Rights Watchdogs and Odd Silence from Muslim Countries — 130

5. Smothering the People's Voice in the Name of National Security — 138

1. One China, Two Systems: Hong Kong and the PRC's Special Administrative Region's Growth, Development, and Destruction — 140
2. Cracking Down on Hong Kong: Beijing's Book Persecution and Unpopular Extradition Bill — 146
3. The Silencing of Hong Kong Protesters: China's June 2020 National Security Law — 154
4. Future of Hong Kong: An Uncertain Path for Businesses, Newspapers, and Freedom-Loving People — 160
5. Linguistic Legacies: Mandarin, Cantonese, Taiwanese - Who Speaks What Language? — 168

6. Democracy's Crossroads: Fear of the Dragon Across the Strait — 174

1. Taiwan's Interconnected Relationship with China: Ownership, Politics, and Economic Ties to China — 168
2. Taiwan's Political Parties: Distinctions between the KMT and DPP — 182
3. 'One China' or an Independent Taiwan? Taipei and Beijing's Clashing Stance on Sovereignty — 188

	4. Taiwan Strait Crises: Historical Firestorms in Sino-Taiwanese Relations	194
	5. U.S.-Taiwan Relations: The Billion Dollar Arms Deal… With Consequences	200

7. Risk and Uncertainty for Sovereign Islands, Sea, and Air   206

1.	Conflict in the East China Sea: Overview of Japan and China's Disputed Senkaku/Diaoyu Islands	208
2.	Conflict Over the Senkaku Islands: Unresolved Disputes that Spilled into 2020	216
3.	Air Defense Identification Zones: East Asian State's Quest to Control Overflight	220
4.	The North Korea Question: Nuclear Powered, Unstable, and Demonstrated Willingness to Act on Impulse	226
5.	South Korean Relations with Allies and Unfriendlies: The Conflux of Coalitions and Instability in East Asia	232

8. Threats on the World's Highest Peaks   238

1.	Strained Sino-Indian Relations: How Border and Resource Conflicts Escalated Through COVID-19	240
2.	Waging a War Over Water: Introduction to China's Dam Construction and Hydrological Data Sharing	248
3.	Weaponizing Himalayan Water Information: China and India's 'Hydrological Data Sharing'	254
4.	China's Investments in Pakistan: A Pawn in the Broader South Asian Conflict	258
5.	China-Bhutan Territorial Conflict Over an Ecological Preserve: Dispute Over the Sakteng Wildlife Sanctuary	264
6.	The Destruction of Tibetan Land and Culture: Borders, Minerals, Water, and Genocide	268

9. China Encroaches on All Sides: Slowly Taking Regional Control   276

1.	States Caught in the Crossfires of Sino-Indian Disputes: Nepal, Bangladesh, and Myanmar	278
2.	More Money Down South: China's Financial and Political Relations with Cambodia, Laos, and Thailand	286
3.	China and Mongolia: Outer Mongolia's Independence and Inner Mongolia's Subjection	294

4. Mongolia's Knight in Shining Armor: China's Economic Aid to Outer Mongolia ... 300
  5. China's Crackdown on Inner Mongolia: Beijing's Policies to Remove Mongolian Culture ... 308
  6. China's BRI Connection in Central Asia: Kazakhstan, Kyrgyzstan, & Tajikistan ... 312
  7. Beijing Eyes Russian Territory: 21st Century Claims on Qing Dynasty Land ... 310

10. "Injustuce Anywhere is a Threat to Justice Everywhere." - Martin Luther King Jr. 326

  1. "Freedom is the Last, Best Hope of Earth." - Abraham Lincoln 328

11. Index 332

Acronyms and Terms

Acronyms and Terms	
3 Buckets of Oil	China's 'Big Three' oil corporations or "Three Buckets of Oil" - PetroChina, Sinopec, and CNOOC
5G	5th generation mobile network
60/40 Rule	Under Philippine law, Philippine government must own at least 60% of capital used in contracts involving natural resources. Furthermore, 60% of the profit must remain with the Philippine government.
99-Year Lease	This was the length of time Great Britain leased Hong Kong after the Opium Wars and the time China leased Hambantota Port in Sri Lanka when Sri Lanka struggled to pay its debt.
ADF	Australian Defense Force
ADIZ	Air Defense Identification Zone
AFP	Armed Forces of the Philippines
AIIB	Asian Infrastructure and Investment Bank
AMM	ASEAN Foreign Ministers' Meeting
Anarchy	The idea that the world lacks any supreme authority or sovereign. In an anarchic state, there is no hierarchically superior, coercive power that can resolve disputes, enforce law, or order the international system.
APEC	Asia-Pacific Economic Cooperation
ARF	ASEAN Regional Forum
ARIA	Asia Reassurance Initiative Act
ASEAN	Association of Southeast Asian Nations - (One Vision, One Identity, One Community) - Regional, intergovernmental association of ten Southeast Asia countries. The 10 member nations include: Brunei, Cambodia, Indonesia, Laos, Malaysia, Myanmar (Burma), the Philippines, Singapore, Thailand, and Vietnam.
ASEAN Plus Three	This cooperative group includes the 10 ASEAN states plus China, Japan, and the Republic of Korea
ASEAN Plus Six	These sixteen countries (the 10 ASEAN states plus Australia, China, India, Japan, South Korea, and New Zealand) form the Regional Comprehensive Economic Partnership.
BRI	Belt and Road Initiative

Acronyms and Terms

CBP	U.S. Customs and Border Protection
CCP	Chinese Communist Party
Century of Humiliation	The approximately one hundred years from 1842, with the Treaty of Nanjing, to October 1, 1949 when the People's Republic of China was formally established.
CGA	Coast Guard Administration
CMREC	China-Mongolia-Russia Economic Corridor
CNOOC	China National Offshore Oil Corporation (Chinese State-Owned Enterprise - SOE)
CNPC	China National Petroleum Corporation (Chinese State-Owned Enterprise - SOE)
CoC	Code of Conduct
COVID-19	The coronavirus COVID-19 pandemic that broke out in the fall of 2019 in Wuhan, China
CPEC	China-Pakistan Economic Corridor
CSIC	China Shipbuilding Industry Corporation (Chinese State-Owned Enterprise - SOE)
DoC	Declaration of the Conduct of Parties in the South China Sea
DPP	Democratic Progressive Party
DPJ	Democratic Party of Japan
EDCA	Enhanced Defense Cooperation Agreement - An agreement signed in 2014 between the U.S. and the Philippines with the goal of supporting U.S. Philippine relations and military cooperation. The EDCA was declared constitutional in 2016.
EEZ	Exclusive Economic Zone – The United Nations Convention on the Law of the Sea (UNCLOS) defines the region as the band extending 200 nautical miles off the shores of a coastal state in which that state has the jurisdiction over the exploration of natural resources and exploitation of marine resources in its adjacent continental shelf.
EU	European Union
Facemask Diplomacy	This initiative was China's effort to sell facemasks to countries worldwide during COVID-19.
FDI	Foreign Direct Investment
First Island Chain	A string of islands from lower Philippines up to the top of Japan that are a near-in region. China hopes to push the U.S. presence outside of this area.
Five Eyes Alliance	An intelligence sharing alliance between Australia, Canada, New Zealand, United Kingdom, and the United States founded in 1941.
FONOPs	Freedom of Navigation Operations
GDP	Gross Domestic Product
GONGOs	Government-Owned NGOs
GPEA	Greenpeace East Asia

Acronyms and Terms

'Gray Zone' Operations	Intense political, economic, informational, and military competition that is just short of war. China uses 'Gray Zone' tactics to "win without fighting" to further its maritime claims and alter the status quo without going to war.
Great Power	The ability of a sovereign state to exert its influence on a global scale.
GRINGOs	Government-Run or Government-Initiated NGOs
Hedging	The management of risk relationships between two opposing parties to protect security and sovereignty by diversifying commitments and simultaneously balancing and engaging. The term 'hedging' is increasingly found in the U.S. strategic discourse, particularly regarding China. The White House 2006 National Security Strategy document stated that the U.S. strategy "seeks to encourage China to make the right strategic choices for its people, while we hedge against other possibilities."
Hegemon	A political state having dominant influence or authority over others. States can have global or regional hegemony.
HYSY	Hiayangshiyou "Ocean Oil" - CNOOC deepwater oil platforms
ICC	International Criminal Court
ICE	U.S. Immigration and Customs Enforcement
ICJ	International Court of Justice
IDF	Indigenous Defense Fighter (Taiwanese Fighter Jet)
IMF	International Monetary Fund
IR	International Relations
IUU	Illegal, unreported, and unregulated fishing practices
JADIZ	Japanese Air Defense Identification Zone
JASDF	Japan Air Self Defense Force
JMSU	Joint Marine Seismic Undertaking – a collaboration between China, the Philippines, and Vietnam to survey for hydrocarbon resources
KADIZ	(South) Korea Air Defense Identification Zone
KIG	Kalayaan Island Group
KMT	Kuomintang
Kowtow	Kneel and touch the ground with the forehead in worship or submission as part of Chinese custom
LAC	Line of Actual Control
LDP	Liberal Democratic Party (Japan)
LNG	Liquefied Natural Gas
Malacanang	The Philippine presidential palace is a high governmental meeting location and residence of the Philippine president. It is incorporated into written text and speeches in the same way as the White House is in the U.S.
Maglev	Magnetic Levitation - A train system that operates using magnets that allow the train to levitate off the track, reducing friction.
MFA (MOFA)	Philippine Ministry of Foreign Affairs

Acronyms and Terms

MIC2025	Made in China 2025
MOU	Memorandum of Understanding
MPA	Marine Protected Area
NATO	North Atlantic Treaty Organization
NBA	National Basketball Association
NGO	Non-Governmental Organization
Nine-Dash Line	China bases its determination of rights to the South China Sea based upon a nine-dash line drawn on a map in 1947. At times, this demarcated map had ten and eleven dashes in a roughly U shape. The boundaries of what they term their 'historic claim' are vague, but roughly encompass about ninety percent of the South China Sea. The ICJ determination in *Philippines v. China* was that, based upon UNCLOS, China has 'no basis' for their claim.
NM	Nautical Miles
NOC	National oil companies
NSC	National Security Council
OBOR	One Belt, One Road
OECD	Organization for Economic Cooperation and Development
ONGC	Indian Oil and Natural Gas Corporation (Indian State-Owned Enterprise - SOE)
ONI	Office of Naval Intelligence
OPEC	Organization of Petroleum Exporting Countries
PAP	Singapore's People's Action Party
Paracel Islands	A disputed archipelago with 130 coral islands and reefs in the South China Sea that is occupied by China and claimed by Taiwan and Vietnam inhabiting a population of over 1,000. They are also called Xisha Islands and Hoang Sa Archipelago.
PCA	Permanent Court of Arbitration
PetroVietnam	Vietnam Oil and Gas Corporation (Vietnamese State-Owned Enterprise - SOE)
PH	The Philippines
PLA	People's Liberation Army (China)
PLAAF	People's Liberation Army Air Force (China)
PLAN	People's Liberation Army – Navy (China)
PLANAF	People's Liberation Army Navy Air Force (China)
PPE	Personal Protective Equipment
R2P	Responsibility to Protect
RCEP	Regional Comprehensive Economic Partnership
RIMPAC	Rim of the Pacific

Acronyms and Terms

RMB	Renminbi (Chinese currency)
Salami Tactics (Salami Slicing)	A process of cutting away at the opposition by utilizing threats and alliances and politically dominating a landscape by slicing the opponent's power piece by piece.
SAR	Special Administrative Region
SCS	South China Sea
Second Island Chain	An extended region into the Pacific Ocean out to Guam from Asia.
Sinopec	China Petroleum & Chemical Corporation (Chinese State-Owned Enterprise - SOE)
SME	Small and Medium-sized Enterprises
SOE	State-Owned Enterprise
SONA	State of the Nation Address
THAAD	Theater High-Altitude Area Defense
Sorties	An air sortie is a military mission where aircraft are sent out on a combat mission.
TPP	Trans-Pacific Partnership
Twitter Fingers	An individual who uses social media rapidly and rabidly, retweeting incessantly.
UN	United Nations
UNCLOS	United Nations Convention on the Law of the Sea – This is an international treaty that was signed in 1982 and came into force in 1994 as an agreement that defines the rights and responsibilities of the world's oceans and seas. As of 2019, 168 parties have joined.
UNDP	United Nations Development Program
USAID	United States Agency for International Development
USD	United States Dollar
VAT	Value-Added Tax
VCP	Vietnamese Communist Party
VFA	Visiting Forces Agreement –This agreement provides guidelines for the conduct and protection of American troops that pass through or work in Philippine territory and the Philippine military who pass through or work in the U.S. This agreement was signed by the U.S. and Philippines in 1998. This was the first military agreement since the U.S. closed its military bases in Subic Bay and Clark Air Base in 1992. This agreement led to the institution of Balikatan (shoulder-to-shoulder) military training exercises, closer coordination on counterterrorism, and security measures.
VPN	Virtual Private Network
Wolf Warrior Diplomacy	The newly introduced, aggressive method of diplomacy used by China in 2020 and named after Chinese blockbuster action films.
WPS	West Philippine Sea
WTO	World Trade Organization

	Acronyms and Terms
WWF	World Wide Fund for Nature, previously known as World Wildlife Fund when founded in 1961.
XUAR	Xinjiang Uyghur Autonomous Region
ZOPFAN	Zone of Peace, Freedom and Neutrality – Declaration signed in 1971 by the foreign ministers of the ASEAN member states.
ZTE	Zhong Xing Telecommunications – a Chinese communications and technology corporation.

Part 1

China's Brand of Global Diplomacy

The CCP's Wolf Warrior Diplomacy

From the outset, this text distinguishes the Chinese Communist Party's (CCP) actions, propaganda, torture, and social control from the vast majority of respectful and respectable Chinese people living in China and abroad. In no way are the contents in this book a negative reflection of our peace-loving, thoughtful, and generous Chinese neighbors and friends. However, there is a brutal, totalitarian faction of the CCP that is bent on dominating the world using means that are not 'win-win' in spirit.

China's propaganda sources describe its 'peaceful rise', though the rise has not been equitable nor peaceful. Rather, China's ascent is provocative, coercive, and threatening. The CCP'S goal is to control the Chinese people first and then take over bits of the rest of the world slice by slice. This imagery clarifies the origin of the term 'salami-slicing'.

Another word used often in this book is 'wolf warrior'. This term stems from the all-time highest grossing Chinese state propaganda film depicting the Chinese nationalistic belief that, "Anyone who offends China, no matter how remote, must be exterminated."[1] Elite Chinese fighters explain in the film, "the Americans are good for nothing."[2] CNN calls it China's "new brand of diplomacy", hence the term "Wolf Warrior Diplomacy".[3] The aggressive style, ferocious debate tactics, and social media actions are suitable to its fierce name.

Leaders around the world have taken notice, but are silenced and threatened by arm-twisting clauses in big money financial contracts. As China increasingly becomes the world's moneylender, Beijing wields great control in calling the shots and making decisions for state leaders who comply with Xi Jinping's campaign, effectively manipulating countries worldwide. Particularly, with the 2020 coronavirus pandemic and countries needing money, the tradeoff seems reasonable for individual states who are handsomely rewarded for abiding by the CCP's demands. The "Century of Humiliation" has ended. China's rise will foretell the future – your future.

---

1 Anthony Kuhn, "Chinese Blockbuster 'Wolf Warrior II' Mixes Jingoism With Hollywood Heroism," *NPR*, August 10, 2017, https://www.npr.org/2017/08/10/542663769/chinese-blockbuster-wolf-warrior-ii-mixes-jingoism-with-hollywood-heroism

2 Helen Raleigh, "Wolf Warrior II Tells Us a Lot about China," *National Review*, July 20, 2019, https://www.nationalreview.com/2019/07/wolf-warrior-ii-tells-us-a-lot-about-china/

3 Ben Westcott and Steven Jiang, "China is Embracing a New Brand of Foreign Policy. Here's What Wolf Warrior Diplomacy Means," *CNN*, May 29, 2020, https://www.cnn.com/2020/05/28/asia/china-wolf-warrior-diplomacy-intl-hnk/index.html

Chapter 1
The Chinese Dream
Change in the World Order

China's Phenomenal Growth

China's economic, social, and military transformation has been nothing less than phenomenal. For forty years, the country's growth has raised 800 million of its citizens out of poverty through rapid industrialization and manufacturing in a range of industry sectors.[1] At one point in China's history, hundreds of millions lived on central communes with little food, barely surviving in harsh living and working conditions.[2] Over the past four decades, China has transitioned from a predominantly agrarian economy to a global market distributor,[3] lifting many to a comparatively high standard of living as people moved off the farmlands and into cities. Urban areas grew increasingly larger; six of China's cities are in the top twenty-five worldwide,[4] more than any other country. Foreign direct investment (FDI) from hundreds of multinational corporations helped to infuse cash, resources, and human capital into the country. While this extraordinary growth has uplifted the mass of citizenry within China, numerous deleterious social and economic costs have been born by countries worldwide. These direct and indirect costs are likely to increase as explained in subsequent chapters.

Change in the World Order

There has been a consistent assumption that welcoming a rising power would not change life as we know it. Similarly, the global economy, production, trade, and interactions would remain the same. In fact, there were great hopes that China might enter the World Trade Organization and become a fair and cooperative partner by integrating into the liberal economic system of the open market. However, that did not happen. China's subsidy system of bolstering companies with state money, free raw materials, and cheap labor necessarily meant that other companies across the planet that pay significant fixed costs could not compete.

To simplify this, if your organization pays an employee $20 per hour for a forty-hour week, they are paying $800 per week or $3,200 per month. If a Chinese company pays an employee $200 per month, or $0 if they live in a concentration camp, the difference is $3,000, not to mention American companies with U.S. employees pay additional costs for benefits. This is why products in many developed countries cost more. China's State-Owned Enterprise (SOE) model is a driving force in this new dynamic, and this has resulted in unfair marketplace competition.

---

1 Press Trust of India, "China Lifting 800 Million People out of Poverty is Historic: World Bank," *Business Standard*, Updated October 13, 2017, https://www.business-standard.com/article/international/china-lifting-800-million-people-out-of-poverty-is-historic-world-bank-117101300027_1.html

2 Facts and Details, "Communes, Land Reform and Collectivism in China," *Facts and Details*, Updated October 2016, http://factsanddetails.com/china/cat2/sub5/item1079.html

3 Yi Wen and Scott Wolla, "China's Rapid Economic Rise: A New Application of an Old Recipe," *Social Education 81*, no. 2 (2017): 93-97, https://www.socialstudies.org/system/files/publications/articles/81021793_0.pdf

4 World Population Review, "World City Populations 2020," *World Population Review*, https://worldpopulationreview.com/world-cities

According to the U.S. Congressional Research Service,

The methods the Chinese government plans to use to achieve its goals have raised concerns among U.S. firms and policymakers because they appear to involve large subsidies, protection of domestic industries, directed policies to purchase technology and IPR from abroad, increased pressure on foreign firms to transfer technology in order to do business in China, and what appears to be a goal of deliberately reducing foreign participation in China's markets.[5]

China's Extended Territorial Claims
Twenty Countries Where China Claims Historic Rights

- BHUTAN
- BRUNEI
- CAMBODIA
- INDIA
- INDONESIA
- JAPAN
- KAZAKHSTAN
- KYRGYZSTAN
- MALAYSIA
- MONGOLIA
- NEPAL
- NORTH KOREA
- PHILIPPINES
- RUSSIA
- SINGAPORE
- SOUTH KOREA
- TAIWAN
- TAJIKISTAN
- TIBET
- VIETNAM

Intellectual Property

Countries, like Germany and France, have become the victims of international property theft. A 2020 report by the European Commission listed China as Priority 1 "for the EU because of the scale and persistence of problems in the area of IPR protection and enforcement."[6]

---

5   Congressional Research Service, "China's Economic Rise: History, Trends, Challenges, and Implications for the United States," *Congressional Research Service*, June 25, 2019, https://fas.org/sgp/crs/row/RL33534.pdf

6   European Commission, "Commission Staff Working Document," *European Commission*, January 8, 2020, https://trade.ec.europa.eu/doclib/docs/2020/january/tradoc_158561.pdf

China sought German and French intellectual property through a technology exchange for a contract to construct its high-speed train.[7] When the German company, Siemens, and French company, Alstom, went into China to help build Beijing's magnetic levitation transportation (maglev), they made a significant amount of money.[8] Enthusiastic about working with China, other German and French companies followed suit. However, what started as a joint venture quickly became alarming as companies lost billions of dollars to China's adapted 'inventions'.[9]

The German company, Hochköppler,[10] wanting to manufacture components, was asked by a Chinese state-owned enterprise (SOE) to send photographs and specifications. The company produced the goods as required. Mastering the technology, the Chinese company vowed to produce trains at one-third of the cost[11] with the encouragement of China's State Council "to learn and absorb foreign advanced technologies while making further innovations."[12] What is more alarming is that the Chinese company, in turn, sold those products to the businesses the German company originally supplied, along with the same photographs, descriptions, and materials.[13] China proudly returned to Germany, presenting copy-cat products that utilized the German company's intellectual property and sold them to the Deutsche Bahn, Germany's railway.[14] The copy-cat phenomenon is so popular in China that Beijing exported its citizens to work for high-tech German companies to take their intellectual property.[15]

There are thousands of similar cases involving China that affect industries around the world. In addition, China's Thousand Talents Program pays high salaries to attract global workers who can bring patent information and product knowledge back to China.[16] One in

---

7   DW Staff, "German High-Speed Rail Technology Soon to be Made in China?" *DW*, August 1, 2006, https://www.dw.com/en/german-high-speed-rail-technology-soon-to-be-made-in-china/a-2115909

8   David Fickling, "Alstom and Siemens Show How Not to Deal With China," *Bloomberg*, February 6, 2019, https://www.bloomberg.com/opinion/articles/2019-02-06/alstom-and-siemens-show-how-not-to-deal-with-china-and-vestager

9   Norihiko Shirouzu, "Train Makers Rail Against China's High-Speed Designs," *The Wall Street Journal*, November 17, 2010, https://www.wsj.com/articles/SB10001424052748704814204575507353221141616

10 Mathias Bolinger, "A Flawed Sino-German Business Connection," *DW*, May 22, 2006, https://www.dw.com/en/a-flawed-sino-german-business-connection/a-2028252

11 DW Staff, "China Masters German Train Technology, Will Cut Costs," *DW*, April 28, 2006, https://www.dw.com/en/china-masters-german-train-technology-will-cut-costs/a-1982476

12 Miao Qing, "Shanghai Maglev Gets Official Approval," *China Daily*, April 27, 2006, http://www.chinadaily.com.cn/bizchina/2006-04/27/content_578061.htm

13 Stephen Evans, "German Firms Fear China Technology Theft," *BBC*, February 8, 2011, https://www.bbc.com/news/12382747

14 Frank Sieren, "Sieren's China: A Slap in the Face for Siemens," *DW*, May 28, 2015, https://www.dw.com/en/sierens-china-a-slap-in-the-face-for-siemens/a-18480773

15 Patricia Weiss and Ludwig Burger, "Exclusive: German Prosecutors Charge Chinese-Born Engineer in Industrial Espionage Case," *Reuters*, November 15, 2018, https://www.reuters.com/article/us-germany-chemicals-espionage-exclusive/exclusive-german-prosecutors-charge-chinese-born-engineer-in-industrial-espionage-case-idUSKCN1NK0UT

16 Ellen Barry and Gina Kolata, "China's Lavish Funds Lured US Scientists What Did it Get in Return," *The New York Times*, February 6, 2020, https://www.nytimes.com/2020/02/06/us/chinas-lavish-funds-lured-us-scientists-what-did-it-get-in-return.html

five companies state that China stole their intellectual property.[17] Furthermore, "more than 80% of the seizures of counterfeit and pirated goods by EU customs authorities originate from China and Hong Kong."[18]

A Different Set of Premises and Logic

The presumption of pre-eminence for any country is dangerous since history has shown that states, peoples, and belief systems are vastly different in form and composition from century to century. If China continues to grow economically, militarily, and politically on the backs of countries throughout the world, the 21st century will mark the end of liberalism, freedom, market economies, as well as possibly any form of political influence of the West.

The British Empire was once vast, spanning most continents. Those glory years are still portrayed in history books with awe. Germany's rise was astonishing in the 1940s as was that of Japan. Afterward, Russia's influence was similarly ominous and growing in the 1940s,

---

17 Eric Rosenbaum, "1 in 5 Corporations Say China Has Stolen Their IP Within the Last Year: *CNBC* CFO Survey," *CNBC*, March 1, 2019, https://www.cnbc.com/2019/02/28/1-in-5-companies-say-china-stole-their-ip-within-the-last-year-cnbc.html

18 European Commission, "Commission Staff Working Document," *European Commission*, January 8, 2020, https://trade.ec.europa.eu/doclib/docs/2020/january/tradoc_158561.pdf

50s, 60s, and 70s. Yet, the U.S. emerged after World War II as a powerful state with a global influence in the world's institutions.

Meanwhile, in 1949, when the People's Republic of China (PRC) was founded, China was a poor, underdeveloped country.[19] Famine, floods, and disease were widespread. Periods during Chairman Mao Zedong's infamous reign actually decreased economic output,[20] though its rise began to take shape when Deng Xiaoping led the country. Year after year afterward, China's gross domestic product (GDP) grew over a span of forty years, averaging 9.5 percent with what the World Bank terms, "the fastest sustained expansion by a major economy in history."[21]

Confidence and nationalism have driven China toward achieving its "Made in China 2025" goals.[22] Ten key sectors targeted for global dominance include:

1. Next-generation information technology
2. High-end numerical control machinery and robotics
3. Aerospace and aviation equipment
4. Maritime engineering equipment and high-tech maritime vessel manufacturing
5. Advanced rail equipment
6. Energy-saving and new energy vehicles
7. Electrical equipment
8. Agricultural machinery and equipment
9. New materials
10. Biopharmaceuticals and high-performance medical devices

In and of themselves, China's goals are noble, though their methods of accomplishing these goals are of grave concern. All countries should have strategic plans to help grow their economy. However, China has implemented these plans and executed them with slave labor,[23] millions of whom are unpaid.[24] Some of the most popular brands around the globe

---

19 Embassy of the People's Republic of China in the Syrian Arab Republic, "China's Socio-Economic Achievements During the Past 60 Years," *Embassy of the People's Republic of China in the Syrian Arab Republic*, October 27, 2009, http://sy.chineseembassy.org/eng/xwfb/t622842.htm

20 U.S. Library of Congress, "The Cultural Revolution, 1966-76," *U.S. Library of Congress*, Accessed on July 31, 2020 from http://countrystudies.us/china/90.htm

21 Wade M. Morrison, "China's Economic Rise: History, Trends, Challenges, and Implications for the United States," *U.S. Congressional Research Service*, June 25, 2020, https://www.everycrsreport.com/files/20190625_RL33534_088c5467dd11365dd4ab5f72133db289fa10030f.pdf

22 Jost Wubbeke, Mirjam Meissner, Max J Zenglein,, Jacqueline Ives, & Bjorn Conrad, "Made in China 2025: The Making of a High-Tech Superpower and Consequences for Industrial Countries," *Metrics Papers on China*, December, 2016, https://assets.documentcloud.org/documents/3864881/Made-in-China-Paper.pdf

23 Peter Bengsten, "China's Forced Labor Problem," *The Diplomat*, March, 2018, https://thediplomat.com/2018/03/chinas-forced-labor-problem/

24 End Slavery Now, "While the Scope is Unclear, at Least a Handful of Chinese Factories Use Forced Labor Comprised of Religious and Ethnic Minorities," *End Slavery Now*, n.d., http://www.endslaverynow.org/act/action-library/learn-about-forced-labor-in-china

use this slave labor[25] to keep prices low and/or increase profits.

Since China derives numerous innovations by taking the intellectual property of companies and individuals across the globe, China will continue to have a competitive advantage in the marketplace. This theft is compounded by subsidies given to energy, financial, and manufacturing industries that decrease their cost of goods sold.[26] Europe reports similar consequences.[27] A German policy report explains that there is a, "distortion of markets and prices through state intervention in the economy,"[28] though they also state, "China is of great importance for German industry. Family businesses, SMEs and listed companies have benefited greatly from China's enormous economic rise and continue to do so today." This conundrum has put states and companies in a dilemma since China's demand is enormous. Access to China's vast marketplace significantly benefits foreign countries and companies that want to sell to Chinese customers. However, the unrecognized, underlying costs are likely to drastically change our present day way of life. As China takes incremental, but increasingly substantial, positions in the international arena, taking intellectual property, and exporting its surveillance-state, inevitable consequences are likely to threaten the world economy.

Technology and intellectual property aside, the social implications are the most alarming. The following chapters will describe how China's intellectual property theft, global manufacturing center creation, non-transparent economic boom, Belt and Road proposition, and inundation of manufactured propaganda could lead to mass surveillance, coerced obedience to the CCP, loss of liberty, an Orwellian social credit system, and normalization of concentration camp labor.

What's at Stake?

First, the CCP is working relentlessly to subject people everywhere to its collective authority and socialist values thereby threatening the West's liberal institutions, cultures, and freedoms. This transition, should it be successful, will be very difficult for those who value freedom and liberty, and will end badly for individuals and enterprises who do not align with the aims of China's leadership.

Second, in a world where intellectual property is not rigorously protected, everyone can share ideas, copy them, and produce new and better replicas, as is occurring is occurring in China. However, if we do not want the state to own our thoughts and creations, then this new world order is, at best, highly problematic.

---

25 Julian Kossoff, "'Virtually the Entire Apparel Industry' — From Gap to H&M to Adidas — Is Profiting From Forced Uighur Labor, Activists Say," *Business Insider*, July 23, 2020, https://www.businessinsider.com/uighur-forced-labor-global-brands-profited-activists-letter-2020-7

26 Capital Trade Incorporated, "An Assessment of China's Subsidies to Strategic and Heavyweight Industries," *Capital Trade Incorporated*, n.d. https://www.uscc.gov/sites/default/files/Research/AnAssessmentofChina%27sSubsidiestoStrategicandHeavyweightIndustries.pdf

27 Federation of German Industries (BDI), "Partner and Systemic Competitor – How Do We Deal with China's State-Controlled Economy?," *Federation of German Industries (BDI)*, English translation, 2019, https://english.bdi.eu/publication/news/china-partner-and-systemic-competitor/

28 Ibid.

Third, social credit obedience, lack of transparency, and propaganda for the good of the social order is part of Beijing's 'socialism with Chinese characteristics' strategy. This outcome can be the new world order or not, depending on our commitment to defend the liberal democratic world order.

Chapter 2

The Howl of the 'Wolf Warriors'

Aggressive Twitter Strategy and Raging Battle with Words

Introduction

Wolf Warrior **is a modernized term in the Chinese lexicon** that has stirred and emboldened the Chinese people. The concept holds a powerful place in 2020's society, signifying both China's aggressive stance on the world stage and their rabid control of the global media narrative.

The People's Liberation Army (PLA) prepares and intensively trains special operations forces. Similarities exist between China's Snow Wolf Commando Unit (SWCU) warriors previously led by Qu Liangfeng and the term 'Wolf Warrior', which may have been the inspiration for the film's name. This elite force, known for its tenacity, was deployed on the most difficult missions including hostage rescues, counterterrorism, and dangerous situations.[1] Executing the most complex tasks, this elite fighting unit focuses on simulating the maneuvers of foreign countries, militaries, and mercenaries to defend China's interests abroad. The bravery and honor exhibited by members of this exceptionally-trained PLA unit has sparked excitement in a generation of citizens and diplomats.

President Xi Jinping widely and unapologetically promotes nationalism, loyalty, and patriotism along with the Chinese Dream of becoming the world's economic and military powerhouse. He encourages his citizens to rise to the challenge, achieve success, and combat dissent. In turn, he has poured resources into his Belt and Road Initiative, military enhancements, and technology infrastructure.

Sparked by respect and inspired by movies portraying Wolf Warrior heroism, China's netizens have come to the foreground to do their part, spawning a new age of Internet celebrities. One Wolf Warrior artist, Wuheqilin, who portrayed an Australian soldier with a bloodied knife on an Afghan child, has more than a million followers.[2] Motivated by patriotism, the devoted masses have come to the rescue to combat media information sources or individuals who speak or write in a way that is contrary to the Chinese Communist Party (CCP) message.

Wielding social media like a powerful sword, the Internet has gained prominence in its 'fight for China'. During 2020, China's Wolf Warriors rose to prominence, impacting foreign relations globally and promoting leaders such as Chinese Foreign Ministry Spokesman, Zhao Lijian, to new heights.[3] According to Australia's Peter Jennings, "China's ambitions will make 2021 the year of the wolf warrior."[4]

---

1 Tang Yuankai, "Beijing's Answer to Bond," *Beijing Review*, January 17, 2008, http://www.bjreview.com.cn/print/txt/2008-01/13/content_95925.htm

2 Ryan Woo, "'Wolf Warrior' Artist Turns New Chapter in Chinese Propaganda Artwork," *Reuters*, December 2, 2020 https://www.reuters.com/article/us-australia-china-image-artist/wolf-warrior-artist-turns-new-chapter-in-chinese-propaganda-artwork-idUSKBN28C1CR

3 Bloomberg News, "Welcome to Wolf-Warrior Diplomacy," *Bloomberg*, December 3, 2020, https://www.bloomberg.com/news/newsletters/2020-12-04/welcome-to-wolf-warrior-diplomacy

4 Peter Jennings, "China's Ambitions Will Make 2021 the Year of the Wolf Warrior at the Door," *The Australian*, December 23, 2020, https://www.theaustralian.com.au/commentary/chinas-ambitions-will-make-2021-the-year-of-the-wolf-warrior-at-the-door/news-story/7d5f2c498f81c2dbbe51e6867443575c

Wolf Warrior Propaganda

'Wolf Warriors' intentionally strike with widespread bombardments on news sites and social media that support China's viewpoints with posts, articles, reports, and political statements. China's domestic and international communication, diplomacy, cooperation, and transparency are championed by the CCP's growing 'Wolf Warrior' movement.

Through widely promoted propaganda, Beijing reiterates its rallying cry to its people, demonstrating to the rest of the world that China is a rising force while cautioning governments to heed their warning to 'tread carefully'. Beijing has warned the world not to speak negatively or there will be consequences. One of those warnings has been issued through its new weapon - a powerful, aggressive cyber-crusade.

The Century of Humiliation is over!

'Wolf Warriors' figuratively wave China's flag proudly throughout its domestic, diplomatic, and global agenda. 'Wolf Warrior' diplomacy is aggressive and swift, using combative language that forcefully denounces any criticism of China. Since Twitter is banned in China, it is ironic that contentious tweets are one of the harshest weapons unsheathed.

This movement has been consistently molded and permanently chiseled into the minds of the Chinese people through their CCTV propaganda and devotion to nationalism. China's remarkable economic rise has fueled this passionate stance. Moreover, the People's Liberation Army's military dominance is evident in marching across its territories and sailing across its regional seas to project China's power after a century of war, theft, betrayal, destruction, shame, and loss. The concept of 'Wolf Warrior' diplomacy is a product of patriotism. To comprehend how the 'Wolf Warrior' impacts China's relations with the rest of the world, it is necessary to understand the brand of nationalism that forms the foundation for deploying these militant social media warriors.

'Wolf Warrior' Narrative in Wolf Warrior 2

As a reflection of cultural pride and nationalism, the term 'Wolf Warrior' stems from the heroic 2017 Chinese film, *Wolf Warrior 2*, an action-packed patriotic drama. In order to promote Beijing's ideals, China sought to expand its soft power globally by demonstrating its strength through visual media. *Wolf Warrior 2* was credited with soft power success[5] when it became China's highest grossing action film of all time.[6]

The Economist reviewed elemental scenes from the Chinese movie that have been assimilated into China's actions and motives in recent foreign policy interactions. They note that the film's protagonist, Leng Feng, portrays China as a fearless, dauntless, and

---

5   Dongyao Nie, "Patriotic Films Win Soft Power for Chinese Government," *Pacific Council on International Policy*, October 11, 2018, https://www.pacificcouncil.org/newsroom/patriotic-films-win-soft-power-chinese-government

6   Viola Zhou, "Patriotic Action Movie Wolf Warrior 2 Tops China's Box Office for 2017 but Foreign Films Gain Ground," *South China Morning Post*, January 1, 2018, https://www.scmp.com/news/china/economy/article/2126366/chinas-box-office-hits-us86-billion-2017-boosted-service-fees

Wolf Warrior Attack

indefatigable nation through Leng's heroic actions.[7] Leng Feng is a veteran member of China's People's Liberation Army (PLA) special forces.[8] The cinematically portrayed mighty China is formidable as an unstoppable force the rest of the world dare not antagonize.

The movie portrays a sudden coup of well-armed fighters mercilessly shooting defenseless everyday Africans and Chinese workers in town. After hundreds are murdered, Leng Feng whisks away two of his African friends to the Chinese embassy.

Later, after an attack by African mercenaries, a factory filled with both Chinese and African employees gathered. The Chinese factory owner called to his African friends, "Everyone here is my employee. I'm taking them all with me." Leng Feng follows, displaying a spirit of Chinese-African unity, "Everyone here leaves together."

Shortly afterward, the factory was surrounded in a brutal attack by African mercenaries led by the American antagonist. In another scene, African mercenaries burst into the factory compound heavily armed and powered by tanks. Leng Feng, armed with a homemade crossbow saves the day. Helped by the Chinese factory owner and the Chinese factory manager, they defend the employees who huddled in an underground shelter.

---

7   The Economist, "China's "Wolf Warrior" Diplomacy Gamble," *The Economist,* May 28, 2020, https://www.economist.com/china/2020/05/28/chinas-wolf-warrior-diplomacy-gamble

8   Evan Osnos, "Making China Great Again," *The New Yorker*, January 1, 2018, https://www.newyorker.com/magazine/2018/01/08/making-china-great-again

Nearby Chinese ships finally save the day. As American ships flee the African coast, the People's Liberation Army (PLA) head straight into the pandemic-stricken warzone. While the U.S. cowardly departs, China valiantly arrives at the battle zones to save the Chinese and African refugees.

In one climactic scene, Leng's vengeful, American adversary looks at him disdainfully and says, "People like you will always be inferior to people like me." Immediately, Leng Feng frees himself, pounces on him, and punches him to death. He denounces his American enemy rival as Chinese missiles wipe out another wave of oncoming mercenary tanks. Later, Leng enters the warzone and waves a Chinese flag high in the air as he leads throngs of people to safety. As the battle scene pacifies with Leng's presence, astonished commanders shout, "Hold your fire! It's the Chinese!"[9]

The Film's Tagline:

"Though far away, anyone who affronts China will pay."[10]

Thus, Leng triumphs, extinguishing the futile idea that Americans are more powerful than the Chinese. While emphasizing that Americans are evil and disgusting, the movie emblazons the vivid image that the Chinese are heroes. In a final comment, the movie caption says, "To the citizens of the People's Republic of China: When you find yourself in danger in a foreign country, never give up hope. China's strength will always support you."

The story shows that China's bravery is highly regarded by nations around the world who desperately need protection from the Americans. With *Rambo*-style heroics and Jackie Chan moves, the amiable Leng Feng overcomes any challenge. Moreover, China is depicted as impressively prepared and capable of overcoming any obstacle merely with its well-equipped manpower.

Despite the integration of *Wolf Warrior 2* into China's modern philosophy, concerns have bubbled to the surface regarding China's peaceful and magnanimous diplomacy. In attempting to spread goodwill around the world, the portrayal in this harsher characterization undermines this message. Thus, critics have questioned that thematic elements have been excluded from China's benevolent international stance and quest to reclaim a central role in the world.[11] The 'Wolf Warrior' depiction of conquest is designed to amplify the confidence and pride of the Chinese people.

However, *The Economist* also suggests that "the film is strikingly respectful of international law." After Leng Feng shares cell phone video footage of the bloody battle scenes to the Chinese ship off the coast, China's People's Liberation Army Navy (PLAN) contact the

---

9   The Economist, "China's "Wolf Warrior" Diplomacy Gamble," *The Economist*, May 28, 2020, https://www.economist.com/china/2020/05/28/chinas-wolf-warrior-diplomacy-gamble

10 Prabhash K. Dutta, "Wolf Warrior Diplomacy: The Chinese Game of Covid-19 Cover-Up," *India Today*, December 3, 2020, https://www.indiatoday.in/news-analysis/story/wolf-warrior-diplomacy-the-chinese-game-of-covid-19-cover-up-1746283-2020-12-03

11 Nick Schifrin and Katrina Yu, "How President Xi Jinping is Transforming China at Home and Abroad," *Pulitzer Center,* September 27, 2019, https://pulitzercenter.org/reporting/how-president-xi-jinping-transforming-china-home-and-abroad

United Nations for approval to launch a missile attack. A Chinese radio operator awaits the ambassador's approval, announcing, "Sir we have received authorization from the United Nations!"[12] The movie presents China's cooperation with other nations and reverence for the international community, although in actuality, Beijing's provocations with other countries have amounted to contentious acts, aggressive tactics, and violations of international laws.[13]

Nevertheless, as explained by Chinese media outlet, *Xinhua*, *Wolf Warrior 2* stimulates Chinese patriotism.[14] Proud and respectful Chinese citizens revere this movie, seeking to assimilate its tenets of leadership, authority, and power shown in this cinematically-depicted representation of China through 'Wolf Warrior diplomacy' and 'Wolf Warriors' in the media.

'Wolf Warrior Diplomacy'

'Wolf Warrior diplomacy' refers to China's rising assertiveness in conveying its diplomatic agenda, primarily being executed through Twitter posts. 'Wolf Warrior diplomats', as proponents and executors of China's new boldness, emerged on the world stage in 2020 and have used fierce 'Twitter fingers'[15] ever since. This army of 'diplomats' express their disapproval of disparaging comments toward China, through threats and condemnations reminding leaders and citizens of other nations that they should not interfere with China's goals.[16]

The Hong Kong Free Press identifies three factors that have motivated China's assertiveness: "Xi Jinping's foreign policy ambitions; new incentives for assertiveness; and a generational shift at the Ministry of Foreign Affairs (FOMA)."[17] When asked about 'Wolf Warrior diplomacy', Chinese foreign minister Wang Yi said that China's diplomats "never pick a fight or bully others, but we have principles and guts." He added, "We will push back against any deliberate insult to resolutely defend our national honour and dignity."[18]

The coronavirus pandemic created challenges for China. As China attempted to cover up the virus and deflect blame to other countries, its 'Wolf Warriors' went en masse, confronting any individual or country who blamed China for inflicting the coronavirus on the world to boost its manufacturing force. China, feeling cornered, increased its Twitter presence,

---

12 The Economist, "China's "Wolf Warrior" Diplomacy Gamble," *The Economist*, May 28, 2020, https://www.economist.com/china/2020/05/28/chinas-wolf-warrior-diplomacy-gamble

13 Steve Mollman & Heather Timmons, "China Has No Respect for International Law, Its Neighbors, or Marine Life, A Tribunal Rules," *Quartz*, July 12, 2016, https://qz.com/729524/chinas-activities-in-the-south-china-sea-are-illegal-and-destroying-the-environment-an-international-court-finds/

14 Xinhua, "China Focus: 'Wolf Warrior 2' Stimulates Country's Patriotism," *Xinhua*, August 15, 2017, http://www.xinhuanet.com//english/2017-08/15/c_136528713.htm

15 Desmond U. Patton, David Pyrooz, Scott Decker, William R. Frey, and Patrick Leonard, "When Twitter Fingers Turn to Trigger Fingers: A Qualitative Study of Social Media-Related Gang Violence," *International Journal of Bullying Prevention 1*, (2019): 205-217, https://link.springer.com/article/10.1007/s42380-019-00014-w

16 James Landale, "Coronavirus: China's New Army of Tough-Talking Diplomats," *BBC News*, May 13, 2020, https://www.bbc.com/news/world-asia-china-52562549

17 Ibid.

18 The Economist, "China's "Wolf Warrior" Diplomacy Gamble," *The Economist*, May 28, 2020, https://www.economist.com/china/2020/05/28/chinas-wolf-warrior-diplomacy-gamble

converting Twitter into "a weapon for 'wolf warrior' diplomats whose tweets are popularized by an army of bots."[19]

These "principles and guts" are evident in tweets that Chinese diplomats have fervently and feverishly posted. In particular, young Chinese diplomats Zhao Lijian, Hua Chunying, and Zha Liyou have been notably recognized for their status updates online and demonstrating that China's younger generation of diplomats will not be silenced.

In response to criticism on how China handled the coronavirus (COVID-19) pandemic, on February 16, 2020, Zha Liyou, China's consul-general, tweeted, "You speak in such a way that you look like part of the virus and you will be eradicated just like virus. Shame on you."[20] In response to Twitter direct messages from *The Economist*, Zha wrote that his "sole purpose" was telling China's "true story."[21]

In May 2020, Zhao Lijian tweeted, "Pompeo said that he stands with the people of Hong Kong. He is flattering himself. In fact, he stands with the so-called Hong Kong independence forces and violent radicals. China is firmly opposed to foreign interference in China's domestic affairs."[22]

That one tweet was not the end of Zhao Lijian's fiery Twitter rampage. On July 9, 2019, 22 nations, including the U.S., sent a message to the United Nations urging China to stop the "arbitrary detention and restrictions on freedom of movement of Uyghurs, and other Muslim and minority communities in Xinjiang."[23] Shortly after, Zhao tweeted, "US & most of these 22 countries invaded Iraq on so-called credible evidence of chemical weapons, bombed Afghanistan, Libya, Syria ... How can they claim to be champions of Muslims in China's Xinjiang where the majority of the Muslims are living in peace & prosperity? Shameless hypocrites!"[24]

Following his previous tweet, Zhao added, "If you're in Washington DC, you know the white never go to the SW area, because it's an area for the black & Latin. There's a saying 'black in & white out', which means that as long as a black family enters, white people will quit, & price of the apartment will fall sharply."[25]

---

19 Prabhash K Dutta, "Wolf Warrior Diplomacy: The Chinese Game of Covid-10 Cover-Up," *India Today*, December 3, 2020, https://www.indiatoday.in/news-analysis/story/wolf-warrior-diplomacy-the-chinese-game-of-covid-19-cover-up-1746283-2020-12-03

20 The Economist, "China Finds a Use Abroad for Twitter, a Medium it Fears at Home," *The Economist*, February 20, 2020, https://www.economist.com/china/2020/02/20/china-finds-a-use-abroad-for-twitter-a-medium-it-fears-at-home

21 Ibid.

22 Lijian Zhao (@zlj517), "Pompeo said that he stands with the people of Hong Kong. He is flattering himself. In fact, he stands with the so called Hong Kong independence forces and violent radicals. China is firmly…," *Twitter*, May 29, 2020, 9:27PM, https://twitter.com/zlj517/status/1266586988380995585

23 Reuters, "Xinjiang Camps: UN Ambassadors Urge China to End Detention of Uygurs in Open Letter," *South China Morning Post*, July 10, 2019, https://www.scmp.com/news/china/diplomacy/article/3018075/xinjiang-camps-un-ambassadors-urge-china-end-detention-uygurs

24 Laura Zhou, "Former US National Security Adviser Susan Rice Calls Chinese Diplomat Zhao Lijian 'A Racist Disgrace' After Twitter Tirade," *South China Morning Post*, July 15, 2019, https://www.scmp.com/news/china/diplomacy/article/3018676/susan-rice-calls-chinese-diplomat-zhao-lijian-racist-disgrace

25 Ibid.

In response, former U.S. National Security Advisor, Susan Rice, tweeted, "You are a racist disgrace. And shockingly ignorant too. In normal times, you would be PNGed for this. Ambassador Cui, I expect better of you and your team. Please do the right thing and send him home."[26] Rice abbreviated persona non grata, signifying an unwelcome diplomat, as "PNG" and urged the Chinese ambassador to the U.S., Cui Tiankai, to send Lijian home.

Firing back, Lijian tweeted, "You are such a disgrace, too. And shockingly ignorant, too. I am based in Islamabad. Truth hurts. I am simply telling the truth. I stayed in Washington DC 10 years ago. To label someone who speak the truth that you don't want to hear a racist, is disgraceful & disgusting."[27] All tweets were removed shortly after.[28]

Through all of the tweets that Chinese diplomats send, it has become abundantly clear that their goal is to chastise any opposition to China's rising global power, especially the United States. Another notable 'Wolf Warrior diplomat', Lu Shaye, also took to the media, replying to the backlash regarding China's response to COVID-19. He told French newspaper *L'Opinion* in April 2020, "Every time the Americans make an allegation, the French media always report them a day or two later. They howl with the wolves, to make a big fuss about lies and rumors about China."[29]

The Foreign Ministry's Communist Party secretary, Qi Yu, reaffirmed the purpose of 'Wolf Warrior diplomats', sharing in a December 2019 essay that they must "firmly counterattack against words and deeds in the international arena that assault the leadership of China's Communist Party and our country's socialist system."[30]

Nevertheless, the backbone providing support for 'Wolf Warrior diplomats' actions is President Xi Jinping's push for China's nationalistic agenda and strong presence on the world stage.[31] Replying to a Twitter direct message from *The Economist*, the Chinese ambassador to Austria, Li Xiaosi, shared that President Xi Jinping directly requested for "Chinese diplomats to tell China's stories well and present a true, multidimensional and panoramic view of China."[32]

---

26 Nayanima Basu, "Who's More Racist? Former US NSA and Chinese Diplomat in Pakistan Fight on Twitter," *ThePrint*, July 15, 2019, https://theprint.in/diplomacy/whos-more-racist-former-us-nsa-and-chinese-diplomat-in-pakistan-fight-on-twitter/263274/

27 Demond Cureton, "Tempers Flare as Chinese Envoy Triggers Susan Rice on Twitter Over Race, Xinjiang Uighur Accusations," *Sputnik News*, Updated September 7, 2019, https://sputniknews.com/world/201907151076253052-tempers-flare-as-chinese-envoy-triggers-susan-rice-on-twitter-over-race-xinjiang-uighur-accusations/

28 The Economist, "China Finds a Use Abroad for Twitter, a Medium it Fears at Home," *The Economist*, February 20, 2020, https://www.economist.com/china/2020/02/20/china-finds-a-use-abroad-for-twitter-a-medium-it-fears-at-home

29 Chun Han Wong & Chao Deng, "China's 'Wolf Warrior' Diplomats Are Ready to Fight," *The Wall Street Journal*, May 19, 2020, https://www.wsj.com/articles/chinas-wolf-warrior-diplomats-are-ready-to-fight-11589896722

30 Ibid.

31 Zhiqun Zhu, "Interpreting China's 'Wolf-Warrior Diplomacy'," *The Diplomat*, May 15, 2020, https://thediplomat.com/2020/05/interpreting-chinas-wolf-warrior-diplomacy/

32 The Economist, "China Finds a Use Abroad for Twitter, a Medium it Fears at Home," *The Economist*, February 20, 2020, https://www.economist.com/china/2020/02/20/china-finds-a-use-abroad-for-twitter-a-medium-it-fears-at-home

With information solely coming from Chinese diplomats' Twitter accounts, a true "panoramic view of China" is questionable. It is essential to note that Twitter has been blocked for the Chinese people to use for a decade,[33] allowing the communist party to share one-sided messages to the rest of the world, without any other perspective.[34] China's absolute censorship facilitates the spread of its well-constructed, coordinated propaganda.

'Wolf Warriors' in the Media

As Chinese leaders and representatives epitomize the 'Wolf Warrior' image, state media, journalists, and other writers have sought to establish access points to present truly "multidimensional" viewpoints. However, access cannot be obtained, given the stifling

Wolves and Twitter Fingers
China's Wolf Warriors Tweet Until They're Heard

---

33   The Economist, "China Finds a Use Abroad for Twitter, a Medium it Fears at Home," *The Economist*, February 20, 2020, https://www.economist.com/china/2020/02/20/china-finds-a-use-abroad-for-twitter-a-medium-it-fears-at-home

34   Jeff Kao, ProPublica, and Mia Shuang Li, "How China Built a Twitter Propaganda Machine Then Let It Loose on Coronavirus," *ProPublica*, March 26, 2020, https://www.propublica.org/article/how-china-built-a-twitter-propaganda-machine-then-let-it-loose-on-coronavirus

of voices through censorship. Media and news platforms are designed to spread China's nationalistic messages through crafted propaganda. Regarding Twitter, access is only provided for diplomats,[35] yet many others in China look for Virtual Private Networks (VPNs) and other digital routings to share perspectives and protect digital information. Naturally, not everyone in China is a diplomat and permitted to tweet. However, the potential for internet freedom has become a beacon of hope for journalists who seek to convey their brand of patriotism to the rest of the world.

The head of the Chinese Foreign Ministry's information department, Hua Chunying, wrote in July 2019, "In order to win the right to speak, we must take the initiative and actively shape it."[36] Chinese careerists seeking to get a leg up in the journalism world have taken it upon themselves to "actively shape" the media, trying to gain any noteworthy opportunities to condemn Western nations and silence anti-China rhetoric.

However, although the goal of nationalists is to spread Chinese ideologies to the rest of the world,[37] the primary obstacle is the Great Firewall,[38] the Chinese government's digital fortress that censors and blocks posts, articles, and other news from being shared without permission.

Surprisingly, the Chinese people have not held their tongues in silence to the internet restrictions, as they have when faced with other government-imposed regulations in the past. In the spring of 2020, Hua tweeted, "I can't breathe." He attached a tweet by U.S. State Department spokesperson, Morgan Ortagus, criticizing China's Hong Kong policies. Shortly afterward, millions of Chinese citizens flooded the news, saying, "I can't tweet," to let the world know that Twitter still remains blocked for the general populace.[39]

The only way to bypass the Great Firewall is through the use of a Virtual Private Network (VPN). However, the Chinese government outlawed the use of VPNs in 2018 and has said they will fine, arrest, and charge citizens for "accessing the international internet through illegal channels."[40] Yet, millions of Chinese citizens protested the Chinese government's arrest of a citizen who bypassed the Great Firewall in May 2020, an unprecedented movement against Beijing.[41]

---

35 Gerry Shih, "Banned at Home, Twitter Becomes a New Tool for Chinese Diplomats Abroad," *The Washington Post*, July 9, 2019, https://www.washingtonpost.com/world/asia_pacific/banned-at-home-twitter-becomes-a-new-tool-for-chinese-diplomats-abroad/2019/07/09/bc61e040-a21f-11e9-a767-d7ab84aef3e9_story.html

36 The Paper, "Hua Chunying Wrote an Article in The Study Times: Occupy the Moral Commanding Heights and Enhance International Discourse Power," *The Paper*, July 12, 2019, https://www.thepaper.cn/newsDetail_forward_3900567

37 Brian Wong, "China's Two-Pronged Diplomacy," *The Diplomat*, September 12, 2020, https://thediplomat.com/2020/09/chinas-two-pronged-diplomacy/

38 Douglas Heaven, "China's Great Firewall and the War to Control the Internet," *NewScientist*, March 12, 2019, https://www.newscientist.com/article/mg24132210-400-chinas-great-firewall-and-the-war-to-control-the-internet/

39 Fergus Ryan, "China's Online Warriors Want More Gates in the Firewall," *Foreign Policy*, June 29, 2020, https://foreignpolicy.com/2020/06/29/china-great-firewall-wolf-warrior-nationalism/

40 Gao Feng, "Fine for VPN Use Sparks Rare Backlash on Chinese Internet," *Radio Free Asia*, May, 21, 2020, https://www.rfa.org/english/news/china/vpn-punishments-05212020103537.html

41 Ibid.

In addition, many media and news personalities have vocalized their desire for internet freedom to spread nationalistic messages of their own. One example is Cao Kefan, a media personality at Shangai Media Group and a delegate of the National People's Congress. Cao told reporters that he submitted a bill that would grant special permission to selected and trusted media workers to have access over the Great Firewall and "speak China's voice" to the rest of the world.[42]

Cao hopes, "In the future, we can gradually expand these opportunities to even more people. We should encourage more influential people in different fields to represent themselves in international media, spread their ideas, and engage with others, showing the world China's tolerance and openness."[43] Cao and others alike seek to have independent access in the media to spread, share, and inform others on their perspective of China in the world and demonstrate their ardent loyalty to Xi Jinping's ambitions in their profession.

Conclusion

The COVID-19 pandemic was a test of the strength of 'Wolf Warrior diplomacy'. Nevertheless, Chinese 'Wolf Warrior diplomats' have pressed harder through the COVID-19 pandemic,[44] utilizing a concerted effort to spread information at the push of a few buttons. These determined forces of citizenry continue to convey China's fearless, hardened, and aggressive position in the world with the global community, particularly in 2020, as they countered accusations that the COVID-19 disease emanated from China or that their PPE products were defective.

China pushed to create alternate narratives for the origin of the disease. Lijian Zhao offered the United States as a culprit in a Tweet. Then, China blamed Italy and Spain.[45] In December 2020, China blamed India, while maintaining a narrative that the Chinese were "efficient" and "vigilant" in combatting the disease.[46]

Additionally, opening the doors to social media platforms and news outlets is the only way for ordinary citizens to become a 'Wolf Warrior' of their own. Needless to say, with more users able to post, the number of outgoing attacks will skyrocket. As the Chinese people gain greater access to reach the rest of the world and spread China's ideologies, new philosophies, beliefs, and principles will filter into the minds of its citizens. Social control and propaganda machines do not work as well when people have widespread access to information and transparency in the media. Though Beijing has yet to make any move toward granting citizens internet access, the new generation of 'Wolf Warriors' may lead to unpredictable changes – only time and tweeting will tell.

---

42 Fergus Ryan, "China's Online Warriors Want More Gates in the Firewall," *Foreign Policy*, June 29, 2020, https://foreignpolicy.com/2020/06/29/china-great-firewall-wolf-warrior-nationalism/

43 Ibid.

44 Anna Schecter, "China Launches New Twitter Accounts, 90,000 Tweets in COVID-19 Info War," *NBC News*, May 20, 2020, https://www.nbcnews.com/news/world/china-launches-new-twitter-accounts-90-000-tweets-covid-19-n1207991

45 Ibid.

46 Prabhash K Dutta, "Wolf Warrior Diplomacy: The Chinese Game of Covid-10 Cover-Up," *India Today*, December 3, 2020, https://www.indiatoday.in/news-analysis/story/wolf-warrior-diplomacy-the-chinese-game-of-covid-19-cover-up-1746283-2020-12-03

What's at Stake?

First, tit-for-tat Twitter battles are likely to stay provided that the new rules of 'diplomacy' mean lashing out at one another with harsh, inflammatory words on the global stage. However, the 'twitter finger' dam broke and the water is surging downstream. There is no way to recapture that water. Thus, it is likely that Twitter battles, as petty and abhorrent as they can be, are here to stay.

Second, 'Wolf Warriors' are on the loose; they are howling loudly. Reporters must ask tough questions, be clear on the issues, and have a keen sense of being played by coercive rhetoric. What is at stake is a public that may be unaware of these propaganda tactics and unable to discern the truth from the lies.

Third, students of life should study philosophy and logic. Much of this deep thinking has been lost in the decimation of liberal arts departments. However, 'Wolf Warriors' use logic as striking points that are filled with fallacies. Many of these fallacies are heard in the media and important to note.

1. Appeal to Ignorance (Argumentum Ad Ignoratum) – stating that a proposition is true, since it has not been proven false. Example: Claiming that there is no torture, because the victim did not tell you.

2. Argument by Force (Argumentum Ad Baculum) – carrying a stick to coerce a desired result. Example: You will denounce your citizenship or else your family will be murdered.

3. Circular Reasoning (Petitio Principii) – the premises presume the conclusion. Example: China is the best country, because it is better than other countries.

4. Guilt by Association (Argumentum Ad Hominem) – an argument stating that one person is corrupt because they are friends with a person who was found guilty. Example: Everyone who protests is violent, since some are violent.

5. Bandwagon Appeal (Argumentum Ad Populum) – correctness is interpreted by following the crowd. Example: Every person should get the new Apple iPhone since the phone is so popular.

These are only a few of the many fallacies that can be used to shape people's thinking. Others include red herrings, a slippery slope, and half-truths. More of these fallacies are being introduced through social media to lure people into following what may seem logical and true when, in fact, it is false, misleading, or deceptive.

Fourth, what is at stake is a world of people who are unaware that these communication tactics and means of manipulation are being used against them.

Chapter 3
Salami Slicing with 'Chinese Characteristics'
Inch-by-Inch, Stealthily Taking Control of the Planet

Salami Slicing

Introduction

China's win-win strategy is designed for Beijing to win both at home and abroad. One aspect of this strategy is achieved through salami attacks, slicing off thin units of opposition, and claiming 'historic rights' to territory, inch-by-inch, as if it were salami. With its thousands of years of history, China views the future on a long-term basis. Dominating the planet, extending social control, and installing its 'Socialism with Chinese Characteristics' cannot be done all at once. Slow and incremental progress is in the best, long-term interest of China - subtle, sure-footed, and tactful. In a carefully executed way, China has taken little by little, calmly biding its time so as not to appear too bold, arrogant, or overconfident.

As such, China builds alliances and friendships through benevolence, generosity, and support while only taking one step forward. Since countries strive for a prosperous future and envision their continued improvement in transportation, communication, and industry, foreign direct investment (FDI) is the lifeblood of each states' prospective development. By working individually, one-by-one, with countries, Beijing can directly appeal to specific state needs, financial incentives, and leadership desires. Furthermore, by providing capital and support, China can also control how the country will vote in the United Nations and in other international bodies by exchanging capital investment for favorable votes. In the United Nations, China needs laws to be adapted to Beijing's socialist ambitions one phrase at a time. In order to overcome opposition to these incremental changes in the global rule of law, thin salami slices in wording make small amounts of progress in the short term, but great headway in the long run so as not to be conspicuous.

Origin and Tactics

The term "salami slicing" was coined when the Hungarian Communist Party took control of power in the late 1940s. The 'cynically candid leader', Matyas Rakosi, explained how he won, one slice at a time.[1] He secretively attacked candidates, political parties, and organizations, manipulating the rhetoric and causing confusion. After ensuring a sense of anarchy in his opponent's organizations, "cutting them off like slices of salami,"[2] he used this divide-and-conquer strategy to achieve victory. Throughout his candidacy, he portrayed each opponent with terms that would make the citizenry dislike those groups, peeling them away one by one.

Salami tactics are veiled offers and slick messaging with hidden motives. The incremental infiltration into opposition groups is slow, but deft in its process. The insidious nature of attack results in devastating consequences, unknown when the first outstretched arm or circumvented election is initiated. Every initial display of good faith is carefully constructed.

China utilizes this "salami slicing" technique to gain leverage over countries and alter elections. With the façade of a substantial gift and "win-win" rhetoric, China offers states and companies significant amounts of money, mostly in loans, that they cannot refuse.[3] Contracts are written with China's interests squarely in mind, sometimes as a lure for support, acknowledgment, or soft power, other times requiring the Chinese language to be spoken on projects and Chinese laborers to be used.[4]

In Beijing's African investment projects, Chinese laborers are brought in to complete the work,[5] explaining to the Africans that it is not easy to train people to operate their specialized machinery. Since the instructions are in Mandarin, there is a language barrier, making it difficult to employ African technicians.[6] Unwilling to translate the specifications and technical details into the country's language, Chinese laborers are necessitated. Those who do not know Mandarin cannot follow the requirements without significant help. Thus, to build soft power, the Chinese teach the Africans Mandarin after hours and provide access to Chinese television, music, and reading materials.[7]

Furthermore, re-payments are often slated to be returned in commodities needed by

---

1 Matyas Rakosi, "How We Took Over Hungary," *CVCE*, Originally published in 1952, https://www.cvce.eu/content/publication/2002/7/22/9a19d06e-4163-4f31-b2c9-1bc9e65a380a/publishable_en.pdf

2 Time Magazine, "Hungary: Salami Tactics," *Time Magazine*, April 14, 1952, http://content.time.com/time/magazine/article/0,9171,857130,00.html

3 Willard Cheng, "Duterte Heads Home From China with $24 Billion Deals," *ABS CBN News*, October 21, 2016, https://news.abs-cbn.com/business/10/21/16/duterte-heads-home-from-china-with-24-billion-deals

4 Ethan B. Kapstein & Jacob N. Shapiro, "Catching China by the Belt (and Road)," *Foreign Policy*, April 20, 2019, https://foreignpolicy.com/2019/04/20/catching-china-by-the-belt-and-road-international-development-finance-corp-beijing-united-states/

5 Tang Xiaoyang, "Does Chinese Employment Benefit Africans? Investigating Chinese Enterprises and their Operations in Africa," *African Studies Quarterly*, December, 2016, http://asq.africa.ufl.edu/files/v16a8.Tang_.HD_.pdf

6 Lucy Corkin, Christopher Burke, and Martyn Davies, "China's Role in the Development of Africa's Infrastructure," *The John Hopkins University, School of Advanced International Studies*, n.d., https://sais.jhu.edu/sites/default/files/China's-Role-in-the-Development-of-Africa's-Infrastructure.pdf

7 Paul Nantulya, "Grand Strategy and China's Soft Power Push in Africa," *Africa Center for Strategic Studies*, August 30, 2018, https://africacenter.org/spotlight/grand-strategy-and-chinas-soft-power-push-in-africa/

China, like minerals or oil,[8] alleviating the state from a monetary transaction. Scott Wingo reported that "between 29 and 32 percent of Chinese lending to developing countries since 2000 has been collateralized with natural resources. Borrowing countries in most cases repay these loans in oil, metals or agricultural commodities."[9] Delinquent loans trigger penalties or restructuring, sometimes with added debt or higher interest rates. Thus, in some cases debt grows until the state is no longer able to pay[10] and is required to relinquish state-owned corporations, capital, or infrastructure.[11]

For a moment, imagine that, China donates money to one political party or a few political groups in some country in order to sew discontent, create anxiety, or throw the country into a firestorm of riots, chaos, and confusion. Political blocs are hypothetically developed, which create movements that spur even greater demise. This dynamic plays well in the Chinese media where the recharged CCTV propaganda machine revs its engines to splash headlines of that country's degradation and how nobody would want to live there. Slice by slice, the political machine propagates disorder and anarchy until the organizational structures of that country collapse. If this demise is in a democratic country, this brand of authoritative socialism may appear compelling or enticing to China.

The use of salami tactics continues to be evident in the South China Sea, with Beijing's territorial expansion and incremental construction of fortified military bases on artificially-manufactured islands. Meanwhile, the world watches, unwilling to call China's 'bluff'. At first, many believed Beijing's expansion and coercive efforts were a bluff or a test. However, China has not stopped.

The first slice was 'merely' to gain approval from the UNESCO Intergovernmental Oceanographic Commission to survey the islands.[12] The request was innocent. However, they started surveying, moving and encroaching slowly on one island, then staked ground on surrounding islands. China never left. The next slice occurred when China claimed those same islands, taking control away from Vietnam.[13] Then, China began constructing so-called benign structures.

China claimed that they were just creating these buildings to help stranded boaters.[14] Later, they said that the structures were for tourists and those interested in marine life. In the next salami slice, they scooped up the coral and underwater sediment, piling the material on the rocks and sand before pouring concrete over the 'islands' to create helicopter pads, airplane landing strips, radar stations, airplane hangars, missile launch sites, bunkers,

---

8   Scott Wingo, "How Will China Respond When Low Income Countries Can't Pay Their Debts," *The Washington Post*, June 30, 2020, https://www.washingtonpost.com/politics/2020/06/30/how-will-china-respond-when-low-income-countries-cant-pay-their-debts/

9   Ibid.

10 Maria Abi-Habib & Keith Bradsher, "Poor Countries Borrowed Billions from China. They Can't Pay It Back," *The New York Times*, May 18, 2020, https://www.nytimes.com/2020/05/18/business/china-loans-coronavirus-belt-road.html

11 Elaine K. Dezenski, "Below the Belt and Road," *Foundation for Defence of Democracies*, May 6, 2020, https://www.fdd.org/analysis/2020/05/04/below-the-belt-and-road/

12 Min Gyo Koo, *Island Disputes and Maritime Regime Building in East Asia* (Dordrecht: Springer, 2009), 154.

13 M. Taylor Fravel, *Strong Borders, Secure Nation: Cooperation and Conflict in China's Territorial Disputes* (Princeton: Princeton University Press, 2008), 183–185.

14 Ibid.

barracks, refueling stations, etc.[15] Then, while the world stood by, they placed military patrols, planes, boats, and vehicles on the island.

Now, with the slices of salami already cut, it is nearly impossible to turn the clock back, even though numerous countries are finally awake. At this point, China has military bases scattered throughout the South China Sea, and they are prepared to launch attacks on any country that threatens their illegal land grab.

China's 'historic claim' was deemed illegal in *Philippines v. China* by the International Court of Justice.[16] Despite this, China ignored the international court which ruled that land and sea rights of each country's Exclusive Economic Zone (EEZ) are protected by the United Nations Convention on the Law of the Sea (UNCLOS). In order to circumvent this ruling, afterward, China stated that it would work with each state separately, which amounted to a divide and conquer process. Although the Philippines brought the case to the court and won, President Rodrigo Duterte agreed to cooperate with China rather than accepting the international court ruling in its favor.[17] Furthermore, China is now working to stack international organizations and international courts with its own designates or proxies through its agreements buried in Belt and Road deals.[18]

China's efforts to peel off land and resources from states has not ended with the South China Sea conflict. In fact, that was just the beginning. This effort has been repeated in Mongolia, Tibet, Hong Kong, Vietnam, and the overtaking of infrastructure in Africa and Asia. Salami tactics are being implemented in India, Japan, Hong Kong, Brunei, Bhutan, U.S., Australia, and elsewhere. China's expansion is not over yet.

An Indian news source commented that China's salami-slicing tactics, by acting against India on multiple fronts, displays a complete disregard for previous agreements and India's good faith in attempting to achieve peace.[19] Other commentators point to incidents during the COVID-19 pandemic, such as the sinking of a Vietnamese vessel and provocations with Malaysian and Indonesian vessels in 2020 along with the incursion and loss of life when China attacked troops on the Indian border. China appears to be increasingly willing to engage militarily.[20]

---

15 Asia Maritime Transparency Initiative," China Island Tracker," *Asia Maritime Transparency Initiative*, n.d., https://amti.csis.org/island-tracker/china/

16 PCA, "PCA Case No. 2013-19 In the Matter of the South China Sea Arbitration," *PCA*, July 12, 2016, https://docs.pca-cpa.org/2016/07/PH-CN-20160712-Award.pdf

17 Xinhua, "China, Philippines Reach Important Consensus Through Diplomatic Consultation," *Xinhua*, July 26, 2019, http://www.xinhuanet.com/english/2019-07/26/c_138261164.htm

18 Kristine Lee, "It's Not Just the WHO: How China Is Moving on the Whole U.N.," *Politico*, April 15, 2020, https://www.politico.com/news/magazine/2020/04/15/its-not-just-the-who-how-china-is-moving-on-the-whole-un-189029

19 Shankhyaneel Sarka, "China's 'Salami-Slicing Tactics' Displays disregard for India's Efforts at Peace" *Hindustan Times*, June 6, 2020, https://www.hindustantimes.com/world-news/china-s-salami-slicing-tactics-displays-disregard-for-india-s-efforts-at-peace/story-ujHFW5zcwTbKiP7j0QghGL.html

20 Lt. Gen. Utpal Bhattacharyya, "Salami Slicing Not Effective Anymore. Is China Prepared For Full-scale Combat?," *Outlook*, June 22, 2020, https://www.outlookindia.com/website/story/opinion-stealthy-slicing-was-effective-earlier-but-not-anymore-is-china-prepared-for-full-scale-combat/355232

Conclusion

While these places seem far away, China has not stopped. Beijing's next effort is being projected to countries worldwide through their satellite and 5G surveillance systems. By connecting people worldwide to its Internet surveillance system, Beijing can exert social control on people through their phone and computer, deciding who can be connected and what they can access.

Furthermore, Beijing is seeking to overtake the islands in the South China Sea, one by one in proper salami tactic style. Stephen Walt of Harvard University stated, "Just taking a tiny bite each time, at what point do you say, Stop! You can't have any more…and, I am willing to take the salami away…That is very difficult to do if the steps are small enough."[21] However, while the world hunkered down during the pandemic, China moved in on all fronts, no longer taking inches but aggressively moving in multiple directions with large leaps.

What's at Stake?

First, geopolitical spheres of influence extend far past China's borders as Beijing deploys its 'salami slicing' tactics worldwide.

Second, 'salami slicing' impacts countries globally. State sovereignty and financial independence are no longer issues of just one nation under the influence of China. With Beijing's extended reach, China has gained leverage and control over a potentially dangerous number of countries.

Third, Beijing holds significant influence over government leaders. 'Salami sliced' nations are thus handicapped by regional disputes and local issues. What's at stake here is that, throughout the negotiations, China has the upper hand.

---

21   *Belfer Center*, "Stephen Walt: China's Salami Tactics," October 27, 2015, video, 1:53, https://www.youtube.com/watch?v=cRGdGZNC5nk

Chapter 4

Chasing Tigers and Flies While Hunting Down Foxes

The CCP's Scrutiny, Harassment, and Elimination

Introduction

Even at the highest ranks of the Chinese elite, discipline and obedience are demanded. Political challengers within the Chinese Communist Party (CCP) are being removed from their offices and sentenced en masse. To take down tigers, top CCP leaders who are rivals of President Xi, local authorities gather any kind of incriminating evidence from down-line staff. Conformity to Chinese Communist Party (CCP) principles is expected on all levels. In the opaque atmosphere of China's 'rule of law', those in power can 'eliminate' anyone suspected of the CCP's amorphous term, 'corruption'.[1] Even Jack Ma, billionaire and co-founder of Alibaba, has been silenced and not seen for months.[2]

With the goal to stay out of the snares of the rulers, uncertainty and fear are rampant. Anyone living in China could be under suspicion. Without freedom of speech or freedom of thought, any comments that are deemed subversive to the Chinese Communist Party (CCP) are scrutinized. If considered improper, the individual's rights can be stripped by the Central Commission for Discipline Inspection (CCDI). *Human Rights Watch* offers video testimony and notes,

> The shuanggui system, which functions beyond the reach of China's criminal justice system, gives the CCDI the authority to summon any of the Communist Party's 88 million members to account for allegedly ill-gotten gains at a "designated location at a designated time." Those summoned are deprived of liberty for days, weeks, or months, during which time they are repeatedly interrogated and often tortured. Typically, shuanggui detention ends when the official confesses to corruption or other alleged disciplinary violations; some are then transferred to the regular criminal justice system for prosecution.[3]

On February 23, 2020, Chinese real estate tycoon, Ren Zhiqiang, vanished. He had been a long time critic of President Xi, once saying that he, "saw not an emperor standing there exhibiting his 'new clothes' but a clown stripped naked who insisted he continued being emperor."[4] Xu Zhiyong, a prominent activist, was put in a secret detention facility without access to a lawyer in February 2020.[5] He had once stated,

> I wish our country could be a free and happy one. Every citizen need not go against their conscience and can find their own place by their virtue and talents; a simple and happy society, where the goodness of humanity is expanded to the maximum, and the evilness of humanity is constrained to the minimum; honesty, trust, kindness, and

---

1. Nathaniel Taplin, "China's Corruption Paradox," *The Wall Street Journal*, November 1, 2019, https://www.wsj.com/articles/chinas-corruption-paradox-11572600605

2. Helen Davidson, "Where is Jack Ma? Chinese Tycoon Not Seen Since October," *The Guardian*, January 5, 2021, https://www.theguardian.com/business/2021/jan/05/where-is-jack-ma-chinese-tycoon-not-seen-since-october-alibaba

3. Human Rights Watch, "'Special Measures' - Detention and Torture in the Chinese Communist Party's Shuanggui System," *Human Rights Watch*, n.d., https://www.hrw.org/zh-hans/node/297068

4. Irwin Cotler and Judith Abitan, "The Chinese Communist Party's Culture of Corruption and Repression Has Cost Lives Around the World," *The Globe and Mail, Opinion*, April 14, 2020, https://www.theglobeandmail.com/opinion/article-the-chinese-communist-partys-culture-of-corruption-and-repression-has/

5. Verna Yu, "China Activist Who Called Xi Clueless on Coronavirus Faces Years in Jail for 'Subversion'," *The Guardian*, March 7, 2020, https://www.theguardian.com/world/2020/mar/08/china-activist-who-called-xi-clueless-on-coronavirus-faces-years-in-jail-for-subversion

helping each other are everyday occurrences in life; there is not so much anger and anxiety, a pure smile on everyone's face.[6]

For Li Qiang, the Lianyungang Party Secretary, when ominous 'investigators' swooped in after one of his 2014 speeches, he was never seen in public again.[7] Nearly 75,000 party members have been similarly 'investigated' by the CCDI.[8] Tigers and flies are netted by "reining in power in a cage" where 'rule of law' is disregarded.[9]

In 2013, President Xi Jinping announced that the CCDI would strike "tigers and flies".[10] 'Tigers' referred to the higher-ranking CCP officials, while the 'flies' connoted those on the lower ranks.[11] In his speech, President Xi promised to root out all rivals and "unhealthy tendencies", adding, "We must have the resolve to fight every corrupt

---

6   Liu Yong, "Xu Zhiyong: Featured in Mr. Fashion," *China Digital Times*, August 4, 2009, https://chinadigitaltimes.net/2009/08/brother-chinese-activist-held-for-tax-evasion/

7   Wang Feng, Yifei Chen, & Patrick Boehler, "Tigers and Flies, How Two Years of Graft Probes Have Shaken China's Political Elite," *South China Morning Post*, November 6, 2014, https://multimedia.scmp.com/china-corruption/

8   Ibid.

9   Human Rights Watch, "'Special Measures' - Detention and Torture in the Chinese Communist Party's Shuanggui System," *Human Rights Watch*, n.d., https://www.hrw.org/zh-hans/node/297068

10 Tania Branigan, "Xi Jinping Vows to Fight 'Tigers' And 'Flies' in Anti-Corruption Drive," *The Guardian*, January 22, 2013, https://www.theguardian.com/world/2013/jan/22/xi-jinping-tigers-flies-corruption

11 Minnie Chan, "75,000 Party Cadres Probed for Graft, But More 'Big Tigers' Unlikely, Says Analyst," *South China Morning Post*, October 5, 2014, https://www.scmp.com/news/china/article/1609789/75000-party-cadres-probed-graft-more-big-tigers-unlikely-says-analyst

phenomenon, punish every corrupt official and constantly eliminate the soil which breeds corruption, so as to earn people's trust with actual results."[12]

The ultimate message instilled in Chinese nationalists is discipline. *BBC* reported that, by 2017, official data shows 1.34 million "tigers and flies" had been accused and faced consequences at all levels; the military has not been spared.[13] More than sixty generals have been sacked, including two top generals, Fang Fenhui and Zhang Yan, who have 'disappeared.'[14]

Operation Fox Hunt

Launched in 2014, Beijing's commitment to expand its 'anti-corruption' effort abroad by locating 'foxes', the term used to describe Chinese Communist Party (CCP) members who have 'escaped' overseas.[15] Chinese authorities announced that they have a 'zero-tolerance stance'.[16]

Discontent and concern has grown within the ranks of Chinese citizens who fear being harshly disciplined, imprisoned for life,[17] or killed for disagreeing with Xi. Some prominent families in China's elite have fled.[18] China announced its crackdown as a way to silence critics, improve domestic perceptions of government, and reassure foreign companies that trade in China is safe.[19] In searching for China's foxes, *Beijing News* reported that they nabbed and 'repatriated' a Chinese national in Thailand and one in Nigeria.[20] Picked off, one-by-one, Fox Hunt stings have happened in Australia,[21] as well as Africa, Asia, Europe, the Middle East, and in both North and South America.[22] *Xinhua* reported that they picked off more than 3,000 foxes in 120 countries so far.[23]

---

12 Sophie Beach, "Xi Jinping Fights Corruption Among 'Tigers' and 'Flies'," *China Digital Times*, January 22, 2013, https://chinadigitaltimes.net/2013/01/xi-jinping-takes-anti-corruption-fight-to-tigers-and-flies/

13 BBC News, "Charting China's 'Great Purge' Under Xi," *BBC News*, October 23, 2017, https://www.bbc.com/news/world-asia-china-41670162

14 Ibid.

15 Goh Sui Noi, "China to Keep Up Hunt for Tigers, Foxes," *The Straits Times*, March 23, 2017, https://www.straitstimes.com/asia/east-asia/china-to-keep-up-hunt-for-tigers-foxes

16 Ben Blanchard, "Corruption Cases in China Jumped One-Third in 2016," *Reuters*, March 11, 2017, https://af.reuters.com/article/worldNews/idAFKBN16J01S

17 Saikiran Kannan, "Operation Fox Hunt: China's Global Witch-Hunt Against Dissenters," *India Today*, July 13, 2020, https://www.indiatoday.in/news-analysis/story/operation-fox-hunt-china-s-global-witch-hunt-against-dissenters-1699869-2020-07-13

18 Ibid.

19 FTI Consulting, "Chasing Foxes: What the Chinese Anti-Corruption Hunt Means for Australian Business," *FTI Consulting*, n.d., https://www.fticonsulting-asia.com/~/media/Files/apac-files/insights/articles/chasing-foxes-grip-article.pdf

20 South China Morning Post, "How the Elite 'Fox Hunt' Police Taskforce Scours the World for Fugitives Who Have Fled Overseas," *South China Morning Post*, n.d., https://www.scmp.com/news/china/article/1620587/how-elite-fox-hunt-police-taskforce-scours-world-fugitives-who-have-fled

21 Angus Grigg & Lisa Murray, "Untold Story: China's Operation Fox Hunt and the Capture of Zhang Jianping," *Financial Review*, June 18, 2016, https://www.afr.com/world/untold-story-chinas-operation-fox-hunt-and-the-capture-of-zhang-jianping-20160616-gpk1i9

22 Thomas Joscelyn, "How China Tries to Intimidate Its Dissidents Living Overseas," *Foundation for Defense of Democracies*, July 8, 2020, https://www.fdd.org/analysis/2020/07/08/how-china-intimidates-dissidents-overseas/

23 Xinhua, "3,317 Fugitives Abroad Captured in China's 'Fox Hunt'," *Xinhua Net*, November 2, 2017, http://www.xinhuanet.com/english/2017-11/02/c_136723754.htm

As of July 2020, together, China and Hong Kong had extradition treaties with more than fifty countries, though in July 2020, Canada suspended its extradition treaty with Hong Kong.[24]

Conclusion

The diaspora of Chinese citizens leaving China with significant assets is resulting in an even stronger arm reaching into countries and threatening former citizens. Beijing is blackmailing Chinese nationals to force their return, offering them two choices: return to China or commit suicide.[25] Christopher Wray, U.S. FBI Chief, explained in a July 2020 news conference,

---

24 Matthew Strong, "Concern Mounts Over 52 Countries Having Extradition Treaties with China or Hong Kong," *Taiwan News*, July 4, 2020, https://www.taiwannews.com.tw/en/news/3960108

25 Julian Borger, "China Blackmailing Dissenters in US to Return Home – FBI Chief," *The Guardian*, July 7, 2020, https://www.theguardian.com/us-news/2020/jul/07/china-christopher-wray-operation-fox-hunt

Since 2014, Chinese General Secretary Xi Jinping has spearheaded a program known as "Fox Hunt." Now, China describes Fox Hunt as some kind of international anti-corruption campaign—it is not. Instead, Fox Hunt is a sweeping bid by General Secretary Xi to target Chinese nationals whom he sees as threats and who live outside China, across the world. We're talking about political rivals, dissidents, and critics seeking to expose China's extensive human rights violations.

Hundreds of the Fox Hunt victims that they target live right here in the United States, and many are American citizens or green card holders. The Chinese government wants to force them to return to China, and China's tactics to accomplish that are shocking. For example, when it couldn't locate one Fox Hunt target, the Chinese government sent an emissary to visit the target's family here in the United States. The message they said to pass on? The target had two options: return to China promptly, or commit suicide. And what happens when Fox Hunt targets refuse to return to China? In the past, their family members both here in the United States and in China have been threatened and coerced, and those back in China have even been arrested for leverage.[26]

What's at Stake?

First, there is great concern for the many Chinese who live and work in the United States and elsewhere. The lives and livelihoods of Chinese-American citizens, Chinese permanent residents, and Chinese students could be endangered if they are caught in Beijing's sting. In July 2020, Christopher Wray, U.S. FBI Chief, stated in a broad-ranging speech, "If you believe the Chinese government is targeting you—that you're a potential Fox Hunt victim—please reach out to your local FBI field office."[27]

Second, if Beijing can threaten Chinese nationals in countries where there is no extradition treaty like Australia, Canada, and the United States, the threat must be even more intense in other countries.

Third, if Chinese authorities, with their long arm, can round up or threaten the masses who have a pro-democracy stance regarding Hong Kong, they may be able to locate people of any nationality across the world who stand with Hong Kong, Taiwan, and/or Tibet and harass them into submission wherever they live, or 're-educate' them in one of their concentration camps in Xinjiang Province, discussed later in this book.

---

26 Christopher Wray, "The Threat Posed by the Chinese Government and the Chinese Communist Party to the Economic and National Security of the United States," *Federal Bureau of Investigation*, July 7, 2020, https://www.fbi.gov/news/speeches/the-threat-posed-by-the-chinese-government-and-the-chinese-communist-party-to-the-economic-and-national-security-of-the-united-states

27 Ibid.

Chapter 5
The Fortune 500's Kowtow to China
Kneeling in Submission to China

Introduction

Kneeling and touching one's head to the ground in docile obedience to the Chinese magistrate was historically required of commoners who wanted to trade with China, as well as foreign representatives who came to discuss business or make a request to the dynastic leader. The Chinese emperor recognized representatives from barbarian states' kowtowing to him as "a symbolic recognition of their inferiority" and "acknowledgement of their status of a vassal state."[1] This act of meek capitulation often included paying a tribute. After bowing to acknowledge Chinese superiority and primacy, delegations often brought gifts, riches, or exotic products from their countries to show respect. With these acts of submission, China defended its claim to be the Middle Kingdom and the center of the world's hierarchy, demanding subordination from foreigners whom they called 'barbarians'.

Formalized during the Ming dynasty (1368-1644), barbarians kowtowed and paid tribute in deference before obtaining permission to trade. In the 1800s, some representatives from Great Britain did not oblige the Chinese emperor Qianlong,[2] who considered himself the "son of heaven".[3] He became angered by the Westerner's lack of respect. Despite the degradation and indignity China endured during the Century of Humiliation, kowtowing was expected for centuries and continues to be expected in other forms of loyalty, respect, and obedience today.[4] Meanwhile, Chinese citizens and foreigners alike must show respect at all times to President Xi and the CCP or face harsh consequences. President Xi Jinping talks

Kowtowing to Xi Jinping

---

1 Khong Y., "The American Tributary System," *Chinese Journal of International Politics* 6, no. 1 (2013): 1-47
2 Internet Modern History Sourcebook, "Emperor Qian Long's Letter to King George III, 1793," *Internet Modern History Sourcebook*, n.d., http://academics.wellesley.edu/Polisci/wj/China/208/READINGS/qianlong.html
3 Ulrich Theobald, "Tianzi, The Son of Heaven," *China Knowledge*, February 28, 2019, http://www.chinaknowledge.de/History/Terms/tianzi.html
4 Howard W. French, *Everything Under the Heavens: How the Past Helps Shape China's Push for Global Power* (New York: Alfred A. Knopf, 2017).

about the use of carrots and sticks to reinforce China's moral authority since, "Leaders in Beijing understand that it is important to demonstrate goodwill now and then."[5]

China's 21st Century Demands to Corporations

The expectation to kowtow is not limited to 'barbarians'. In the 21st century, corporations who operate their businesses in China must oblige the Chinese Communist Party. In January 2018, the Marriott corporation was required to shut down its websites and apps in China as punishment for disrespecting China's sovereignty[6] by publishing a survey with Taiwan and Tibet as separate countries.[7] China ordered the suspension of its hotels and demanded an apology.[8] In August 2020, the Shanghai Cyberspace Authority ordered Marriott "to conduct a comprehensive self-examination and rectification to completely clean up illegal content."[9]

Marriott was not the only company to face a backlash from Beijing. After not including Taiwan on a map, Christian Dior made its apologies widely known as it groveled to placate China, stating,[10] "Dior ultimately respects and upholds the one-China principle [of sovereignty], strictly safeguards China's sovereignty and territorial integrity, and treasures the feelings of the Chinese people." The handbag maker and clothing designer, Coach, also apologized for selling a shirt that says "Hong Kong – HONG KONG" and "Taipei, Taiwan"[11] and pulled these clothing products off the shelves across the globe. The Chinese fashion model for the company apologized, "I am sorry for the damage caused to the public for my poor choice of brand," saying, "I love my motherland and I resolutely safeguard national sovereignty."[12]

Donatella Versace also apologized on Instagram after the company identified Hong Kong and Macau as countries. She stated, "Never have I wanted to disrespect China's National Sovereignty and this is why I wanted to personally apologize for such inaccuracy and for

---

5 Michael Thim, "Xi Jinping's Rhetoric on Taiwan May Have Been Gentler, But His Bag of Carrots and Sticks Remains the Same," *South China Morning Post*, July 25, 2018, https://www.scmp.com/comment/insight-opinion/hong-kong/article/2156622/xi-jinpings-rhetoric-taiwan-may-have-been-gentler

6 Pei Li & Brenda Goh, "Shanghai Temporarily Closes Marriott Website in China After Questionnaire Gaffe," *Reuters*, January 11, 2018, https://www.reuters.com/article/us-china-marriott/shanghai-temporarily-closes-marriott-website-in-china-after-questionnaire-gaffe-idUSKBN1F00UT?il=0

7 Abha Bhattarai, "China Demanded Marriott Change its Website. The Company Complied.," *The Washington Post*, January 18, 2018, https://www.washingtonpost.com/news/business/wp/2018/01/18/china-demanded-marriott-change-its-website-the-company-complied/

8 AP News, "China Orders Marriott to Suspend Website, App in Map Furor," *AP News*, January 11, 2018, https://apnews.com/cf56a1ffc53049118b5a14424c5fc0e6/China-orders-Marriott-to-suspend-website,-app-in-map-furor

9 Ibid.

10 Alexandra Ma, "Dior Groveled to China After It Used a Map that Didn't Show Taiwan as Part of the Country. Here are Other Times Western Brands Caved After Offending the Communist Party," *Business Insider*, October 17, 2019, https://www.businessinsider.com/western-companies-apologize-china-communist-party-list-2019-10

11 Harriet Amurao, "Versace's New T-Shirt Is All Sorts Of Problematic," *Fashion Industry Broadcast*, August 21, 2019, https://fashionindustrybroadcast.com/2019/08/21/versaces-new-t-shirt-is-all-sorts-of-problematic/

12 Xu Qing, "US Fashion Brand Coach Apologizes for Territorial Blunder After Model Liu Wen Quits," *Shine*, August 12, 2019, https://www.shine.cn/news/nation/1908120037/

any distress that it might have caused."¹³ The fashion company, Zara, apologized for listing Taiwan as a country. Zara's representative expressed regret, saying that they would undergo "self-examination".¹⁴ After Swarovski also included a map with Taiwan, the company posted on Facebook, "Swarovski has always firmly respected China's National Sovereignty and territorial integrity, providing the Chinese market with unified worldwide services and products."¹⁵

After being scolded, Medtronic, a medical equipment manufacturer, apologized for calling Taiwan a country.¹⁶ "It's hard not to see it as part of the wider trend where nationalist issues are being emphasized very deliberately as part of the new era."¹⁷

These companies were only a few of those who immediately 'kowtowed' to Beijing, after being threatened that they would not be able to enter Chinese markets without changing their behavior, stance, or marketing. Airlines that listed Taiwan as its own country also

Airlines Nabbed for Naming Taiwan and /or Tibet

---

13 Lucy Handley, "Versace, Givenchy and Coach Say Sorry Over Chinese T-shirt Anger," *CNBC*, August 12, 2019, https://www.cnbc.com/2019/08/12/versace-givenchy-and-coach-say-sorry-over-chinese-t-shirt-anger.html

14 The Economist, "China is Getting Tougher on Taiwan," *The Economist*, January 18, 2018, https://www.economist.com/china/2018/01/18/china-is-getting-tougher-on-taiwan

15 Swarovski. 2019. "Considering the recent happenings in China, Swarovski takes full responsibility...," *Facebook*, August 12, 2019. https://www.facebook.com/SWAROVSKI.global/photos/considering-the-recent-happenings-in-china-swarovski-takes-full-responsibility-a/10156422249192647

16 Brenda Goh & John Ruwitch, "China Cracks Down on Foreign Companies Calling Taiwan, Other Regions Countries," *Reuters*, January 12, 2018, https://www.reuters.com/article/us-china-delta/china-cracks-down-on-foreign-companies-calling-taiwan-other-regions-countries-idUSKBN1F10RC?il=0

17 Ibid.

followed suit. China's Civil Aviation Administration admonished 44 Airlines, including, American, British Airways, Delta, Qantas, and United among others for listing Taiwan as its own country.[18] China forced Emirates airline to remove Taiwanese pins from their uniforms.[19] Hong Kong Airlines were forced to replace their designation of Taiwan with the destination, Taiwan, China.[20] Qantas admitted 'oversight' in its designation of Taiwan. Most offenders immediately bowed to China's demand to remove or rename Taiwan, fearful of punishment and banishment.[21]

The NBA Kowtows to China

In another sensational display of Chinese totalitarianism and determination for countries to kowtow, Daryl Morey of the Houston Rockets tweeted his support for the pro-democracy residents of Hong Kong, saying, "Fight For Freedom Stand With Hong Kong".[22] China's authoritarian backlash was played out in dramatic fashion. Morey deleted his tweet, explaining that his personal views were not the views of the NBA, though it was too late.

China's streaming media platforms vowed never to show Houston Rockets games again, though over a half a billion people in China watch NBA games.[23] Morey apologized, saying that he regretted posting the tweet and that he "deeply offended many of our friends and fans in China, which is regrettable."[24] Chinese authorities even asked the NBA to fire Morey.[25]

Chinese officials proceeded to tear down NBA banners and posters[26] and "China's state broadcaster and Tencent responded by…refusing to air all NBA preseason games."[27] Beijing's drastic steps sent a clear message to anyone who dared to support Hong Kong or back the pro-democracy movement.

Lebron James criticized Morey's pro-democracy sentiment. "In Hong Kong, protesters burned James jerseys, shot baskets at a hoop with his face on the backboard…including a

---

18. Michael Mazza, "China's Airline Censorship Over Taiwan Must Not Fly," *NIKKEI Asian Review*, July 31, 2018, https://asia.nikkei.com/Opinion/China-s-airline-censorship-over-Taiwan-must-not-fly

19. One Mile At A Time, "China Forces Emirates Crews To Remove Taiwanese Flags From Uniforms," *One Mile At a Time*, May 30, 2017, https://onemileatatime.com/emirates-crews-taiwan-flag/

20. Jennifer Creery, "All Hong Kong Airlines Change Taiwan's Destination Name To 'Taiwan, China' on Deadline Set by Beijing," *Hong Kong Free Press*, July 25, 2018, https://hongkongfp.com/2018/07/25/hong-kong-airlines-change-taiwans-destination-name-taiwan-china-deadline-set-beijing/

21. Erika Kinetz, "Airlines Obey Beijing's Demand to Call Taiwan Part of China," *AP News*, May 22, 2018, https://apnews.com/6f55419ce6a9449687b91f3fdfb3417d

22. Dan Wetzel, "Why the NBA Cowered to its Chinese Overlords," *Yahoo Sports*, October 7, 2019, https://sports.yahoo.com/why-the-nba-cowered-to-its-chinese-overlords-171046325.html

23. Derek Wallbank and Alfred Cang, "How a Quickly-Deleted Tweet About China Got Pretty Much Everyone Mad at the NBA," *Time Magazine*, October 7, 2019, https://time.com/5694150/nba-china-hong-kong/

24. Yanan Wang, "NBA's Reaction to Morey Tweet Differs in English, Chinese," *AP News*, October 7, 2019, https://apnews.com/9c3df9a26a464a86990b59f89602b854

25. Des Bieler, "Adam Silver Says China Asked NBA to Fire Rockets Daryl Morey," *The Washington Post*, October 17, 2019, https://www.washingtonpost.com/sports/2019/10/17/adam-silver-says-china-asked-nba-fire-rockets-daryl-morey/

26. Brad Sullivan, "Report: Posters for Lakers Games in China Taken Down, Sparking Fears of Cancellation," *Lakers Daily*, October 9, 2019, https://lakersdaily.com/posters-for-lakers-games-china-taken-down-sparking-fears-cancellation/

27. Alexandra Ma, "Dior Groveled to China After It Used a Map that Didn't Show Taiwan as Part of the Country. Here are Other Times Western Brands Caved After Offending the Communist Party," *Business Insider*, October 17, 2019, https://www.businessinsider.com/western-companies-apologize-china-communist-party-list-2019-10

depiction of him embracing Chinese cash."[28] Shaquille "Shaq" O'Neal publicly defended Morey, saying, "Daryl Morey was right...We, as American people, do a lot of business in China...And they know and understand our values and we understand their values. And one of our best values here in America is free speech. We're allowed to say what we want to say, and we're allowed to speak up about injustices, and that's just how it goes."[29]

The question remains what the NBA would do. China made it clear that until the NBA repudiated Morey, they would cease showing NBA games in China. Fans accused the NBA of kowtowing to China, putting their profits first. Fans questioned if American sponsors would kowtow to China as well.[30] Daryl Morey ultimately resigned as the general manager of the Houston Rockets, effective November 1, 2020 after thirteen seasons.[31]

Conclusion

These incidents were not the first, and definitely not the last. Beijing continues to influence company's decisions. In a subtle incident, Amazon told its employees to delete TikTok, an entertainment app owned by Chinese company ByteDance, from their phones because of "security risks",[32] but then backtracked and stated the email announcement was sent "in error".[33] Nevertheless, these incidents involving major corporations 'kowtowing' to Beijing are alarming. Because major companies depend on Chinese markets for their production, manufacturing, operation, and sales, China has large corporations wrapped around its finger to stand with Beijing's policies and ambitions.

What's at Stake?

First, according to J. Michael Cole, scholar with the China Policy Institute, "If Beijing does not encounter red lines, it can only keep asking for more."[34]

Second, without boundaries, China will exert its influence over intellectual property, website content, and values of companies worldwide.

Third, if China can tell non-Chinese corporations, sports leagues, and executives what they can and cannot do, wherever they live, the power and influence they exert worldwide can force everyone to kowtow.

---

28 Sopan Deb, "LeBron James Faces Backlash Unseen Since 'The Decision'," *The New York Times*, October 15, 2019, https://www.nytimes.com/2019/10/15/sports/basketball/lebron-china-burned-jerseys.html

29 Rosie Perper, "China and the NBA are Coming to Blows over a Pro-Hong Kong Tweet. Here's Why.," *Business Insider*, October 22, 2019, https://www.businessinsider.com/nba-china-feud-timeline-daryl-morey-tweet-hong-kong-protests-2019-10

30 Chris Isidore, "The NBA Faces a No-Win Situation in China. Here's What It Stands to Lose," *CNN Business*, October 8, 2019, https://www.cnn.com/2019/10/08/business/daryl-morey-tweet-nba-china/index.html

31 Tim MacMahon, "Daryl Morey Stepping Down as Houston Rockets GM," *ESPN*, October 15, 2020, https://www.espn.com/nba/story/_/id/30120824/daryl-morey-stepping-houston-rockets-gm-sources-say

32 Mike Isaac & Karen Weise, "Amazon Backtracks from Demand That Employees Delete TikTok," *The New York Times*, July 10, 2020, https://www.nytimes.com/2020/07/10/technology/tiktok-amazon-security-risk.html

33 Brian Fung & Zachary Cohen, "Amazon Tells Employees to Delete TikTok Immediately—Then Takes It Back," *CNN Business*, July 10, 2020, https://www.cnn.com/2020/07/10/tech/amazon-tiktok/index.html

34 Erika Kinetz, "Airlines Obey Beijing's Demand to Call Taiwan Part of China," *AP News*, May 22, 2018, https://apnews.com/6f55419ce6a9449687b91f3fdfb3417d

Chapter 6
Nibbling Away
Gobbling Up Each Tasty Bite of Asia Around its Perimeter

Introduction

China is placing its stake in territories throughout Asia. Few states in Asia are left untouched by China's reach and determined approach. Ever since Xi Jinping was elected as the President of the People's Republic of China (PRC) on March 14, 2013, he has bolstered China's position and extended Beijing's reach. With an increase in its military budget and a dizzying array of new vessels, China is now a global superpower and on its way to hegemony in Asia. In the north, south, east, and west, China's economic, political, and military power can be felt. The remainder of this book will cover these topics in depth. For now, this chapter offers a preview.

Hong Kong and Taiwan

The hope for Hong Kong's autonomy until 2047 is all but gone. As *Vox* explains, China's new control is an 'official death sentence'.[1] Protests are banned, free speech is outlawed, and hundreds have been taken into custody. This authoritative domination is likely to be the same future for Taiwan, which is under China's One Country, Two Systems approach.[2] Beijing intends to sweep Taiwan fully under its wing at its next opportunity; reunification of Taiwan with China will not be stopped by any force.[3] The Chinese news sources insist that supporting Taiwan is 'wicked',[4] since Taiwan will never be independent.[5]

Still, Taiwan is self-governing and has been for more than seventy years. Beijing has attempted to exert financial, diplomatic, and military pressure with military overflight, ships encroaching in the Taiwan Strait, and threats to fishing vessels. Even with the political pressure and ability to block Taiwan's admission to international governing bodies, President Tsai Ing-wen has managed to gain support from several countries, even if unofficially, and, with it, a multibillion-dollar purchase of weapons. The U.S. sent high-level officials to visit Taiwan in August 2020.[6] In September 2020, Keith Krach, U.S. Undersecretary for Economic Affairs, went to Taiwan while China showed its displeasure by flying warplanes overhead.[7]

---

1   Jen Kirby, "'It is an Official Death Sentence for Hong Kong': China Moves to Pass National Security Law," *Vox*, May 21, 2020, https://www.vox.com/2020/5/21/21266419/hong-kong-china-national-security-law-protests

2   A.K., "What is China's "One Country, Two Systems" Policy?," *The Economist*, June 30, 2019, https://www.economist.com/the-economist-explains/2019/06/30/what-is-chinas-one-country-two-systems-policy

3   Xinhua, "China's Reunification Cannot be Stopped by Any Force: Spokesperson," *XinhuaNet*, May 20, 2020, http://www.xinhuanet.com/english/2020-05/20/c_139072434.htm

4   Xinhua, "Opinion: Washington's Wicked Motives behind Provocative Taiwan Trip," *XinhuaNet*, August 10, 2020, http://www.xinhuanet.com/english/2020-08/10/c_139279720.htm

5   Xinhua, "Mainland Slams Taiwan Official's 'Taiwan Independence' Remarks," *XinhuaNet*, June 22, 2020, http://www.xinhuanet.com/english/2020-06/22/c_139159054.htm

6   Gerry Shih, "Taiwan and U.S. to Hold Highest-Level Meeting Since 1979 as China Tensions Soar," *The Washington Post*, August 4, 2020, https://www.washingtonpost.com/world/asia_pacific/taiwan-and-us-to-hold-highest-level-contact-since-1979-as-china-tensions-grow/2020/08/04/63d84cb4-d6be-11ea-a788-2ce86ce81129_story.html

7   John Xie, "China Sends Warplanes Over Taiwan as US Envoy Visits," *VOA News*, September 18, 2020, https://www.voanews.com/east-asia-pacific/voa-news-china/china-sends-warplanes-over-taiwan-us-envoy-visits

Nepal and Bhutan

China's ambitions have expanded. Kathmandu is a key partner in China's 'Belt and Road Initiative' as China invests in Nepal's infrastructure.[8] Meanwhile, China questioned why Nepalese nationals were joining the Indian army in August 2020,[9] which Beijing sees as a threat to its expansion efforts.[10]

China has territorial claims on Nepal as well and seeks to 'correct' boundaries as Beijing continues to encroach on Nepalese territory, nibbling bite by bite each year on Nepal's land.[11] In response, angry Nepalese burned images of Xi Jinping in effigy.[12] Even more heartbreaking and enraging for the Nepalese, in May 2020, Chinese media announced that

---

8 Anbarasan Ethirajan, "India and China: How Nepal's New Map is Stirring Old Rivalries," *BBC News*, June 10, 2020, https://www.bbc.com/news/world-asia-52967452

9 Times Now, "'Why are Gurkhas joining Indian Army?': China Wants Nepal NGO to Audit," *The Economic Times*, August 12, 2020, https://economictimes.indiatimes.com/news/defence/why-are-gurkhas-joining-indian-army-china-wants-nepal-ngo-to-audit/videoshow/77503103.cms?from=mdr

10 Ibid.

11 Vasudevan Sridharan, "Nepal Protesters Burn Xi Jinping Effigies Over China's Alleged Border Encroachment," *South China Morning Post*, November 12, 2019, https://www.scmp.com/week-asia/politics/article/3037449/protesters-nepal-burn-effigies-chinas-xi-jinping-over-alleged

12 Nepal Monitor, "Chinese President's Xi's Effigy Burned in Sarlahi," *Nepal Monitor*, November 10, 2019, https://nepalmonitor.org/reports/view/26688

Mount Everest is Chinese territory.[13] Reports in June 2020 stated that China also considered some Nepalese villages part of Chinese territory, saying, "Questions are being raised in the media about Nepal's villages falling under Chinese territory in Tibet, about Huawei 5G towers on the north side of Mt Everest, about Chinese language teachers coming to Nepal, and the online meeting between the Communist Parties of China and Nepal."[14]

Bhutan's situation is not considerably different. China now also claims part of Bhutan. When Bhutan made a request to create the Sakteng Wildlife Sanctuary, China protested saying that the region within Bhutan was part of China.[15] Bhutan protested this claim.[16] China had never before made this claim so the demand was a new attempt to encroach further south. China claims that its livestock have grazed in Bhutan and thus China has a 'historic right' to the region. India attempted to become involved in these negotiations, though this angered China as it gave CCP diplomats less control of the proceedings and Beijing requested that India stay out of the discourse.[17]

The Himalayas – India

In the Himalayas, China's need for water and desire to control natural resources has resulted in deadly clashes in 2020. China and India are two nuclear powerhouses; both countries have approximately 1.4 billion people. To put that into context, combined, these two countries have more than seven times as many people as the entire population of both the United States and Canada. Geographically, China and the U.S. are approximately the same size, while India is approximately one-third smaller. In another context, that means that approximately the same number of people live in China and India, though India is extremely compact.

The McMahon Line, the demarcation between Tibet and India, was agreed to in the 1914 Simla Accord. China claims a 'historic right' to a larger expanse of land on the grounds that there are historic maps showing that, once upon a time, China had more territory. While the Line of Actual Control (LAC) is the boundary, China is now contesting that agreement and has sought to expand its territory into India. Although Sino-Indian agreements that granted legal recognition to the LAC were signed by China and India in 1993, 1996, and 2013, they have since been violated.[18]

---

13 NDTV, "Chinese Media Post on Mount Everest Sparks Twitter Fight With Nepal," *NDTV*, May 10, 2020, https://www.ndtv.com/world-news/chinese-media-cgtn-tweet-on-mount-everest-sparks-twitter-fight-with-nepal-2226439

14 Surendra Phuyal, "Nepal Also Has Boundary Issues with China," *Nepali Times*, June 25, 2020, https://www.nepalitimes.com/latest/nepal-also-has-boundary-issues-with-china/

15 Felix K. Chang, "No Sanctuary: China's New Territorial Dispute with Bhutan," *Foreign Policy Research Institute*, July 29, 2020, https://www.fpri.org/article/2020/07/china-territorial-dispute-bhutan/

16 NDTV, "Bhutan Rejects China's New Claim Over Its Territory, Sends Demarche: Report," *NDTV*, July 22, 2020, https://www.ndtv.com/world-news/bhutan-rejects-chinas-new-claim-over-its-territory-sends-demarche-report-2266673

17 Xinhua, "Full Text of Facts and China's Position Concerning Indian Border Troops' Crossing of China-India Boundary," *ChinaDaily*, August 3, 2017, https://www.chinadaily.com.cn/world/2017-08/03/content_30341027.htm

18 Pranab Dhal Samanta, "Chinese Action Violates 1993, 1996, and 2013 Border Agreements," *The Economic Times*, June 18, 2020, https://economictimes.indiatimes.com/news/defence/chinese-action-violates-1993-1996-and-2013-border-agreements/articleshow/76405795.cms

These agreements state that "No activities of either side shall overstep the Line of Actual Control."[19] However, Chinese troops cross the LAC's agreed upon 2 km boundary each year, though in June 2020, the clashes became deadly and twenty Indian soldiers were killed.[20] Meanwhile, the first article of the 1993 agreement says, "Neither side shall use or threaten to use force against the other by any means. Pending an ultimate solution to the boundary question between the two countries, the two sides shall strictly respect and observe the line of actual control between the two sides."[21] China crossed the line again in August 2020 on the opposite side of a lake considered part of India.[22] The second requirement is, "Each side will keep its military forces in the areas along the line of actual control to a minimum level compatible with the friendly and good neighbourly relations between the two countries."[23] In September 2020, both India and China accused the other side of firing shots across the border,[24] the first time this has been thought to have happened since 1975.[25]

Southeast Asia

In the South China Sea, China has artificially constructed and militarized once-submerged coral reefs and sandbars. In 2020, it established two administrative districts.[26] Among other takeovers in the South China Sea, China took the Paracel Islands and Johnson Reef from Vietnam, Scarborough Shoal and Mischief Reef from the Philippines and asserted its claim over 80-90% of the waterway. According to the United Nations Convention on the Law of the Sea, signed by each of the regional countries, states are granted 200 nautical miles off of their coastline which extend into the South China Sea

---

19 Peace Agreements Database, The University of Edinburgh, "Agreement on the Maintenance of Peace and Tranquility along the Line of Actual Control in the India-China Border Areas," *The University of Edinburgh*, n.d., https://www.peaceagreements.org/view/286

20 BBC News, "India-China Clash: 20 Indian Troops Killed in Ladakh Fighting," *BBC News*, June 16, 2020, https://www.bbc.com/news/world-asia-53061476

21 Signed by R.L. Bhatia and Tang Jiaxuan, "Agreement on the Maintenance of Peace and Tranquility Along the Line of Actual Control in the India-China Border Areas," *PeaceAgreements.org*, Signed on September 7, 1993, https://www.peaceagreements.org/viewmasterdocument/286

22 Jeffrey Gettlemen, Sameer Yasir, and Hari Kumar, "India and China Face Off Again at Border as Troops Move In," *The New York Times*, August 31, 2020, https://www.nytimes.com/2020/08/31/world/asia/india-china-troops-border.html

23 Signed by R.L. Bhatia and Tang Jiaxuan, "Agreement on the Maintenance of Peace and Tranquility Along the Line of Actual Control in the India-China Border Areas," *PeaceAgreements.org*, Signed on September 7, 1993, https://www.peaceagreements.org/viewmasterdocument/286

24 Joanna Slater, Niha Masih, and Gerry Shih, "Shots Fired on the India-China Border for the First Time in Decades as Tensions Flare," *The Washington Post*, September 8, 2020, https://www.washingtonpost.com/world/asia_pacific/shots-fired-on-the-india-china-border-for-the-first-time-in-decades-as-tensions-flare/2020/09/08/d8c5a020-f195-11ea-8025-5d3489768ac8_story.html

25 Jessie Yeung, "China is Doubling Down on its Territorial Claims and That's Causing Conflict Across Asia," *CNN*, September 30, 2020, https://www.cnn.com/2020/09/26/asia/china-asia-territorial-claims-conflicts-explainer-intl-hnk-scli/index.html

26 Rachel Winston and Ishika Sachdeva, *Raging Waters in the South China Sea: What the Battle for Supremacy Means for Southeast Asia* (Irvine: Lizard Publishing, 2020).

(UNCLOS),[27] also claimed by China. These claimant states include Brunei, Malaysia, the Philippines, Taiwan, and Vietnam, though Indonesia and Singapore have rights to their EEZs protected by UNCLOS as well.

Despite the 2016 ruling in the *Philippines v. China* arbitral case presented to the International Court of Justice[28] that said China had 'no basis' for its claim,[29] Beijing's military and construction arm continued its development of military bases in the South China Sea. China ignored and further violated the tribunal's outcome. Widespread protests ensued as runways, missile silos, radar stations, weapons caches, barracks, desalination plants, and more were placed on these islands. Regardless of the ruling, China claims sovereignty and continues to assert its claim resorting to violence (ramming vessels, preventing fishing, thwarting oil drilling efforts) and shining lasers in pilots' eyes.

In July 2020, the U.S. formally rejected China's claims.[30] Other countries, like Australia have dismissed China's nine-dash line claim as well.[31] In 2020, these waters heated up, with countries angry over Beijing's aggression and foreign countries defending freedom of the navigation. This inflamed China's ire and prompted the People's Liberation Army (PLA) in August 2020 to fire ballistic missiles into the South China Sea as a warning.[32] The *Global Times*, a China-sponsored media source explains, "Chinese society must therefore have real courage to engage calmly in a war that aims to protect core interests, and be prepared to bear the cost," continuing, "we must win."[33]

Japan – The Senkaku Islands

On a few small Japanese islands, China has staked another claim. These islands are claimed by Japan (Senkaku), Taiwan (Tiaoyutai), and China (Diaoyu). Using the same argument that once, long ago, fishermen fished around the islands, China makes its claim based upon a 'historic right', calling the islands its "inherent territory".[34] After Japan conducted a 1885 survey, the Japanese claimed sovereignty over the Senkakus.[35] The area is a

---

27 United Nations, "United Nations Convention on the Law of the Sea," *United Nations*, 1982, https://www.un.org/Depts/los/convention_agreements/texts/unclos/unclos_e.pdf

28 Permanent Court of Arbitration, "The South China Sea Arbitration (The Republic of Philippines v. The People's Republic of China)," *Permanent Court of Arbitration*, July 12, 2016, https://pcacases.com/web/sendAttach/2086

29 Ibid.

30 Michael R. Pompeo, "U.S. Position on Maritime Claims in the South China Sea," *U.S. Department of State*, July 13, 2020, https://www.state.gov/u-s-position-on-maritime-claims-in-the-south-china-sea/

31 Reuters Staff, "Australia Says China's South China Sea Claims are Unlawful," *Reuters*, July 25, 2020, https://www.reuters.com/article/us-australia-china/australia-says-chinas-south-china-sea-claims-are-unlawful-idUSKCN24Q09D

32 Steven Lee Myers and Keith Bradsher, "China Fires Missiles into South China Sea, Sending U.S. a Message," *The New York Times*, September 18, 2020, https://www.nytimes.com/2020/08/27/world/asia/missiles-south-china-sea.html

33 Hu Xijin, "China Must Be Militarily and Morally Ready for a Potential War," *Global Times*, September 11, 2020, https://www.globaltimes.cn/content/1200595.shtml

34 The Sasakawa Peace Foundation, "China's 'Diaoyu Dao White Paper' and Territorial Claims," *The Sasakawa Peace Foundation*, September 12, 2016, https://www.spf.org/islandstudies/readings/b00008r.html

35 Tadashi Ikeda, "Getting Senkaku History Right," *The Diplomat*, November 26, 2013, https://thediplomat.com/2013/11/getting-senkaku-history-right/

fisherman's paradise and vessels from China and Japan frequently clash.[36] There are also other valuable natural resources like oil, gas, and mineral deposits below the sea that are coveted by all three countries.[37]

In 2020, China increased overflights of the area and sent in coast guard vessels to the islands as it probed Japanese defenses to search for opportunities to gain access and take over the Senkaku Islands.[38] China's takeover would be unconscionable to Japan, but possibly more dangerous for Taiwan since the islands are 221 km from Taipei (1,890 km from Tokyo and 638 km from Shanghai). Furthermore, the U.S. has a 1960 agreement with Japan to defend Japan from attack.[39] Thus, an attack by China on Japan's islands could spark an all-out great power war.

Conclusion

The countries highlighted in this chapter are only a few that will be discussed further in the subsequent parts of this book. China has encroached on the territories of more than a dozen states during the COVID-19 pandemic and its expanding reach is unlikely to subside.

What's at Stake?

First, it is nearly a foregone conclusion that Hong Kong, Tibet, and Inner Mongolia will ever be pried away from China, though the islands of Taiwan and Japan are likely to be overtaken next if the world does not wake up.

Second, the South China Sea is currently being watched by a number of countries. Meanwhile, dangerous incursions, highlighted in *Raging Waters in the South China Sea* (book 1 of this series), have been increasingly provocative.

Third, clashes in India and protests in Nepal and Bhutan are but a few places where China has set its sights and is nibbling away as people worldwide have their focus on their economies, managing the impact of the coronavirus pandemic, and other social issues.

---

36   Ankit Panda, "Japanese Naval Ship Involved in Collision With Chinese Fishing Vessel in East China Sea," *The Diplomat*, March 31, 2020, https://thediplomat.com/2020/03/japanese-naval-ship-involved-in-collision-with-chinese-fishing-vessel-in-east-china-sea/

37   Shantanu Roy-Chaudhury, "The Senkaku Islands Dispute," *International Policy*, August 1, 2016, https://intpolicydigest.org/2016/08/01/senkaku-islands-dispute/

38   David Axe, "China is Probing Japan's Defenses over the Disputed Senkaku Islands," *Forbes*, August 19, 2020, https://www.forbes.com/sites/davidaxe/2020/08/19/china-is-probing-japans-aerial-defenses-over-the-disputed-senkaku-islands/#724e2bc97dab

39   Ministry of Foreign Affairs of Japan, "Treaty of Mutual Cooperation and Security Between Japan and the United States of America," *Ministry of Foreign Affairs of Japan*, n.d., https://www.mofa.go.jp/region/n-america/us/q&a/ref/1.html

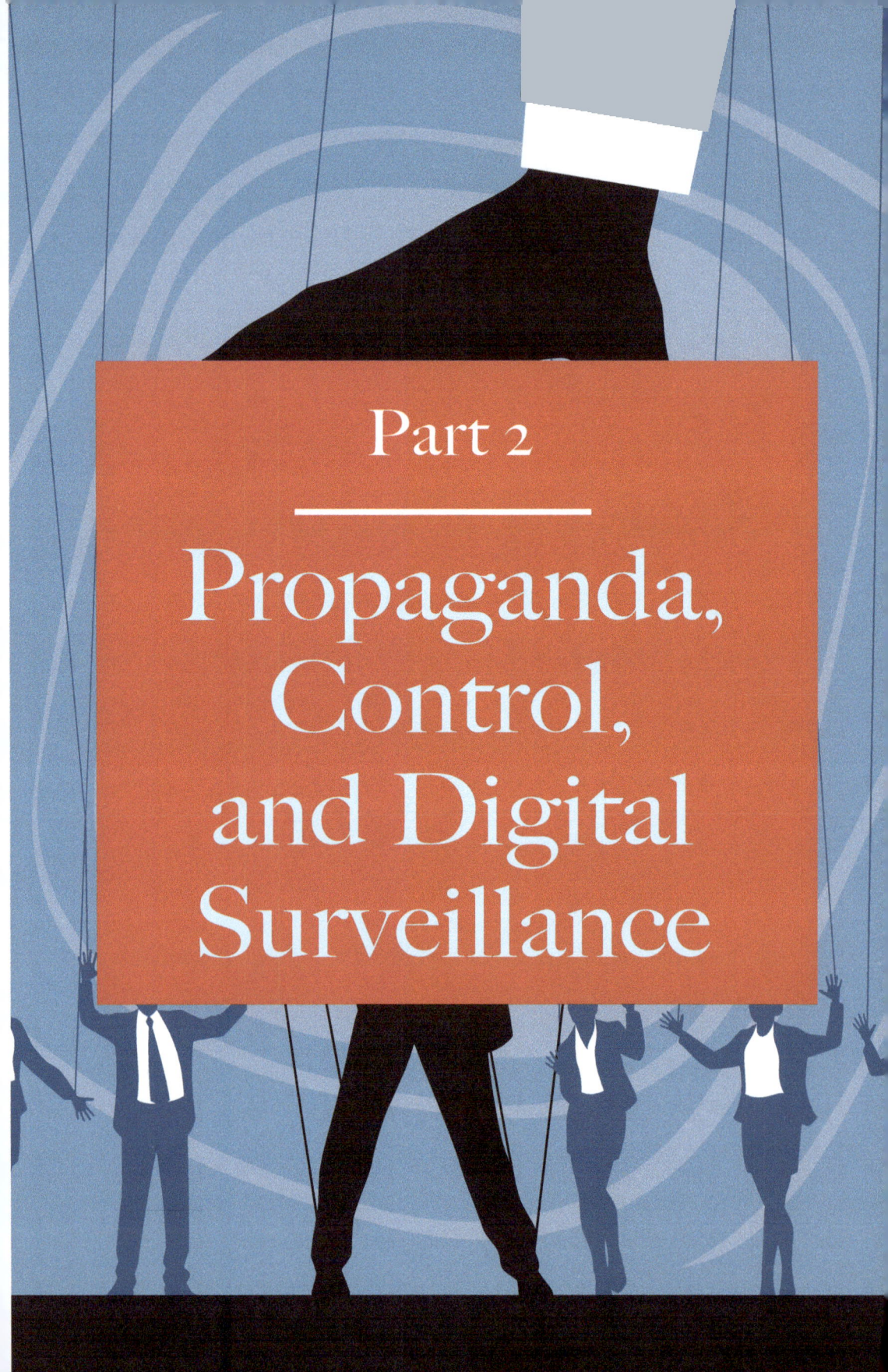

Censorship, Monitoring, and Social Control

We are being controlled by information pumped into us by groups attempting to influence our beliefs. Disinformation enters through the news, social media, and bots. This is not just happening in China, it is happening worldwide. Philippine President Rodrigo Duterte canceled the rights to an entire television station whose information he opposed. U.S. news stations selectively provide sources, commentary, and interviews depending upon their political bent – left and right. However, in China, there is an entire unit devoted to propaganda in state-owned, state-controlled, and state-dictated broadcasts. Furthermore, thousands of 'wolf warriors' are intent on scrubbing out the truth by shaming corporations and officials and harassing those who disagree with China.

Chinese television screens were erased of content during CNN's October 7, 2020 broadcast of the U.S. Vice Presidential debate when they discussed China's cover-up of the coronavirus outbreak.[1] The screen turned to colorful stripes. Automated accounts, pretending to represent real people, are increasingly being used by propaganda-distributing machines. False narratives drown out the facts. Information on websites are being transmitted to China and included in its growing bank of data.

Social control is inherent in socialist systems where all members must comply with directives and follow the orders of a supreme disseminator of information and rules. In Qingdao, every resident was forced to be tested and faced with the possibility of quarantine. Social control does not end with mere testing but extends to China's blocking of information and extreme social credit system discussed in the next chapters.

Dr. Martin Luther King, Jr., wrote the article, "The Purpose of Education", warning us to think intensively and critically. He spoke about propaganda and cautioned Americans of threats to society. Dr. King said, "We are prone to let our mental life become invaded by legions of half-truths, prejudices, and propaganda."[2] We should heed his words.

---

1. Ben Westcott, Adam Renton, and Laura Smith-Spark, "October 8 Coronavirus News," *CNN*, Updated October 9, 2020, https://www.cnn.com/world/live-news/coronavirus-pandemic-10-08-20-intl/index.html

2. Martin Luther King Jr., "The Purpose of Education," *Morehouse College in 1948, Posted on The Seattle Times*, 1948, https://projects.seattletimes.com/mlk/words-education.html

Propaganda, Control, and Digital Surveillance | Part 2

Chapter 1

No Place to Hide From China's 5G Network

Tracking, Scanning, Lurking, Watching, Punishing

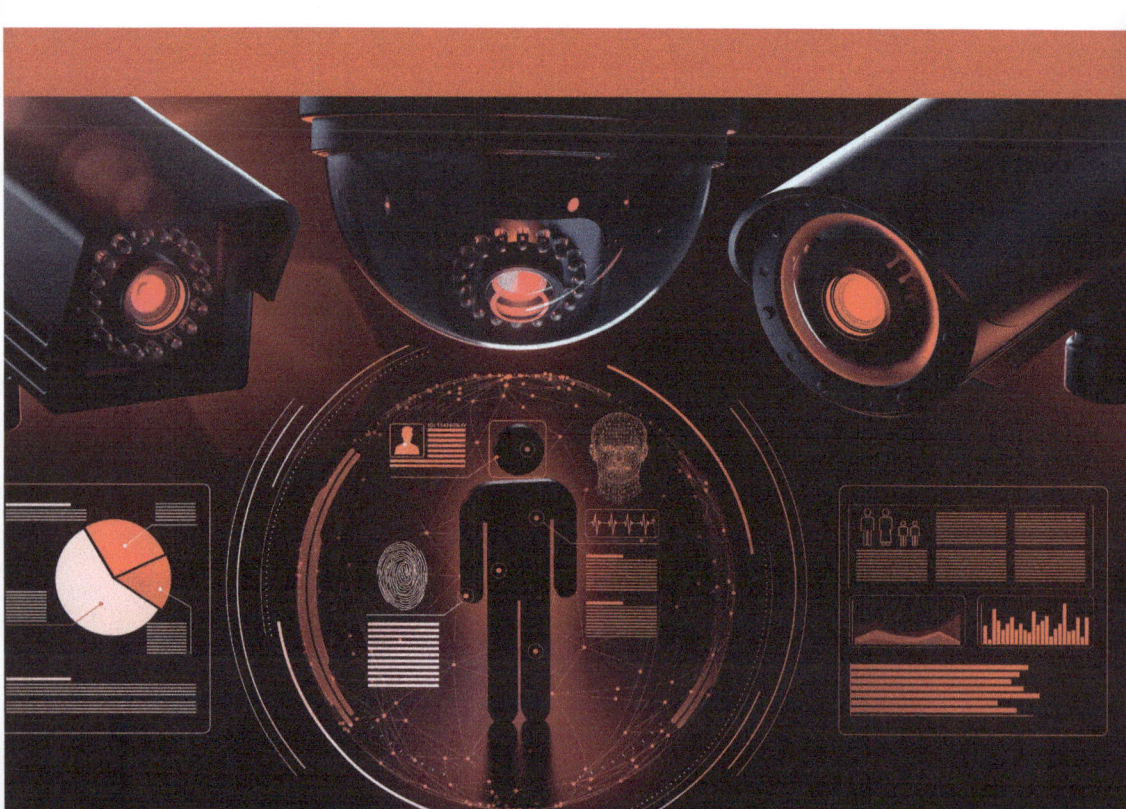

Introduction

Technology is rapidly changing, adapting, and improving. This innovation is particularly exhibited in the enhanced, next-gen 5G (fifth generation) version that is slated to yield fast speeds, wide-coverage, and fewer transmission gaps. The ability to reach speeds up to twenty times faster[1] has become increasingly attractive to users in the digital era, a period in which computer usage is on the rise, more people are working from home,[2] and videoconferencing has become a staple to both work and school life.[3]

The 5G network transformation is designed to offer faster download speeds, additional capacity, and a wider-range of connectivity to billions of devices in the area of artificial intelligence, virtual reality, and the Internet of Things.[4] This fifth-generation technology (5G), initially launched in 2019, is expected to be globally-accessible by 2025.[5] Specially-adapted 5G devices will allow for efficient organization, instantaneous network connections, and better connectivity overall which will even follow users on-the-go through advanced antenna beam steering.[6]

Leader of the Pack

Although there are numerous advantages, challenges abound. The Chinese version of 5G has been a topic of discussion since its release in 2019. China is moving swiftly to ensure that they are the front-runner for the distribution of 5G. Just as Germany and Japan were the two victors of 2G and 3G, respectively, China is similarly aiming to lead the charge as the premiere 5G provider by exporting the network ahead of the United States. China has already installed 5G capacity to about fifty cities across the globe.[7] Its rapid deployment of 5G has created controversies between nations to the extent that some have offered conspiracy theories that the 5G network is the cause of the spread of the coronavirus pandemic.[8]

---

1 Alex Fitzpatrick, "Everything You Need to Know About 5G," *Time*, May 23, 2019, https://time.com/5594360/what-to-know-about-5g/

2 Global Work Place Analytics, "Work-At-Home After Covid-19—Our Forecast," *Global Work Place Analytics*, 2020, https://globalworkplaceanalytics.com/work-at-home-after-covid-19-our-forecast

3 Sarah Perez, "Videoconferencing Apps Saw a Record 62M Downloads During One Week in March," *TechCrunch*, March 30, 2020 https://techcrunch.com/2020/03/30/video-conferencing-apps-saw-a-record-62m-downloads-during-one-week-in-march/

4 Qualcomm, "Everything You Need to Know About 5G," *Qualcomm*, n.d., https://www.qualcomm.com/invention/5g/what-is-5g

5 Eileen Yu for By The Way, "Global 5G Population to Hit 2.6B in 2025: Ericsson," *ZD Net*, November 26, 2019, https://www.zdnet.com/article/global-5g-population-to-hit-2-6b-in-2025/

6 EMF Explained 2.0, "5G Explained - How 5G Works," *EMF Explained 2.0*, n.d., http://www.emfexplained.info/?ID=25916

7 Xinhua, "China Focus: Top Mobile Operators Switch on Commercial 5G Services," *Xinhuanet*, October 31, 2019, http://www.xinhuanet.com/english/2019-10/31/c_138518626.htm

8 Jorge Noguera, "Coronavirus and the 5G Conspiracy Theories," *Diario AS*, April 27, 2020, https://en.as.com/en/2020/04/27/other_sports/1587985559_381491.html

No Place to Hide
China's Surveillance State

A January 2020 article in The Atlantic explains,

Some of the world's leading telecom-equipment manufacturers, including Huawei and ZTE, are Chinese companies with murky ownership structures and close ties to China's authoritarian one-party government. Many in the U.S. national security establishment rightly fear that these companies' equipment could allow Beijing to siphon off sensitive personal or corporate data. Or it could use well-concealed kill switches to cripple Western telecom systems during an active war. The mere threat of this activity would endow China's leadership with geopolitical leverage at all times.[9]

The 5G network comes with inherent security risks. The United States, under the Trump administration, has made it clear that no U.S. company should, or will be able to, do business with Huawei, a Chinese telecommunications distributor, due to security reasons.[10] The U.S. has also warned the U.K. about allowing Huawei 5G technology into the country; the British did not listen. Instead, they said that will limit Huawei use and also restrict its

---

9 Lindsay Gorman, "5G Is Where China and the West Finally Diverge," *The Atlantic*, January 5, 2020, https://www.theatlantic.com/ideas/archive/2020/01/5g-where-china-and-west-finally-diverge/604309/

10 Michael R. Pompeo, "The United States Further Restricts Huawei Access to U.S. Technology," *U.S. Department of State*, August 17, 2020, https://www.state.gov/the-united-states-further-restricts-huawei-access-to-u-s-technology/

products to industries that are not security-sensitive.[11]

The decision for the U.K. to allow the operation of Huawei to enter their networks did not sit well with some U.S. officials. For example, Matthew Pottinger, Deputy National Security Adviser, likened the actions taken by the U.K. to this illustration. He commented, "Can you imagine a situation where, in the '80s, Ronald Reagan and Margaret Thatcher have a conversation, and they say, 'You know, I think we should have the KGB come and build all of our telecommunications and computer network systems because they're offering a great discount'."[12]

In November 2020, the U.K. set out a roadmap to remove Huawei from its 5G network. A national security telecommunications bill would remove 'high risk' vendors in a regulatory framework to protect U.K. infrastructure.[13] The Telecommunications Bill would require all communications providers to comply and pay penalties for non-compliance.[14]

Warnings from Business Leaders

Business leaders have sounded the alarm on small and large stages. George Soros, speaking at the World Economic Forum said,

> China is not the only authoritarian regime in the world, but it is the wealthiest, strongest, and technologically most advanced. This makes Xi Jinping the most dangerous opponent of open societies. That's why it's so important to distinguish Xi Jinping's policies from the aspirations of the Chinese people. The social credit system, if it became operational, would give Xi total control over the people. Since Xi is the most dangerous enemy of the open society, we must pin our hopes on the Chinese people, and especially on the business community and a political elite willing to uphold the Confucian tradition.[15]

The 'social credit' system is like Big Brother on steroids. Each person's actions are monitored. The likes of social control through the social credit system are beyond comprehension. Meanwhile, there is no doubt that artificial intelligence is a vehicle for great promise but also for enormous potential for forced capitulation. Sergey Brin, one of Google's founders, warned that China could threaten the internet, thwart civil liberties, and impose government surveillance that filtered and blocked information flow.[16]

---

11 Tom Newton Dunn (@tnewtondunn), "Breaking: Boris Johnson is controversially allowing Huawei into Britain's new 5G mobile network despite also formally designating it 'a high risk vendor'...", *Twitter*, January 28, 2020, 4:01AM, https://twitter.com/tnewtondunn/status/1222127542255128576

12 Jonathan Swan, "Huawei Threatens America's Closest Relationship," *AXIOS*, January 26, 2020, https://www.axios.com/huawei-5g-trump-boris-johnson-china-05338af0-00a9-4950-80b6-21ddd0a44d50.html

13 BBC, "Huawei Ban: UK to Impose Early End to Use of New 5G Kit," *BBC*, November 30, 2020, https://www.bbc.com/news/business-55124236

14 Baker McKenzie, "UK Government Proposes Telecommunications (Security) Bill to Remove High Risk 5G Providers and Introduce Strict New Controls on Telecoms Network Security," *Lexology*, December 3, 2020, https://www.lexology.com/library/detail.aspx?g=8c91b0ea-e44d-48a6-8915-2c58fa2ff848

15 George Soros, "Remarks Delivered at the World Economic Forum," *George Soros Website*, January 24, 2019, https://www.georgesoros.com/2019/01/24/remarks-delivered-at-the-world-economic-forum-2/

16 Josh Horwitz, "Without Sergey Brin, Google Has Lost its Healthy Fear of Authoritarianism," *Quartz*, August 6, 2018, https://qz.com/1347623/without-sergey-brin-google-has-lost-its-fear-of-authoritarian-china/

This Concern is Not About a Trade War

Most people believe that the United States and other countries have rejected China's 5G network as a result of the U.S.-China trade war and associated disputes between the two governments. While it is true that the two countries have locked horns, China's 5G network poses a legitimate and ominous security threat. Yet, since China gained a strategic advantage in developing these technologies; many companies that produce 5G technology in 2020 and 2021 are controlled by the Chinese government.[17] This means that the Chinese government can reroute information to their data mining centers and potentially control information and people at their will. Furthermore, they can dictate how companies run their affairs and demand that corporations put a back door to its hardware or software so that the Chinese government can obtain remote access of its users.

The U.S. Department of Defense's Defense Innovation Board report stated, "Evidence of backdoors or security vulnerabilities have been discovered in a variety of devices globally." They went further to explain, "Many of these seem to be related to requirements from the Chinese intelligence community pressuring companies to exfiltrate information about domestic users."[18] These backdoors have been found both in camera software and handsets.[19]

Although China is believed to be using this media access to spy on its own people, the truth is that nothing is going to stop its intelligence operations from redirecting these traps to spy on citizens of foreign countries once they are shipped and installed globally. Huawei's reach is global, with surveillance equipment distributed to approximately 230 cities, extending from Asia to Europe and Africa.[20]

Furthermore, with the Chinese government's enthusiasm regarding the export of its 5G technology by subsidizing prices to increase sales of its network equipment, this security problem has created a tangled web around the world.[21]

Conclusion

A solution is not near. In fact, the insidiousness of data transfer and security compromises may worsen long before governments realize the threat. The issue of threats may have been the reason Singapore chose Ericsson and Nokia over Huawei in June 2020 due to security threats, though Singapore is still reliant on Chinese technology and Huawei will still be used for their smaller networks.[22]

---

17 Dan Strumpf, "Where China Dominates in 5G Technology," *The Wall Street Journal*, February 26, 2019, https://www.wsj.com/articles/where-china-dominates-in-5g-technology-11551236701

18 What Phone Plans, "Could Your Chinese Smartphone Be Spying On You?," *What Phone Plans*, n.d., https://whatphone.com.au/guide/your-chinese-smartphone-spying-you

19 Ibid.

20 L.A. Times, "How China Cornered The Facial Recognition Surveillance Market," *L.A. Times*, December 09, 2019, https://www.latimes.com/business/story/2019-12-09/china-facial-recognition-surveillance

21 Elise Thomas, "As the West Warns of Chinese Cyber Spies, Poorer Nations Welcome Gifts With Open Arms," *Wired*, June 11, 2018, https://www.wired.co.uk/article/china-hacking-cyber-spies-espionage

22 Muhammad Faizal Abdul Rahman, "Singapore Decides on 5G Networks: Is Huawei Banned?," *The Diplomat*, July 2, 2020, https://thediplomat.com/2020/07/singapore-decides-on-5g-networks-is-huawei-banned/

In a U.S. State Department comment, Secretary of State, Mike Pompeo declared,

> The tide is turning against Huawei as citizens worldwide are waking up to the danger of the Chinese Communist Party's surveillance state... The momentum in favor of secure 5G is building. The more countries, companies, and citizens ask whom they should trust with their most sensitive data, the more obvious the answer becomes: not the Chinese Communist Party's surveillance state.[23]

With time, 5G technology is likely to become a security risk that will be career-ending for some and life-threatening for others. Although the U.S. technical standards committee has started the discussion on 6G,[24] the challenges we face today will continue while we wait for the next iteration of technology to arrive. Still, great uncertainty exists in determining whether next-generation innovation will solve the present-day security issues.

What's at Stake?

First, 5G is here and its processing speed is faster. China is deploying its political, technology, and marketing forces to drive countries into China's 5G network so that the CCP can lurk in the digital background, watching over citizenry everywhere.

Second, this 5G threat is so real that George Soros said that China's mass surveillance system would give China "total control" over its people.[25] Potentially, with the spread of 5G, China would have total global control over all people within Huawei and China's other digital networks.

Third, to be clear, this is not a question of who gets more business and which country will be more economically prosperous from their business dealings. This is a question of a 'Big Brother' surveillance state controlling through its pervasive artificial intelligence network and draconian social credit system (more in another chapter).

Fourth, companies are canceling social media accounts,[26] and state leaders are censoring or closing down television[27] and social media[28] with information in which they do not agree.

---

23 Michael R. Pompeo, "The Tide Is Turning Toward Trusted 5G Vendors," *U.S. Department of State*, June 24, 2020, https://www.state.gov/the-tide-is-turning-toward-trusted-5g-vendors/

24 Martijn Rasser, "Setting the Stage for U.S. Leadership in 6G," *Lawfare*, August 13, 2019, https://www.lawfareblog.com/setting-stage-us-leadership-6g

25 Tom Simonite, "The 'Mortal Danger' of China's Push Into AI," *Wired*, January 24, 2019, https://www.wired.com/story/mortal-danger-chinas-push-into-ai/

26 Adam Liptak, "Can Twitter Legally Bar Trump? The First Amendment Says Yes," *The New York Times*, January 9, 2021, https://www.nytimes.com/2021/01/09/us/first-amendment-free-speech.html

27 RSF, "RSF Unveils 20/2020 List of Press Freedom's Digital Predators," *RSF*, Updated March 12, 2020, https://rsf.org/en/news/rsf-unveils-202020-list-press-freedoms-digital-predators

28 Jason Gutierrez, "Duterte's Shutdown of TV Network Leaves Void Amid Coronavirus Crisis," *The New York Times*, May 14, 2020, https://www.nytimes.com/2020/05/14/world/asia/duterte-philippines-tv-network-ABS-CBN.html

Chapter 2
China's Surveillance
China's Networks – Who Are They Watching?

Introduction

Few would be surprised to know that China spies on its citizens. Data collected by PreciseSecurity.com shows that the top three countries with the largest surveillance networks are China, the U.S., and Germany. By 2019, China soared to the top, ranking the networks highest with four times more cameras installed its territory than in the United States.[1] A *CNN Business* report stated that by 2021, China is projected to install 571 million cameras throughout China, six times that of the United States.[2] Still, that may be an underestimate since 600 million cameras were planned to be connected by 2020.[3]

Surveillance Cameras Everywhere

A recent report shows that, due to the importance of monitoring its citizens during the COVID-19 pandemic, China has installed surveillance cameras outside of people's front doors and, in many cases, inside their homes too.[4] Also, they have invented an overarching, technically-advanced surveillance facial recognition camera to spot someone in a crowd.[5]

Chinese facial recognition companies lead the pack in supplying 5G and surveillance services in the growing international market with their advantage over other countries in, "a massive domestic market and an authoritarian system where privacy often takes a back seat."[6] Even more concerning is that Chinese companies are in initial phases of a larger-scale emotion-tracking initiative through artificial intelligence.[7] In classrooms, they, "track attendance and to catch students dozing, playing on their phones or talking in class."[8] This development was put in place to ensure compliance with laws and emphasize China's seriousness is in capturing citizens' moves and motives.

Privacy is all but gone. The Chinese government insists that camera installations inside and outside of homes are a way to control the coronavirus pandemic. People who are quarantined at home for two weeks are watched through cameras installed outside their door

---

1　AiT News Desk, "Top 10 Countries And Cities By Number Of CCTV Cameras," *AiThority*, December 5, 2019, https://www.aithority.com/news/top-10-countries-and-cities-by-number-of-cctv-cameras/

2　Nectar Gan, "China is Installing Surveillance Cameras Outside People's Front Doors ... and Sometimes Inside Their Homes," *CNN*, April 28, 2020, https://www.cnn.com/2020/04/27/asia/cctv-cameras-china-hnk-intl/index.html

3　CBS News, "China's Behavior Monitoring System Bars Some From Travel, Purchasing Property," *CBS News*, April 24, 2018, https://www.cbsnews.com/news/china-social-credit-system-surveillance-cameras/

4　Nectar Gan, "China is Installing Surveillance Cameras Outside People's Front Doors ... and Sometimes Inside Their Homes," *CNN*, April 28, 2020, https://www.cnn.com/2020/04/27/asia/cctv-cameras-china-hnk-intl/index.html

5　Anthony Cuthbertson, "China Invents Super-Surveillance Cameras That Can Spot Someone Within a Crowd of Thousands," *Independent UK*, October 2, 2019, https://www.independent.co.uk/life-style/gadgets-and-tech/news/china-surveillance-camera-facial-recognition-privacy-a9131871.html

6　L.A. Times, "How China Cornered The Facial Recognition Surveillance Market," *L.A. Times*, December 09, 2019, https://www.latimes.com/business/story/2019-12-09/china-facial-recognition-surveillance

7　Financial Times, "Emotion Recognition is China's New Surveillance Craze," *Financial Times*, October 31, 2019, https://www.ft.com/content/68155560-fbd1-11e9-a354-36acbbb0d9b6

8　L.A. Times, "How China Cornered The Facial Recognition Surveillance Market," *L.A. Times*, December 09, 2019, https://www.latimes.com/business/story/2019-12-09/china-facial-recognition-surveillance

Propaganda, Control, and Digital Surveillance | Part 2

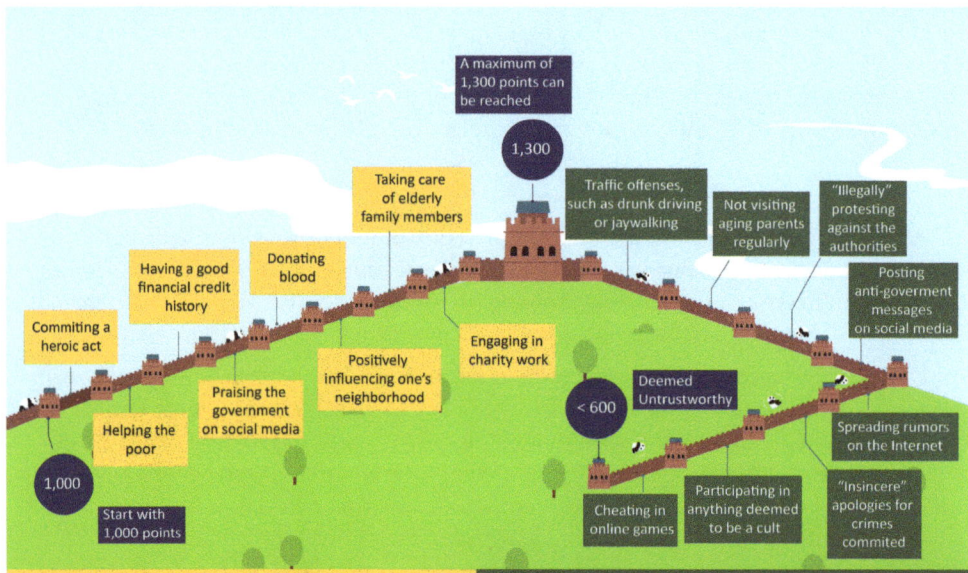

HIGH SCORES CAN LEAD TO

- Priority for school admissions and employment
- Easier access to cash loans and customer credit
- Free gym facilities
- Cheaper public transport
- Shorter wait times in hospitals
- Fast track promotion at work
- Jumping the queue for public housing
- Tax breaks
- Discount on energy bills
- Access to better hotels
- Deposit-free bicycle and car hire

PUNISHMENTS CAN LEAD TO

- Less access to credit
- Denial of licenses, permits and access to some social services
- Exclusion from booking flights or high-speed train tickets
- Restricted access to public service
- Ineligibility for goverment jobs
- Public shaming
- Slower internet
- Dog taken away

and some doors have equipment that sounds an alarm if a person leaves the premises "trying to escape".[9]

A 34-year-old Irish expat who lived through this experience said that the installation of cameras outside their home is, "an incredible erosion of privacy…It just seems to be a massive data grab. And I don't know how much of it is actually legal."[10]

If this trend continues without control, a time will come when everyone, even some outside of China, will be wary of their actions. As it is now, the Chinese government rates its citizens. While this may sound like a Sci-Fi film, this is a reality.[11] China's social credit was first tested in 2009 and formally introduced by Wen Jiabao, China Premier, in 2011.[12] People in China are given a social credit score based on the actions they take and how the government trusts those actions.[13]

Furthermore, the Chinese people cannot get information from numerous sources outside of China given that Beijing's Great Firewall, a term coined by *Wired*,[14] blocks Facebook, Instagram, Twitter, WhatsApp, Google, *Bloomberg, The Wall Street Journal, The New York Times*, and other widely available tools. Over time, China has blocked over 10,000 websites.[15]

Monitoring and Scoring

Just when it feels that China has done enough in installing millions of surveillance cameras all over the country, they are seeking to lead the effort to become the first country to implement a pervasive system of algorithmic surveillance. China states that this surveillance system is necessary to help reduce crime and terrorism.[16] At the same time, the individual civil liberties of its citizens are sacrificed as people do not have the luxury of making choices that suit them in terms of their personal beliefs, politics, religion, and other individual and sensitive matters.[17]

---

9   Jamie P., "Coronavirus Update: China Finds a Smart Alarm System to Track Down Self-Isolated Chinese Citizens Trying To Escape," *Tech Times*, February 27, 2020, https://www.techtimes.com/articles/247632/20200227/watch-coronavirus-update-china-finds-smart-alarm-system-track-down.htm

10 Nectar Gan, "China is Installing Surveillance Cameras Outside People's Front Doors … and Sometimes Inside Their Homes," *CNN*, April 28, 2020, https://www.cnn.com/2020/04/27/asia/cctv-cameras-china-hnk-intl/index.html

11 Anna Mitchell and Larry Diamond, "China's Surveillance State Should Scare Everyone," *The Atlantic*, February 2, 2018, https://www.theatlantic.com/international/archive/2018/02/china-surveillance/552203/

12 Amanda Lee, "Explainer – What is China's Social Credit System and Why is it Controversial?," *South China Morning Post*, August 9, 2020, https://www.scmp.com/economy/china-economy/article/3096090/what-chinas-social-credit-system-and-why-it-controversial

13 Alexandra Ma, "China Has Started Ranking Citizens With a Creepy 'Social Credit' System — Here's What You Can Do Wrong, and The Embarrassing, Demeaning Ways They Can Punish You," *Business Insider*, October 29, 2018, https://www.businessinsider.com/china-social-credit-system-punishments-and-rewards-explained-2018-4

14 Geremie R. Barme and Sang Ye, "The Great Firewall of China," *Wired*, June 1, 1997, https://www.wired.com/1997/06/china-3/

15 Xinmei Shen, "The Story of China's Great Firewall, the World's Most Sophisticated Censorship System," *Abacus*, November 7, 2019, https://www.scmp.com/abacus/who-what/what/article/3089836/story-chinas-great-firewall-worlds-most-sophisticated

16 Reuters Staff, "China to Strengthen Surveillance, Security in Anti-Terror Push," *Reuters*, April 13, 2015, https://www.reuters.com/article/us-china-security/china-to-strengthen-surveillance-security-in-anti-terror-push-idUSKBN0N507C20150414

17 Paul Mozur and Aaron Krolik, "A Surveillance Net Blankets China's Cities, Giving Police Vast Powers," *The New York Times*, December 17, 2019, https://www.nytimes.com/2019/12/17/technology/china-surveillance.html

This plan to watch over global citizens is one reason why India banned 59 Chinese apps and services, including TikTok and WeChat.[18] China denies tracking individual's information, though the government controls these apps and all other information going in and out of its state-owned enterprises (SOE).[19] After the deaths of 20 Indians at the India-China border over disputed land, many Indians called for a boycott on Chinese goods and the cancelation of Chinese contracts.[20] Other platforms blocked included Weibo, Alibaba's UC Browser, and e-commerce sites.[21]

The problem is not just that Chinese citizens suffer from a lack of freedom of expression, both on and off the internet, but also that such repressive technologies will surely find its way to other authoritarian regimes around the world. The concern for citizens worldwide is that this wave of surveillance is a tsunami and it is about to engulf whole cities. By reaching its tentacles into states on each continent, millions of people will suffer the same fate as the Chinese citizens. Eventually, these surveillance actions will jeopardize democracy, freedom, and justice around the world.

An Extreme Even Orwell Could Not Have Imagined

A brawl that led to the murder of Uyghur toy factory workers was the match that lit a tinderbox of tensions between the Chinese and Uyghurs. In the capital of Xinjiang Province, Urumqi, Uyghur Muslims protested until a riot broke out, leaving thousands dead or injured. This 2009 incident was a key turning point in the massive crackdown of the Uyghurs.[22]

Conclusion

Though life essentially turned to normal with people going to work and students going to classes,[23] in Urumqi, Beijing unleashed even harsher restrictions on the predominantly Muslim population. With approximately 22 million people in Xinjiang Province, "Community officials continue to go door to door, sealing doors with paper strips, tape and in some cases metal bars, to prevent residents from leaving their homes."[24] Calling the situation a 'war time' state, Beijing cracked down. In Xinjiang Province, as many as two

---

18 Manish Singh, "What India's TikTok Ban Means for China," *TechCrunch*, July 8, 2020, https://techcrunch.com/2020/07/08/what-indias-tiktok-ban-means-for-china/

19 Emily Feng, "China Intercepts WeChat Texts From U.S. And Abroad, Researchers Say," *NPR*, August 29, 2019, https://www.npr.org/2019/08/29/751116338/china-intercepts-wechat-texts-from-u-s-and-abroad-researcher-says

20 French Press Agency, "India Moves to Boycott Chinese Goods After Border Clash," *Daily Sabah*, June 25, 2020, https://www.dailysabah.com/world/asia-pacific/india-moves-to-boycott-chinese-goods-after-border-clash

21 BBC News, "Ban on Chinese Apps, Including TikTok, Surprises India Content Makers," *BBC News*, June 30, 2020, https://www.bbc.com/news/world-asia-india-53232486

22 Erin Handley, "How China's Mass Detention of Uyghur Muslims Stemmed From the 2009 Urumqi Riot," *Australian Broadcasting Corporation (ABC) News*, July 4, 2019, https://www.abc.net.au/news/2019-07-05/china-xinjiang-urumqi-riots-10th-anniversary-uyghur-muslims/11270320

23 Javier C. Hernandez, "In China, Where the Pandemic Began, Life Is Starting to Look ... Normal," *The New York Times*, August 23, 2020, https://www.nytimes.com/2020/08/23/world/asia/china-coronavirus-normal-life.html

24 Emily Feng, "China Calls It A 'Wartime Mode' COVID-19 Lockdown. And Residents Are Protesting," *NPR*, August 26, 2020, https://www.npr.org/sections/goatsandsoda/2020/08/26/906206090/china-calls-it-a-wartime-mode-covid-19-lockdown-and-residents-are-protesting

million people are locked up in concentration camps. Yet, this is not the first time the minority population has been locked down. Residents were unable to leave their homes without severe punishment,[25] including being handcuffed to their homes and having their social credit scores go down when yelling for help.[26]

ABC reported, "They have shared photos of front doors with pieces of paper stuck to them, which would tear if a resident attempted to open the door to leave. Some photos also appeared to show doors with wires attached to the handles to prevent them from being opened."[27] The architect of this lockdown is the same Chen Guanguo who took control of Tibet's lockdowns and imprisoned up to two million Uyghur Muslims in concentration camps.[28]

What's at Stake?

First, cameras are everywhere in China recording information for Beijing. While there are also cameras in the U.S., the cameras in China record all moves and diminish Chinese citizens' social credit scores causing them to lose benefits, security, and freedom just by violating a 'crime' like leaving a dog off a leash, cheating at a video game, or not praising Xi Jinping.

Second, it is easy to think that these types of excessive social controls could not possibly happen in the West. However, it could and it might if data is transferred from computers, cameras, phones, or other devices through back door technology.

---

25 Nectar Gan, "Xinjiang Capital in 'Wartime' Lockdown Over Spike in Coronavirus Cases," *CNN*, July 20, 2020, https://www.cnn.com/2020/07/20/asia/coronavirus-xinjiang-urumqi-intl-hnk/index.html

26 Lily Kuo, "Xinjiang Residents Handcuffed to Their Homes in Covid Lockdown," *The Guardian*, August 25, 2020, https://www.theguardian.com/world/2020/aug/25/xinjiang-residents-handcuffed-to-their-homes-in-covid-lockdown

27 Bang Xiao and Michael Walsh, "China's Xinjiang Residents Yell from Balconies as Strict Coronavirus Lockdown Drags On," *ABC*, August 25, 2020, https://www.abc.net.au/news/2020-08-25/xinjiang-yell-from-balconies-over-strict-coronavirus-lockdown/12589440

28 William Zheng, "Architect of China's Muslim Camps Chen Quanguo Expected to Stay on in Xinjiang For Now," *South China Morning Post*, March 24, 2019, https://www.scmp.com/news/china/politics/article/3003047/architect-chinas-muslim-camps-chen-quanguo-expected-stay

Chapter 3
China's Global Digital Pandemic

Dual Power Digital Weaponry–The Great Firewall and The Great Cannon

Introduction

The Great Firewall of China is a digital blockade that prevents access to websites around the world.[1] As China's technologies have improved, the Great Firewall now reaches in and threatens Hong Kong and Macau disrupting their previous autonomy and "One Country, Two Systems" pledge. Internet use is monitored, and censorship removes access to both foreign websites and those within China that are not flattering to the CCP.

The Great Firewall is designed to 'protect' Chinese citizens from receiving news, images, and content by blocking devices that access 'illegal' websites like Twitter, Facebook, and Instagram. Citizens are, thus, shielded from the outside world and any politically undesirable information that may contradict Beijing's objectives. Additionally, the Great Firewall boosts China's economy by increasing access to Chinese companies while minimizing access to services offered, developed, and sold in China by non-Chinese companies.[2] Search engine strategies allow the amplification and suppression of results. Thus, Chinese companies are given greater opportunities to market and sell.

In essence, the Great Firewall monitors Internet flow and then prohibits content from entering or exiting. Google is blocked.[3] While China does provide Baidu, a similar search provider, available content is limited, curated, or manipulated as part of a larger propaganda machine.[4] Additionally, China has created a more ominous force than the Great Firewall's defensive mechanism. The 'Great Cannon' is an offensive weapon that maneuvers behind the Great Firewall. This digitized explosive machine is not fired often due the negative publicity generated by its deployment of each salvo, shot into Internet space.

CNN explains, "Imagine an eavesdropper on a party line: when one party says something objectionable, the eavesdropper shouts into the line until everyone hangs up."[5] The Great

---

1 Elizabeth C. Economy, "The Great Firewall of China: Xi Jinping's Internet Shutdown," *The Guardian*, June 29, 2018, https://www.theguardian.com/news/2018/jun/29/the-great-firewall-of-china-xi-jinpings-internet-shutdown

2 Alexander Chipman Koty, "China's Great Firewall: Business Implications," *China Briefing*, June 1, 2017, https://www.china-briefing.com/news/chinas-great-firewall-implications-businesses/

3 Paige Leskin, "Here are all the Major US Tech Companies Blocked Behind China's 'Great Firewall,'" *Business Insider*, October 10, 2019, https://www.businessinsider.com/major-us-tech-companies-blocked-from-operating-in-china-2019-5

4 Simon Denyer, "China's Scary Lesson to the World: Censoring the Internet Works," *Washington Post*, May 23, 2016, https://www.washingtonpost.com/world/asia_pacific/chinas-scary-lesson-to-the-world-censoring-the-internet-works/2016/05/23/413afe78-fff3-11e5-8bb1-f124a43f84dc_story.html

5 Nicolas Weaver, "How China's 'Great Cannon' Works -- and Why We Should Be Worried," *CNN*, June 5, 2015, https://www.cnn.com/2015/06/04/opinions/china-great-cannon/index.html

Cannon adds a new layer to Chinese censorship which maliciously attacks users and prevents free speech.

China controls and harnesses what The Citizen Lab, a Canadian research laboratory, calls "The Great Cannon".[6] This elusive mass of 'explosive' power attacks users through the Internet. The digital resource launches distributed denial-of-service attacks using proxy warriors that latch onto websites, shooting a widespread discharge of ammunition, targeting specific content providers.

With the goal of disrupting any objectionable operations, the website faces a blizzard of 'cannon fire' that slows or stops communication. Furthermore, the Great Cannon of China has the ability to monitor websites by redirecting traffic.

These Great Cannon attacks began in 2015, when Beijing's servers targeted sites that allowed access of content to pass through the Great Firewall, a digital guard dog in China that prevents content from being received. Hundreds of sites are not allowed and illegal to be used in China.

When GitHub and GreatFire were blasted by the Great Cannon in 2015,[7] a warning bell went off. A GreatFire report pointed to Baidu as the source of the 2015 attack, though Baidu denied the accusation.[8] The threat impacted millions of users and sounded an alarm. Those who championed an open, accessible Internet were at risk. GitHub is a U.S.-based subsidiary of Microsoft that tracks bugs, provides hosting, and offers task management support. GitHub is a popular, relatively benign Silicon Valley organization that also allows programmers to share code and has no malicious intent toward Beijing. GreatFire, on the other hand, is a non-profit organization composed of Chinese expats who assist Chinese Internet users[9] to access blocked content and "bring transparency to the Great Firewall of China,"[10] including news sources like *BBC*, *The New York Times*, and Google.

---

6   Bill Marczak, Nicholas Weaver, Jakub Dalek, Roya Ensafi, David Fifield, Sarah McKune, Arn Rey, John Scott-Railton, Ron Deibert, and Vern Paxson, "China's Great Cannon," *The Citizen Lab*, April 10, 2015, https://citizenlab.ca/2015/04/chinas-great-cannon/

7   Jon Russell, "'Great Cannon' is China's New Weapon that Shoots Down Internet Sites," *Tech Crunch*, April 10, 2015, https://techcrunch.com/2015/04/10/china-great-cannon/

8   Bill Marczak, Nicholas Weaver, Jakub Dalek, Roya Ensafi, David Fifield, Sarah McKune, Arn Rey, John Scott-Railton, Ron Deibert, and Vern Paxson, "China's Great Cannon," *The Citizen Lab*, April 10, 2015, https://citizenlab.ca/2015/04/chinas-great-cannon/

9   Great Fire, "Apple Censoring Tibetan Information in China," *GreatFire*, June 10, 2019, https://en.greatfire.org/blog/2019/jun/apple-censoring-tibetan-information-china

10   Tom Jowitt, "Microsoft Claims 'System Error' Blocks Chinese Bing Search Results," *Silicon UK*, February 12, 2014, https://www.silicon.co.uk/workspace/microsoft-chinese-bing-result-138908

Attacks to other digital sites were chronicled in 2017. In 2019, a major Great Cannon incident led to the shutdown of communication between Hong Kong activists.[11] The Great Cannon hurled its mighty JavaScript code into insecure connections of pro-democracy activists who were staging and coordinating anti-government demonstrations.[12]

Transparency is a foreign concept in China and access to information is consistently thwarted. Companies that seek to work with China are obliged to censor information and give up intellectual property rights. GreatFire spells out Apple's stance[13] saying, "Apple claims to defend human rights, yet thousands of apps are selectively made unavailable in App Stores around the world," including *Bloomberg*, *Pinterest*, and *Reddit*.[14] Apple states that "194 apps were removed in China for legal reasons"[15] since they contain vile, pornographic, or betting information objectionable to Beijing. What they really mean is that if Chinese representatives tell them to take content down, it must be removed, like the removal of podcasts Beijing demanded to be taken down in June 2020.[16]

Conclusion

The concern is that continued use of this Internet attack could lead to a global digital pandemic. While China's censorship is primarily aimed at content flowing in and out of China, the weaponry could have powerful, global consequences. The Great Firewall undermines civil liberties and freedom of speech. However, the restrictions have been complicit in enabling fearsome human rights violations, particularly with the Falun Gong, Uyghurs in Xinjiang Province, and those who attempt to surmount the wall to see over the other side. Yet, a giant offensive malware blast could infect computers everywhere with a virus that is unstoppable and has no vaccine to prevent the attack.

What's at Stake?

First, the Great Cannon's capabilities are advancing with China's 5G technology. A massive cyber-attack or cyber-pandemic could cripple world affairs.

Second, as China develops its facial recognition technology, Beijing's reach will increase, particularly since technology is ubiquitous in modern society.

Third, Internet restrictions imposed on Chinese citizenry makes propaganda, fake news, and unique perspectives dangerously one-sided, cutting off the rest of the world.

---

11 Davey Winder, "China Fires 'Great Cannon' Cyber-Weapon at the Hong Kong Pro-Democracy Movement," *Forbes*, December 5, 2019, https://www.forbes.com/sites/daveywinder/2019/12/05/china-fires-great-cannon-cyber-weapon-at-the-hong-kong-pro-democracy-movement/#3e718df87c85

12 Alex Hern, "GreatFire Activist Urges Western Firms to Help End Chinese Censorship," *The Guardian*, April 14, 2016, https://www.theguardian.com/world/2016/apr/14/greatfire-activist-urges-western-firms-to-help-end-chinese-censorship

13 Ibid.

14 GreatFire, "Apple Censorship", *GreatFire*, n.d., https://applecensorship.com/free-speech/?l=en

15 Mark Gurman, "Apple Removes Two Podcast Apps From App Store at China's Request," *Bloomberg*, June 11, 2020, https://www.bloomberg.com/news/articles/2020-06-11/apple-pulls-pocket-casts-from-app-store-at-china-s-request

16 Ibid.

Chapter 4
Social Credit Rating & China's Surveillance State
Dystopian Social Acceptance – Obey or Face Consequences

Introduction

China's nationwide, sophisticated social credit system put into effect on a comprehensive scale, brings together the best practices of civilian monitoring and surveillance. These clandestine, dystopian tactics have been tested throughout the country for just over a decade. Each element of society – individual, organizational, business, and governmental – are all given a score. The social credit system has three interconnected components – a master database, a blacklisting system, and a punishment and rewards mechanism.[1] The numerical value of credits or demerits an individual or group receives determines a set of rewards and punishments to ensure that all levels of society are kept in line with the moral and ethical guidelines determined by the Chinese Communist Party (CCP).

Any individual can view these scores to determine their worth, morality, trustworthiness, and loyalty to the CCP.[2] The vast surveillance network continuously churns information to track all actions and transactions. Facial recognition matches individuals to their ranking system.[3]

China's Social Credit Rollout

China's rollout of its 'Social Credit' rating (shehui xinyong tixi) in 2020 seems benign. After all, U.S. citizens also have a score to determine creditworthiness based upon their debt, credit, and payment records. However, China's ultra-intrusive scoring system goes just to the edge of imagination. Digging deeper into the details, this score includes ratings based upon personal qualities deemed good and bad by the Chinese Communist Party (CCP).

Pilot programs began in 2009 with an expansion of efforts in forty-two cities nationwide. Each city created their own system with varying social control mechanisms to determine positive and negative behaviors. The systemwide administration of this "social sorting"[4] program was set for late 2020.[5] This unique experiment impacts individuals, companies, and governmental entities, each receiving its own score.

The CCP explained this score to the people on CCTV (Chinese television) as a win-win for everyone. The translation of a Chinese State Council document states,

> Its inherent requirements are establishing the idea of [a] sincerity culture, and carrying forward sincerity and traditional virtues, it uses encouragement to keep trust and constraints against breaking trust as incentive mechanisms, and its objective is raising the honest mentality and credit levels of the entire society....

---

1   Trivium, "Understanding China's Social Credit System," *Trivium*, August 27, 2019, https://socialcredit.triviumchina.com/what-is-social-credit/

2   Nicole Kobie, "The Complicated Truth About China's Social Credit System," *Wired*, June 7, 2019, https://www.wired.co.uk/article/china-social-credit-system-explained

3   NBC News, "Social Credit System Coming to China, with Citizens Scored on Behavior | *NBC Nightly News*," May 11, 2019, video, 2:33, https://www.youtube.com/watch?v=NOk27I2EBac

4   David Lyon, "Surveillance, Security and Social Sorting: Emerging Research Priorities," *International Criminal Justice Review* 17, no. 3 (2007): 161-170.

5   Louise Matsakis, "How the West Got China's Social Credit System Wrong," *Wired*, July 29, 2019, https://www.wired.com/story/china-social-credit-score-system/

Further enhance the content of sincerity education in all levels and all kinds of education and training. Forcefully launch activities to let universal education and propaganda about credit enter enterprises, enter classrooms, enter communities, enter villages and enter households.

Build and use morality classrooms well, and advocate value views and moral norms of patriotism, respecting labour, sincerity, amity, etc. Launch mass activities for moral judgment, conduct analysis and evaluation of instances where there was a lack of sincerity and credit was not stressed, and guide people towards sincerity and trust-keeping, morality and upholding courtesy.[6]

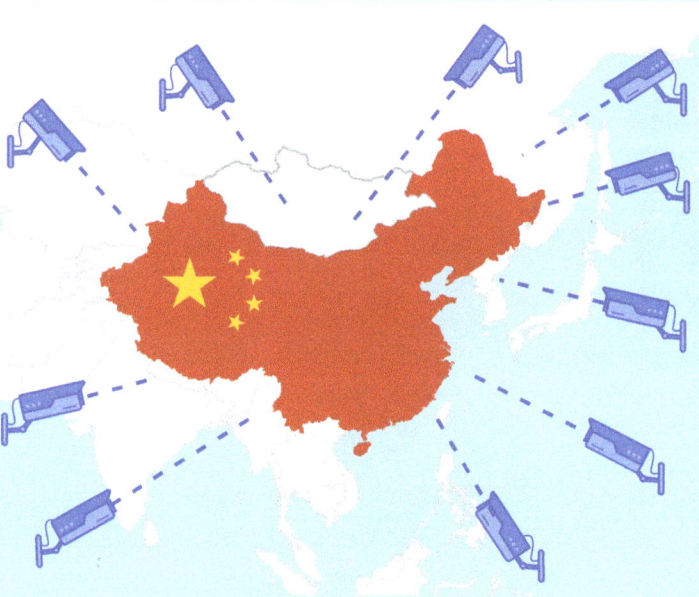

Individuals will be able to determine the 'goodness' of a friend or potential dating partner. Colleges will know the 'honesty' of students. Companies will be able to determine the 'trustworthiness' of customers. Lenders will know the 'creditworthiness' of borrowers. The government will know the 'loyalty' of individuals and companies to the CCP.

---

6 State Council, "Planning Outline for the Construction of a Social Credit System (2014-2020)," *China Copyright and Media*, Updated April 25, 2015, https://chinacopyrightandmedia.wordpress.com/2014/06/14/planning-outline-for-the-construction-of-a-social-credit-system-2014-2020/

Monitoring

All aspects of daily life are being monitored through camera, phone, computer, internet traffic, and other digital technologies.[7] For the past decade, China has increasingly monitored[8] its citizens in a pervasive attempt to exert greater social control on the people to adapt, conform, and obey the norms and laws of society. Placing a high priority on this effort, the CCP has attempted to mitigate the threat to China's social, financial, and political system, while strengthening its security state. [9]

In Tibet and Xinjiang Province, surveillance and monitoring are inescapable with cameras mounted even in mosques and temples.[10]

Daily Life

Imagine you are jaywalking across the street with your dog, but your dog is not on a leash; you just received two violations.[11] Then, you do not pick up your dog's poop and put your soda can in the receptacle for paper products; two more violations. You are not having a good day. Worse, you do not visit your parents regularly and play loud music in public; two more violations. The result is that the government may take your dog away and you may not be able to ride public transportation, take the high-speed railway, or buy a plane ticket. A 2016 *Black Mirror* episode available on *Netflix* entitled "Nosedive" portrays an extreme, but interesting, dramatic portrayal of social credit played out in society.

Every action will be monitored and evaluated. Positive actions will boost a score while negative actions will decrease the score. Citizens will be judged every day as to whether they are socially beneficial to society or social harmful. Financial, social, and moral behaviors will be monitored constantly through government, financial, legal, friendships, purchase histories, online searches, content posted, driving record, as well as the way individuals treat family and others at home, work, and in the community.

Examples of ways to increase a score may include the following:

- paying bills on time
- caring for elderly family
- socializing with high social score individuals
- donating money, blood, or books
- volunteering in the community
- committing a heroic act

---

7   Alexandra Ma, "China is Building a Vast Civilian Surveillance Network — Here are 10 Ways it Could Be Feeding its Creepy 'Social Credit System'," *Business Insider*, April 29, 2018, https://www.businessinsider.com/how-china-is-watching-its-citizens-in-a-modern-surveillance-state-2018-4

8   Tara Francis Chan, "Parts of China are Using Facial Recognition Technology that can Scan the Country's Entire Population in One Second," *Business Insider*, March 26, 2018, https://www.businessinsider.com/china-facial-recognition-technology-works-in-one-second-2018-3?r=UK

9   Yuhua Wang and Carl Minzner, "The Rise of the Chinese Security State," *The China Quarterly* 222, (2015): 339.

10 Frank Langfitt, "In China, Beware: A Camera May Be Watching You," *NPR*, January 29, 2013, https://www.npr.org/2013/01/29/170469038/in-china-beware-a-camera-may-be-watching-you

11 Sophia Yan, "Pick Up Poo or We Take the Dog: Chinese City Rolls Out 'Social Control' System for Petowners," *The Telegraph UK*, October 30, 2018, https://www.telegraph.co.uk/news/2018/10/30/pick-poo-take-dog-chinese-city-rolls-social-credit-system-pet/

- posting positive comments about the CCP
- getting good evaluations at work
- being a good student in school
- turning in those who violate the rules
- preventing unacceptable religious practices
- telling on a cheater

Scores can decrease by:

- not paying bills
- breaking promises
- being disrespectful
- not properly sorting trash
- playing loud music in public spaces
- spreading rumors or making false statements
- using a VPN
- gambling or pornography
- playing video games too long
- performing poorly at work or school
- traffic violations
- jaywalking
- drunk driving
- insincere apologies
- participating in a cult
- walking a dog without a leash or not picking up their poop
- protesting or speaking out against the government
- supporting Hong Kong or Taiwan independence

Rewards and punishments incentivize individuals to follow the prescribed rules and live by societal expectations.

Rewards may include:

- lower taxes
- access to jobs
- lower interest loans
- improved healthcare
- access to better public schools and universities
- promotions at work
- passes to movies, gyms, and museums
- priority admissions to events, schools, and programs
- discounts at theaters, hotels, buses, boats, and trains

Punishments may include[12]

- slower Internet connection speeds
- higher taxes
- spending limits
- blacklisting
- denial of licenses, permits, and accounts
- distancing from friends and family who do not want their score lowered

---

12 Alexandra Ma, "China has Started Ranking Citizens with a Creepy 'Social Credit' System — Here's What You Can Do Wrong, and the Embarrassing, Demeaning Ways They Can Punish You," *Business Insider*, October 29, 2018, https://www.businessinsider.com/china-social-credit-system-punishments-and-rewards-explained-2018-4

- lack of access to gyms, events, and organizations
- public shaming in hotels, restaurants, bars, road intersections, and apps
- restrictions on school entrance and job opportunities for the entire family
- the inability to get a visa to leave the country, the inability to travel on buses, boats, trains, or planes

Chinese Society

An enormous amount of information is being collected on an unprecedented scale. By monitoring all citizens and organizational entities, the CCP can regulate, control, promote, or restrict behaviors for the benefit of the society. Driven by data and controlled by a massive artificial intelligence model, society can be encouraged to act in appropriate ways. The threat, as Rogier Creemers explains, is "if trust is broken in one place, restrictions are imposed everywhere."[13]

Chinese society is focused on the collective good of the people rather than the freedom and liberty of the individual, which makes this plan more palatable to the citizenry. However, imagine that China's digital technology, facial recognition, 5G surveillance, satellites, and data collection are spread to other countries through the purchase of China's cameras, phones, computers, and Wi-Fi technology. This huge social credit experiment could be replicated in authoritarian states globally before it comes to the rest of the world.

China's propaganda machine has churned out broadcasts as to why this effort benefits everyone. The idea of zhixing nan, "enforcement is difficult", runs like a current through society that some fear cannot be solved without strict management, and drastic measures. Furthermore, China is committed to stamping out corruption, which is broadly defined as any unpatriotic act that is disloyal to China, the CCP, or Xi Jinping.

Conclusion

Trust and safety are important to the Chinese people and these qualities must be earned. Many Chinese people are concerned, and thus, the CCP seeks to weed out those who are immoral, unethical, and corrupt, as defined by strict adherence to Beijing's dictates while denouncing all other beliefs or allegiances. The idea is that cheaters and violators should be removed or, at a minimum, kept away from the rest of society.

It is important to note that, though this social credit system is a reality, the details are ambiguous. There is not enough authoritative information to definitively conclude the future or consequences of this initiative. Nevertheless, much is at stake.

---

13 Rogier Creemers, "China's Social Credit System: An Evolving Practice of Control," *SSRN*, May 9, 2018, https://papers.ssrn.com/sol3/papers.cfm?abstract_id=3175792

What's at Stake?

First, with the implementation of this social credit system, every individual and entity's reputation and daily living experience may be altered.

Second, as this grand, ambitious experiment is rolled out and enhanced, the tentacles of China's reach can latch onto personal information, one individual and country at a time.

Third, censorship has eliminated any ideology contrary to the CCP's vision. Therefore, concerns about the ramifications of the social credit system have not widely surfaced and are unlikely to do so soon given the pervasiveness of the CCP's digital reach.

Finally, privacy is thrown out the window as ratings and numbers become the citizenry's primary regard. Jobs, homes, hotels, cars, safety, and security, are determined by a social credit score, and this will mean that no citizen can escape any fate that Beijing designates for them.

Propaganda, Control, and Digital Surveillance | Part 2

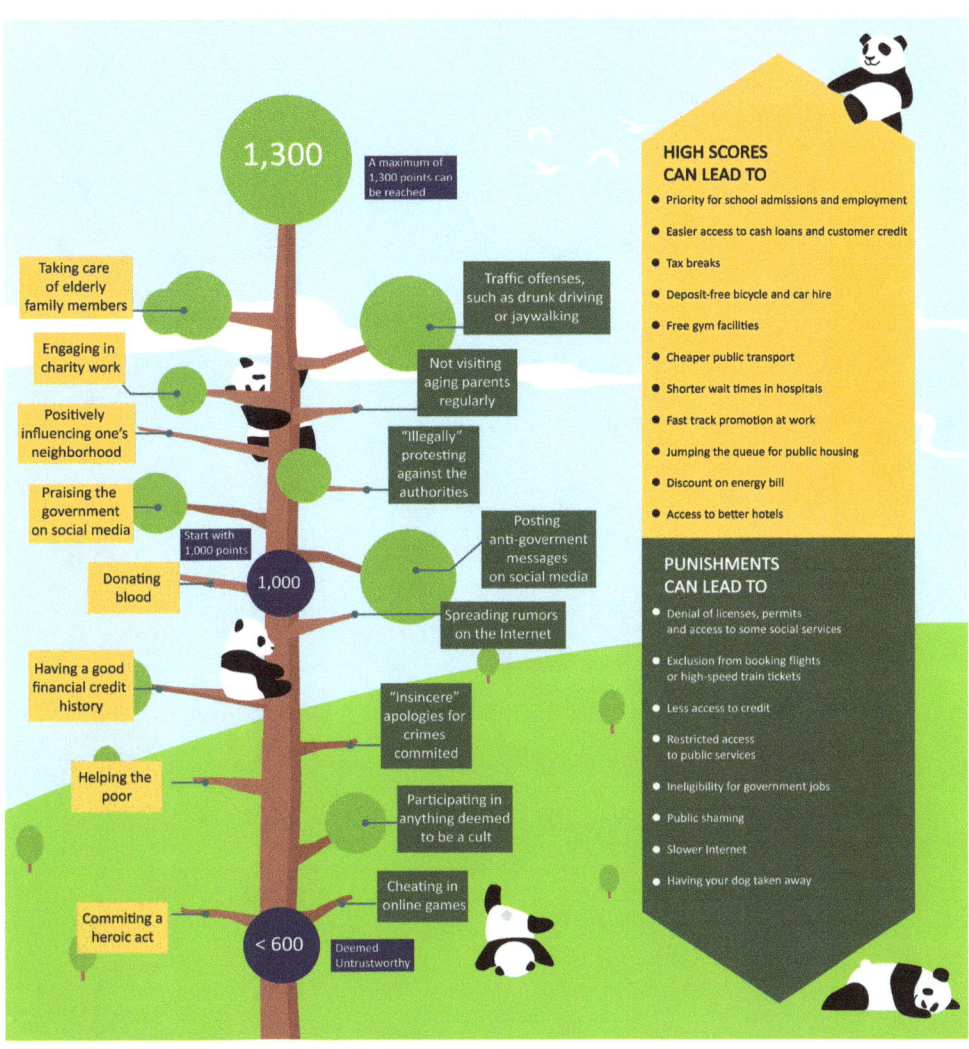

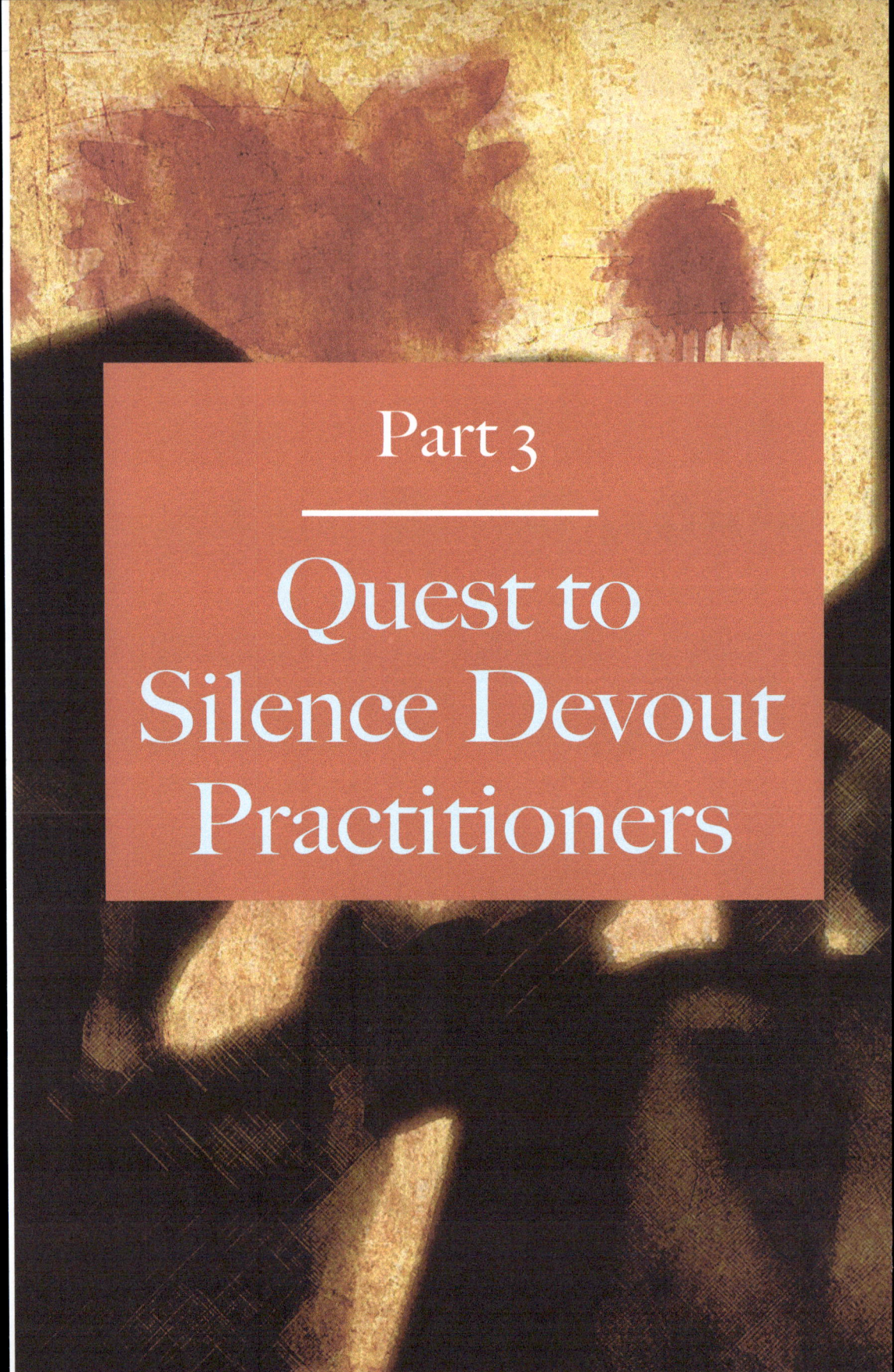

Part 3

Quest to Silence Devout Practitioners

Suppressing Religion and Stifling Freedom of Speech

China has amassed a campaign against religion, wiping out individual's spiritual practices. Compliance is required. The goal is for the Chinese people to adhere to atheist-socialism. Outside religious beliefs are undesirable. Religion and religious practices that gain traction and corral the masses are extinguished, like those of the Falun Gong. The Chinese Communist Party (CCP) members set a goal to have all people believe solely in its social and political system. In 2017, Beijing directed 90 million members of the CCP to shun religion.[1] Chinese President Xi Jinping and other members of the CCP have announced that the goal is for the Chinese to be "unyielding Marxist atheists".[2]

Churches have been demolished. Temples have been razed. Religious practices have been denied. Even groups that practice meditation have been viciously persecuted. Violations have included imprisonment, organ harvesting, and 're-education'.

These are hard to imagine in today's society. Tibetan monks have been threatened for decades. Their cries have been largely unheard. Over time, even some ardent advocates have given up the rallying cry for the Buddhist monks. However, in 2020, hundreds of thousands of Tibetans were subject to forced indoctrination and retraining for the world's mass production factories and labor encampments.

Read reports, listen to testimonies, and learn about what is happening. There are plenty of sources in this chapter to follow up on any topic that grabs your curiosity. In particular, today, the most incredible and horrific events are occurring in Xinjiang Province, which is covered in the subsequent sections.

---

1. The Economic Times, "China's Communist Party Asks Members to Give Up Religion," *The Economic Times*, July 19, 2017, https://economictimes.indiatimes.com/news/international/world-news/chinas-communist-party-asks-members-to-give-up-religion/articleshow/59666001.cms

2. Charlie Campbell, "China's Leader Xi Jinping Reminds Party Members to Be 'Unyielding Marxist Atheists,'" *Time Magazine*, April 25, 2016, https://time.com/4306179/china-religion-freedom-xi-jinping-muslim-christian-xinjiang-buddhist-tibet/

Chapter 1

What is Religious Persecution, Harassment, and Torture?

Freedom of Religion is Extinguished as People are Imprisoned

United States Commission on International Religious Freedom (USCIRF) Report

In 2020, the following results were determined.[1]

1. There are an estimated **1,300 concentration camps** in Xinjiang Province.
2. People are sent to concentration camps for wearing a beard, refusing alcohol, or other signs of "religious extremism".
3. Former inmates report **torture, rape, and sterilization**.
4. Nearly **500,000 Muslim children** have been taken from their families to be re-educated.
5. Falun Gong practitioners were taken into custody in 2019 for meditation exercises and distributing literature about their beliefs.
6. **Organ harvesting** of the Falun Gong practitioners occurred "on a significant scale".
7. **Mosques have been damaged or destroyed**.
8. Signs in Arabic have been removed from Muslim businesses.
9. Monks and nuns, refusing to denounce the Dalai Lama have been tortured and imprisoned.
10. More than 150 **Tibetans have self-immolated** in protest.
11. Protestant churches have been **raided or shut down**.
12. Pastors have been imprisoned with "subversion of state power".
13. Bishops have been harassed and coerced to follow Xi Jinping.
14. **Cash bounties were offered to informants** of underground churches.
15. **Crosses have been removed** and youth are banned from participating in religion.
16. Images of Jesus Christ and the Virgin Mary have been **replaced with pictures of Xi Jinping**.
17. Buddhist, Daoist, and Confucian statues were **demolished**.

---

1 U.S. Commission on International Religious Freedom, "Annual Report of the U.S. Commission on International Religious Freedom," *U.S. Commission on International Religious Freedom*, April, 2020, https://www.uscirf.gov/sites/default/files/USCIRF%202020%20Annual%20Report_Final_42920.pdf

Consequences

Totalitarian regimes claim the whole person – mind, body, and spirit - with the goal of destroying beliefs.[2] The consequences for those in China who hold a non-Marxist belief system are devastating. In an August 2020 *Foreign Affairs* article, Michael McFaul, former U.S. Ambassador to Russia, wrote, "The CCP under Xi runs a ruthless and oppressive dictatorship. It stifles individual freedoms, jails dissidents and rivals, and has sent countless Uighurs and other minorities to internment camps in what some experts have classified as cultural genocide."[3] In China, repression, discrimination, and imprisonment is endemic in society as churches are destroyed, religious leaders are silenced, and members are tortured. Testimonies from Uyghurs,[4] members of religious minorities,[5] and the Falun Gong,[6] are alarming, including,[7]

> Twenty prisoners live in one small room.
>
> The captured are handcuffed, their heads shaved, every move is monitored by ceiling cameras.
>
> A bucket in the corner of the room is their toilet.
>
> The daily routine begins at 6 a.m. They are learning Chinese, memorizing propaganda songs and 'confessing' to invented sins and violations they did not commit.
>
> Prisoners range in age from teenagers to elderly.
>
> Their meals are meager: cloudy soup and a slice of bread.
>
> Torture – affixed to chairs with metal nails, fingernails pulled out, prodded with electric shocks – takes place in the "black room."
>
> Punishment is a constant.
>
> The prisoners are forced to take unknown pills and receive injections for disease prevention, the staff tell them, but in reality they are the human subjects of medical experiments.
>
> Many of the inmates suffer from cognitive decline. Some of the men have become sterile.
>
> Women are routinely raped.

---

2   Doug Bandow, "Religious Persecution Around the Globe: A Guide," *The American Spectator*, May 3, 2020, https://spectator.org/religious-persecution-around-the-globe-a-guide/

3   Michael McFaul, "Xi Jinping is Not Stalin," *Foreign Affairs*, August 10, 2020, https://www.foreignaffairs.com/articles/united-states/2020-08-10/xi-jinping-not-stalin

4   Hong Kong Free Press. "In Full: 'I Begged Them to Kill Me' - Ex-Xinjiang Detainee Mihrigul Tursun Gives Testimony in the US." *YouTube video*, 8:08. December 3, 2018, https://www.youtube.com/watch?v=dsd1NkCKaNg

5   Jerry Dykstra, "Key Chinese House Church Leader's Testimony," *The Christian Broadcasting Network*, n.d., https://www.cbn.com/spirituallife/biblestudyandtheology/discipleship/persecution_112702.aspx?mobile=false&q=spirituallife/biblestudyandtheology/discipleship/persecution_112702.aspx

6   Faluninfo, "U. S. Congress Hears Testimony on Thousands of Falun Gong Killings for Organs," *Falun Dafa Infocenter*, September 14, 2012, https://faluninfo.net/u-s-congress-hears-testimony-on-thousands-of-falun-gong-killings-for-organs/

7   David Stavrou, "A Million People Are Jailed at China's Gulags. I Managed to Escape. Here's What Really Goes on Inside," *Haaretz*, October 17, 2019, https://www.haaretz.com/world-news/.premium.MAGAZINE-a-million-people-are-jailed-at-china-s-gulags-i-escaped-here-s-what-goes-on-inside-1.7994216

In a testimony to the *Christian Broadcasting Network (CBN)*, one Chinese Christian explained that the Chinese government forced foreign missionaries to leave and were attacked, criticized, and scolded. He further explained that some martyred themselves for Christ or were sent to jail, while others who were scared, denied Jesus, escaped overseas or betrayed friends, brothers, and sisters.[8]

Condemned by Human Rights Groups

Beijing has instituted extreme measures that are condemned by human rights groups, like the United Nations Human Rights Council, as inhumane.[9] The persistent abuse is done in a bid to restrict Chinese citizens and completely streamline their religious views to one path: the worship of Xi.[10]

China takes an increasingly aggressive approach to controlling religious activity within its borders in what basically has amounted to a series of escalating human rights violations.[11] There are countless stories of Uyghur Muslims being detained arbitrarily,[12] Tibetan monks being kicked out of their homes, temples destroyed,[13] and crosses burned.[14] Throughout history, the tendency for societies and groups within societies to alienate and suppress subcultures is, sadly, a recurring theme. For example, the Armenian genocide,[15] which began in 1915 was partly ethnic cleansing and the belief by the Ottoman Empire that Armenians were 'infidels'.[16]

Throughout the past decade, religious persecution in China, including harassment and torture, have taken many different forms. Persecution and harassment are generally based on ethnic origin or religious affiliation, arising either as a result of religious bigotry (when the members of a dominant religious group denigrate minority religious affiliations) or an attempt by a government to suppress or control a religious group that is perceived as a threat

---

8   Jerry Dykstra, "Key Chinese House Church Leader's Testimony," *The Christian Broadcasting Network*, n.d., https://www.cbn.com/spirituallife/biblestudyandtheology/discipleship/persecution_112702.aspx?mobile=false&q=spirituallife/biblestudyandtheology/discipleship/persecution_112702.aspx

9   United Nations Human Rights, "Human Rights by Country: China," *United Nations Human Rights Office of the High Commissioner*, n.d., https://www.ohchr.org/EN/countries/AsiaRegion/Pages/CNIndex.aspx

10 Simon Denyer, "Jesus Won't Save You — President Xi Jinping Will, Chinese Christians Told," *The Washington Post*, November 14, 2017, https://www.washingtonpost.com/news/worldviews/wp/2017/11/14/jesus-wont-save-you-president-xi-jinping-will-chinese-christians-told

11 Sarah Cook, "Worsening Religious Persecution in China Requires Stronger U.S. Response," *Freedomhouse*, March 20, 2020, https://freedomhouse.org/article/worsening-religious-persecution-china-requires-stronger-us-response

12 Lindsay Maizland, "China's Repression of Uighurs in Xinjiang," *Council on Foreign Relations*, June 30, 2020, https://www.cfr.org/backgrounder/chinas-repression-uighurs-xinjiang

13 Emily Walker, "China's Oppression of Tibetans Has Dramatically Increased," *New Internationalist*, February 4, 2016, https://newint.org/features/web-exclusive/2016/02/04/chinas-oppression-of-tibetans-has-dramatically-increased

14 Javier C. Hernandez, "As China Cracks Down on Churches Christians Declare 'We Will Not Forfeit Our Faith,'" *The New York Times*, December 25, 2018, https://www.nytimes.com/2018/12/25/world/asia/china-christmas-church-crackdown.html

15 Robert Fisk, "Robert Fisk: Let Me Denounce Genocide from the Dock," *The Independent*, October 14, 2006, https://www.independent.co.uk/voices/commentators/fisk/robert-fisk-let-me-denounce-genocide-dock-6231049.html

16 History.com Editors, "Armenian Genocide," *History.com*, October 31, 2019, https://www.history.com/topics/world-war-i/armenian-genocide

to its security or its interests. This intolerance is evidenced in China's control of its citizens as they observe their religious practices - a process the Chinese government labels 'sinicization'.[17]

Conclusion

Persecution is often top-down, from leaders to citizens. Adopting the dominant religion or belief system is fashionable in an attempt to attract favor from those in power and avoid being alienated or ostracized. Thus, when everyone falls in lock-step with the national dictates, rulers can impose their will and beliefs on their subjects in the form of restrictive policies against subordinated religious groups.

The rise of religious persecution in China in its current form can be traced back to the rise of the Chinese Communist Party (CCP).[18] In particular, silencing of the masses began during the time of Mao Zedong's Cultural Revolution, a period in Chinese history when all forms of religious activity were banned.

What's at Stake?

First, religious persecution has been around for thousands of years and still exists. Individuals throughout the ages have suffered. We can only hope that as we move on, we will learn from history.

Second, evidence supports the notion that the number of religious people in China is on the rise, including men and women who practice folk religions and several other banned faiths. Meanwhile, China has one of the world's largest populations of religious prisoners.[19] Imprisonment is likely to increase.

Third, the freedom to practice religion in China is all but eliminated, though not yet. In October 2020, the Vatican and China extended their agreement, allowing the Pope to appoint Bishops to China with the CCP's approval, even though there are no official relations between the Holy See and China since they severed ties shortly after 1949.[20]

---

17 Alexandra Ma, "Jailing Muslims, Burning Bibles, and Forcing Monks to Wave the National Flag: How Xi Jinping is Attacking Religion in China," *Business Insider*, August 10, 2019, https://www.businessinsider.com/how-xi-jinping-is-attacking-religion-in-china-2018-11?IR=T

18 TRT World, "13 Things to Know About Religious Persecution in China," *TRT World*, March 2, 2017, https://www.trtworld.com/asia/13-things-to-know-about-religions-persecution-in-china-308451

19 Eleanor Albert and Lindsay Maizland, "Religion in China," *Council on Foreign Relations*, September 25, 2020, https://www.cfr.org/backgrounder/religion-china

20 Nicole Winfield, "Vatican, China Extend Bishop Agreement Over US Opposition," *AP News*, October 22, 2020, https://apnews.com/article/beijing-china-pope-francis-europe-vatican-city-5c5f822b98317f1bb5002887e383473f

Chapter 2
China's Church Demolitions
Remodeling Buildings, Cultures, and Social Norms

Introduction

From 1966 to 1976, Chairman Mao Zedong launched China's Cultural Revolution as a movement to re-educate and re-define Chinese cultural values. The country had just emerged from the Great Leap Forward, an expensive, failed attempt to shift China's predominantly agrarian economy toward industrialization, in which approximately 30 million people died.[1] Alongside this demoralizing initiative was a devastating nationwide famine, compounded by droughts and floods. Wanting to raise the tide of the lowered morale and deep despair, Mao embarked on a mission to challenge his citizens to embrace his vision of China and eliminate the capitalist elements of society.

Mao launched a class struggle. Chinese youth, the Red Guard, were deployed to remove symbols of the past and identify those who were disloyal. Mao demanded obedience, requiring every citizen to read his *Little Red Book* as he purged society of the elite scholars, scientists, landlords, and rich farmers. The goal of Mao's socialist society was to create equality and level the playing field so that everyone had a share in the country's success with no individual or group having more than others. In the Cultural Revolution, Mao envisioned a large-scale nationwide effort to reignite his downtrodden people, the proletariat, with a nationalistic pride while teaching the younger generation the virtues of Communist Party values.

Chairman Mao's initiative was bolstered by killing, ransacking, and the persecution of Christians through the campaign to get rid of the 'Four Olds": old traditions, old customs, old culture, and old ideas. In Mao's campaign, churches were destroyed from the inside and redesigned to be used as storerooms, factories, or homes. Any remaining religious book,[2] figure, or article was burned. Christians were considered "enemies of the people"[3] and Catholics were targeted as high-level suspects for counter-revolutionary activity.

The institution of Christianity was inherently viewed as a threat since the intent of missionaries was to sway the hearts and minds of people who Mao sought to control. Additionally, Christianity embodied a vestige of Western culture that China wanted to eradicate. As such, the Cultural Revolution resulted in the removal of crosses, as well as the tearing down and destruction of statues, temples, shrines, heritage sites, artwork, and, ironically, anything cultural.

Xi's Mao-Like Initiatives

Decades later in the 2000s, President Xi Jinping rode into his leadership, lassoing and tearing down any remaining cultural and religious symbols with similar ropes. He instructed local officials to demolish churches, repaint over prayers, hang portraits of Xi Jinping on walls, and both remove crosses and destroy statues.[4]

---

1 LALKAR, "Revisiting alleged 30 million famine deaths during China's Great Leap," *LALKAR*, November/December 2012, https://www.lalkar.org/article/634/revisiting-alleged-30million-famine-deaths-during-chinas-great-leap

2 Daniel Schwartz, "The Books Have Been Burning," *CBC*, September 10, 2010, https://www.cbc.ca/news/world/the-books-have-been-burning-1.887172

3 Sergio Ticozzi, "The Persecution of Catholics During the Cultural Revolution," *AsiaNews.it*, May 17, 2016, http://www.asianews.it/news-en/The-persecution-of-Catholics-during-the-Cultural-Revolution-37513.html

4 Steven W. Mosher, "How China's Xi Jinping Destroyed Religion And Made Himself God," *The New York Post*, February 1, 2020, https://nypost.com/2020/02/01/how-chinas-xi-jinping-destroyed-religion-and-made-himself-god/

Religion Under Attack
Persecution of the Faithful in China

Furthermore, in a particularly forceful demonstration of authority and determination to wipe out Islam from the country, President Xi directed the Chinese Communist Party (CCP) to oversee the persecution of the Uyghur Muslims in Xinjiang Province. Islamophobia became widespread and individual rights vanquished from Muslim citizens on the grounds that 'they are all terrorists'. While the 9/11 terrorist attacks in New York City contributed to this fear, China faced its own terrorist threats, including:

1. October 28, 2013 – Car bomb explosion in Tiananmen Square
2. March 1, 2014 – Mass knifing attack at the Kunming, Yunnan railway station
3. May 22, 2014 – Car bomb at an outdoor market in Urumqi, Xinjiang Province
4. September 30, 2015 – Explosion of 17 package bombs in Guangxi Province
5. November 2015 – Islamic State killing of a Chinese teacher and a hostage [5]

---

[5] Murray Scot Tanner & James Bellacqua, "China's Response to Terrorism," *CAN Analysis & Solutions*, June 2016, https://www.uscc.gov/sites/default/files/Research/Chinas%20Response%20to%20Terrorism_CNA061616.pdf

The effort in Xinjiang Province started slowly. First, Xi banned women from wearing hijabs and long dresses and men from having beards.[6] Next, he forced the Muslims to eat pork and drink alcohol and removed Halal foods.[7] He then stopped the practice of Islam, stripping expressions of Islamic faith, including domes and minarets.[8] Public use of Arabic script was outlawed as was the teaching of Arabic in schools.[9] A large proportion of the population in Xinjiang Province were sent to concentration camps to be confined in a prison-like environment and re-educated.

These incidents are not isolated as similar actions and demolitions have occurred in other areas of China as well, including Inner Mongolia, Henan, and Ningxia.[10] The sweeping campaign to remove religious freedom is not unique to the Muslims. China targets Buddhists[11] and Christians[12] by demolishing temples and churches in order to 'cleanse' the nation of any diversity in belief. Still, over 100 million Christians live in China[13] while 245 million Buddhists reside there as well.[14]

Xi Jinping continued with religious cleansing by replacing images of the Madonna and Child with self-portraits. *Bitter Winter* reports that a Catholic church in Ji'an that was named "The True and Original Source of the Universe" was painted over with the name "Follow the Party, Obey the Party, and Be Grateful to the Party" with a Chinese flag planted at the church doors.[15] In 2019, local officials removed the Virgin Mary and the Christ Child painting and hung a portrait of Xi right at the center of a wall so that all worshipers would hail to their new God, Xi Jinping.[16] Shortly after, officials stole the church's keys from worship leaders, locked the doors and windows, and banned the congregation from entering again.[17]

---

6   Saphora Smith, "China Bans Veils and 'Abnormal' Beards in Western Province of Xinjiang," *NBC News*, April 1, 2017, https://www.nbcnews.com/news/world/china-bans-veils-abnormal-beards-western-province-xinjiang-n741501

7   Jon Sharman, "China 'Forcing Muslims to Eat Pork and Drink Alcohol' For Lunar New Year Festival," *Independent UK*, February 7, 2019, https://www.independent.co.uk/news/world/asia/china-muslims-xinjiang-pork-alcohol-lunar-new-year-spring-festival-uighur-islam-a8767561.html

8   Steven Lee Myers, "A Crackdown on Islam is Spreading Across China," *The New York Times*, September 21, 2019, https://www.nytimes.com/2019/09/21/world/asia/china-islam-crackdown.html

9   Al Jazeera, "Arabic, Muslim Symbols Ordered Taken Down in China's Capital," *Al Jazeera*, July 31, 2019, https://www.aljazeera.com/news/2019/7/31/arabic-muslim-symbols-ordered-taken-down-in-chinas-capital

10 BBC News, "China Mosque Demolition Sparks Standoff in Ningxia," *BBC News*, August 10, 2018, https://www.bbc.com/news/world-asia-china-45140551

11 Shen Xinran, "Hundreds of Policemen Sent to Demolish Buddhist Temples," *Bitter Winter*, July 2, 2020, https://bitterwinter.org/hundreds-of-policemen-sent-to-demolish-buddhist-temples/

12 Ian Johnson, "Decapitated Churches in China's Christian Heartland," *The New York Times*, May 22, 2016, https://www.nytimes.com/2016/05/22/world/asia/china-christians-zhejiang.html

13 Asia Harvest, "How Many Christian Are in China?", *Asia Harvest*, n.d., https://asiaharvest.org/how-many-christian-are-in-china/

14 Yang Si Qi, "Life in Purgatory: Buddhism Is Growing in China, But Remains in Legal Limbo," *Time Magazine,* March 16, 2016, https://time.com/4260593/china-buddhism-religion-religious-freedom/

15 Tang Zhe, "Xi Jinping Portraits Replace Catholic Symbols in Churches," *Bitter Winter*, November 25, 2019, https://bitterwinter.org/xi-jinping-portraits-replace-catholic-symbols

16 Steven W. Mosher, "How China's Xi Jinping Destroyed Religion And Made Himself God," *The New York Post*, February 1, 2020, https://nypost.com/2020/02/01/how-chinas-xi-jinping-destroyed-religion-and-made-himself-god/

17 Tang Zhe, "Xi Jinping Portraits Replace Catholic Symbols in Churches," *Bitter Winter*, November 25, 2019, https://bitterwinter.org/xi-jinping-portraits-replace-catholic-symbols/

The Chinese Patriotic Catholic Association in Jiangxi's Poyang County was destined for the same fate as local officials ordered the closure of religious activities and threatened the elders' retirement pensions if they did not comply.[18] Pictures of Xi Jinping and Mao Zedong replaced the cross and a painting of the Virgin Mary. In the state-run Three-Self Church in Luoyang city, Xi painted over the Ten Commandments and replaced them with his own quotes.[19]

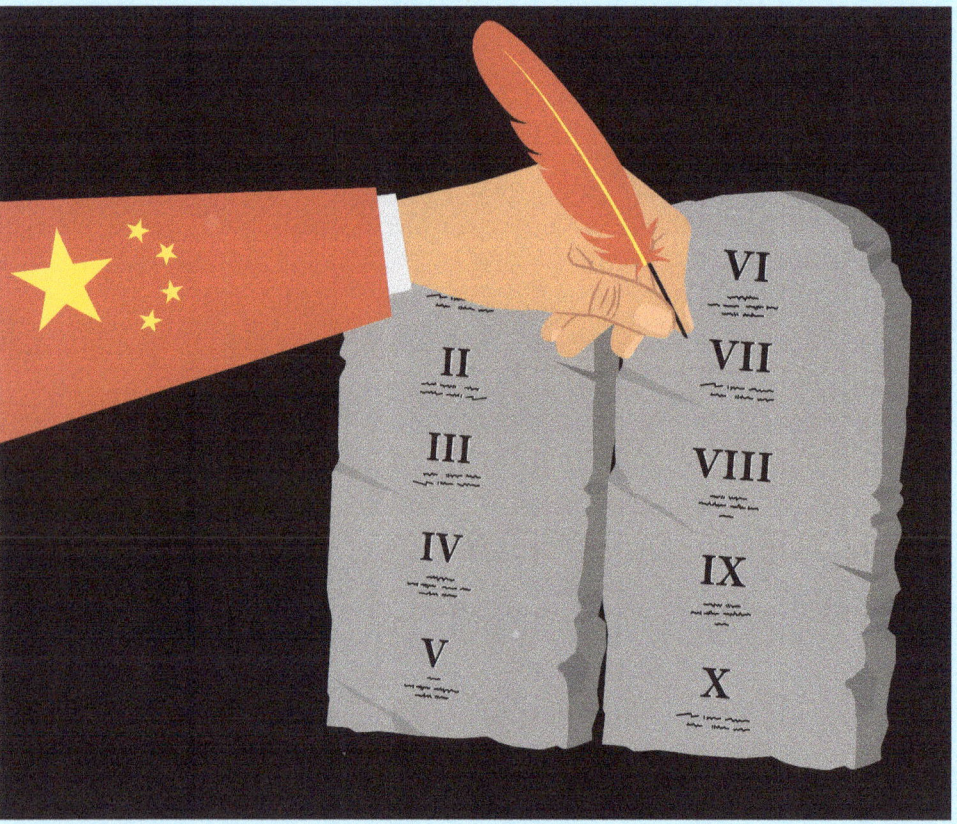

18 Tang Zhe, "Xi Jinping Portraits Replace Catholic Symbols in Churches," *Bitter Winter*, November 25, 2019, https://bitterwinter.org/xi-jinping-portraits-replace-catholic-symbols/

19 Tang Feng, "Xi Jinping's Quotes Replace the Ten Commandments in Churches," *Bitter Winter*, September 14, 2019, https://bitterwinter.org/xi-jinpings-quotes-replace-the-ten-commandments/

In his campaign for religious cleansing, Xi Jinping set out to replace centuries of religious traditions and beliefs centered on Buddha's preaching. Rather than hearing Buddha's enlightened 'Thought' resonating through the Buddhist temple, Xi Jinping's recorded voice now echoes in the chambers.[20]

While Article 35 of the Chinese constitution outlines freedom of expression, on February 1, 2020, Xi implemented the "Control Measures for Religious Groups", a law that regulated all religious practices and commanded that they abide by Beijing's rules for church, prayer, and congregations.[21] Based on these standards, any program sponsored by a religious community must be approved by the Religious Affairs Office. These religious groups are required to "spread the principles and policies of the Chinese Communist Party" and educate "religious staff and religious citizens to support the leadership of the Chinese Communist Party."[22]

Conclusion

The CCP tightly monitors religion in China. Although recognizing Buddhism, Catholicism, Daoism, Islam, and Protestantism, Beijing is aware that there are numerous banned faiths that continue to be practiced. As more Chinese citizens practice religion and China's constitution declares its "freedom of religious belief", millions are persecuted for their faith.

A Chinese Catholic priest observed, "In practice, your religion no longer matters, if you are Buddhist, or Taoist, or Muslim or Christian: the only religion allowed is faith in the Chinese Communist Party."[23] China's new laws complement the other manners in which officials regulate church preaching. These include editing the Bible to ensure a proper number of quotations from Xi Jinping. Furthermore, the CCP's narrative is shaping the way worship is conducted nationwide, including pledging allegiance to the CCP.[24]

---

20 Steven W. Mosher, "How China's Xi Jinping Destroyed Religion And Made Himself God," *The New York Post*, February 1, 2020, https://nypost.com/2020/02/01/how-chinas-xi-jinping-destroyed-religion-and-made-himself-god/

21 STNN translated from Chinese to English, "Measure for the Administration of Religious Groups," *STNN*, December 30, 2019, http://m.stnn.cc/pcarticle/703584

22 Wang Zhicheng, "New Administrative Measures For Religious Groups: Total Submission To The Chinese Communist Party," *AsiaNews*, December 31, 2019, http://www.asianews.it/news-en/-New-administrative-measures-for-religious-groups:-total-submission-to-the-Chinese-Communist-Party-%E2%80%8B-48919.html

23 Ibid.

24 Steven W. Mosher, "How China's Xi Jinping Destroyed Religion And Made Himself God," *The New York Post*, February 1, 2020, https://nypost.com/2020/02/01/how-chinas-xi-jinping-destroyed-religion-and-made-himself-god/

What's at Stake?

First, under Xi Jinping's rule, state and religion are not independent of one another. Rather, religion must abide by government regulations and newly instituted proclamations that ensure loyalty to Beijing, which must override one's commitment to faith.

Second, along with China's surveillance activities, monitoring actions, and increasing police presence, the Chinese people are being held accountable to all CCP laws; the regulation of religion is just another mechanism in which Beijing strives to impose control on its population.

Chapter 3
The Persecution of the Falun Gong
China's 'Unprecedented Persecution'

Introduction to Falun Gong

Amidst China's ethnic and religious cleansing efforts to eradicate diverse beliefs that may threaten Beijing, Jiang Zemin took extreme measures by extending his long arm of oppression over the Falun Gong, practitioners of a moral and spiritual movement.

Those who practice Falun Gong are involved in peaceful, slow-moving meditations and exercises. Meditators sit in rows with their legs crossed, backs straight, and minds focused. The goal of Falun Gong is to nurture "truthfulness, compassion, and forbearance",[1] while creating the best 'xining', or personal moral character.[2]

Falun Gong emerged in China in the 1980s during the Qigong boom. Qigong was a breathing and exercise meditation with many health benefits for participants.[3] Qigong-inspired principles were translated into the Falun Gong movement by Li Hongzhi, Falun Gong's leader and primary teacher of the practice, in May 1992.[4]

Li Hongzhi was born into an ordinary family of scholars in 1951.[5] When he was four years old, Master Qun Jue of the Buddha School chose Li Hongzhi to be the only disciple of his generation to train in Master Qun Jue's Buddhist principles.[6] At eight years old, Li Hongzhi learned the meaning of "Truthfulness-Compassion-Forbearance", the three principles he translated into Falun Gong[7].

At twelve years old, Li Hongzhi was taught by a new master in the Tao School, learning ancient teachings of the Tao. Throughout his life, he was taught by various different masters in different religious philosophies. What Li Hongzhi took from this mixed cultivation of ideology was that he needed to find a practice in which ordinary people could engage to teach them goodness of heart, improvement of health, and a focus on the betterment of humankind.[8]

Falun Gong has no hierarchical structure, meaning there were no administrators, officials, churches, or designated places of worship. As such, Li Hongzhi's writings and spiritual beliefs, rooted in Falun Gong, provide a central authority.[9]

---

1 James Griffiths, "Why China Fears the Falun Gong," *Global Post*, July 14, 2014, https://www.pri.org/stories/2014-07-14/why-china-fears-falun-gong

2 Ibid.

3 J.Y., "What is Falun Gong?," *The Economist*, September 5, 2018, https://www.economist.com/the-economist-explains/2018/09/05/what-is-falun-gong

4 James Griffiths, "Why China Fears the Falun Gong," *Global Post*, July 14, 2014, https://www.pri.org/stories/2014-07-14/why-china-fears-falun-gong

5 Falun Dafa, "A Chronicle of Major Historic Events during the Introduction of Falun Dafa to the Public," *Falun Dafa*, October 8, 2004, http://en.minghui.org/emh/articles/2004/10/8/53286.html

6 Ibid.

7 Ibid.

8 Ibid.

9 James Griffiths, "Why China Fears the Falun Gong," *Global Post*, July 14, 2014, https://www.pri.org/stories/2014-07-14/why-china-fears-falun-gong

Beijing's Narrative of Falun Gong

The primary misconception with Falun Gong is that the movement originates from religious ideology. Furthermore, others have argued that Falun Gong is a 'cult', a narrative Beijing fervently pushes. Because of Li Hongzhi's Buddhist and Taoist background and the simultaneous 1960's religious uprisings in the West,[10] Falun Gong was often perceived as a religious group rather than a practice focused on exercise for the mind and body.

The Chinese government initially praised the many health benefits the Chinese people received from Falun Gong, often widely broadcasted on CCTV. Even further, the government praised Li for "promoting rectitude in society".[11]

By 1999, it was estimated that China had 100 million Falun Gong followers.[12] However, at that same time, the Chinese-state media began publishing articles attacking Qigong and Falun Gong, saying it was a dangerous "feudal superstition".[13] Many CCTV stations followed suit, reporting that Falun Gong was a threat to Chinese society. The news was inundated with this new politically-motivated warning to practitioners and those considering the practice.

---

10 James Griffiths, "Why China Fears the Falun Gong," *Global Post*, July 14, 2014, https://www.pri.org/stories/2014-07-14/why-china-fears-falun-gong

11 Ibid.

12 Friends of Falun Gong, "The Unprecedented Persecution," *Friends of Falun Gong*, n.d., http://fofg.org/the-unprecedented-persecution/

13 James Griffiths, "Why China Fears the Falun Gong," *Global Post*, July 14, 2014, https://www.pri.org/stories/2014-07-14/why-china-fears-falun-gong

The Turning Point for the Falun Gong

In response to an April 1999 article deriding the Falun Gong, the practitioners peacefully protested holding a sit-in outside the offices of a Tianjin newspaper. Roughly 300 police arrived to the offices to break up the Falun Gong meditation; forty-five Falun Gong practitioners were arrested.[14] This act of government aggression launched the turning point in Beijing's Falun Gong persecution.

On April 25, 1999, over 10,000 Falun Gong practitioners gathered in Beijing in front of the Zhongnanhai government compound to protest the media and authoritarian harassment. Party General Secretary Jiang Zemin was outraged by the scale of the protest, demanding that Falun Gong be "defeated".[15] Jiang sought to eradicate Falun Gong from Chinese society.

The Chinese government deployed all their forces to abolish this movement. On June 10, 1999, the Chinese Communist Party created the 610 Office, a government organization designed to monitor, track, and arrest Falun Gong members.[16] On July 20, 1999, security forces detained several thousand Falun Gong followers. On July 22, 1999, Falun Gong was declared illegal for "advocating superstition, spreading fallacies, hoodwinking people, inciting and creating disturbances, and jeopardizing social stability."[17]

Launching the 'Unprecedented Persecution'

Shortly after China banned the practice of Falun Gong,[18] the government instigated what became known as the 'unprecedented persecution',[19] attacking anyone who practiced this form of meditation in China.

The Chinese government tortured, murdered, brainwashed, imprisoned, raped, slandered, robbed, impoverished, and forced into labor millions of citizens who they caught practicing Falun Gong.[20] Tens of thousands of meditation practitioners have since been detained and hundreds have died in the Chinese government's custody.[21] In addition to these torturous conditions, tens of thousands have been killed by the government in order to harvest their organs and sell them to ready buyers.[22]

---

14 James Griffiths, "Why China Fears the Falun Gong," *Global Post*, July 14, 2014, https://www.pri.org/stories/2014-07-14/why-china-fears-falun-gong

15 Ibid.

16 Falun Dafa Club, "Persecution in China," *Falun Dafa Club*, n.d., http://sites.bu.edu/dafa/persecution-in-china/

17 James Griffiths, "Why China Fears the Falun Gong," *Global Post*, July 14, 2014, https://www.pri.org/stories/2014-07-14/why-china-fears-falun-gong

18 J.Y., "What is Falun Gong?," *The Economist*, September 5, 2018, https://www.economist.com/the-economist-explains/2018/09/05/what-is-falun-gong

19 Friends of Falun Gong, "The Unprecedented Persecution," *Friends of Falun Gong*, n.d., http://fofg.org/the-unprecedented-persecution/

20 Andrew Jacobs, "China Still Presses Crusade Against Falun Gong," *The New York Times*, April 27, 2009, https://www.nytimes.com/2009/04/28/world/asia/28china.html?_r=0

21 Ibid.

22 Falun Dafa Club, "Persecution in China," *Falun Dafa Club*, n.d., http://sites.bu.edu/dafa/persecution-in-china/

In a 2020 report, doctors from top Chinese hospitals admitted to removing organs from the Falun Gong.[23] The black market for organs is thriving, and China is attempting to meet global demand. In July 2020, Chinese doctors were jailed for illegal organ harvesting.[24] Organs have been transported worldwide. Some organs from China are thought to be in European hospitals. Witnesses have testified before the U.K. tribunal that trafficked organs and human tissue have come from Chinese ethnic minorities including Uyghurs and Falun Gong members.[25]

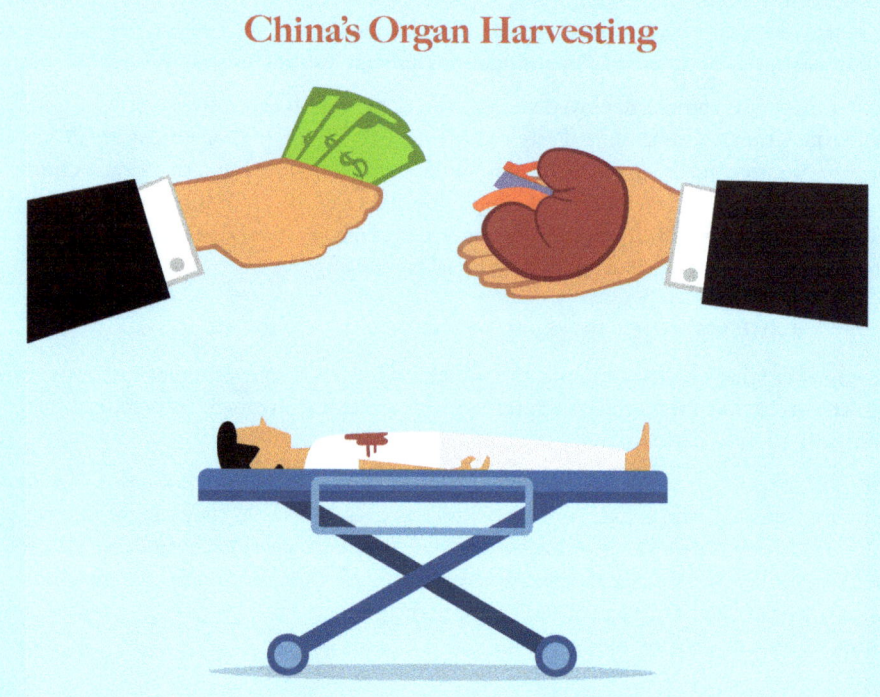

In response to the media's light cast on China for harvesting Falun Gong organs, on July 26, 2006, the Chinese Embassy stated,

> China has issued a regulation on human organ transplants, explicitly banning the sale of organs and introducing a set of medical standards for organ transplants in an effort to guarantee medical safety and the health of the patients.

---

23 Gareth Lacobucci,. "Chinese Doctors Admitted in Undercover Calls that Harvested Organs Were Available, Informal Tribunal Finds," *BMJ*, March 3, 2020, https://www.bmj.com/content/368/bmj.m859

24 BBC, "Chinese Doctors Jailed for Illegal Organ Harvesting," *BBC News*, November 27, 2020, https://www.bbc.com/news/world-asia-china-55097424

25 Miriam Karmali, "OPINION: Forced Organ Harvesting Could Be Making Its Way Into the UK Health System," *Thomson Reuters Foundation News*, August 28, 2020, https://news.trust.org/item/20200828082140-xyga1

Falun Gong is an anti-science, anti-humanity, and anti-evil cult which has been banned in China in accordance with law. It uses religion, Qigong or other things as camouflage to brainwash and control the practitioners. It preaches that human[s] can, through psychological meditation, form invisible magic wheels inside their bodies, cure their illness without medical treatment. It spreads Dooms Day theory, boasts that Li Hongzhi, founder of Falun Gong, is the most powerful God, claiming the sole power to foresee and avert the many unseen disasters that threaten the world.[26]

It is believed that the Chinese government began this episode of persecution because they feared the coalescence and possible unity of a powerful and growing group.[27] They may have believed that Falun Gong events hosted in Beijing were part of a future political uprising.[28] Regardless, the Chinese government inflicted gruesome torture and violence on a peaceful meditation group with no concrete reason to attack Falun Gong followers.

The International Community's Response

The international community continues to condemn China for this exact reason. In July 2020, 600 lawmakers from thirty different countries signed a joint statement to stop China's "systematic and brutal campaign to 'eradicate' the spiritual discipline of Falun Gong."[29] Furthermore, on July 20, 2020, the U.S. Department of State issued a press statement on the 21st anniversary of Falun Gong oppression. Mike Pompeo said,

> We call on the PRC government to immediately end its depraved abuse and mistreatment of Falun Gong practitioners, release those imprisoned due to their beliefs, such as Ma Zhenyu, and address the whereabouts of missing practitioners. Twenty-one years of persecution of Falun Gong practitioners is far too long, and it must end.[30]

Furthermore, the U.K. has similarly and repeatedly condemned China. In December 2017, thirty-three U.K. cabinet members signed on the motion, "That this House calls on the Government of the United Kingdom of Great Britain and Northern Ireland to condemn the persecution of Falun Gong and the crime of harvesting organs from Falun Gong practitioners and other prisoners of conscience in China."[31]

---

26 Embassy of the People's Republic of China in Canada, "Chinese Embassy's Statement on the Issue of Falun Gong," *Embassy of the People's Republic of China in Canada*, July 26, 2006, http://ca.china-embassy.org/eng/mtfw/press2/t265055.htm

27 Friends of Falun Gong, "The Unprecedented Persecution," *Friends of Falun Gong*, n.d., http://fofg.org/the-unprecedented-persecution/

28 Leeshai Lemish, "Why is Falun Gong Banned?," *NewStatesman*, August 19, 2008, https://www.newstatesman.com/blogs/the-faith-column/2008/08/falun-gong-party-chinese

29 Marco Respinti, "More than 600 Lawmakers Denounce China on the Anniversary of Falun Gong Repression," *Bitter Winter*, July 20, 2020, https://bitterwinter.org/more-than-600-lawmakers-denounce-china-on-the-anniversary-of-falun-gong-repression/

30 Michael R. Pompeo, "21st Anniversary of the PRC Government's Persecution of Falun Gong," *U.S. Department of State*, July 20, 2020, https://www.state.gov/21st-anniversary-of-the-prc-governments-persecution-of-falun-gong/

31 House of Commons, UK Parliament, "Falun Gong and Harvesting Organs," *UK Parliament*, December 12, 2017, https://edm.parliament.uk/early-day-motion/51146

In September 2020, the U.K. attempted to close the gaps that allow human tissue to be imported from China without being documented or traced.[32] Criticism partially stemmed from surgical mesh implants, criticized for safety and effectiveness, and the need for regulation.[33] Research on human organs to resolve concerns may have come from non-consenting individuals. The U.K. continues to consider ways to close the gaps. Amnesty International has spoken out against China on multiple occasions, sharing stories of torture and abuse of many practitioners.[34]

Conclusion

China has yet to listen to the rest of the world and end its abuse of the Falun Gong. This 'unprecedented persecution' has brutally demonstrated Beijing's willingness to oppress and incriminate any religious, spiritual, ethnic, or nationalistic group that they see as a threat to their ambitions.

What's at Stake?

First, freedom cannot be expressed in a nation which launches religious, spiritual, and ideological cleansing initiatives. The idea of freedom in thought and belief is eradicated through Beijing's persecution.

Second, Chinese-state media controls the narrative of the Falun Gong, depicting the peaceful group as a threat to society. Propaganda which spins the perception of the Falun Gong enables the human rights abuses of the group.

Third, many members of the international community and global citizens are unaware of this persecution. Without transparency in media and awareness through headlines, the world's blind eye endangers the lives of thousands of Chinese practitioners.

---

32 Bukky Balogun & Elizabeth Rough, "Medicines and Medical Devices Bill 2019-21," *U.K. Parliament House of Commons Library*, September 4, 2020, https://commonslibrary.parliament.uk/research-briefings/cbp-8699/

33 Ibid.

34 Amnesty International, "China: Falun Gong Practitioner at Risk of Torture: Qin Wei," *Amnesty International,* June 17, 2016, https://www.amnesty.org/en/documents/asa17/4275/2016/en/

Chapter 4

Cleansing of Oppositional Thought

CCP Institutes "Control Measures" Demanding Members to be "Unyielding Marxist Atheists"

Introduction

In July 2020, the Ministry of Justice of the People's Republic of China offered a report at a Central Political and Legal Committee forum, to remove subversion through discipline by

1. completely cutting off the cancer growing among the CCP
2. removing the black sheep
3. ensuring absolute loyalty
4. political and legal purity and reliability.[1]

In a 2020 reflection of Mao and Xi's forward movement to fireproof their power, Xi has instituted strict and fearsome controls to protect against CCP turbulence.[2] Xi Jinping told CCP members that they must be "unyielding Marxist atheists" and move forward with efforts to stamp out religion, demolish churches, and bulldoze anyone in protest.[3] These rules have been imposed on all foreign and domestic businesses in China as well. The nature of these instituted guidelines require serious consideration and education.

Removing Black Sheep
China Removes and Throws Out Anyone Who is Disloyal

---

1. Ministry of Justice Government Website (translated into English), "The National Political and Legal Team Education and Rectification Pilot Blew the Assembly Call," *Ministry of Justice of the People's Republic of China*, July 30, 2020, http://www.chinalaw.gov.cn/news/content/2020-07/30/zfyw_3253482.html
2. Chris Buckley, "'Drive the Blade In': Xi Shakes Up China's Law-and-Order Forces," *The New York Times*, August 20, 2020, https://www.nytimes.com/2020/08/20/world/asia/china-xi-jinping-communist-party.html
3. Charlie Campbell, "China's Leader Xi Jinping Reminds Party Members to Be 'Unyielding Marxist Atheists,'" *Time Magazine*, April 25, 2016, https://time.com/4306179/china-religion-freedom-xi-jinping-muslim-christian-xinjiang-buddhist-tibet/

Given the severity of the punishments, some directives include political stances in line with China's geopolitical aims, foreign affairs disputes, and territorial claims. Private businesspeople are told to "weaponize their minds with [Xi's] socialism ideology."[4]

Although obeying Beijing's requirements within China is obligatory, increasingly, Xi Jinping has used hardball tactics to advance CCP objectives coercing officials, demanding compliance, using financial leverage, ramming vessels, pointing lasers at pilots, and taking increasing control of international governing bodies.[5] Furthermore, Beijing is asserting its sovereignty in territorial disputes, through 'China's power grab' in the South China Sea, East China Sea, India, Bhutan, Nepal, west of China, and other areas.

Xi Jinping explained that all CCP members must learn the basic theories of Marxism for the 19th Central Political Bureau's fifth collective study.

[U]nswervingly strive for the lofty ideals of communism and the common ideals of socialism with Chinese characteristics. The "Communist Manifesto" revealed the inevitable trend that human society will eventually move towards communism, laying the theoretical foundation for Communists to firm up their ideals and beliefs and stick to their spiritual home. ... As long as we have mastered the basic principles of Marxism, we will be able to deeply realize that the realization of communism is a long historical process that is gradually achieved one by one. It requires several generations of continuous struggle, arduous struggle, and unremitting struggle; we can deeply understand China Socialism with characteristics is the only way to realize the great rejuvenation of the Chinese nation, and it is also the successful path for the Chinese Communists to lead the people in pursuing lofty ideals and opening up a bright future.[6]

Loyalty is Demanded

As Chen Yixin, Secretary-General of the Central Political and Legal Affairs Commission, presented the CCP's policy, he exclaimed, "Root out the harmful members of the herd," and "Root out 'two-faced people' who are disloyal and dishonest to the party."[7] With sharp words, Xi Jinping emphasized his cutting manifesto. Rule of law in China means something very different than in the West since the legal framework rests in the hands of the CCP, who proclaim, "the handle of the knife is firmly in the hands of the party and the people."[8]

---

4   Laura He, "Xi Jinping wants China's Private Companies to Fight Alongside the Communist Party," *CNN Business*, September 22, 2020, https://www.cnn.com/2020/09/22/business/china-private-sector-intl-hnk/index.html

5   Denny Roy, "'Xi Jinping Thought on Diplomacy' Fails to Impress – or Reassure," *The Diplomat*, April 2, 2020, https://thediplomat.com/2020/04/xi-jinping-thought-on-diplomacy-fails-to-impress-or-reassure/

6   Xi Jinping, "Learning the Basic Theories of Marxism is a Compulsory Course for Communists," *Qiushi*, November 15, 2019, http://www.qstheory.cn/dukan/qs/2019-11/15/c_1125234267.htm

7   Beijing News, "Chen Yixin: The Education and Rectification of the National Political and Legal Team is a "Yan'an Rectification Style"," *Ifeng*, July 8, 2020, http://news.ifeng.com/c/7xwhnCdD5zm

8   Samuel Wade, "Xi's Sharp Words "Ominous" For Legal Reform," *China Digital Times*, February 10, 2015, https://chinadigitaltimes.net/2015/02/xis-sharp-words-ominous-legal-reform/

Quest to Silence Devout Practitioners | Part 3

Cleansing of Oppositional Thought
"Control Measures" Instituted as a Warning
CCP Members are Told to be "Unyielding Marxist Athiests"

Liu Zhiqiang, businessman and member of the Chinese People's Political Consultative Conference, remarked that all levels of the CCP must reunify, strengthening their sense of purpose, eliminating 'bad horses', removing 'stubborn diseases', and build an 'iron army of politics and law'.[9]

Xi Jinping's Domination

President Xi Jinping seems to be intent on reviving this extreme ideology. Since he took office in March 2013, he replaced images of the Virgin Mary and baby Jesus with pictures of himself,[10] sent Muslims to concentration camps, which the government calls 'vocational training centers',[11] and painted over the Ten Commandments with quotes from Xi Jinping.[12] Chinese citizens are essentially forced to view Xi as their god.[13] As such, Chinese subjects offer their prayers to him. Some foreign observers have called this surge of power and authority a growing 'personality cult', reminiscent of the days of Mao Zedong, whose picture was in every home.[14]

In modern day China, citizens are allowed to practice religion under the condition that customs and traditions are practiced in accordance with the rules set by the Chinese Communist Party.[15] The Chinese government, in an attempt to 'sinicize' religion in China, has set up the United Front Work Department,[16] tasked with the responsibility of overseeing and controlling the five officially sanctioned religious organizations.[17]

The Chinese Constitution

Freedom of some religious practices may be banned, although Chinese citizenry continue to think on their own. Still, violations of individuals' freedom of thought, conscience, and belief continue, made possible by a cleverly constructed loophole in the Chinese constitution.

---

9 Ministry of Justice Government Website (translated into English), "The National Political and Legal Team Education and Rectification Pilot Blew the Assembly Call," *Ministry of Justice of the People's Republic of China*, July 30, 2020, http://www.chinalaw.gov.cn/news/content/2020-07/30/zfyw_3253482.html

10 Steven W. Mosher, "How China's Xi Jinping Destroyed Religion and Made Himself God," *New York Post*, February 1, 2020, https://nypost.com/2020/02/01/how-chinas-xi-jinping-destroyed-religion-and-made-himself-god/

11 Reuters, "China Shows Off Xinjiang 'Vocational Education Training Centres' Despite Global Concern," *Global News*, January 7, 2019, https://globalnews.ca/news/4823673/china-xinjiang-education-centres/

12 Catholic News Agency, "Chinese Churches Made to Replace Ten Commandments with Xi Jinping Quotes," *Catholic News Agency*, September 23, 2019, https://www.catholicnewsagency.com/news/chinese-churches-made-to-replace-ten-commandments-with-xi-jinping-quotes-72313

13 Asia News, "The Fruits of Sinicization: Worshiping the 'God' Xi Jinping," *AsiaNews.it*, November 16, 2018, http://www.asianews.it/news-en/The-fruits-of-sinicization:-worshiping-the-'god'-Xi-Jinping-45496.html

14 Letters, "Why Xi Jinping Personality Cult in China Brings Back Memories of Mao," *South China Morning Post*, August 7, 2018, https://www.scmp.com/comment/letters/article/2158612/why-xi-jinping-personality-cult-china-brings-back-memories-mao

15 Eleanor Albert and Lindsay Maizland, "Religion in China," *Council on Foreign Relations*, Updated September 25, 2020, https://www.cfr.org/backgrounder/religion-china

16 Julia Bowie and David Gitter, "The CCP's Plan to 'Sinicize' Religions," *The Diplomat*, June 14, 2018, https://thediplomat.com/2018/06/the-ccps-plan-to-sinicize-religions/

17 U.S. Department of State, "2019 Report on International Religious Freedom: China (Includes Tibet, Xinjiang, Hong Kong, and Macau)," *U.S. Department of State*, 2019, https://www.state.gov/reports/2019-report-on-international-religious-freedom/china/

In the Constitution of The People's Republic of China of 1982, Article 36 states that "Citizens of the People's Republic of China enjoy freedom of religious belief. No state organ, public organization or individual may compel citizens to believe in any religion; nor may they discriminate against citizens who believe in or do not believe in any religion. The state protects normal religious activities..."[18] This protection seems to extend only to those religions that have submitted to the absolute control of the government via the State Administration for Religious Affairs.[19]

In June 2020, a village official in Lin county, administered by the prefecture-level city of Lüliang in the northern province of Shanxi, repeatedly notified villagers through social media to remove all religious symbols from their homes. He stated that the cross symbolized heterodox teachings, which should be purged as per orders from higher authorities. If not, they will be held criminally accountable. The official stressed that impoverished households must replace the symbols with images of Xi Jinping.[20]

Conclusion

China is controlled by the CCP and led by Xi Jinping, whose authority is absolute and unconditional. Xi Jinping has created a climate of fear in China using the same techniques on political opponents as he has on those who practice religion.[21] As those who do not obey the CCP are arrested, Xi warns all to "drive the blade in" and "scrape poison off the bone."[22]

When asked who the knife Xi Jinping wields is to stab, responses included,

- "Whoever displeases the Secretary's eye."
- "Whoever offends the Secretary's mistress!"
- "Whoever resists forced demolitions."
- "Whoever calls for disclosure of officials' financial assets!"
- "Whoever dares speak truth!"[23]

---

18 The State Council, The People's Republic of China, "Constitution of The People's Republic of China," *The State Council of the People's Republic of China*, Updated November 20, 2019, http://english.www.gov.cn/archive/lawsregulations/201911/20/content_WS5ed8856ec6d0b3f0e9499913.html

19 Eleanor Albert and Lindsay Maizland, "Religion in China," *Council on Foreign Relations*, Updated September 25, 2020, https://www.cfr.org/backgrounder/religion-china

20 Zhang Feng, "Christians Must Worship President Xi to Get Social Welfare," *Bitter Winter*, September 30, 2020, https://bitterwinter.org/christians-must-worship-president-xi-to-get-social-welfare/

21 James Palmer, "Xi's Latest Purge Reflects Climate of Fear," *Foreign Policy*, August 19, 2020, https://foreignpolicy.com/2020/08/19/xi-jinping-latest-purge-climate-fear-china-ccp/

22 Chris Buckley, "'Drive the Blade In': Xi Shakes Up China's Law-and-Order Forces," *The New York Times*, August 20, 2020, https://www.nytimes.com/2020/08/20/world/asia/china-xi-jinping-communist-party.html

23 Samuel Wade, "Xi's Sharp Words "Ominous" For Legal Reform," *China Digital Times*, February 10, 2015, https://chinadigitaltimes.net/2015/02/xis-sharp-words-ominous-legal-reform/

What's at Stake?

First, what is at stake is freedom of thought, faith, and conscience.

Second, all people who enter China must beware if they are free thinking individuals.

Third, stakes are high for those who do business in China as well. What is at stake is a business community that has been warned to "weaponize their minds" and push Xi Jinping's totalitarian belief system, foreign policy, and Marxist-atheist policies throughout their corporate enterprise.

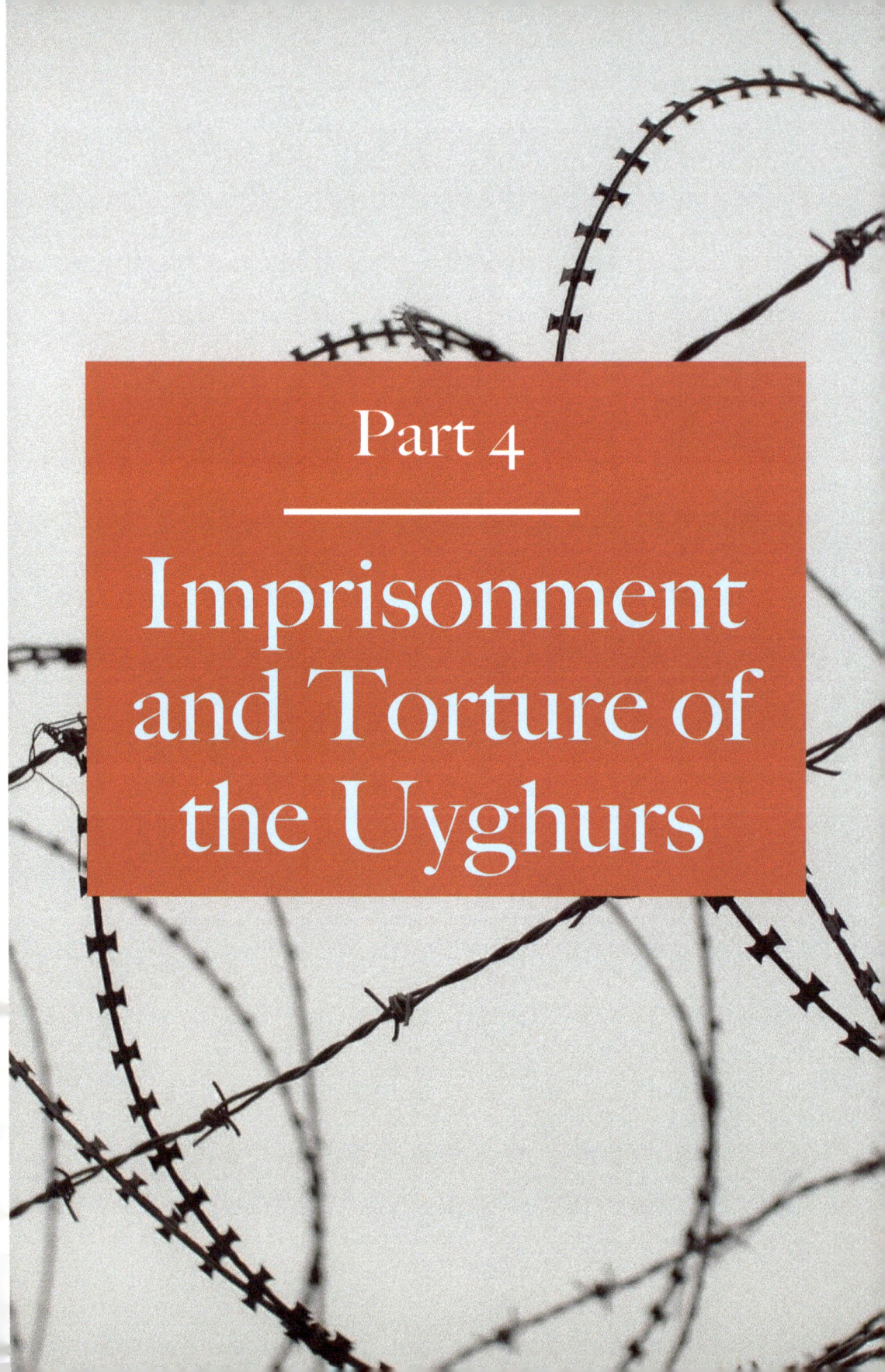

Part 4

Imprisonment and Torture of the Uyghurs

Absolute Control: The Rise of Concentration Camps to "Re-Educate" Uyghur Muslims

While no religious group is beyond the reach of the Chinese Communist Party (CCP), the Muslim Uyghurs (Uighurs) are being 're-educated' beyond what is conceivable. Concentration camps have been built throughout Xinjiang Province.

Located in Western China, Xinjiang Province may seem inhospitable to some. Xinjiang is enclosed by high mountains. The Taklamakan Desert is located in the central region. While there can be snow to the north and in the highest elevations, the desert can reach temperatures as high as 120 degrees Fahrenheit. Still, the Uyghur Muslims have lived in this location, what they call East Turkestan, for centuries. The Uyghur Empire was once almost the size and scope of China's land mass today.

While history is said to repeat itself, this refrain is true. During World War II, concentration camps were abolished; the torture ended, or so we thought. Today, concentration camps are being used to imprison the masses in Xinjiang Province. Two million people are thought to be imprisoned and enslaved. Their children are taken to orphanages to be 're-educated' separately in order to change the Muslim Uyghur societal culture, learn Mandarin, embrace the teachings of Xi Jinping, and obey all CCP laws and directives.

Torture, forced injections, rape, abortions, infanticide, and forced labor are only some of the actions of the Chinese authorities. Sterilization is being conducted on the Muslim prisoners to prevent a next generation of Uyghurs and replace them with 'superior' Han.

How can today's society let the ashes rise and repeat history again? Yet, many Muslim countries are silent. Many family members who have escaped Xinjiang Province are speaking out. Who is listening?

Chapter 1
Disclaimer and Trigger Warning

Disclaimer and Trigger Warning

Before reading this section, it is important to note that China is not the only nation in violation of human rights. Worldwide, governments have engaged in countless numbers of human rights offenses, including wars on drugs, torture and abuse, police brutality, unsafe working conditions, and child labor. The Universal Declaration of Human Rights, defined by the United Nations in December 1948 provides basic standards to protect universal human freedom and justice.

The Philippines has been admonished by numerous organizations for its 'War on Drugs'[1] where law enforcement officers have been granted permission to kill suspected drug dealers.[2] In Vietnam, prostitution brothels are commonplace, with 14,000 in Saigon.[3] Furthermore, 75,000 drug addicts and prostitutes have been placed in "rehab" camps, putting thousands at risk for HIV/AIDS without treatment.[4] Bangladeshi workers, many of whom are children forced to work extremely long hours, are unpaid.[5] In Africa, Uganda has established "internally displaced persons camps" where it is estimated that over 500,000 have died.[6]

The United States has also been cited for violating these standards by disproportionately incarcerating people of color at a higher rate than any other race.[7] Additionally, the U.S. Immigration and Customs Enforcement (ICE) has been accused of human rights violations.[8]

United for Human Rights, an organization whose charter states that they defend the U.N. Declaration of Human Rights, estimates that at least 81 countries are guilty of abuse and torture, and 54 nations hold unfair trials.[9] In other areas of this book, human rights violations from the Philippines and other South and Southeast Asian states are discussed. However, in this section, the book is focused on China's crimes against humanity that have been challenged by other governments and the United Nations.

Rape is discussed in the following chapters.

---

1   United Nations, "The Universal Declaration of Human Rights," *United Nations*, December 10, 1948, https://www.un.org/en/universal-declaration-human-rights/

2   BBC News, "Philippines Drugs War: UN Report Criticises 'Permission to Kill'," *BBC News,* June 4, 2020, https://www.bbc.com/news/world-asia-52917560

3   Goffredo Parise, "The Sexual Warfare Of Saigon's Bar Girls," *Maclean's*, February 1, 1968, https://archive.macleans.ca/article/1968/2/1/the-sexual-warfare-of-saigons-bar-girls

4   United for Human Rights, "Human Rights Violations," *United for Human Rights*, n.d., https://www.humanrights.com/what-are-human-rights/violations-of-human-rights/

5   International Programme on the Elimination of Child Labour (IPEC), "Bangladesh Child Labour Data Country Brief," *International Labour Office*, n.d.

6   United for Human Rights, "Human Rights Violations," *United for Human Rights*, n.d., https://www.humanrights.com/what-are-human-rights/violations-of-human-rights/

7   NAACP, "Criminal Justice Fact Sheet," *NAACP*, n.d., https://www.naacp.org/criminal-justice-fact-sheet/

8   Stanford Law School, "The Case to Abolish ICE: Human Rights Abuse & Federal Immigration Enforcement," *Stanford Law School*, May 15, 2018, https://law.stanford.edu/event/case-abolish-ice-human-rights-abuse-federal-immigration-enforcement/

9   United for Human Rights, "Human Rights Violations," *United for Human Rights*, n.d., https://www.humanrights.com/what-are-human-rights/violations-of-human-rights/

Chapter 2

The Uyghurs of Xinjiang Province

Background on China's Muslim Minority Group

Introduction

In 2012, **President Xi Jinping stood** in front of the press at the Great Hall of the People in Beijing and said, "During the long process of history, by relying on our own diligence, courage and wisdom, Chinese people have opened up a good and beautiful home where all ethnic groups live in harmony and fostered an excellent culture that never fades."[1] Yet, in a dramatic contradiction, in April 2017,[2] President Xi opened up "re-education camps" in the Xinjiang Uyghur Autonomous Region (XUAR) to quell what he perceived was terrorism, insolence, and extremism.

The Uyghur people, a predominantly Muslim group, were rounded up and taken against their will to concentration camps designed to marginalize, entrap, and re-concentrate the Uyghurs (Uighurs), along with other Muslim minority groups, within China.[3] It is important to understand the history of Islam in China and how Beijing's modern-day perception of Muslims has changed since the religion's first introduction into China's melting pot.

---

1 BBC News, "Full Text: China's New Party Chief Xi Jinping's Speech," *BBC News*, November 15, 2012, https://www.bbc.com/news/world-asia-china-20338586

2 Scott Busby, "Testimony of Deputy Assistant Secretary Scott Busby," *Senate Foreign Relations Committee*, December 4, 2018, https://www.foreign.senate.gov/imo/media/doc/120418_Busby_Testimony.pdf

3 World Without Genocide, "Genocide of Uyghurs in Western China," *World Without Genocide*, n.d., http://worldwithoutgenocide.org/genocides-and-conflicts/genocide-of-the-uyghurs-in-western-china

Islam's Roots in China

While 21st century Islam in China is a target of Beijing's religious and ethnic cleansing, Muslim religious practices have been practiced in the nation since its first arrival around 620 AD.[4] Four companions of the Islamic prophet Muhammad arrived in China to establish a trade relationship and spread Islam's ideology.[5]

In 651 AD, Muhammad's uncle, Saad ibn Abi Waqaas, was sent on an official visit to China by Uthman, Islam's third caliph ruler. Tang dynasty Emperor Gaozong, then-leader of China, welcomed him with open arms.[6] Following Saad's visit, Emperor Gaozong ordered the Memorial Mosque to be constructed in honor of Muhammad; China-Islam relations began blossoming. Between 651 to 798 AD, it is estimated that 39 Arabian envoys[7] went on official visits to China, furthering the relationship between the Chinese government and Islamic traders.

In the Tang and Song Dynasties (618-1279), the diffusion of Islam from Arabia into China was largely achieved along China's two silk roads, a land and sea trade network that connected China, Central Asia, and the Middle East.[8]

Many of the Arabian and Persian traders who went to China settled along the coast, especially in Chang'an, the former Chinese capital. Upon receiving government permission, the traders lived in Guangzhou, Yangzhou, Quanzhou, Hangzhou and began building mosques and tombs in the cities. After many years, the Muslims married local residents and had children together, raising the first Chinese Muslim generation.

The Muslims in China attempted to avoid any conflict between their Islamic beliefs and practices with traditional Chinese customs. In fact, they contributed greatly to the scientific and cultural prospects of China.

The Origin of the Hui

The Mongols conquered the Islamic regions in Central and Western Asia, ending the Abbasid dynasty of the Arabian Empire (1258) and starting the Yuan dynasty. In the Yuan and the following Ming dynasty, trade and transportation from the West to China was so accessible that Islam spread along the trade routes with ease. Strong diplomatic relations and frequent trade exchanges between the West and China were fostered. In the Yuan dynasty, trade items from Muslims in Central Asia, along with the construction of mosques and tombs, made transportation easy for Mongolian, Han, and Uyghur people to convert to the Islamic religion. Those from prior nationalities who converted to Islam were called the Hui.

Toward the end of the Yuan dynasty and the beginning of the Ming dynasty, the number of Hui people living in China skyrocketed. To continue the spread of Islam, Chinese

---

4   Wee Kek Koon, "A Brief History of Islam in China – Including a Moment of Prominence," *South China Morning Post*, May 11, 2020, https://www.scmp.com/magazines/post-magazine/short-reads/article/3083114/brief-history-islam-china-brief-prominence-near

5   Cheyanne, "Islam in China," *China Highlights*, October 25, 2019, https://www.chinahighlights.com/travelguide/islam.htm

6   Ibid.

7   Light of Islam, "Brief Introduction to Islam in China," *Light of Islam*, December 25, 2006, http://www.islam.org.hk/eng/eIslamInChina05.asp

8   Ibid.

Nearly Two Million Uyghurs Tortured and Persecuted in Concentration Camps

Muslims integrated Islamic education into Chinese society, known as Islamic Mosque Education. In addition, the Hui translated Islamic scriptures into Chinese. Thus, the interconnectivity of Islam and traditional Chinese practices normalized Chinese-Islamic philosophies in society.

The Rise of Anti-Islam Sentiment

While the Hui nationality remained prevalent in China, during the Manchu and Qing dynasties (1644-1911),[9] Han Chinese and Hui engaged in frequent ethnic and religious conflicts with one another. The Han Chinese, now 92% of China's population,[10] have a written history dating back to 1,000 BC[11] that has revolved around a chauvinistic sentiment reflecting Han Chinese superiority to other ethnicities.[12]

A fervent nationalism rose within the Han Chinese toward the end of the Ming dynasty (1644). A *Journal of Contemporary China* article suggests that CCP nationalists have distorted

---

9 Haiyun Ma, "The Anti-Islamic Movement in China," *Hudson Institute*, June 13, 2019, https://www.hudson.org/research/15095-the-anti-islamic-movement-in-china

10 The Economist, "The Upper Han," *The Economist*, November 19, 2016, https://www.economist.com/briefing/2016/11/19/the-upper-han

11 Gavin Van Hinsbergh, "The Han — China's Majority Ethnic Group," *China Highlights*, February 17, 2019, https://www.chinahighlights.com/travelguide/nationality/han.htm

12 Haiyun Ma, "The Anti-Islamic Movement in China," *Hudson Institute*, June 13, 2019, https://www.hudson.org/research/15095-the-anti-islamic-movement-in-china

and sensationalized China's strength to inspire today's citizens with historical glory.[13] Even so, there was tension with Muslims at points along China's history and this may have led to the Han's sense of superiority.

With the rise of the Manchu-led Qing dynasty, a sense of 'Hui-phobia',[14] now the equivalent of Islamophobia, rose. The Manchus sought to conquer as much foreign land as possible, including Hui and Muslim regions.

Furthermore, in the Manchu-led Qing dynasty, Han Confucian officials served as government leaders and implemented a strict imperialist policy to take over indigenous Muslim lands, subjecting residents to their rule by force. With this new order, Han Confucian leaders became the predominant political and legal forces of China who implemented 'Hui-phobic' policies. At the same time, Han Chinese scholars described the Hui people as "foreigners" and subjugated them to a lesser socioeconomic and political status than the Han.[15] Later, as all foreigners in China were considered barbarians, racism and xenophobia grew.[16]

Who Are the Uyghurs?

The Uyghurs were once a nomadic tribe from the Altai Mountains dating back a millennia ago. While assimilating in Central Asia, they emerged as a Muslim minority group in the Mongul Empire.

Many lived in the untamed territories to the west of China in what they called East Turkistan, gaining independence which was backed by Joseph Stalin in 1933 and 1934. Later, for a short time in 1949, the Uyghurs gained independence from China. These instances of independence were short-lived and soon the People's Republic of China (PRC) gained control of Xinjiang, folding the region into China's territory. Many of the Uyghurs who lived in Eastern China moved west to Xinjiang and settled together.

Originally, practitioners of Islam assimilated in Xinjiang Province in the 10th and 11th centuries prior to the emergence of Muslim group distinctions with the arrival of those from regional nations.[17]

Most of these Muslims speak Uyghur, a Turkic language. The largest population of Uyghurs, eleven million, are estimated to live in China's autonomous Xinjiang Province.[18]

---

13 Haiyang Yu, "Glorious Memories of Imperial China and the Rise of Chinese Populist Nationalism," *Journal of Contemporary China* 23, no. 90 (2014), https://doi.org/10.1080/10670564.2014.898907

14 Haiyun Ma, "The Anti-Islamic Movement in China," *Hudson Institute*, June 13, 2019, https://www.hudson.org/research/15095-the-anti-islamic-movement-in-china

15 Ibid.

16 Yuehua Dong, "Racism, Religion, and Governmentality in China: The Muslim Rebellion in the 19th Century," Thesis, (Uppsala Universitet, 2016), http://uu.diva-portal.org/smash/record.jsf?pid=diva2%3A935679&dswid=-2512

17 Haiyun Ma, "The Anti-Islamic Movement in China," *Hudson Institute*, June 13, 2019, https://www.hudson.org/research/15095-the-anti-islamic-movement-in-china

18 Anna Fifield, "China Celebrates 'Very Happy Lives' in Xinjiang After Detaining 1 Million Uighurs," *The Washington Post*, July 30, 2019, https://www.washingtonpost.com/world/china-celebratesvery-happy-lives-in-xinjiang-after-detaining-a-million-uighurs/2019/07/30/0e07b12a-b280-11e9-acc8-1d847bacca73_story.html

In 2020, an estimated 1-2 million Uyghurs are thought to be held in internment or concentration camps in Xinjiang.[19]

In modern China, anti-Islamic sentiment and xenophobia have resurged, making the Uyghurs and other Muslim minority groups a target of Beijing's persecution. In 1949, the established People's Republic of China (PRC) classified the Chinese population into fifty-six ethnic nationalities, the Han Chinese population being the largest.[20]

During Mao Zedong's Cultural Revolution, the Communist Party committed large-scale acts of violence against all ethnic groups in China, including the Muslims.[21] In 1991, as the Soviet Empire collapsed, Central Asian Muslim republics formed. China's anti-Islamic sentiment rose once again in the late 1990s when the Chinese began to correlate the Islamic religion to the "three evil forces": separatism, extremism, and terrorism.[22] With this inherent bias toward those who practice Islam, the Chinese began oppressing Muslims both implicitly, with how they treated Muslims differently than Han-Chinese, and explicitly through a shift in policy that oppresses Muslims.

Conclusion

As of June 2020, the estimated population of Xinjiang was reported to be 24 million, with 10.5 million who are Uyghur.[23] The Muslim population in China is greater than 20 million.[24] Around 3,000 Uyghurs live in Australia[25] and between 1,500-5,000 live in the United States.[26]

What's at Stake?

First, the Uyghur internment camps threaten liberty, human rights, and freedom of the Uyghur Muslims.

Second, what is most alarming is the lack of outcry on Beijing's cultural genocide that includes rape, organ harvesting, and forced labor for the prisoners of these camps.

Third, the world's complacency is emboldening Beijing to unforeseen heights.

---

19 Lily Kuo, "China Transferred Detained Uighurs to Factories Used by Global Brands – Report," *The Guardian*, March 1, 2020, https://www.theguardian.com/world/2020/mar/01/china-transferred-detained-uighurs-to-factories-used-by-global-brands-report

20 Haiyun Ma, "The Anti-Islamic Movement in China," *Hudson Institute*, June 13, 2019, https://www.hudson.org/research/15095-the-anti-islamic-movement-in-china

21 Ibid.

22 Ibid.

23 Congressional Research Service, "Uyghurs in China," *Congressional Research Service*, July 13, 2020, https://fas.org/sgp/crs/row/IF10281.pdf

24 James Palmer, "There Are More Than 20 Million Muslims in China. For Some, Piety is a Dangerous Political Act," *Vox*, July 15, 2016, https://www.vox.com/2016/7/15/12170178/uighur-muslims-china-ramadan

25 Biwa Kwan, "Uighur 'Human Rights Crisis': Australia Urged to Impose Sanctions on China," *SBS News*, December 9, 2018, https://www.sbs.com.au/news/uighur-human-rights-crisis-australia-urged-to-impose-sanctions-on-china

26 Omer Kanat, "China's Cross-Border Campaign to Terrorize Uyghur Americans," *The Diplomat*, August 29, 2019, https://thediplomat.com/2019/08/chinas-cross-border-campaign-to-terrorize-uyghur-americans/

Chapter 3
Defining Moment
How the 2009 Uyghur Massacre Changed Xinjiang

Introduction

China's perception of Islam changed dramatically over time. At one time, the nation valued the Muslim religion and both Islamic trade and cultural diversity. Gradually, China adopted an anti-Islam stance as the Han Chinese sought to eradicate religious diversity from the nation. With the rise of anti-Islamic sentiment, the Uyghurs became a target of xenophobia and persecution. A research study published in the *Asian Journal of Communication*, compiling 15,427 news reports about Muslims, showed that negative views of Islam is rampant, and that Muslim Chinese experience extraordinary racism.[1]

The 2009 Uyghur Massacre

The Han Chinese have cracked down on the Uyghurs since the 1990s, enforcing strict security and surveillance over the population to impede their freedoms.[2] Though the Uyghurs have always resented Han Chinese rule, in 2009, a series of riots localized in the northern city of Urumqi on the China-Kazakhstan border included bombings, protests, and chaos between the Muslim Uyghurs and the Han Chinese.

In July 2009, rumors surfaced that a Uyghur immigrant worker sexually assaulted a Han Chinese woman. Following those allegations, Chinese workers cornered and beat two Uyghur factory workers to death and several were injured.[3] Footage of the killings were released online, prompting large-scale protests; approximately 1,000 rioters took to the street.[4] On July 5, 2009, a day that is known as the Uyghur Massacre, mobs of Han Chinese citizens used sticks and metal bars to beat any Uyghurs they found on the streets of Urumqi. Chinese authorities reported that 197, mostly Han Chinese, were killed and roughly 1,700 were injured.[5]

Though sources differ on the total number of casualties, there is little information on the total Uyghur casualty rate and death toll in China-controlled media sources. Yet, observers recall first-hand accounts of armored vehicles ramming and running over people along with gunfire from Chinese law enforcement pointed at the crowds.

Stripping Rights, Culture, and Privacy

Anti-Muslim sentiment had become China's cultural norm. However, xenophobia toward the Muslims grew. With the majority of the Chinese Muslims living in Xinjiang province, the focal point of hatred became centralized.

---

1 Luwei Rose Luqiu and Fan Yang, "Islamophobia in China: News Coverage, Stereotypes, and Chinese Muslims' Perceptions of Themselves and Islam," *Chinese Journal of Communication 13*, no. 3 (2018): 598-619, https://www.tandfonline.com/doi/full/10.1080/01292986.2018.1457063

2 Edward Wong, "Riots in Western China Amid Ethnic Tension", *The New York Times*, July 5, 2009, https://www.nytimes.com/2009/07/06/world/asia/06china.html

3 Tania Branigan, "Ethnic Violence in China Leaves 140 Dead," *The Guardian*, July 6, 2009, https://www.theguardian.com/world/2009/jul/06/china-riots-uighur-xinjiang

4 Erin Handley, "How China's Mass Detention of Uyghur Muslims Stemmed from the 2009 Urumqi Riots," *Australia Broadcasting Corporation (ABC) News*, July 4, 2019, https://www.abc.net.au/news/2019-07-05/china-xinjiang-urumqi-riots-10th-anniversary-uyghur-muslims/11270320

5 Ibid.

Meanwhile, China felt as if the population in Xinjiang Province needed to be more Chinese, speak Mandarin, and live the cultural norms of the Han Chinese people. However, the Uyghurs had maintained their own culture for centuries. Their food was different; their practices were different; they spoke their own language. In order to fully integrate them into the population, Beijing made the decision to bring in waves of Han Chinese, incentivizing them by giving them government subsidies to move to the region and then offering them housing when they arrived.

At first, many were housed in Uyghur homes. This served a dual purpose. First, it allowed the Xinjiang residents to 'learn' how to be Chinese with the guidance of the newly transplanted Chinese who lived in their homes. Second, it allowed them to learn the language, since Mandarin was now spoken in the home. Finally, the cohabitating residents provided an opportunity for these new 'guests' to spy on the Uyghurs so they did not act out of line with the new expectations.

Afterward, those who did not comply or adapt were believed to need a more formal 're-education'. Cameras were installed throughout the region and in the home. Next, all cell phones needed to be turned over so that a chip could be imbedded to monitor all of their digital activities. QR codes were put outside of their home.[6] Also, the Chinese government closed the Uyghur stores, disallowed group gatherings, and removed their places of worship.

13 Tons of Human Hair
Shipment Seized in July 2020 From the Port of New York

---

6 Sigal Samuel, "China's Crackdown on Muslims is Being Felt Beyond Its Borders," *Vox*, March 30, 2019, https://www.vox.com/future-perfect/2019/3/30/18287532/china-uighur-muslims-internment-camps-turkey

Conclusion

Hundreds of thousands of Uyghurs have been rounded up and sent to camps where they are coerced into forced manual labor for multinational corporations. Furthermore, while being indoctrinated into Chinese language and laws, they are forced to renounce Islam and their customary religious practices. Additionally, many are tortured to involuntarily submit to the surgical extraction of their organs and the removal of their hair. The CCP stripped the Uyghurs of their rights as they transported them to locked, guarded, and isolated concentration camps.

In June 2020, the U.S. Customs and Border Protection seized a shipment of hair at the Port of New York. This shipment, arriving from Xinjiang Province, contained 13 tons of human hair worth over $800,000.[7] This is the second reported hair shipment by the U.S. Customs and Border Patrol and is believed to have come from Uyghur prisoners.

What's at Stake?

First, though the following chapter thoroughly explains the fate of the Uyghurs in concentration camps, it is critical to note that all liberty and freedom for the Uyghurs vanished once the CCP began kidnapping, torturing, and imposing their beliefs on the Muslim group.

Second, China's 'salami slicing' initiative in which Beijing seeks to control dozens of other nations is especially alarming since the concentration camps in Xinjiang Province could be replicated in any other country.

Third, what is transpiring in Xinjiang Province is a gross violation of human rights.

---

7   U.S. Customs and Border Protection, "CBP Detains Chinese Shipment of Suspected Forced Labor Products Made with Human Hair," *U.S. Customs and Border Protection*, July 1, 2020, https://www.cbp.gov/newsroom/national-media-release/cbp-detains-chinese-shipment-suspected-forced-labor-products-made

Chapter 4
Uyghur Internment Camps
The Imprisonment of the Uyghurs in Concentration Camps

Introduction

After China forcibly removed Uyghur Muslims from their homes, Beijing attempted to smooth the global backlash, stating that the Uyghurs are being housed in "re-education camps". The Xinjiang government chairman, Shohrat Zakir, stated that the Uyghurs are living in "free vocational training" centers that make life more "colorful".[1]

This "colorful" life that China promises the Uyghurs strips away all freedom of expression and religion and exploits the Muslim group for economic profit in forced labor and organ harvesting facilities. Confined within four walls and crammed with dozens of 'cellmates', the Uyghurs' lives are anything but "colorful".

Nevertheless, through a carefully crafted narrative, Beijing broadcasts to the rest of the world about their uniquely interwoven, "colorful" tale about how the Uyghurs are granted new opportunities, experiences, and protection. In China's fairytale, the Uyghurs would have been 'suffering' if not for the knight in shining armor that defines China's altruism and hospitality.

Re-Education with Chinese Characteristics

Shohrat Zakir claims the Uyghurs in these internment camps "will advance from learning the country's common language, to learning legal knowledge and vocational skills." Zakir furthered that the camps are designed "to get rid of the environment and soil that breeds terrorism and religious extremism and stop violent terrorist activities from happening." In his statement, he added, "Many trainees have said that they were previously affected by extremist thought and had never participated in such kinds of art and sports activities, and now they have realized that life can be so colorful."

China publicly claims that Xinjiang Province is at risk for Islamic extremist groups to infiltrate or attack, and that is why Xinjiang is under a strict lockdown.[2] Rukiya Maimati, a Communist party functionary working in Western Xinjiang, wrote in a message, "Fully understand that this task is in order to save your relatives and your families."[3] She added that "this is a special kind of education for a special time."[4]

At the frontline of the crackdown in Xinjiang is Chen Quanguo, China's former hard-line party chief in Tibet who now serves as the chief enforcer in Xinjiang after being promoted to the 25-member Politburo, the party leadership council governing China.[5] Chen is known

---

1 Xiang Bo, "Full Transcript: Interview with Xinjiang Government Chief on Counterterrorism, Vocational Education and Training in Xinjiang," *Xinhua Net*, October 16, 2018, http://www.xinhuanet.com/english/2018-10/16/c_137535821.htm

2 Chris Buckley, "The Leaders Who Unleashed China's Mass Detention of Muslims," *The New York* Times, October 13, 2018, https://www.nytimes.com/2018/10/13/world/asia/china-muslim-detainment-xinjang-camps.html

3 Ibid.

4 Ibid.

5 Ibid.

as the "architect"[6] for the internment camps. He gained traction in the Chinese government through close-knit relations with Xi Jinping. In February 2016, Chen spoke of Xi as the "core" of the party leadership. Chen has been rewarded with higher positions of power because of his loyalty to Xi.[7]

When Chen was a leader in Tibet, he tightened regulations and increased police presence in the general public, policies he carried over into Xinjiang Province. In Lhasa, the capital of Tibet, alone, Chen established 156 "convenience police stations".[8] Furthermore, Chen made ordinary citizens hand in their passports and ask for permission in order to travel.

These same policies from Tibet have been introduced to Xinjiang Province, thanks to Chen. In Tibet and Xinjiang Province, Chen is known for implementing ironclad control with incentives of economic rewards for community surveillance and informing on targeted individuals.[9] China also offered hefty rewards for reporting 'terrorists'.[10] Furthermore, he has established "convenience police stations" across many cities. The capital of Xinjiang Province, Urumqi, is expected to have 949 of its own "convenience police stations" under Chen's rule. Furthermore, Chen has also made the Uyghurs in Xinjiang turn in their passports to local authorities, as he did when overseeing Tibet, for 'safekeeping'.[11]

Nevertheless, a key element to note is that Xinjiang Province is a vital transport corridor in China's new Belt and Road Initiative (BRI), a Chinese infrastructure development project, including railroads that connect dozens of nations through a trade and shipping network. Xinjiang is an essential part of China's BRI and the passageway of economic activity running throughout East Asia. Xinjiang offers a convenient thoroughfare between China, Afghanistan, India, Kazakhstan, Kyrgyzstan, Russia, and Pakistan. Therefore, China must protect and monitor the region in order to control its trade network.[12] China helps to accomplish this goal by confining the Uyghurs in internment camps.

To add another element of the economic value of this strategic location, the Xinjiang Uyghur Autonomous Region contains forty percent of China's coal reserves,[13] 122 important

---

6   Jun Mai, "From Tibet to Xinjiang, Beijing's Man for Restive Regions Chen Quanguo is the Prime Target of US Sanctions," *South China Morning Post*, December 13, 2019, https://www.scmp.com/news/china/politics/article/3041810/tibet-xinjiang-beijings-man-restive-regions-chen-quanguo-prime

7   Ibid.

8   Tibetan Review, "Party Boss Chen Quanguo Replicating His Tibet Policy in Xinjiang," *Tibetan Review*, December 13, 2016, https://www.tibetanreview.net/party-boss-chen-quanguo-replicating-his-tibet-policy-in-xinjiang/

9   Ibid.

10 Michael Martina and Hugh Lawson, "China Offers Hefty Rewards for 'Terrorism' Tips in Xinjiang," *Reuters*, September 9, 2014, https://www.reuters.com/article/us-china-xinjiang/china-offers-hefty-rewards-for-terrorism-tips-in-xinjiang-idUSKBN0H41O620140909

11 Tibetan Review, "Party Boss Chen Quanguo Replicating His Tibet Policy in Xinjiang," *Tibetan Review*, December 13, 2016, https://www.tibetanreview.net/party-boss-chen-quanguo-replicating-his-tibet-policy-in-xinjiang/

12 Shabir Hashmi, "Xinjiang at the Heart of Belt, Road," *China Daily*, September 2, 2019, http://global.chinadaily.com.cn/a/201909/02/WS5d6c84d0a310cf3e355692ce.html

13 Edward Wong, "China Invests in Region Rich in Oil, Coal and Also Strife," *The New York Times*, December 21, 2014, https://www.nytimes.com/2014/12/21/world/asia/china-invests-in-xinjiang-region-rich-in-oil-coal-and-also-strife.html

minerals,[14] and one-third of the country's oil and natural gas reserves.[15] China has a vested interest in ensuring that the people of the Xinjiang Uyghur Autonomous Region (XUAR) never seek independence.

Xinjing Province
China's Uyghur Concentration Camps

Confinement, Forced Labor, and Renouncing Islam

The Uyghurs are co-mingled in tiny, confined living areas within prison-like internment camps where children are separated from their parents, women are raped, and the Han Chinese monitor every move they make. The Western view of freedom is a completely foreign concept that has no place in a totalitarian society where all citizens are expected to conform. Passports are taken away and they cannot escape. Tech companies are instructed to monitor Uyghur's mobile devices.[16] Hijabs are prohibited from being worn. Practicing Muslim culture and associated customs are considered illegal.

---

14 China Through A Lens, "Xinjiang's Natural Resources", *China Through A Lens,* n.d., http://www.china.org.cn/english/MATERIAL/139230.htm

15 Zachary Torrey, "The Human Costs of Controlling Xinjiang," *The Diplomat,* October 10, 2017, https://thediplomat.com/2017/10/the-human-costs-of-controlling-xinjiang/

16 Simon Denyer, "Former Inmates of China's Muslim 'Reeducation' Camps Tell of Brainwashing, Torture," *The Washington Post,* May 17, 2018, https://www.washingtonpost.com/world/asia_pacific/former-inmates-of-chinas-muslim-re-education-camps-tell-of-brainwashing-torture/2018/05/16/32b330e8-5850-11e8-8b92-45fdd7aaef3c_story.html?noredirect=on

Article 35 of China's constitution states, "Citizens of the People's Republic of China enjoy freedom of speech, of the press, of assembly, of association, of procession, and of demonstration."[17] That statement should ring out as a blaring contradiction of China's anti-freedom and anti-liberty stance toward minority groups and those who speak out against the CCP.

In order to gain any semblance of normal living conditions, the Uyghurs must renounce Islam and pledge their loyalty to the CCP.[18] In China's efforts to commit cultural genocide, the state has taken the initiative to put the Uyghurs in "re-education" facilities to work in a way that is chillingly reminiscent of the "Arbeit Macht Frei" (work sets you free) dictum of Nazi Germany.[19]

In the internment camps, numerous reports indicate that Uyghurs are forced into hard labor to manufacture goods for large companies. Others are sent to detention camps for further brainwashing. The Australian Strategic Policy Institute estimates that between 2017 and 2019, more than 80,000 Uyghurs were transferred to work in factories or detention camps.[20] The Chinese government states that they are in "vocational training programs"[21] to prepare for work outside of the camps when they are done with their 'training', though they are unpaid and unable to leave.

Reports describe eighty-three global brands that benefit from the Uyghur's forced and slave labor, including Apple, Gap, Huawei, Nike, Samsung, Sony, Volkswagen, and BMW.[22] In July 2020, the U.S. State Department warned large U.S. companies that there would be "risks" in continuing to exploit slave laborers in Xinjiang Province.[23] China says these warnings hurt the global supply chain and Beijing would continue to fight back.[24] The battle between China and those who condemn its forced labor has been ongoing and is unlikely to be resolved.

---

17   The National People's Congress of the People's Republic of China, "Constitution of the People's Republic of China," *The National People's Congress of the People's Republic of China*, December 4, 1982, http://www.npc.gov.cn/zgrdw/englishnpc/Constitution/node_2825.htm

18   Simon Denyer, "Former Inmates of China's Muslim 'Reeducation' Camps Tell of Brainwashing, Torture," *The Washington Post*, May 17, 2018, https://www.washingtonpost.com/world/asia_pacific/former-inmates-of-chinas-muslim-re-education-camps-tell-of-brainwashing-torture/2018/05/16/32b330e8-5850-11e8-8b92-45fdd7aaef3c_story.html?noredirect=on

19   Krakow Direct, "Arbeit Macht Frei – Auschwitz Gate," *Krakow Direct*, n.d., https://krakowdirect.com/arbeit-macht-frei-auschwitz-gate/

20   Vicky Xiuzhong Xu, Danielle Cave, Dr. James Leibold, Kelsey Munro, & Nathan Ruser, "Uyghurs For Sale," *Australian Strategic Policy Institute*, March 1, 2020, https://www.aspi.org.au/report/uyghurs-sale

21   Chun Han Wong, "China Says Majority of Xinjiang Detainees Released, but Activists Question Claim," *The Wall Street Journal*, July 30, 2019, https://www.wsj.com/articles/china-offers-rare-update-on-detainees-in-xinjiang-detention-camps-11564490302

22   Vicky Xiuzhong Xu, Danielle Cave, Dr. James Leibold, Kelsey Munro, & Nathan Ruser, "Uyghurs For Sale," *Australian Strategic Policy Institute*, March 1, 2020, https://www.aspi.org.au/report/uyghurs-sale

23   U.S. Department of the Treasury, "Treasury Sanctions Chinese Entity and Officials Pursuant to Global Magnitsky Human Rights Accountability Act," *U.S. Department of the Treasury*, July 9, 2020, https://home.treasury.gov/news/press-releases/sm1055

24   Roxanne Liu & Meg Shen, "China Says U.S. Warnings Over Xinjiang Hurt Global Supply Chain," *Reuters*, July 14, 2020, https://www.reuters.com/article/us-usa-trade-china-xinjiang/china-says-u-s-warnings-over-xinjiang-hurt-global-supply-chain-idUSKCN24F1L6

Furthermore, video footage released about the internment camps reveals that the Uyghurs are forced to live in "jail-like" conditions. Each room has metal bars for doors, with some rooms housing up to fifteen people at once.[25] In a YouTube video from *Bitter Winter*, Chinese propaganda posters cover the walls in the footage. Sayings include, "Be grateful" and "Follow the guidance of Xi Jinping's thought on socialism with Chinese characteristics for a new era, and untiringly strive to realize the Chinese dream of a great rejuvenation of the Chinese nation."[26]

The underlying root of China's detention camps is its desire to cleanse the Uyghur Muslims from its nation. To eradicate further generations of Uyghurs, China has begun excising or blocking the reproduction capabilities for Muslim women. For the purposes of 'family planning', some of the Uyghurs are sterilized. Mihrigul Tursun testified before the U.S. Congressional Commission on China about these horrific conditions.[27]

Freedom From Slavery and Persecution
Ethnic Cleansing of Uyghur Muslims in Xinjiang Province

---

25 Alexandra Ma, "Shocking Footage Purportedly Shows Cells Inside Prison Camp Where China Oppresses Muslim Minority," *Business Insider*, November 27, 2018, https://www.businessinsider.com/china-camps-for-muslims-look-like-jail-cells-in-purported-video-2018-11

26 Ibid.

27 Eli Meixler, "'I Begged Them to Kill Me.' Uighur Woman Tells Congress of Torture in Chinese Internment Camps," *Time Magazine*, November 29, 2018, https://time.com/5467628/china-uighur-congress-torture/

They forced us to take some unknown pills and drink some kind of white liquid. The pill caused us to lose consciousness and reduced our cognition level. The white liquid caused loss of menstruation in some women and extreme bleeding in others and even death. I was also forced to take some unknown drugs. They checked my mouth with their fingers to make sure I swallowed them. I felt less conscious and lethargic, and lost appetite after taking these drugs.[28]

Forced Sterilization and Rape of Uyghur Women

Chinese men rape the women and then either remove the women's reproductive system or abort the children before they are born.[29] These stories are repeated, though limited testimonies are available since few escape. Constantly under scrutiny, escapees are threatened by the Chinese who vow to kill their families.[30]

Radio Free Asia first reported in October 2019 that the Chinese government assigned and paid Chinese men to sleep in Uyghur women's beds when their husbands were away in detention camps.[31] This system, known as the "Pair Up and Become Family", was an initiative designed to monitor the Uyghur families, calling the Han Chinese men "relatives" of the women.[32]

Nevertheless, Uyghur activists have shed light on the 'mass rape' of the Uyghur women through the "Pair Up and Become Family" program where the Han Chinese men are paid to sleep in the women's homes. One U.S.-based Uyghur activist, Rushan Abbas, whose own family is in a Uyghur detention camp, notes that women are forced into submission to the Han Chinese men and often coerced into marriage.[33]

Abbas comments, "Neither the girls nor their families can reject such a marriage because they will be viewed [by Chinese authorities] as Islamic extremists for not wanting to marry atheist Han Chinese," adding that "they have no choice but to marry them." Abbas furthers, "[The Han Chinese] have been raping Uighur women in the name of marriage for years."[34]

In addition to forced marriage and sexual activity, the Chinese government is enforcing regulations to sterilize women's reproductive capability so that they are physically or

---

28 Mihrigul Tursun, "Hearing: The Communist Party's Crackdown on Religion in China," *Congressional-Executive Commission on China*, November 28, 2018, https://www.cecc.gov/sites/chinacommission.house.gov/files/documents/REVISED_Mihrigul%20Tursun%20Testimony%20for%20CECC%20Hearing%2011-28-18_0.pdf

29 Rosie Perper, "'This is Mass Rape': Uighur Activist Condemns Program Said to Pay Chinese Men to Sleep with Uighur Women to Promote 'Ethnic Unity'," *Business Insider*, December 24, 2019, https://www.insider.com/uighur-activists-mass-rape-chinese-men-xinjiang-2019-12

30 CBSN, "Rare Look Inside China's Internment Camps Holding More than 1 Million Muslims," *CBSN on YouTube*, June 18, 2019, https://www.youtube.com/watch?v=ujk8spsLA_Q

31 Shohret Hoshur, "Male Chinese 'Relatives' Assigned to Uyghur Homes Co-sleep With Female 'Hosts'," *Radio Free Asia*, October 31, 2019, https://www.rfa.org/english/news/uyghur/cosleeping-10312019160528.html

32 Ibid.

33 Rosie Perper, "'This is Mass Rape': Uighur Activist Condemns Program Said to Pay Chinese Men to Sleep with Uighur Women to Promote 'Ethnic Unity'," *Business Insider*, December 24, 2019, https://www.insider.com/uighur-activists-mass-rape-chinese-men-xinjiang-2019-12

34 Ibid.

genetically unable to have children for future generations of Uyghurs. In the 2019 family budget planning of Hotan, a large county with a population of 2.53 million, a "performance target" figure of 14,872 sterilizations per year was set.[35] Guma, a smaller county with 322,000 citizens, set a similar "performance target", striving to implement 5,970 intrauterine contraception devices (IUD) and 8,064 female sterilizations for the year.[36]

China's attempts at sterilization and birth prevention are seeing results. While between 2018 and 2019, China's entire national birth rate declined only 4.2%, in Xinjiang, the birth rates declined 24%. Furthermore, the birth rates in ethnic majority regions in Xinjiang fell between 30-56%.[37]

U.N. Definition of Genocide

Article II of the United Nations Convention on the Prevention and Punishment of the Crime of Genocide, a document that outlines its specific criteria, states that one form of genocide is "imposing measures intended to prevent births within the [targeted] group."[38] Many analysts recognize China's persecution of the Uyghurs as genocide. Meanwhile, Beijing has attempted to wash away the Uyghur culture from China's Xinjiang society under the guise of protecting the Chinese nation and preparing the Uyghurs for a brighter future.

In July 2020, U.S. Customs and Border Protection (CBP) officers in the port of New York confiscated over 13-tons of wigs and weaves supposedly made out of human hair.[39] The CBP officers seized the products from China as they believed the human hair came from the Uyghur concentration camps in Xinjiang Province. This incident was the second of its kind in 2020 alone.[40]

To put this in perspective, if a woman's hair typically weighs one ounce, then 13-tons of human hair equates to 416,000 people. If this was the second time, then it is possible that 832,000 heads of women's hair were removed and shipped to the United States, not to mention other countries where shipments may have been sent. If there are an equal number of men imprisoned then there are a minimum of 1.6 million people imprisoned and that is only with the shipments to the U.S. that they found. If just one shipment was missed in the U.S. and only one in Europe, the number could easily be more than three million.

In addition to raping, sterilizing, and forcing 'birth control' on the Uyghurs, many reports reveal that China may be inhumanely harvesting these inmates' organs and selling their body parts to buyers in other nations. It is believed that the Uyghurs confined in

---

35 Adrian Zenz, "China's Own Documents Show Potentially Genocidal Sterilization Plans in Xinjiang," *Foreign Policy*, July 1, 2020, https://foreignpolicy.com/2020/07/01/china-documents-uighur-genocidal-sterilization-xinjiang/

36 Ibid.

37 Ibid.

38 United Nations, "Genocide", *United Nations Office on Genocide Prevention and the Responsibility to Protect,* n.d., https://www.un.org/en/genocideprevention/genocide.shtml

39 CBS News, "Hair Weaves from Chinese Prison Camps Seized by U.S. Customs," *CBS News*, July 3, 2020, https://www.cbsnews.com/news/hair-weaves-chinese-prison-camps-uighur-muslims-seized-u-s-customs/

40 Allison Gordon, "13-Ton Shipment of Human Hair, Likely from Chinese Prisoners, Seized," *CNN*, July 2, 2020, https://www.cnn.com/2020/07/02/us/china-hair-uyghur-cpb-trnd/index.html

concentration camps are 'medically examined' in order to have organs removed to be sold for transplants.[41] Saudi Arabia has been accused of buying 'Halal organs' from China that were 'slaughtered on demand' in cruel, gruesome ways.[42]

What's at Stake?

First, subjugated to slave labor, eating non-Halal foods, harvesting organs, constant surveillance, forced sterilization, mass rape, conversion 'therapy', unconscionable incarceration, and obligatory loyalty to the CCP, the "colorful" life China promised in its propaganda is predominantly black with highlights of gray and blood red.

Second, the gross violation of ethics, principles, privacy, and human dignity has become a dire humanitarian crisis. However, many world leaders have chosen to turn a blind eye under duress and pressure from China's economic strength.

Third, the vague and lackluster responses from the international community have sent a weak message to China that only a few nations are willing to challenge its human rights abuses and incarceration of the Uyghurs.

Fourth, the acceptance of concentration camps means there is no limit or repercussion to Beijing's influence, power, and ambitions.

---

41 Benedict Rogers, "The Nightmare of Human Organ Harvesting in China," *The Wall Street Journal*, February 5, 2019, https://www.wsj.com/articles/the-nightmare-of-human-organ-harvesting-in-china-11549411056

42 Keoni Everington, "Saudis Allegedly Buy 'Halal Organs' from 'Slaughtered' Xinjiang Muslims," *Taiwan News*, August 25, 2020, https://www.taiwannews.com.tw/en/news/3862578

Imprisonment in Concentration Camps

Chapter 5

The International Response to China's Persecution of the Uyghurs

Human Rights Watchdogs and Odd Silence from Muslim Countries

Introduction

Though China has artfully crafted a politically-correct narrative to conceal the horrific treatment of the Uyghurs confined in internment camps, some world leaders and governments have spoken out, while others have been strangely quiet. A loud uproar in a few countries has resulted in a war of sanctions. Nevertheless, the international community has yet to project a unified stance against the human rights crisis. This chapter discusses the different responses from global organizations and governmental entities that have contributed to the issue of disunity.

Silencing the Uyghur Muslims

U.S. UIGHUR Act and Sanctions

The United States has engaged in ongoing efforts to end Beijing's torture, brainwashing, and imprisonment in Xinjiang Province. In 2019, the U.S. House of Representatives overwhelmingly supported the UIGHUR Act, which would sanction Chinese officials for their human rights abuses. The bill passed the U.S. Senate by unanimous consent on May 14, 2020 and by the U.S. House of Representatives by a vote of 413-1 on May 27, 2020. This bill was signed by President Trump into law June 17, 2020.[1]

---

1   Eleanor Albert, "Trump Signs Uyghur Human Rights Act into Law," *The Diplomat*, June 18, 2020, https://thediplomat.com/2020/06/trump-signs-uyghur-human-rights-act-into-law/

Chinese foreign ministry spokeswoman Hua Chunying responded to the bill, saying it "deliberately defames the human rights situation in Xinjiang and discredits Beijing's efforts to fight against extremism and terrorism in the region."[2] She claimed, "The core of the Xinjiang issue [in China] is not human rights, ethnic minority or religion; instead, the core is anti-terrorism and anti-separatism." Hua threatened, "We warn the US that Xinjiang is China's internal affairs and has no room for foreign forces."[3]

In passing the UIGHUR Act, the U.S. State Department is required to appoint a "special coordinator" in Xinjiang. The President must submit a list of Chinese officials complicit in the Uyghur internment camps to be sanctioned. Many U.S. officials agreed that Chen Quanguo, the former-Tibet security official and "architect" of the camps, would be on the list.[4]

China responded to the U.S.' pledge to sanction complicit leaders. Beijing's foreign ministry stated, "We again urge the U.S. side to immediately correct its mistakes and stop using this Xinjiang-related law to harm China's interests and interfere in China's internal affairs."[5]

The statement continued, "Otherwise China will resolutely take countermeasures, and all the consequences arising therefrom must be fully borne by the United States."[6] These countermeasures soon went into effect. In July 2020, China sanctioned U.S. senators Ted Cruz and Marco Rubio for speaking out against the Uyghur crisis in Xinjiang. The two took to Twitter to respond. Rubio tweeted, "The Communist Party of #China has banned me from entering the country. I guess they don't like me?"[7] Cruz tweeted, "Bummer. I was going to take my family to Beijing for summer vacation, right after visiting Tehran."[8]

Furthermore, in late July 2020, the U.S. Treasury Department imposed sanctions on the Xinjiang Production and Construction Corps and two important officials involved in the development of Xinjiang Province's concentration camps, Peng Jiarui and Sun Jinlong.[9] When explaining the sanctions on the government entity and the two officials, Secretary Steven T. Mnuchin affirmed, "As previously stated, the United States is committed to using the full breadth of its financial powers to hold human rights abusers accountable in Xinjiang and across the world."[10]

---

2   Owen Churchill & Kristin Huang, "China Protests as US House Passes Uygur Bill Demanding Sanctions Over Human Rights Abuses in Xinjiang Camps," *South China Morning Post*, December 4, 2019, https://www.scmp.com/news/china/politics/article/3040466/us-house-passes-uygur-law-demanding-sanctions-china-over-human

3   Ibid.

4   Ibid.

5   Aljazeera, "Trump Signs Bill for Sanctions on China Officials over Uighurs," *Aljazeera*, June 17, 2020, https://www.aljazeera.com/news/2020/06/trump-signs-bill-sanctions-chinese-treatment-uighurs-200617205702511.html

6   Ibid.

7   Thomas Colson, "China Has Imposed Retaliatory Sanctions on Its US Critics, Including Senators Ted Cruz and Marco Rubio," *Business Insider*, July 14, 2020, https://www.businessinsider.com/china-announces-sanctions-us-senators-ted-cruz-and-marco-rubio-2020-7

8   Ted Cruz (@tedcruz), "Bummer. I was going to take my family to Beijing for summer vacation, right after visiting Tehran", *Twitter*, July 13, 2020, 7:22AM, https://twitter.com/tedcruz/status/1282681821356933121?lang=en

9   Ana Swanson and Edward Wong, "U.S. Adds Sanctions over Internment of Muslims in China," *The New York Times*, July 31, 2020, https://www.nytimes.com/2020/07/31/us/politics/sanctions-china-xinjiang-uighurs.html

10 U.S. Department of the Treasury, "Treasury Sanctions Chinese Entity and Officials Pursuant to Global Magnitsky Human Rights Executive Order," *U.S. Department of the Treasury*, July 31, 2020, https://home.treasury.gov/news/press-releases/sm1073

Nations File Reports to the U.N.

The U.S. and China have strained relations over the Uyghur crisis. Other nations have become involved in the effort to stop the enslavement as well. In December 2019, the European Parliament passed a resolution that criticizes Chinese actions in Xinjiang. The resolution states,

> [Parliament] urges the Chinese Government to put an immediate end to the practice of arbitrary detention without charge, trial or conviction for a criminal offense of members of the Uyghur and Kazakh minorities, to close all camps and detention centers, and to immediately and unconditionally release those detained.[11]

Furthermore, in July 2019, officials from twenty-two nations came together and submitted a document to the U.N. Human Rights Council condemning China's forced political indoctrination and human rights abuses. The report demanded the "freedom of movement of Uighurs and other Muslim and minority communities in Xinjiang."[12] The signatories included Australia, Britain, Canada, France, Germany, and Japan.[13]

International Response

---

11   RFA's Uyghur Service, "European Parliament Passes Resolution Condemning China on Treatment of Uyghurs in Xinjiang," *Radio Free Asia*, December 19, 2019, https://www.rfa.org/english/news/uyghur/resolution-12192019145547.html

12   Agence France-Presse, "More Than 20 Ambassadors Condemn China's Treatment of Uighurs in Xinjiang," *The Guardian*, July 10, 2019, https://www.theguardian.com/world/2019/jul/11/more-than-20-ambassadors-condemn-chinas-treatment-of-uighurs-in-xinjiang

13   Ibid.

However, after twenty-two nations spoke out on China's actions, thirty-seven ambassadors from other countries delivered their own letter to the United Nations, supporting China's initiative for, what they see as "counter-terrorism and de-radicalization".[14] The most shocking part of this document is that many Muslim countries were signatories in favor of China's Uyghur concentration camp policies and practices, despite the indiscriminate incarceration of Muslims just by virtue of practicing Islam.

The signers included Pakistan, Saudi Arabia, Egypt, Cuba, Algeria, United Arab Emirates, Qatar, Nigeria, Angola, Togo, Tajikistan, Philippines, and Belarus. It is important to note that Indonesia, Turkey, and Malaysia withheld their signatures.[15]

The thirty-seven countries agreed that in the Uyghur internment camps, "the fundamental human rights of people of all ethnic groups there are safeguarded."[16] Furthermore, these nations agreed, "We also appreciate China's contributions to the international human rights cause."[17]

The Deafening Silence from Muslim Countries and the Reason

First and foremost, it is necessary to understand that the Muslim countries who signed the document approving of China's "anti-terrorism" efforts are primarily doing so because of Beijing's promised incentive of investments and fear of China's backlash.[18] China's investments are vital to economies whose low credit scores may make them unable to otherwise gain infrastructure loans. Additionally, the Belt and Road Initiative benefits many African and Eurasian nations' economic capacity and transportation capabilities. China's loan handout is too appealing for these nations to get on China's bad side.[19]

Turkey, in 2019, was the one nation who did condemn China's Uyghur concentration camps.[20] In a Turkish Foreign Ministry statement, spokesman Hami Aksoy stated,

> It is no longer a secret that more than one million Uighur Turks incurring arbitrary arrests are subjected to torture and political brainwashing in internment camps and prisons. Uighurs who are not detained in these camps are under heavy pressure.

---

14 The Washington Post, "Muslim Countries Joined China in Defending its Cultural Genocide of Uighurs: Aren't They Ashamed?," *The Washington Post*, July 20, 2019, https://www.washingtonpost.com/opinions/global-opinions/muslim-countries-joined-china-in-defending-its-cultural-genocide-of-uighurs-arent-they-ashamed/2019/07/20/0a7d62b4-aa3f-11e9-86dd-d7f0e60391e9_story.html

15 Ibid.

16 Xinhua Net, "Spotlight: Ambassadors From 37 Countries Issue Joint Letter to Support China on its Human Rights Achievements," *Xinhua Net*, July 13, 2019, http://www.xinhuanet.com/english/2019-07/13/c_138222183.htm

17 Ibid.

18 Tamara Qiblawi, "Muslim Nations are Defending China as it Cracks Down on Muslims, Shattering Any Myths of Islamic Solidarity," *CNN*, July 17, 2019, https://www.cnn.com/2019/07/17/asia/uyghurs-muslim-countries-china-intl/index.html

19 Alexandra Ma, "Why the Muslim World Isn't Saying Anything About China's Repression and 'Cultural Cleansing' of its Downtrodden Muslim Minority," *Business Insider*, August 26, 2018, https://www.businessinsider.com/why-muslim-countries-arent-criticizing-china-uighur-repression-2018-8

20 Ben Westcott & Hira Humayun, "Turkey Condemns China's 'Torture and Political Brainwashing' in Xinjiang," *CNN*, February 10, 2019, https://www.cnn.com/2019/02/10/asia/turkey-china-uyghur-xinjiang-intl/index.html

> Our kinsmen and citizens of Uighur origin living abroad cannot get news from their relatives in the region. Thousands of children have been removed from their parents and became orphans.
>
> The reintroduction of internment camps in the XXIst century and the policy of systematic assimilation against the Uighur Turks carried out by the authorities of China is a great shame for humanity.
>
> We expressed our views on the tragedy in the Xinjiang region to the Chinese authorities at all levels.[21]

However, later in 2019, even Turkey folded. *Foreign Policy* explains that Beijing angrily threatened to withhold economic opportunities. Erdogan backtracked, deciding instead to 'revive' Turkey's historic links to China in his effort to gain monies China is offering from the Belt and Road Initiative.[22] Erdogan sought avenues to resuscitate his economy after a political defeat in early 2019. The *South China Morning Post* explains,

> [H]is administration faces an uphill battle to support Turkey's ailing lira, which has roughly halved in value against the US dollar over the past two years.
>
> Earlier this year, Chinese ambassador to Turkey Deng Li said that many Chinese companies were looking to invest in Turkey, including the country's plans for a third nuclear power plant.
>
> But Deng added that economic ties with China could be at risk if Ankara continued to criticise Beijing's treatment of Uygurs.[23]

Previously, in 2009, then prime-minister Recep Tayyip Erdogan said China was enabling "a kind of genocide" and furthered, "We have difficulty understanding how China's leadership can remain a spectator in the face of these events."[24] In response, Chinese media sources issued statements threatening Turkey to take back their remarks, warning them not to "twist facts". China continues to hold the looming threat of economic distress over Muslim nations in order to keep them in line.

The problem with Muslim countries remaining silent is that they are complicit in allowing China to oppress its people, culture, and religion.

---

21 Hami Aksoy, "Statement of the Spokesperson of the Ministry of Foreign Affairs, Mr. Hami Aksoy, in Response to a Question Regarding Serious Human Rights Violations Perpetrated Against Uighur Turks and the Passing Away Of Folk Poet Abdurehim Heyit," *Republic of Turkey Ministry of Foreign Affairs*, February 2019, http://www.mfa.gov.tr/sc_-06_-uygur-turklerine-yonelik-agir-insan-haklari-ihlalleri-ve-abdurrehim-heyit-in-vefati-hk.en.mfa

22 Azeem Ibrahim, "Muslim Leaders Are Betraying the Uighurs," *Foreign Policy*, July 8, 2019, https://foreignpolicy.com/2019/07/08/muslim-leaders-are-betraying-the-uighurs/

23 Jun Mai, "Turkish President Recep Tayyip Erdogan's 'happy Xinjiang' Comments 'mistranslated' in China," *South China Morning Post*, July 22, 2019, https://www.scmp.com/news/china/diplomacy/article/3019630/turkish-president-recep-tayyip-erdogans-happy-xinjiang

24 Alexandra Ma, "Why the Muslim World Isn't Saying Anything About China's Repression and 'Cultural Cleansing' of its Downtrodden Muslim Minority," *Business Insider*, August 26, 2018, https://www.businessinsider.com/why-muslim-countries-arent-criticizing-china-uighur-repression-2018-8

Conclusion

A now famous and widely quoted poem by German theologian Martin Niemoller reads:

> First they came for the socialists, and I did not speak out – because I was not a socialist.
>
> Then they came for the trade unionists, and I did not speak out – because I was not a trade unionist.
>
> Then they came for the Jews, and I did not speak out – because I was not a Jew.
>
> Then they came for me – and there was no one left to speak for me.

As the saying goes, if no one speaks out against egregious torture and other unconscionable wrongdoings, by allowing the continued expansion of Uyghur concentration camps, few will be left to challenge the oppressor. Muslim nations that have chosen to remain silent, while also officially supporting China's Muslim genocide, are hanging their own people out to dry. Ultimately, this leaves their people with the grave possibility of harm and almost certain vulnerability when Beijing comes for them.

While momentum is slowly building as more nations protest and sanction Beijing over the mass-confinement of the Uyghurs, advocates must continue pressing for Uyghur freedom. Many global citizens are unaware of the cultural genocide, treatment, and conditions the Uyghurs are forced to endure. To obtain freedom for the Uyghur population, an international outcry must be heard on all corners of the planet. Basic unalienable human rights must be heard loudly enough to motivate leaders to speak out and end this mass enslavement.

What's at Stake?

First, freedoms, including religion, expression, culture, ideology, and belief systems, are endangered.

Second, China's mass oppression and imprisonment of Muslims is a horrific and alarming threat to human rights worldwide. While Beijing's oppression is presently concentrated in China, the potential for Xi Jinping to expand his reach is great. If the international community does nothing, what will stop him?

Third, nations that remain silent to the oppression and religious persecution of the Muslims have sent a dangerous message to Beijing that its concentration camps in Xinjiang Province will be ignored.

Fourth, without awareness and public protests of China's gross violation of ethics and human rights, millions of Muslims' lives are in danger and possibly everyone else who seeks a world where there is freedom as well.

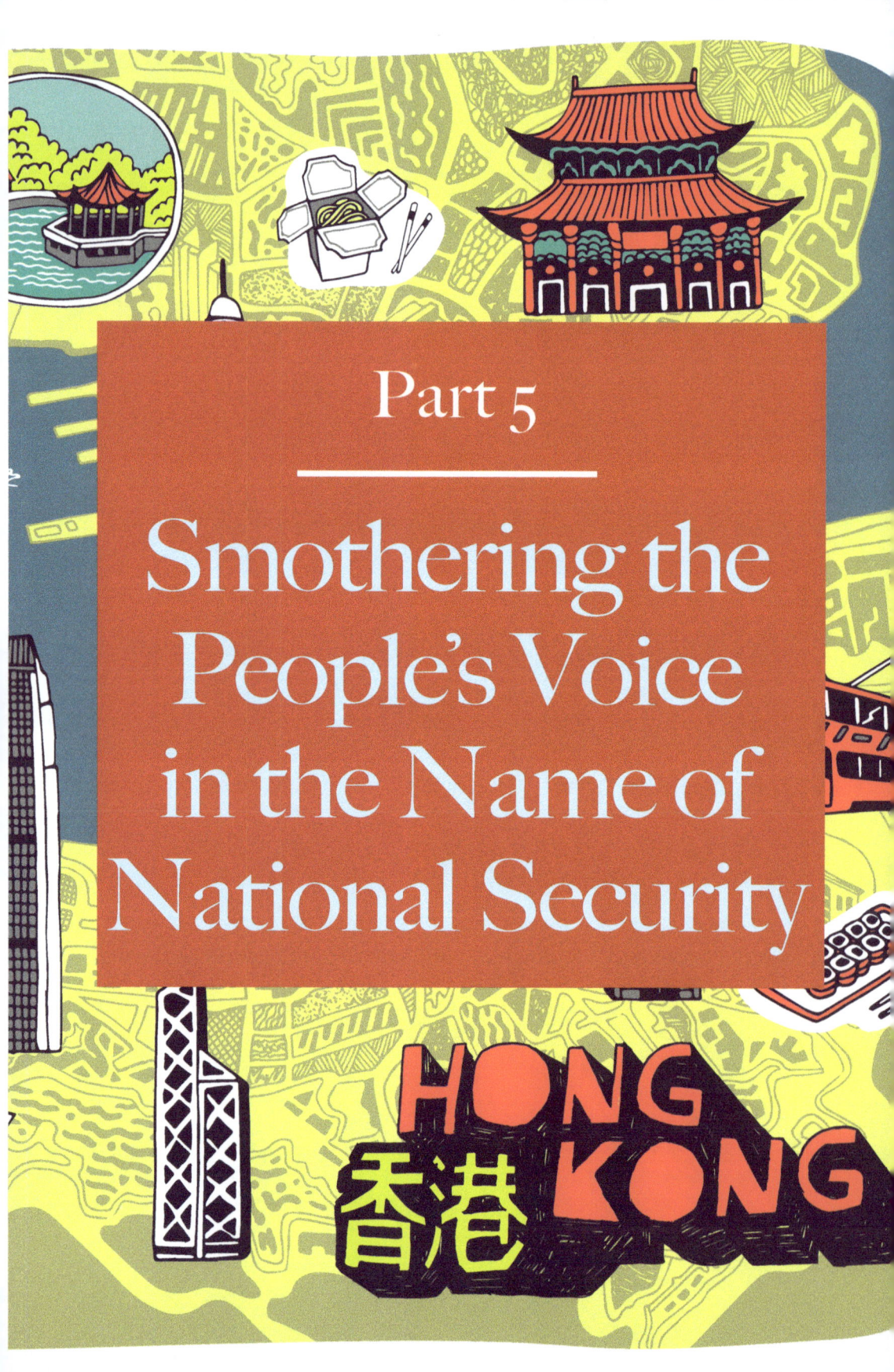

Part 5

Smothering the People's Voice in the Name of National Security

Last Cry for Help: The Loss of Freedom in Hong Kong

Hong Kong was once an economic force full of vibrant people who loved their city and cherished their freedom. The city was once energetic and bustling with businesses, entertainment, clubs, and shops full of people excited about their future. Though tourists might not have noticed, the opening of the 2020s did not usher in a better future, but one that was darker and bleaker than the past. Fear was now rampant. Freedom of speech that was generally guaranteed in the news and on the streets was no longer assured. Hong Kong citizens were punished for speaking out.

In 2021, Hong Kongers lived in fear. Furthermore, with the June 30, 2020 National Security Law, Hong Kong citizens had a justifiable reason to be afraid. Many obtained citizenship in the U.K. and moved. Some gave up their U.K. citizenship option to remain and fight for the Hong Kong they envisioned for the future.

Beijing's claim to a peaceful rise abruptly ended. China's overpowering political takeover clarified what would happen if any political unit or its citizens spoke out or went against China's totalitarian plans. Despite China's attempt to reshape the narrative about COVID-19, PPE failures, surveillance, or its concentration camps in Xinjiang Province, the actions Beijing took in Hong Kong provided a clear view into what is likely to happen in the future.

Hong Kong's promise became overshadowed by Beijing's crackdown, violence, and imprisonment of activists. Anyone who protested, spoke out, or wrote about China was threatened with punishment. Hong Kong is no longer autonomous. Some call the National Security Law "the end of Hong Kong," and so we begin this part for you to learn more.

Chapter 1

One China, Two Systems

Hong Kong and the PRC's Special Administrative Region's Growth, Development, and Destruction

Introduction

There have been very few days in the past decade when Hong Kong has not been in the news. Hong Kong's focal point on the world stage as a multinational business center, along with its proximity to the South China Sea, made this territory a regional powerhouse. Approximately 7.5 million people live in this small, densely populated area of about 426 sq. mi. With more skyscrapers than anywhere in the world, tall buildings reach toward the clouds in a dazzling array of colors that dance in the night sky. These brilliant lights once held a beacon of hope that the future of Hong Kong and the world would be free, peaceful, and independent. The dreams of residents and corporations that invested in Hong Kong faded with China's iron fist clamping down on free speech, changing the political fabric, and imposing draconian laws that remove individual and corporate freedoms.

Hong Kong Special Administrative Region of the People's Republic of China

From the Beginning...

The opium trade of the 1800s was devastating to China. Westerners took advantage of the Chinese who had become addicted to the poppy extract. Chinese leaders of the Qing dynasty attempted to prevent the influx of opium into the country, demanding that Western traders leave. The Daoguang Emperor banned the opium trade and rejected proposals to legalize opium. He called for the seizure of the drugs at the port of Canton, which is now Guangzhou. The Chinese, under the direction of the Governor of Hunan, Lin Tse-hsu

Unequal Treaties
Dividing Up China's Ports

(Zexu),[1] demanded the destruction of 20,000 bales of opium in 1839,[2] which lit a fire on the conflict. However, an underground of corruption kept the flow of opium coming. In attempting to stop the illegal opium trade, Chinese soldiers and small vessels attempted to fend off the larger and more sophisticated military, weaponry, and naval power with little chance of success in the First Opium War.

Chinese and British ships first clashed in 1839, leading to British warships and merchant ships arriving in Canton (Guangzhou) in 1840. Fighting continued as the British bombarded fortresses and fought in numerous battles. In one of the early settlement agreements, China agreed to cede Hong Kong to the British Empire and pay an indemnity.[3] These battles ended in a negotiated treaty, often referred to by the Chinese as one of the 'unfair' or 'unequal' treaties.

Treaty ports were established after the First Opium War with the Treaty of Nanjing, the

---

1   Reuters, "CHRONOLOGY: Timeline of 156 Years of British Rule in Hong Kong," *Reuters*, June 27, 2007, https://www.reuters.com/article/us-hongkong-anniversary-history/chronology-timeline-of-156-years-of-british-rule-in-hong-kong-idUSSP27479920070627

2   Kallie Szczepanski, "Why Did China Lease Hong Kong to Britain?," *ThoughtCo.*, June 9, 2020, https://www.thoughtco.com/china-lease-hong-kong-to-britain-195153

3   Jack Patrick Hayes, "The Opium Wars in China," *Asia Pacific Curriculum*, n.d., https://asiapacificcurriculum.ca/learning-module/opium-wars-china

first of the unequal treaties, signed on August 29, 1842, wherein China ceded Hong Kong to Great Britain. A Second Opium War was fought later, which led to additional ports being opened. The Kowloon Peninsula was ceded to the British after the Second Opium War within the Convention of Peking agreement.[4] This period, beginning with the First Opium War, started China's 'Century of Humiliation'.

Later, Great Britain, led by Queen Victoria, brokered a 99-year lease of Hong Kong with China. Hong Kong's lease to the British was drawn up on June 9, 1898, after ceding the surrounding islands. In 1984, Margaret Thatcher, then British Prime Minister, and Zhao Ziyang, the PRC's third Premier from 1980 to 1987, negotiated an agreement that Hong Kong would remain semi-autonomous for 50 additional years when the lease ended.[5]

Hong Kong's 99-year lease lasted from June 9, 1898, until June 30, 1997.[6] The 1984 agreement stated that the region would remain semi-autonomous for a 50-year period, known as 'borrowed time' from 1997 to 2047.[7] Though 2047 is decades away, China's 'One Country, Two Systems' agreement with a "high degree of autonomy" has been violated.[8]

After the 1997 turnover, some feared that Beijing would renege,[9] but life in Hong Kong was relatively unchanged until recently; two decades passed with few sparks. The five-decade honeymoon period thereafter abruptly ended with a series of abductions.

Joint Declaration – "One Country, Two Systems"[10]

Both Prime Minister, Margaret Thatcher, and Chinese Premier, Zhao Ziyang, signed the 50-year agreement which was registered at the United Nations for the period from 1997 to 2047.

Contained within this mutually agreed upon Joint Declaration, the Hong Kong Special Administrative Region (SAR) "will enjoy a high degree of autonomy, except in foreign and defence affairs which are the responsibilities of the Central People's Government". Laws in force in 1997 were expected to remain essentially unchanged along with the social

---

4 Reuters, "CHRONOLOGY: Timeline of 156 Years of British Rule in Hong Kong," *Reuters*, June 27, 2007, https://www.reuters.com/article/us-hongkong-anniversary-history/chronology-timeline-of-156-years-of-british-rule-in-hong-kong-idUSSP27479920070627

5 Kallie Szczepanski, "Why Did China Lease Hong Kong to Britain?," *ThoughtCo.*, June 9, 2020, https://www.thoughtco.com/china-lease-hong-kong-to-britain-195153

6 Steven Vines, "A Lease No One Thought Would Run Out," *Independent*, January 3, 1997, https://www.independent.co.uk/news/world/a-lease-no-one-thought-would-run-out-1281384.html

7 Greg Torode, "Explainer: Hong Kong's 'Borrowed Time' - Worry About 2047 Hangs Over Protests," *Reuters*, August 23, 2019, https://www.reuters.com/article/us-hongkong-protests-explainer/explainer-hong-kongs-borrowed-time-worry-about-2047-hangs-over-protests-idUSKCN1VD0S6

8 Tuan N. Pham, "What the Year of the Rat Holds for China," *The Diplomat*, January 18, 2020, https://thediplomat.com/2020/01/what-the-year-of-the-rat-holds-for-china/

9 John McDermott, "The Rule of Law in Hong Kong after 1997," *Digital Commons at Loyola Marymount University and Loyola Law School*, January 1, 1997, https://digitalcommons.lmu.edu/ilr/vol9/iss2/2/

10 Digital Commons at Loyola Marymount University and Loyola Law School, "Official Publication: Sino-British Joint Declaration on the Question of Hong Kong," *Digital Commons at Loyola Marymount University and Loyola Law School*, January 1, 1984, https://digitalcommons.lmu.edu/cgi/viewcontent.cgi?article=1071&context=ilr

and economic systems, existing rights, and freedom of religion, speech, assembly, strike, movement, travel, research, and lifestyle.[11]

The Hong Kong government would be composed of "local inhabitants". Protections were to include private property and foreign investment, while the semi-autonomous region will "retain the status of an international financial centre" with independent finances.[12]

No Ordinary Dates: June 4th, June 30th, and July 1st

June 4, 1989 – The Tiananmen Square Massacre

July 1, 1997 – Turnover of Hong Kong to Beijing

June 30, 2020 – Xi Jinping Signs National Security Law

The Tiananmen Square Massacre was one of the most horrific shows of a state's force and Beijing's willingness to stamp out dissent that has been witnessed in the past forty years. Gatherings grew. Student groups protested. The people called for freedom of speech and less censorship.[13] Estimates say that one million people arrived in Beijing demanding change.[14] Congregating on Tiananmen Square, students staged a sit-in and a Hunger Strike Declaration.[15] China's leaders' responses vacillated, ranging from considering the people's request for change all the way to crushing the people in the streets. Ultimately, the hardliners won. Tanks rolled in, literally squashing humans under tanks and opening fire on the protesters,[16] turning its military might on its own people.[17] A recently-released British diplomatic cable says that 10,000 people were massacred.[18] China gained its hardline control and silenced its people.

The Turnover of Hong Kong to Beijing was expected, but the reality of what was to come afterward was not. At first, everything seemed normal. Hong Kongers did not experience much of a change. With 'business as usual', foreign workers traveled and lived in the city without much difference.

In typical Beijing-style, Chinese authorities showered pleasantries regarding how they would abide by "One Country, Two Systems" and that the people of Hong Kong would still

---

11 Digital Commons at Loyola Marymount University and Loyola Law School, "Official Publication: Sino-British Joint Declaration on the Question of Hong Kong," *Digital Commons at Loyola Marymount University and Loyola Law School*, January 1, 1984, https://digitalcommons.lmu.edu/cgi/viewcontent.cgi?article=1071&context=ilr

12 Ibid.

13 BBC News, "Timeline: Tiananmen Protests," *BBC News*, June 2, 2014, https://www.bbc.com/news/world-asia-china-27404764

14 BBC News, "Tiananmen Square: What Happened in the Protests of 1989?," *BBC News*, June 4, 2019, https://www.bbc.com/news/world-asia-48445934

15 Index on Censorship, "Tianamen Square," *SagePub*, n.d., https://journals.sagepub.com/doi/pdf/10.1080/03064228908534708

16 The Editors of Encyclopaedia Britannica, "Tiananmen Square Incident," *Encyclopaedia Brittanica*, n.d., https://www.britannica.com/event/Tiananmen-Square-incident

17 Ben Wescott, "Tiananmen Square Massacre: How Beijing Turned on its Own People," *CNN News*, June 3, 2019, https://www.cnn.com/2019/06/02/asia/tiananmen-square-june-1989-intl/index.html

18 BBC News, "Tiananmen Square Protest Death Toll 'Was 10,000'," *BBC News*, December 23, 2017, https://www.bbc.com/news/world-asia-china-42465516

retain their freedom through the next fifty years.[19] Encroachment was slow and subtle, one inch at a time, using "Salami Slicing Tactics", also exemplified in its encroachment into the South China Sea, Africa, and each of the countries in which Beijing slices off sovereignty bit by bit.

The National Security Law was a giant leap, subverting Hong Kong legislative bodies and, instead, lowering its hammer and sickle on Hong Kong, Macau, and Taiwan with a level blow. The coronavirus pandemic provided the perfect decoy since the rest of the world focused on their own countries and barely watched the news in Asia. Many of the provisions despised in the Extradition Law that led to massive protests in previous years were buried in this 66-article law. Furthermore, the National Security Law, drafted in stealth fashion and kept secret from the public until published, took away civil and political freedom.[20] This tactic ignored a fundamental requirement in the international 'rule of law' – laws should be as transparent as rights.

What's at Stake?

First, Hong Kong will never be the same. The National Security Law has threatened all of Hong Kong's businesses, markets, and citizenry.

Second, citizens' rights have been taken away in dramatic fashion. The concept of freedom, once cherished by Hong Kongers, no longer exists and this has widespread implications for the future.

Third, business owners may never again trust their ability to conduct their work without caution, surveillance, and imprisonment.

---

19 Matthew Campbell, "What Happens to Hong Kong When 'One Country, Two Systems' Expires in 2047," *Bloomberg*, August 27, 2019, https://www.bloomberg.com/news/articles/2019-08-27/countdown-to-2047-what-will-happen-to-hong-kong-quicktake

20 Helen Regan, "China Passes Sweeping Hong Kong National Security Law," *CNN News*, June 30, 2020, https://www.cnn.com/2020/06/29/china/hong-kong-national-security-law-passed-intl-hnk/index.html

Chapter 2

Cracking Down on Hong Kong

Beijing's Book Persecution and Unpopular Extradition Bill

Introduction

At the stroke of midnight, July 1, 1997, Hong Kong transferred from British rule to Chinese rule. In an agreement, the Chinese government pledged to preserve Hong Kong's capitalist system for fifty years. On June 30, 1997, a grand handover ceremony was broadcast worldwide from the Hong Kong Convention and Exhibition Centre with chief executives from both Britain and China in attendance. At first, previously held concerns seemed unfounded until a series of 'disappearances' of booksellers in 2015 sounded an alarm. There was a public outcry as Hong Kong citizens believed the booksellers were 'kidnapped' from Hong Kong, placed in extrajudicial detention, and put in mainland China's custody. These originally unexplained 'kidnappings', later confirmed to be accurate, were not the end of the 'disappearances' that galvanized the Hong Kong public's growing concern that they were no longer safe. A National Security Law, passed on June 30, 2020, further enhanced China's ability to arrest anyone at any time for nearly any reason.

Chinese Authorities Kidnap Hong Kong Booksellers

Freedom to read was central to Hong Kong life. Freedom to think, speak, and assemble was also sacrosanct. However, these are not rights that are freely granted in China, where thousands of books are banned. Severe punishments are given to those who distribute written materials about Chinese leaders, politics, Bibles, Falun Gong, Tibet, Xinjiang, the Dalai Lama, or the Tiananmen Square Massacre.[1] Whole sections of popular books were edited out.[2] In July 2020, China went on a nationwide rampage to discard books considered politically incorrect with the goal of consolidating writings and teachings around Chinese patriotism.[3] In one situation, scholars signed a petition for Cambridge University Press to push back on China's request to block access to hundreds of articles China did not want released.[4]

In 2019, China's book burnings were reinstated and "a campaign launched in October by the Ministry of Education that called on school libraries across China to remove books that supposedly smeared the Chinese Communist Party (CCP) and its leaders or that harmed 'society's order.'"[5] This type of censorship, book burnings, and removal of books from schools did not exist in Hong Kong where citizens felt free to read whatever they liked.

---

1 Dan Strumpf, "Hong Kong Libraries Pull Books for Review Under China's Security Law," *The Wall Street Journal*, July 5, 2020, https://www.wsj.com/articles/hong-kong-libraries-pull-books-for-review-under-chinas-security-law-11593963424

2 Alexa Olesen, "Chinese Censorship of Western Books Is Now Normal. Where's the Outrage?," *Foreign Policy*, June 5, 2015, https://foreignpolicy.com/2015/06/05/chinese-censorship-western-books-where-is-the-outrage/

3 Huizhong Wu, "In Echo of Mao Era, China's Schools in Book-cleansing Drive," *Reuters*, July 9, 2020, https://www.reuters.com/article/us-china-books-insight/in-echo-of-mao-era-chinas-schools-in-book-cleansing-drive-idUSKBN24A1R5

4 Elizabeth Redden, "Outrage Over University Press Caving in to Chinese Censorship," *Inside Higher Ed*, August 21, 2017, https://www.insidehighered.com/news/2017/08/21/cambridge-university-press-blocks-access-300-plus-articles-request-chinese-censors

5 James Palmer, "Why is China Burning Books?," *Foreign Policy*, December 11, 2019, https://foreignpolicy.com/2019/12/11/china-burning-book-censorship-online-outrage/

That was until 2015 when 863 'repatriating fugitives' from 68 countries were captured by the Chinese government,[6] less than two decades into Hong Kong's semi-autonomous 50-year period.

Causeway Bay Books, a Hong Kong bookstore that specialized in literature critical of the Communist Party, became China's target. Lam Win-kee, the bookstore's owner, became a point-person for China's wrath. In 2015, Lam suddenly disappeared and was whisked away to a secret Chinese prison.[7] Lam was later forced to confess on Chinese state television to the crime of smuggling contraband. After being taken by Chinese' special forces',[8] Lam was released from a secret Chinese prison and now lives in Taiwan running a new bookstore after crowdfunding monies to provide the resources to get started.[9]

Two of the other kidnapped and imprisoned booksellers, Cheung Chi-ping and Lui Por, were also released. Gui Minhai and Lee Bo were the owners and managers of a publishing house. Lee Bo was forced to confess in a televised interview and compelled to renounce his British citizenship.[10] Lee Bo was released. However, the captivity of Gui Minhai was very different.

Gui Minhai, who holds a Swedish passport, was taken while vacationing in Thailand and is still being kept against his will.[11] After a response from the international community that condemned China's "brutal intervention",[12] Beijing began accusing Stockholm of "grossly" meddling in China's affairs and threatening Sweden.[13] In another threat, Gui Congyou, Ambassador of the People's Republic of China to Sweden, remarked about Swedish media, "The 86kg boxer, out of goodwill to protect the lightweight boxer, advises him to leave and mind his own business, but the latter refuses to listen, and even breaks into the home of the heavyweight boxer. What choice do you expect the heavyweight boxer to have?"[14]

---

6   Jiayang Fan, "The Case of the Missing Hong Kong Book Publishers," *The New Yorker*, January 8, 2016, https://www.newyorker.com/news/daily-comment/the-case-of-the-missing-hong-kong-book-publishers

7   Al Jazeera, "The Saga of the Kidnapped Bookseller of Hong Kong | The Listening Post (Feature)," February 7, 2020, video, 2:27, https://www.youtube.com/watch?v=Vh_eT7LzAOg

8   Elizabeth Joseph & Katie Hunt, "Missing Hong Kong Bookseller: I Was Kidnapped by Chinese 'Special Forces'," *CNN News*, June 16, 2016, https://www.cnn.com/2016/06/16/asia/china-hong-kong-booksellers/index.html

9   BBC News, "Hong Kong Bookseller Who Defied China Raises $100,000 in a Day for New Shop," *BBC News*, September 6, 2019, https://www.bbc.com/news/world-asia-49612785

10 AFP in Hong Kong, "'Missing' Hong Kong Bookseller Lee Bo Says he will Give Up British Citizenship," *The Guardian*, February 29, 2016, https://www.theguardian.com/world/2016/feb/29/missing-british-bookseller-appears-on-television

11 BBC News, "Gui Minhai: Hong Kong Bookseller Gets 10 Years Jail," *BBC News*, February 25, 2020, https://www.bbc.com/news/world-asia-china-51624433

12 Tom Phillips, "Sweden Condemns China's 'Brutal' Detention of Bookseller Gui Minhai," *The Guardian*, February 5, 2018, https://www.theguardian.com/world/2018/feb/06/sweden-condemns-chinas-brutal-detention-of-bookseller-gui-minhai

13 Tom Phillips, "'A Very Scary Movie': How China Snatched Gui Minhai on the 11.10 Train to Beijing," *The Guardian*, February 21, 2018, https://www.theguardian.com/world/2018/feb/22/how-china-snatched-gui-minhai-train-beijing-bookseller-hong-kong

14 Zhuang Pinhui, "China's Ambassador to Sweden Summoned After He Hit Out at 'Smears' in Latest Outburst Against Beijing Critics," *South China Morning Post*, January 18, 2020 https://www.scmp.com/news/china/diplomacy/article/3046689/chinas-ambassador-sweden-hits-out-smears-latest-outburst

Anna Lindstedt, who was formerly the Swedish envoy to China, Vietnam, and Mexico, was put on trial in June 2020 with the possibility of being imprisoned for two years because she attempted to free Gui Minhai.[15] Imprisoning a bookseller is one thing, but a diplomat is quite another.

Introducing the Extradition Bill

The kidnappings of booksellers and other 'accomplices' were just the prelude to an even more alarming act. Beijing wanted permission to kidnap, extradite, and convict any Hong Kong resident who acted or said anything against the Chinese Communist Party (CCP). The unpopular extradition bill was submitted in February 2019,[16] triggering the first eruption of protests and concerns from the international community. After presenting the bill to the legislature by Carrie Lam, Beijing's choice as a Hong Kong's Chief Executive, amendments were added to send 'criminal' suspects to China for trial, leaving them at the courts' mercy where victims say they were tortured.[17]

Yet, in between, tens of thousands of protesters took to the Hong Kong streets on April 28, 2019 to oppose removing citizens from Hong Kong, Taiwan, and Macau to be imprisoned in China.[18] Some Hong Kong legislators wrangled over the proposition, saying, "Scrap the evil law."[19] In the media, Carrie Lam pressed forward, insisting that her administration would push through the bill, expediting the process.[20] Members of the international community joined the growing chorus of protests.

There was already an undercurrent of anxiety about the bill, which was publicly displayed. By June 2019, more than a million residents of Hong Kong took to the streets.[21] Hong Kong considered concessions, but this was not enough and could have violated their autonomy. Schools, companies, and officials joined the fight against the extradition law. Yet, in 2019, during the commemoration of the June 4, 1989, Tiananmen Massacre, a Hong

---

15 Agence France-Presse, "Ex-Swedish China Envoy Anna Lindstedt on Trial Over Talks to Free Jailed Bookseller Gui Minhai," *South China Morning Post*, June 5, 2020, https://www.scmp.com/news/world/europe/article/3087783/ex-swedish-china-envoy-anna-lindstedt-trial-over-talks-free

16 Anne Marie Roantree & Delfina Wentzel, "Timeline: Key Dates for Hong Kong Extradition Bill and Protests," *Reuters*, June 30, 2019, https://www.reuters.com/article/uk-hongkong-extradition-timeline/timeline-key-dates-for-hong-kong-extradition-bill-and-protests-idUSKCN1TW14F

17 Ibid.

18 Lea Li, "Protest March Through Hong Kong Against Proposed Extradition Law," *South China Morning Post*, April 28, 2019, https://www.scmp.com/video/3008021/hongkongers-march-protest-against-proposed-extradition-law

19 James Pomfret and Jessie Pang, "Hong Kong Lawmakers Clash Over What Democrats Call 'Evil' Extradition Bill," *Reuters*, May 14, 2019, https://www.reuters.com/article/us-hongkong-politics-extradition/hong-kong-lawmakers-clash-over-what-democrats-call-evil-extradition-bill-idUSKCN1SK12D

20 Jeffie Lam and Gary Cheung, "Has Carrie Lam Lost Hong Kong in Her Bid to Push Through Extradition Bill?," *South China Morning Post*, June 29, 2019, https://www.scmp.com/week-asia/politics/article/3016577/has-carrie-lam-lost-hong-kong-her-bid-push-through-china

21 James Griffiths, Eric Cheung, and Chermaine Lee, "More Than 1 Million Protest in Hong Kong, Organizers Say, Over Chinese Extradition Law," *CNN News*, June 10, 2019, https://www.cnn.com/2019/06/08/asia/hong-kong-extradition-bill-protest-intl/index.html

Hong Kong Protests

Kong teenager was shot in the chest by police.[22] Police brutality raged on in Hong Kong with a volunteer medic lying on the ground with blood running from her eye.[23] Her eye patch later became a symbol of the fight for freedom representing police brutality.[24]

After marches that stopped the city's progress and slowed down work with millions rallying to preserve freedom, Carrie Lam still seemed unstoppable. Then, two million showed up on June 19, 2019.[25] The summer was marred with violence. Activists rebelled. Police pushed back. Activists blocked police headquarters. Carrie Lam refused to step down, though, amid apologies, she suggested that the bill will not be passed.[26] Beijing pushed back

---

22 Sophia Yan, Katy Wong, and Gareth Davies, "Hong Kong Protester Shot in Chest During Demonstrations on China's 70th Anniversary," *The Telegraph*, October 1, 2019, https://www.telegraph.co.uk/news/2019/10/01/china-celebrates-70th-anniversary-hong-kong-braces-dangerous/

23 Ryan Ho Kilpatrick, "'An Eye For An Eye': Hong Kong Protests Get Figurehead in Woman Injured by Police," *The Guardian*, August 16, 2019, https://www.theguardian.com/world/2019/aug/16/an-eye-for-an-eye-hong-kong-protests-get-figurehead-in-woman-injured-by-police

24 Jillian Kay Melchior, "Eye Patch Becomes a Symbol of Freedom in Hong Kong," *The Wall Street Journal*, August 12, 2019, https://www.wsj.com/articles/eye-patch-becomes-a-symbol-of-freedom-11565652051

25 Annie Lee, Fion Li, and Shawna Kwan, "As Many as Two Million Protesters Hit Hong Kong Streets," *Bloomberg*, June 16, 2019, https://www.bloomberg.com/news/articles/2019-06-16/protests-swell-as-hong-kong-rejects-leader-s-compromise

26 BBC News, "Hong Kong Protests: Carrie Lam Sorry for Extradition Controversy," *BBC News,* June 18, 2019, https://www.bbc.com/news/world-asia-48673259

too, insisting that G20 leaders would not be allowed to discuss the strife in Hong Kong, despite desperate calls from activists to "liberate" Hong Kong. The July 1, 2019 anniversary of Hong Kong's turnover led to millions of people gathering to commemorate that day.[27] The summer of 2019 continued with heated exchanges with the pro-democracy movement.

Protestors Declaration - "Five demands, not one less"[28]

At first, the protestors only wanted to remove the extradition bill, which would allow the government to remove any citizen at will for charges including speaking freely or assembling in protest - even retroactively. This component of the bill would mean that approximately two million people in Hong Kong could be taken to a secret prison in China at any time since they had protested. However, as Carrie Lam and the legislature refused to budge on the extradition bill,[29] the numbers of demonstrators grew, and the protestors created the slogan they shouted in the streets, "Five Demands, Not One Less."

The Five Demands

1. Complete withdrawal of the extradition bill from the legislative process
2. Retraction of the "riot" characterization
3. Amnesty for the arrested protestors
4. Establishment of an independent commission of inquiry into police conduct and use of force during the protests
5. Resignation of Carrie Lam

While Carrie Lam, Hong Kong's Chief Executive, did announce the "indefinite suspension" of the bill on June 15, 2019,[30] the legislative council was prepared to resume the discussion. Ultimately, the extradition bill was formally withdrawn on October 23, 2019 - at least for a short time.

While protesting and assembling were allowed under the law, rioting was not. The June 12, 2019 protest was considered a riot. Thus, with the National Security Law and the Extradition Bill, everyone who gathered was faced with the real possibility that they would be jailed for rioting or inciting a riot. Since the penalty was ten years in prison, the protestors demanded that the label be changed to a protest and not a riot.[31]

---

27 TIME Staff, "Enraged Protesters Storm the Legislature on the Anniversary of Hong Kong's Return to Chinese Sovereignty," *Time Magazine*, June 30, 2019, https://time.com/longform/hong-kong-july-1-handover-china-protests-democracy/

28 BBC News, "The Hong Kong Protests Explained in 100 and 500 Words," *BBC News,* November 28, 2019, https://www.bbc.com/news/world-asia-china-49317695

29 The Straits Times, "Carrie Lam Starts Talks but Refuses to Budge on Protesters' Demands," *The Straits Times*, August 28, 2019, https://www.straitstimes.com/asia/east-asia/lam-starts-talks-but-refuses-to-budge-on-protesters-demands

30 Emma Graham-Harrison, "Hong Kong Leader Suspends Extradition Bill Amid Protest Pressure," *The Guardian*, June 15, 2019, https://www.theguardian.com/world/2019/jun/15/hong-kong-leader-carrie-lam-extradition-bill-delay-protests-china

31 Elaine Yu, "Couple Charged with Rioting After Hong Kong Protest Are Found Not Guilty," *The New York Times*, July 24, 2020, https://www.nytimes.com/2020/07/24/world/asia/hong-kong-protests-newlyweds-rioting.html

Furthermore, some pro-democracy leaders were arrested during this period, and the protestors demanded their release.[32] Ultimately, the protests were aggravated by police brutality, illegal searches, and excessive use of force.[33] Several people committed suicide to protest the loss of freedoms.[34] The protestors demanded the resignation of Carrie Lam and to institute a legislature that was representative of the people's will since the "One country, two systems" Joint Declaration stated that free and fair elections would mean that the legislature would be composed of "local inhabitants".

Conclusion

The Extradition Bill was not passed in its original form. However, the offensive teeth in the bill were relocated in the National Security Law. China, thus, had the ability to extradite Hong Kongers to mainland China. The National Security Law was passed on June 30, 2020. Hong Kong citizenry's concern has only grown throughout 2020 as more people have been taken into custody, and residents feel threatened. The U.K. offered many the opportunity to move to Britain, and some have, while others chose to remain and fight the battle for freedom.

What's at Stake?

First, elections are no longer free and fair since pro-democracy candidates cannot be on the ballot. Thus, elections have 'Chinese characteristics'. Beijing's candidates are the only choices to be 'elected'. The word 'elected' has little meaning, though, if people cannot run and many refuse to participate in a fait accompli.

Second, pro-democracy candidates were removed from the ballot. On November 20, 2020, fifteen pro-democracy legislators who were elected to office resigned en masse.[35] On January 6, 2021, Chinese authorities arrested fifty-three pro-democracy leaders, former elected officials, and an American lawyer.[36]

---

32 Kimmy Chung and Karen Zhang, "Hong Kong District Councillors Kick Off New Term With Pledge to Pursue Protesters' Demands Amid Anti-Government Movement," *South China Morning Post*, January 2, 2020, https://www.scmp.com/news/hong-kong/politics/article/3044383/hong-kong-district-councillors-kick-new-term-pledge-pursue

33 Amnesty International, "Hong Kong's Protests Explained," *Amnesty International*, September 2019, https://www.amnesty.org/en/latest/news/2019/09/hong-kong-protests-explained/

34 TIME Staff, "Enraged Protesters Storm the Legislature on the Anniversary of Hong Kong's Return to Chinese Sovereignty," *Time Magazine*, June 30, 2019, https://time.com/longform/hong-kong-july-1-handover-china-protests-democracy/

35 BBC News, "Hong Kong Pro-Democracy Lawmakers Resign After China Ruling," *BBC News*, November 12, 2020, https://www.bbc.com/news/world-asia-china-54899171

36 Natasha Khan, "Hong Kong Police Arrest 53 Opposition Figures Over Alleged Subversion," *The Wall Street Journal*, Updated January 6, 2021, https://www.wsj.com/articles/hong-kong-police-arrest-dozens-of-opposition-politicians-over-alleged-subversion-11609895177

Third, the idea of "One country, two systems" promised fifty years of autonomy. This pledge, endorsed by the Chinese, has been cast aside. Freedom of thought, religion, and literature is literally being burnt to the ground. Citizens are too afraid to speak out since they may be kidnapped and sent away for challenging Beijing's influence.

Fourth, any of the millions of Hong Kongers who protested can be taken into custody and brought back to mainland China for 'trial' and punishment.

Chapter 3
The Silencing of Hong Kong Protesters
China's June 2020 National Security Law

Introduction

On June 30, 2020, just before the July 1st anniversary of Hong Kong's turnover, Beijing pre-empted gatherings or protests with a law that allows for the arrest of protesters and extradition to China to face charges.[1] This law bypassed the Hong Kong legislature and was drawn up in China and signed by Xi Jinping.[2] The National Security Law prohibits "acts of secession, subversion of state power, terrorist activities, and collusion with foreign or external forces to endanger national security."[3] A Microsoft Word document from *Xinhua* provides the text for the National Security Law's Chapter 3, Part 2, Article 22.

Hong Kong National Security Law - Article 22

"Article 22 A person who organises, plans, commits or participates in any of the following acts by force or threat of force or other unlawful means with a view to subverting the State power shall be guilty of an offence:

1. overthrowing or undermining the basic system of the People's Republic of China established by the Constitution of the People's Republic of China;

2. overthrowing the body of central power of the People's Republic of China or the body of power of the Hong Kong Special Administrative Region;

3. seriously interfering in, disrupting, or undermining the performance of duties and functions in accordance with the law by the body of central power of the People's Republic of China or the body of power of the Hong Kong Special Administrative Region; or

4. attacking or damaging the premises and facilities used by the body of power of the Hong Kong Special Administrative Region to perform its duties and functions, rendering it incapable of performing its normal duties and functions.

A person who is a principal offender or a person who commits an offence of a grave nature shall be sentenced to life imprisonment or fixed-term imprisonment of not less than ten years; a person who actively participates in the offence shall be sentenced to fixed-term imprisonment of not less than three years but not more than ten years; and other participants shall be sentenced to fixed-term imprisonment of not more than three years, short-term detention or restriction."

Arrests began immediately. The following day, "Police said 10 people were arrested under the law, including a man with a Hong Kong independence flag and a woman holding a sign displaying the British flag and calling for Hong Kong's independence."[4] Arrests continued

---

1 Emily Feng, "5 Takeaways From China's Hong Kong National Security Law," *NPR*, July 1, 2020, https://www.npr.org/2020/07/01/885900989/5-takeaways-from-chinas-hong-kong-national-security-law

2 Abigail Ng, "China Passes Controversial National Security Law for Hong Kong," *CNBC*, June 30, 2020, https://www.cnbc.com/2020/06/30/china-reportedly-passes-national-security-law-for-hong-kong.html

3 Xinhua, "English Translation of the Law of the People's Republic of China on Safeguarding National Security in the Hong Kong Special Administrative Region," *Xinhua Net*, July 1, 2020, http://www.xinhuanet.com/english/2020-07/01/c_139178753.htm

4 ZEN SOO Associated Press, "Hong Kong Police Make First Arrests Under New Security Law," *ABC News*, July 1, 2020, https://abcnews.go.com/International/wireStory/security-laws-passage-hong-kong-marks-china-rule-71546945

even as risks prevailed. One woman remarked, "It's really the first time that I had a genuine feeling that I would be arrested just because of speaking aloud a slogan or holding a poster on the street."[5] As more activists were rounded up for expressing their freedom of speech, Beijing called Hong Kong an "inalienable" part of China.[6]

Convictions can lead to torture. This fate has been experienced by millions in China who are being 're-educated' in concentration camps. "As one pro-independence protester in his early 20s put it, from Beijing's perspective, there was really no concept of rule of law in Hong Kong that couldn't be overridden, and so anything could be interpreted as lawbreaking."[7] Hong Kong's new law is unlike any measure the citizens have experienced. The consequences have been swift and harsh. Britain has offered a path to citizenship for Hong Kong residents if a resident was a British national in 1997 at the turnover to China.[8]

Jimmy Lai (Lai Chee-Ying), a clothing retailer, media tycoon, and pro-democracy advocate, called the National Security Law a "death knell", saying that "it supersedes our law and our rule of law."[9] In shocking news to the world, Jimmy Lai was arrested on August 10, 2020, as two hundred police officers raided his home.[10] While many were swept up in China's sting to imprison and silence pro-democracy leaders, Agnes Chow Ting, also arrested at her home, was also a key figure in the movement.[11] Fluent in Japanese, English, and Cantonese,[12] she had spoken at events around the world and thus was accused "of 'colluding with foreign forces' under the National Security Law. According to the police, Agnes was accused of calling upon foreign countries to impose sanctions on China on her social media accounts since the enactment of the law."[13]

In December 2020, journalists, educators, judiciary, and pro-democracy sympathizers have been picked up one-by-one in a stifling sweeping swath of arrests. Agnes Chow, Joshua Wong, and Ivan Lam, three student democracy activists, were jailed on December 2, 2020,

---

5   Jen Kirby, "China's New National Security Law and What It Means for Hong Kong's Future, Explained," *Vox*, July 14, 2020, https://www.vox.com/2020/7/2/21309902/china-national-security-law-hong-kong-protests-us-sanctions

6   Anne Marie Roantree, "Hong Kong Police Arrest Four Under New Security Law in Move Slammed by Rights Group," *Reuters*, July 29, 2020, https://www.reuters.com/article/us-hongkong-security/hong-kong-police-arrest-four-under-new-security-law-in-move-slammed-by-rights-group-idUSKCN24U3DQ

7   Helen Regan, "China Passes Sweeping Hong Kong National Security Law," *CNN News*, June 30, 2020, https://www.cnn.com/2020/06/29/china/hong-kong-national-security-law-passed-intl-hnk/index.html

8   Government of the United Kingdom, "Apply for Citizenship if You Have British Nationality," *Government of the United Kingdom*, n.d., https://www.gov.uk/apply-citizenship-british-nationality/hong-kong

9   Helen Regan, "China Imposes Sweeping National Security Law as Hong Kong Marks Handover Anniversary," *Pittsburgh Post-Gazette*, June 30, 2020 https://www.post-gazette.com/news/world/2020/07/01/Hong-Kong-national-security-law-passes-China/stories/202007010064

10 The Washington Post, "Hong Kong Tycoon Jimmy Lai Arrested Under National Security Law," *The Washington Post*, August 9, 2020, https://www.washingtonpost.com/world/asia_pacific/hong-kong-jimmy-lai-arrest/2020/08/09/d7312f20-daa4-11ea-b205-ff838e15a9a6_story.html

11 Rick Noack, "Who Are Jimmy Lai and Agnes Chow, Two of the Hong Kong Democracy Advocates Arrested Monday," *The Washington Post*, August 10, 2020, https://www.washingtonpost.com/world/2020/08/10/who-are-jimmy-lai-agnes-chow-two-hong-kong-democracy-advocates-arrested-monday/

12 Jesse Johnson, "Hong Kong Democracy Activists Press Japan To Reconsider Xi Visit," *The Japan Times*, June 4, 2020, https://www.japantimes.co.jp/news/2020/06/04/national/politics-diplomacy/hong-kong-pro-democracy-activists-press-tokyo-rethink-xis-visit-japan/

13 South China Morning Post, "Hong Kong Opposition Activist Agnes Chow Swept Up in Hong Kong Arrests Under Security Law," August 10, 2020, video, 1:47, https://www.youtube.com/watch?v=g_A91611Rog

The Umbrella Movement
Hong Kong Protesters Come Out in Millions

convicted based on Hong Kong's National Security Law.[14] On December 3, 2020, Jimmy Lai, the 73-year-old editor of Hong Kong's newspaper, *Apple Daily*, was taken as well, denied bail until April 2021. However, on the day before Christmas, Jimmy Lai was released on a 10 million Hong Kong Dollar bail (approximately USD $1.3 million) provided that he not "meet with foreign officials, give any interviews, publish any articles or post on social media, and will have to remain at home and surrender his travel documents."[15]

Jimmy Lai was released on bail. He exclaimed to *NPR*,

"Well, let's put it this way," Lai said.

"If we don't fight, we will lose everything.

---

14 James Griffiths, "With Arrests and a Security Law, Who is Left to Fight for Democracy in Hong Kong?," *CNN*, December 3, 2020, https://www.cnn.com/2020/12/03/asia/hong-kong-democracy-arrests-protest-intl-hnk/index.html

15 Reuters Staff, "HK Court Grants Tycoon Jimmy Lai Bail in National Security, Fraud Case," *Reuters*, December 23, 2020, https://www.reuters.com/article/us-hongkong-security/hk-court-grants-tycoon-jimmy-lai-bail-in-national-security-fraud-case-idUSKBN28X0YG

We will lose the rule of law.

We will lose the human right.

We will lose the way of life that we're used to.

We will lose, you know, the freedom we have.

But if we fight, that might — you know, there may be a chance.

There may be a miracle."[16]

On Christmas Day, 2020, Hong Kong prosecutors filed an urgent appeal to send Jimmy Lai back to prison.[17]

The Future of Hong Kong

The future cannot be predicted, but some breadcrumbs illuminate the likely road of China's victorious question to take over Asia. China uses 'salami slicing' to pick off one small slice at a time until freedoms are gone, territories are relinquished, and the takeover of land and resources is inevitable. These small slices are so thin and under a veiled guise to not alarm anyone. Furthermore, the COVID-19 pandemic provided a cloak to mask its efforts and a 'valid' justification for Beijing since few global citizens were watching, re-focused on their own family's health, community's survival, and country's political ramifications. Additionally, countries were in desperate need of money and supplies that Beijing was willing to loan in exchange for resources, territory, and a future reservoir of indebtedness. The CCP also held out the lure of vaccines.

Conclusion

Consider the protests on July 1, 2019 and July 1, 2020. In the first case, in 2019, millions of people took to the streets to commemorate Hong Kong's turnover to China. In the second case, in 2020, the National Security Law threatened every citizen. If they dared to protest, they would act against the Chinese government and possibly be arrested. A few hundred showed up in 2020,[18] a dramatic difference from the year before. Silencing people by threatening them with possible torture in Chinese jails was an effective tactic.

The fears of the people in 2019 have been born out in the capture of Jimmy Lai and Agnes Chow Ting as criminals for acting against Beijing. Even disrespect for the Chinese flag, the national anthem, or the CCP has a penalty of up to three years in prison.[19] The National Security Law and its dangers to residents have forever changed the city. Hong Kong is no

---

16 Mark Katkov, "Hong Kong Democracy Activist Jimmy Lai Released on Bail," *NPR*, December 23, 2020, https://www.npr.org/2020/12/23/949633411/hong-kong-democracy-activist-jimmy-lai-released-on-bail

17 Chris Lau, "National Security Law: Hong Kong Prosecutors File Urgent Appeal in Bid to Have Media Mogul Jimmy Lai Sent Back to Jail," *South China Morning Post*, December 25, 2020, https://www.scmp.com/news/hong-kong/politics/article/3115315/national-security-law-hong-kong-prosecutors-file-urgent

18 CNN News, "New Security Law Sparks Protests in Hong Kong," *CNN News*, July 2, 2020, https://www.cnn.com/2020/07/01/asia/gallery/hong-kong-unrest-2020/index.html

19 Chris Buckley and Keith Bradsher, "Jail Time for Disrespecting China's Anthem Jumps From 15 Days to 3 Years," *The New York Times*, November 4, 2017, https://www.nytimes.com/2017/11/04/world/asia/china-hong-kong-national-anthem.html

longer autonomous. For the citizens of Hong Kong, freedom and liberty are fading under China's ominous laws. "Going forward, virtually any form of resistance could be treated as illegal under the new law."[20]

What's at Stake?

First, this story is not about Hong Kong. This story is about people everywhere – one salami slice at a time. People who allow the creeping force to enter through purchases or technology or 'cooperation' are likely to face the same perilous consequence. Ask the people of Hong Kong who enjoyed freedom in 1997, 2007, and 2017 what they think now.

Second, free speech movements in Hong Kong that previously rallied global citizens now silence protesters. Those living in Hong Kong fear that they will suffer the same consequence of imprisonment or worse as Jimmy Lai, Agnes Chow, Ivan Lam, and Joshua Wong, as well as hundreds of other publishers, educators, or free thinkers who advocate for freedom.

Third, many journalists have been silenced or told to leave Hong Kong. Thus, news articles on events as they unfold are limited, and the global citizenry has less information regarding current events.

Fourth, the lack of transparency sets a dangerous precedent. Hong Kong news will be filtered through Beijing's propaganda machine and communist principles, despite citizens' efforts to voice their opinions. Fear of imprisonment is enough to control Hong Kong citizenry and force them to abide by whatever future Beijing chooses.

Fifth, lured by the possibility of getting vaccines first, states capitulated to Beijing's demands.[21] The fact that the results were unproven was not a problem.[22]

Sixth, China's Sinovac vaccine has shown to be 50.4% effective, which means that it is not effective in almost half of the cases.[23]

---

20 Tuan N. Pham, "What the Year of the Rat Holds for China," *The Diplomat,* January 18, 2020, https://thediplomat.com/2020/01/what-the-year-of-the-rat-holds-for-china/

21 Abigail Ng, "Developing Nations are First in Line for China's Covid Vaccines. Analysts Question Beijing's Intent," *CNBC,* Updated December 9, 2020, https://www.cnbc.com/2020/12/10/covid-china-may-be-using-its-vaccines-to-expand-its-soft-power.html

22 Sui-Lee Wee and Elsie Chen, "Vaccine Unproven? No Problem in China, Where People Scramble for Shots," *The New York Times,* Updated January 7, 2021, https://www.nytimes.com/2020/11/17/business/china-coronavirus-vaccine-safety.html

23 Samantha Pearson, Luciana Magalhaes, and Chao Deng, "Chinese Covid-19 Vaccine Far Less Effective Than Initially Touted in Brazil," *The Wall Street Journal*, Updated January 12, 2021, https://www.wsj.com/articles/chinas-sinovac-covid-19-vaccine-is-50-4-in-late-stage-brazil-trials-11610470581?mod=djemalertNEWS

Chapter 4
Future of Hong Kong
An Uncertain Path for Businesses, Newspapers, and Freedom-Loving People

Smothering the People's Voice in the Name of National Security | Part 5

Introduction

The economy aside, the most extraordinary impact on Hong Kong is the demoralization of its more than 7.5 million citizens. Most of Hong Kong's residents were raised knowing and internalizing freedom. They went where they wanted, communicated what they thought, and pursued life's course on the path they set. Although questions lingered about the far-off date, 2047, when China would convert Hong Kong to its full charge, until then, autonomy was promised and expected. Many residents even thought that in all ways - economically, politically, and socially - Hong Kong could and would be free again, eventually cutting ties to Beijing and allowing a new city-state to stand as a proud entity with its unique flair, style, and personality.

No Longer Free

Warning signs abounded as Hong Kongers took to the streets to dampen the threat of the fire breathing dragon, spewing flames down their necks just a few miles away. An undercurrent of change slowly crept, like smoke billowing under a door, warning of a fire outside. However, the fire still seemed distant, even when the smoke alarm repeatedly rang with every bill passed and continuous threats to residents, like the booksellers who were taken away by the Chinese authorities.

The disconnect between liberty and totalitarianism bewildered Hong Kong residents. One day, citizens could speak freely. The next day, they could not. Furthermore, the economic future of Hong Kong was impacted in the short term. Fears mounted that the negative impact would last a long time.

Emergency 911 – What You Need to Know about Hong Kong's National Security Law

1. China is now in charge of Hong Kong. All 'legislators' are at the whim of the Chinese Communist Party (CCP). All citizens are at the whim of the sweeping new laws that bypassed normal channels and were put in place June 30, 2020.

2. One troubling component of the law concerns 'endangering national security'. People may be arrested for wide-ranging 'offenses', assets seized, and the city forced into lockdown. Moreover, trials may be conducted in mainland China where some prisoners have been tortured.[1] This vague statement of 'endangering national security' carries a maximum sentence of life in prison. Ambiguous and abstruse, China has free reign to interpret the text broadly:

    - "separatism" (for leaving the country)
    - "subversion" (for speaking out for democracy)
    - "terrorism" (for bringing protection against police)
    - "collusion with a foreign government" (for communicating with an embassy

---

1 Amnesty International, "China: Authorities Must End Ruthless Crackdown on Human Rights Lawyers and Activists," *Amnesty International*, July 7, 2017, https://www.amnesty.org/en/latest/news/2017/07/china-end-ruthless-crackdown-human-rights-lawyers-activists/

or requesting government support)

3. Peaceful protests have been silenced. Non-violent protesters have been charged with various crimes. People who possessed flags, banners, and emblems were arrested. However, even people who held up blank pieces of white paper at a shopping mall were considered dangerous – and then scores of riot police came.[2]

4. Without a warrant, the violator's assets may be frozen, properties searched, and travel prohibited. Information access, including computers, may be required and property taken. Authorities can demand passwords. Any person who violates an order may be taken into custody and imprisoned.[3]

5. Journalists have been provoked; some have been arrested. *Apple Daily* CEO, Jimmy Lai, was arrested in August 2020.[4] Other newspaper leaders and reporters have similarly been threatened. *The New York Times* headline comments, 'We're Almost Extinct': China's Investigative Journalists Are Silenced Under Xi."[5]

Harassed and threatened, journalists have been told that they will lose their media credentials,[6] and some say that it is dangerous even to admit to being an investigative journalist publically.[7] Student reporters have been similarly thwarted.[8] *The New York Times* moved some of its journalists to Seoul, South Korea for their protection.[9] This movement of reporters was replicated by *The Wall Street Journal (WSJ)* as well after China expelled three of their journalists from Beijing.[10] In September 2020, *The Washington Post* pulled its last full-time correspondent out of China.[11]

On December 7, 2020, a *Bloomberg News* reporter in Beijing, Haze Fan, was taken

---

2   Bill Bostock, "Hong Kong Activists are Holding Up Blank Signs Because China Now has the Power to Define Pro-Democracy Slogans as Terrorism," *Business Insider*, July 6, 2020, https://www.businessinsider.com/hong-kong-activists-blank-signs-avoid-china-national-security-law-2020-7

3   Dan Harris, "How to Protect Your Company Information When You Travel to China," *China Law Blog*, December 3, 2019, https://www.chinalawblog.com/2019/12/how-to-protect-your-company-information-when-you-travel-to-china.html

4   Will Ripley and Jenni Marsh, "Hong Kong Media Tycoon Says 'The Fight Has To Go On' after 'Symbolic' Arrest under New Law," *CNN Business*, Updated August 14, 2020, https://www.cnn.com/2020/08/14/media/jimmy-lai-interview-hnk-intl/index.html

5   Javier C. Hernández, "'We're Almost Extinct': China's Investigative Journalists Are Silenced Under Xi," *The New York Times*, July 12, 2019, https://www.nytimes.com/2019/07/12/world/asia/china-journalists-crackdown.html

6   Rachel Cheung and David Pierson, "Hong Kong Journalists Harassed, Arrested and Lose Press Freedoms under New China Law," *Los Angeles Times*, August 15, 2020, https://www.latimes.com/world-nation/story/2020-08-15/hong-kong-media-freedom

7   Javier C. Hernández, "'We're Almost Extinct': China's Investigative Journalists Are Silenced Under Xi," *The New York Times*, July 12, 2019, https://www.nytimes.com/2019/07/12/world/asia/china-journalists-crackdown.html

8   Heidi Lee, "How Hong Kong's Student Reporters Fear Being Silenced under New Police Rules," *Hong Kong Free Press*, October 2, 2020, https://hongkongfp.com/2020/10/02/student-reporters-fear-being-silenced-under-new-police-rules/

9   BBC News, "New York Times to Move Hong Kong Staff to Seoul Over Press Freedom Fears," *BBC News*, July 15, 2020, https://www.bbc.com/news/world-asia-china-53413057

10 The Editorial Board, "First They Came for Hong Kong," *The Wall Street Journal*, July 7, 2020, https://www.wsj.com/articles/first-they-came-for-hong-kong-11594164086

11 Paul Farhi, "Western Journalists are Getting Squeezed out of China by Superpower Tensions," *The Washington Post*, September 16, 2020, https://www.washingtonpost.com/lifestyle/media/journalists-get-caught-in-the-middle-of-souring-us-china-relations/2020/09/16/350f8a52-f6ab-11ea-be57-d00bb9bc632d_story.html

away by security officials, though by Thursday, December 10, 2020, they learned that the journalist was held on suspicion of endangering national security.[12] Other correspondents are concerned, mainly since two Australian TV hosts, Bill Birtles (*Australian Broadcasting Corporation*) and Michael Smith (*Australian Financial Review*), were also detained. Cheng Lei, an Australian business anchor for *CGTN*, who previously served for nine years as *CNBC*'s China correspondent, was being held on the basis of "carrying out criminal activities endangering China's national security."[13] All references of Cheng Lei have been removed from the *CGTN* website and social media."[14] The EU has urged China to release those news reporters, including Haze Fan and Cheng Lei, or give them access to a legal defense according to international law.[15]

6. Social media has been silenced among the people. Also, the new law allows authorities to remove content and obtain user data. Thus, WhatsApp, Twitter, Facebook, and Google suspended the processing of user data, citing that freedom of expression is a human right.[16]

7. People outside of Hong Kong are also susceptible to the law which authorizes a worldwide jurisdiction. Citizens of other countries may be accused, arrested, and prosecuted.

Act of Desperation in the Name of Safety and Security

While the CCP explains that the efforts against Hong Kong are for security, they are likely trying to avoid any future political dissent. An early strike in June 2020 quelled July 1, 2020 protests or gatherings. Furthermore, by preempting social unrest with an all-encompassing law, the move also mitigated against problems for its September 2020 election, preventing pro-democracy candidates from being on the ballot. However, the efforts to remove pro-democracy candidates from the ballot was met with an uproar, particularly after the Hong Kong police arrested those seeking elected positions.[17] Thus, on July 31, 2020, Hong Kong's Chief Executive, Carrie Lam, announced that the election would be postponed until September 2021 "to ensure fairness and public safety...in an open, fair and impartial manner."[18] On the scheduled election day, September 6, 2020, protests erupted; 289 people

---

12 Sol Han, "Bloomberg Journalist Detained in Beijing for Allegedly 'Endangering National Security,'" *CNN Business*, December 11, 2020, https://www.cnn.com/2020/12/11/media/bloomberg-journalist-beijing-intl-hnk/index.html

13 Ibid.

14 Ibid.

15 France24, "EU Urges China to Free Those Detained for Reporting After Bloomberg Employee Held," *France24*, December 13, 2020, https://www.france24.com/en/live-news/20201213-eu-urges-china-to-free-those-detained-for-reporting-after-bloomberg-employee-held

16 Newley Purnell, "Google, Facebook and Twitter Suspend Review of Hong Kong Requests for User Data," *The Wall Street Journal*, Updated July 7, 2020, https://www.wsj.com/articles/whatsapp-to-suspend-processing-law-enforcement-requests-for-user-data-in-hong-kong-11594034580

17 Reuters Staff, "Hong Kong Police Arrest Pro-Democracy Politician Set to Run for Legislature," *Reuters*, July 17, 2020, https://www.reuters.com/article/us-hongkong-security/hong-kong-police-arrest-pro-democracy-politician-set-to-run-for-legislature-idUSKCN24I1KF

18 Zen Soo, "Hong Kong Postpones Elections by a Year, Citing Coronavirus," *AP News*, July 30, 2020, https://apnews.com/article/ap-top-news-democracy-international-news-hong-kong-elections-ece28d6c700f34d496327ae7a66ed2bd

were arrested.[19] The subtle goal was for the future of Hong Kong to be paved with CCP ideologues who would implement the party's program.

Beyond Britain to Chinese Domination

After keeping the text secret,[20] the Hong Kong legislature passed the sweeping National Security Law on June 30, 2020. This broadly-applied and vaguely-defined law[21] offers little room for self-expression. Furthermore, Beijing resoundingly expressed that it would not tolerate any breach or violation. With the One China, Two Systems dismantled, China exerted its sovereignty broadly and mightily. *Time Magazine* called the effect "chilling"- using common language punishable with life in prison, books were purged from libraries, and chants outlawed.[22] Assembly is now illegal, as is the spread of pro-independence information. Pro-independence candidates are no longer able to run for election in an effort to neutralize the movement and silence voices.

Fleeing China is not allowed either. Hundreds of freedom-seeking Hong Kongers have sought asylum in Taiwan. In one case, on August 23, 2020, a dozen protesters fled in a boat from Hong Kong attempting to reach Taiwan, but were picked up when the Chinese Guangdong Coast Guard overtook their boat.[23] On December 17, 2020, Chinese prosecutors, with a 99% conviction rate, indicted the Hong Kong residents who were attempting to flee to Taiwan on the grounds that they were illegally crossing the border, which carries with it two to seven years up to life imprisonment.[24]

Families have demanded access to lawyers in support of those who were taken into custody.[25] When taken to Shenzhen, they were given Chinese government-appointed lawyers.[26] One was a Portuguese national, which might have added pressure from outside

---

19 AP News, "Hong Kong Police Arrest 289 at Protests over Election Delay," *AP News*, September 6, 2020, https://apnews.com/article/bdf4662dc7690907606a9f322b689b5a

20 Gary Cheung and Natalie Wong, "Hong Kong National Security Law: No Reason to Keep Draft Secret, Say Legal Experts," *South China Morning Post*, https://www.scmp.com/news/hong-kong/politics/article/3090629/hong-kong-national-security-law-no-reason-keep-draft-secret

21 Veta Chan, "The One Element of Hong Kong's New Security Law that Concerns Business the Most," *Fortune*, July 16, 2020, https://fortune.com/2020/07/16/hong-kong-business-national-security-law/

22 Laignee Barron, "'It's So Much Worse Than Anyone Expected.' Why Hong Kong's National Security Law Is Having Such a Chilling Effect," *Time Magazine*, July 23, 2020, https://time.com/5867000/hong-kong-china-national-security-law-effect/

23 Shibani Mahtani, "Hong Kong Refugees Captured at Sea Spent Months Plotting Daring Dash to Freedom," *The Washington Post*, August 31, 2020, https://www.washingtonpost.com/world/asia_pacific/hong-kong-boats-refugees-asylum-seekers-national-security-law-taiwan/2020/08/31/2d429170-eb34-11ea-bd08-1b10132b458f_story.html

24 Nectar Gan, James Griffiths, and Eric Cheung, "China Formally Indicts 10 Hong Kong Activists Who Attempted to Flee by Boat to Taiwan," *CNN*, December 17, 2020, https://www.cnn.com/2020/12/17/asia/hong-kong-twelve-indicted-intl-hnk/index.html

25 Wenxin Fan, "China Signals It Will Put 12 Fleeing Hong Kong Residents on Trial," *The Wall Street Journal*, Updated September 30, 2020, https://www.wsj.com/articles/china-signals-it-will-try-12-hong-kong-residents-caught-fleeing-to-taiwan-11601484015

26 Agence France-Presse, "Lawyers Pressured as China Labels Hong Kong Fugitives 'Separatists'," *Courthouse News Service*, September 14, 2020, https://www.courthousenews.com/lawyers-pressured-as-china-labels-hong-kong-fugitives-separatists/

of China on their trial.[27] Mike Pompeo, U.S. Secretary of State, exclaimed that he encouraged China to proceed with due process of the law.[28] Still, the group was charged with 'separatism',[29] which has a sentence of up to life in prison.[30]

Stripped of their passports, other pro-democracy activists have also attempted to flee Hong Kong. This has put pressure on Taiwan, which does not want to antagonize China.[31] China has sent numerous warnings with its daily military overflight provocations within Taiwan's Air Defense Identification Zone (ADIZ) that increased in the fall of 2020. As many as eighteen bombers in a day were flown in Taiwan's airspace, despite warnings by the Taiwanese.[32]

The Cry for Help

October 1, 2019 was termed by democracy activists as a 'day of mourning'.[33] The tears they shed in 2019 were a cry to the world for help. Demonstrators shouted loudly in the streets, "There is no National Day celebration, only a national tragedy."[34] Few around the globe listened.

Hong Kong protesters hung a banner reading "#NotMyNationalDay, Proud to be British since 1841" at the entrance of the British consulate.[35] October 1, 2019, was intended to celebrate China's communist party rule, though the killing of Hong Kong protesters overshadowed Beijing's celebration. One Twitter post read, "Think of it, the biggest mass murderer of the Chinese is the Chinese Communist Party. 70 yrs of mass killings and repression while building the perfect totalitarian cage."[36]

---

27 Austin Ramzy and Elaine Yu, "For Hong Kong Protesters Caught at Sea, Trial in China Is Likely," *The New York Times*, September 29, 2020, https://www.nytimes.com/2020/09/29/world/asia/hong-kong-protesters-china.html

28 Austin Ramzy and Elaine Yu, "For Hong Kong Protesters Caught at Sea, Trial in China Is Likely," *The New York Times*, September 29, 2020, https://www.nytimes.com/2020/09/29/world/asia/hong-kong-protesters-china.html

29 Reuters Staff, "China Calls Hong Kong People Arrested at Sea 'Separatists'," *Reuters*, September 13, 2020, https://www.reuters.com/article/us-hongkong-security-china/china-calls-hong-kong-people-arrested-at-sea-separatists-idUSKBN2640DW

30 BBC News, "Hong Kong Security Law: Life Sentences for Breaking China-Imposed Law," *BBC News*, June 30, 2020, https://www.bbc.com/news/world-asia-china-53238004

31 Reuters Staff, "Flight of Hong Kong Protesters Piles Pressure on Taiwan," *Reuters*, September 30, 2020, https://www.reuters.com/article/us-hongkong-security-taiwan-insight/flight-of-hong-kong-protesters-piles-pressure-on-taiwan-idUSKBN26L1SR

32 Wu Su-wei, "PLA Aircraft Cross into Taiwan's ADIZ," *Taipei Times*, September 19, 2020, https://taipeitimes.com/News/front/archives/2020/09/19/2003743692

33 Time Staff, "Protester Reported Shot as Hong Kong Marks China's National Day with Widespread Unrest," *Time Magazine*, October 1, 2019, https://time.com/5689617/hong-kong-protest-china-national-day-october-1/

34 Holmes Chan, "'Day of Mourning': Protests Erupt Around Hong Kong Districts as China National Day Marred by Tear Gas, Clashes," *Hong Kong Free Press*, October 1, 2019, https://hongkongfp.com/2019/10/01/day-mourning-protests-erupt-around-hong-kong-districts-china-national-day-marred-tear-gas-clashes/

35 Mattha Busby, Martin Farrer, and Naaman Zhou, "Hong Kong Protester Shot in Chest as China National Day Demos Intensify – as it Happened," *The Guardian*, Updated October 1, 2019, https://www.theguardian.com/world/live/2019/oct/01/china-anniversary-nation-marks-70-years-of-communism-amid-hong-kong-protests-live?page=with:block-5d92d71d8f084ab84173036a

36 Twitter Hashtag, "#notmynationalday", 2019, https://twitter.com/hashtag/notmynationalday?lang=en

Hong Kong's Future
Xi Jinping – The Chairman of Everything

Conclusion

On October 1, 2020, those cries were largely silenced by the CCP's national security law that imposed prison sentences for anyone who spoke out. Police filed charges again for pro-democracy leader Joshua Wong,[37] as Hong Kong's leadership cracked down against freedom of speech. More people were charged with offenses ranging from rioting, possession of explosives, collusion with a foreign country. Nathan Law, who shared that the press is no longer free to write in Hong Kong, fled to the U.K. to speak out and advocate for Hong Kong freely in defense of the democracy activists who are being rounded up and imprisoned.[38]

After imprisonment, some Hong Kong activists were removed and transported eighteen miles to Shenzhen, on China's mainland.[39] Their nightmare begins where other Hong

---

37 Reuters Staff, "Hong Kong Democracy Activist Joshua Wong Arrested for 2019 Illegal Assembly," *Reuters*, September 24, 2020, https://www.reuters.com/article/us-hongkong-security-joshuawong-idUSKCN26F13I

38 Linda Mottram, Scott Mitchell, and Barbara Miller, "Wanted by China, Nathan Law is Worried Foreign Journalists Could Soon be Harassed in Hong Kong," *Australian Broadcasting Corporation (ABC News)*, Updated September 17, 2020, https://www.abc.net.au/news/2020-09-17/nathan-law-living-in-exile-censorship-hong-kong-foreign-media/12672282

39 Alice Su and Rachel Cheung, "A Nightmare Comes True for 12 Hong Kongers Arrested at Sea, Now in Chinese Detention," *Los Angeles Times*, September 25, 2020, https://www.latimes.com/world-nation/story/2020-09-25/hong-kong-china-refugees-taiwan-justice-detention

Kongers have been tortured into confessing to crimes.[40] Li Heping was force-fed drugs, chained, and electrocuted while others have simply 'vanished'.[41] As fleeing ramps up, Hong Kong's Chief Executive, Carrie Lam, declares, "The reason for their fleeing Hong Kong is seemingly to escape their legal responsibilities."[42]

For more than a century, the prevailing thought was that Hong Kong was a 'safe-haven' from China's totalitarian control, though that belief is gone.[43]

What's at Stake?

First, Hong Kong's National Security Law has silenced Hong Kong residents and forced democracy activists to go underground.

Second, many more pro-democracy activists are likely to be charged with the crime of speaking out for freedom.

Third, Hong Kong's authoritarian legislative control is stamping out any means to leave the country. In November 2020, pro-democracy legislators resigned en masse in solidarity.[44] Many citizens are being charged and noted as criminals on their documents for past protests that occurred even before the national security law was put in place.

Fourth, Hong Kong is no longer a 'safe-haven'. Taiwan's takeover is next. What is at stake is Taiwan's stance on taking in Hong Kongers who flee China's oppression and China's actions to stop both Hong Kong residents' exodus and exert control over Taiwan's leadership.

---

40 Simon Denyer, "Former British Consulate Worker Tells of Torture by China over Hong Kong," *The Washington Post,* November 19, 2019, https://www.washingtonpost.com/world/asia-pacific/hong-kong-protesters-police-enter-final-phase-of-showdown-as-china-slams-us/2019/11/19/6b571fb2-0b10-11ea-8054-289aef6e38a3_story.html

41 Amnesty International, "China: Authorities Must End Ruthless Crackdown on Human Rights Lawyers and Activists," *Amnesty International,* July 7, 2017, https://www.amnesty.org/en/latest/news/2017/07/china-end-ruthless-crackdown-human-rights-lawyers-activists/

42 ABC, Australian Morning Mail, "Fleeing Hong Kong Ramps Up!," *Australian Morning Mail,* September 18, 2020, https://morningmail.org/fleeing-hong-kong-ramps-up/

43 Ivan Watsonm, Rebecca Wright, and Vanesse Chan, "Hong Kong Was Once a Safe Haven from China. Now Activists are Fleeing the City by Boat to Taiwan," *CNN,* September 15, 2020, https://www.cnn.com/2020/09/14/asia/hong-kong-taiwan-boat-dst-intl-hnk/index.html

44 Emily Feng & Scott Neuman, "Hong Kong's Pro-Democracy Lawmakers Quit Legislature Over Ouster Of Colleagues," *NPR,* November 11, 2020, https://www.npr.org/2020/11/11/933780136/hong-kongs-pro-democracy-lawmakers-quit-legislature-over-ouster-of-colleagues

Chapter 5
Linguistic Legacies
Mandarin, Cantonese, Taiwanese – Who Speaks What Language?

Introduction

Hong Kong recognizes English and Chinese as its official languages, though an array of other dialects are spoken by its citizenry. An estimated eighty-nine percent of Hong Kong residents speak Cantonese, twenty-five percent speak Mandarin, and Hakka and Taiwanese are commonly spoken dialects.[1] Taiwan has twenty-two living languages spoken by the indigenous people.[2] The three most prominent languages in Taiwan, often dubbed "dialects", are the Sinitic, or Chinese, languages: Mandarin, Taiwanese, and Hakka.[3] Since 1911, Mandarin has been recognized as Taiwan's official language,[4] though an estimated eighty-percent of Taiwan residents speak Taiwanese.[5]

The Long-Lasting Cantonese Language in Hong Kong

From 1883 to 1974, during which Hong Kong was a British colony, English was the official language.[6] In 1974, the Cantonese dialect of Chinese became officially recognized. The language is believed to originate in the Eastern Han dynasty (25-220 AD) when the northern Chinese fled their war-struck territories to the south and carried their language with them.[7] Mandarin was recognized in Chinese societies in the 14th century Yuan dynasty (1271-1368 AD) and popularized by the communist party in 1949.[8] Cantonese uses traditional Chinese characters.

There has been much debate over whether or not Hong Kong should implement Mandarin as its official language. This controversy originally centered around Han Chinese customs since the majority of Hong Kong residents are Han.[9] As such, many argued that Hong Kong should shift to educate, write, and speak in Mandarin rather than Cantonese. In 2018, responding to questions regarding whether Mandarin should be taught in Hong Kong schools, Chief Executive Carrie Lam affirmed, "We are speaking Cantonese every day, so this is a non-issue."[10]

---

1   Mark Owuor Otieno, "What Languages Are Spoken In Hong Kong?," *World Atlas*, October 31, 2017, https://www.worldatlas.com/articles/what-languages-are-spoken-in-hong-kong.html

2   Island Folklore, "Taiwan: Folklore Website Maps 22 Languages Spoken on the Island Nation Today?," *Unrepresented Nations & Peoples Organization*, February 3, 2017, https://unpo.org/article/19823

3   Keoni Everington, "Map of Taiwan's Living Languages," *Taiwan News*, February 2, 2017, https://www.taiwannews.com.tw/en/news/3086412

4   Stony Brook You, "Language Use in Taiwan," *Stony Brook University*, n.d., https://you.stonybrook.edu/aas220taiwan/mandarin/

5   Kate Chernavina, "Cantonese and Mandarin in Hong Kong and Taiwan," *Omniglot*, n.d., https://omniglot.com/language/articles/chineseinhongkongandtaiwan.htm

6   China Highlights, "Hong Kong Languages: Background and Helpful Travel Tips," *China Highlights*, n.d., https://www.chinahighlights.com/hong-kong/language.htm

7   Juliana Liu, "Cantonese v Mandarin: When Hong Kong Languages Get Political," *BBC News*, June 29, 2017, https://www.bbc.com/news/world-asia-china-40406429

8   Ibid.

9   Race Relations Unit, "The Demographics: Ethnic Groups," *The Government of Hong Kong Special Administrative Region*, n.d., https://www.had.gov.hk/rru/english/info/info_dem.html

10 Su Xinqi and Sum Lok-kei, "Should Mandarin Replace Cantonese in Hong Kong? No, Says Carrie Lam," *South China Morning Post*, May 3, 2018, https://www.scmp.com/news/hong-kong/politics/article/2144578/should-mandarin-replace-cantonese-hong-kong-says-no

Mandarin, Cantonese, and Taiwanese
'Chinese' Languages in Asia

Taiwan's Linguistic Melting Pot

Cantonese, though, is not spoken as commonly in Taiwan.[11] In fact, *Island Folklore* illustrated a linguistic lineage map of the two main language groups in modern Taiwan today: the Austronesian Language Family and the Sino-Tibetan Language Family.

Some notable distinctions from the *Island Folklore* map are:[12]

1. Austronesian languages emerged from Madagascar, the Philippines, Malaysia, Indonesia, and Polynesian islands (New Zealand, Hawaii, Samoa)
2. Modern Austronesian languages include the Formosan group of languages spoken in Taiwan
3. The three currently spoken Austronesian languages in Taiwan are Yami (Formosan), Ibtayat, and Ivatan
4. The Sino-Tibetan languages emerged from Chinese, Tibetan, Burmese, and other variant languages
5. The three currently spoken Sino-Tibetan languages in Taiwan are Taiwanese, Mandarin, and Hakka

It is essential to recognize that Taiwan's Mandarin roots date back to 1949 when General Chiang Kai-shek implemented "re-Sinicisation" policies to socialize the Taiwanese culture

---

11 Kate Chernavina, "Cantonese and Mandarin in Hong Kong and Taiwan," *Omniglot*, n.d., https://omniglot.com/language/articles/chineseinhongkongandtaiwan.htm

12 Island Folklore, "The Languages of Taiwan," *Island Folklore*, n.d., https://islandfolklore.com/about/taiwan/languages/?platform=hootsuite#jp-carousel-7297

into Chinese identity.[13] Still, in 1946, before the Cultural Revolution, Taiwan attempted to eradicate Japanese culture. The Taiwan Culture Promotion Association was established to "propagate the Three Principles of the People and democracy, transform Taiwanese culture and promote the use of Mandarin."[14] Then-leader Chen Yi asserted, "The Japanese carried out Japanization education, and now we shall counter it by Sinicization."[15]

The South China Morning Post notes that following the loss to Mao Zedong and the citizenry (under Chiang Kai-shek's rule) fleeing to Taiwan,

> Other "softer" measures were implemented that tried to supplant Taiwanese characteristics with Chinese traits: Mandarin and other Chinese dialects became the national languages in education, television and films; buildings were reconstructed in northern Chinese architectural styles; street names in Taipei were replaced with ones that were associated with traditional Confucian values; non-Mandarin speakers were stigmatized and even portrayed as criminals in the media; and local, non-Mandarin cultural expressions were censored, with those judged guilty given corporal punishment.[16]

Conclusion

With China's move to incorporate Hong Kong under its wing, further changes in the social, political, and economic system are likely to occur. One of these will be in the area of language. The predominant language in China is Mandarin. Thus, to integrate under China's umbrella, Hong Kong will probably transition in its language use from English and Cantonese to Mandarin, even though Hong Kong Chief Executive, Carrie Lam, said this would not happen.

Changing from Cantonese to Mandarin would likely begin with the transformation of Hong Kong's education system. Children would learn Mandarin in lower grades and progress through the years, with Cantonese slowly being eliminated from use. Parents might need to learn Mandarin as well. This transition may be quite controversial at first but, over time, would be accepted as the norm. Within the decade, Mandarin is likely to be fully incorporated as the predominant language.

What's at Stake?

First, although the transition away from Cantonese did not happen in 2020, Mandarin is likely to become Hong Kong's official language, aligning with mainland China's culture, policy, and business.

---

13 Anson Au, "Any Attack on the Cantonese Language Will Only Strengthen Hong Kong Identity – Just Look at Taiwan's Experience," *South China Morning Post*, May 15, 2018, https://www.scmp.com/comment/insight-opinion/article/2146238/any-attack-cantonese-language-will-only-strengthen-hong-kong

14 Han Cheung, "KMT Sinicization," *The Ohio State University*, June 12, 2017, https://u.osu.edu/mclc/2017/06/12/kmt-sinicization/

15 Ibid.

16 Anson Au, "Any Attack on the Cantonese Language Will Only Strengthen Hong Kong Identity – Just Look at Taiwan's Experience," *South China Morning Post*, May 15, 2018, https://www.scmp.com/comment/insight-opinion/article/2146238/any-attack-cantonese-language-will-only-strengthen-hong-kong

Second, all signs that are currently in English and communications that are in both English and Cantonese are likely to change to Mandarin. Time will tell.

Third, what is at stake is the further undermining of Hong Kong's independent spirit.

Fourth, the "re-Sinicisation" of Taiwan perpetuates a loss of Taiwanese culture. China continues to push in its efforts to reunify Taiwan. As discussed in the next section, Beijing is facilitated in this effort by using the contention that Taiwan had already been introduced to their dialect.

Part 6

Democracy's Crossroads: Fear of the Dragon Across the Strait

Looming Uncertainty: Taiwan's Quest for Sovereignty

Though just over seventy years old, Taiwan has a thriving economy, remarkable capital city, and rich culture. Taipei, Taiwan's capital, is the seat of government, though China does not recognize the country as a separate entity. Beijing believes the islands of Taiwan are part of its territory according to its 'One China Policy'. Nevertheless, some citizens in Taiwan have sought independence from China, a goal that is unlikely to be realized given Beijing's vehement declarations to the contrary.

The following chapters help create a basic understanding of Taiwan and its relationship with the world, though the issues are much more complicated. However, one point that is important to note is that many countries implicitly acknowledge Taiwan while they do not explicitly make this claim. Subtle support is orchestrated through arms sales, trade, and diplomacy.

Democracy and communism are in a heated battle of words. A blistering fight threatens to explode over the Taiwan Strait, which some believe could be the future site of a military conflict. Increasing tension is gaining strength between Beijing and Taipei. China has warned Taiwan that it will forcibly 'take back its rightful territory'. If so, the United States is likely to be drawn into a war. Meanwhile, China's military capabilities are being developed at an alarming rate, surpassing the United States.

Taiwanese President Tsai Ing-wen won a landslide re-election on January 11, 2020, while walking along a thin tightrope with China. Beijing has offered Taipei appetizing enticements to unify peacefully while at the same time brashly threatening Taiwan with antagonistic warplanes overflight and hostile naval incursions within Taiwan's Exclusive Economic Zone (EEZ).

If China sees Taiwan as its possession and assertively challenges its existence, the two countries will remain at an impasse. Moreover, Hong Kong's National Security Law is a frightening prelude to an eventuality that worries residents of Taiwan. Witnessing the unsettling brutality leveled against Hong Kong citizens after passing the National Security Law and its extradition provisions, it is improbable that Taipei will willingly or easily relinquish control to Beijing. Finally, if the United States lets Taiwan fall, its Asian allies may not be apt to ever again trust Washington's treaty assurances.

Chapter 1

Taiwan's Interconnected Relationship with China

Ownership, Politics, and Economic Ties to China

Introduction

The island of Taiwan, formerly Formosa, has a long history, which will not be thoroughly discussed in this book. However, more recent history is pertinent to this story.

Taiwan/Formosa was never part of the People's Republic of China (PRC), which was formed on October 1, 1949, under Chinese Communist leader Mao Zedong. In 1912, the Republic of China (ROC) was established under Chiang Kai-shek a Chinese military leader who led China out of Japanese occupation but was forced to leave mainland China after the Chinese Civil War. Along with loyalists, military, and legions of others who fled mainland China, Chiang Kai-shek re-established the Republic of China on Taiwan and other islands.

In September 1945, after World War II, the Republic of China (what is now Taiwan) established a provincial government. Both the PRC and ROC lay claim to Taiwan, though the PRC sees Taiwan as a breakaway province. Nevertheless, from 1912 to 1949, the entirety of China and its islands were part of the Republic of China, though when the leaders left mainland China and separated from the PRC, they relocated to the island of Taiwan.

China-Taiwan Geographic Size Comparison

Demographics

Taiwan is a small island nation off the coast of mainland China with a population of over twenty-three million citizens.[1] For perspective, mainland China's distance to Taiwan across the Strait at its shortest point is approximately two-thirds the distance from either Los Angeles to San Diego or the length of Long Island, New York. The Taiwan Strait connects the South China Sea to the East China Sea.

---

1 Worldometer, "Taiwan Demographics," *Worldometer*, n.d., https://www.worldometers.info/demographics/taiwan-demographics/

The nation is composed of several ethnic groups, with the Hoklo Han Chinese accounting for 70 percent of the total population.[2] The next largest ethnic group is the Hakka Han Chinese (14 percent of the population).[3]

Overview of Ownership

Before the 1600s, Taiwan was a self-governing state. In the mid-17th century, Taiwan was a colony of the Netherlands before becoming subject to China's control in the late 17th century after a two-decade intermission of autonomy.[4] In 1895, Japan obtained control over Taiwan after the First Sino-Japanese War, making Taiwan its colony[5] and ruling the state in a constitutional monarchy.[6] After Japan lost World War II, Nationalist Chinese forces (ROC) re-acquired control over Taiwan and later separated from mainland China. Taiwan claimed ownership over both the Chinese mainland and Taiwan's island-state.[7] The Republic of China has vacillated in its position with mainland China based on its leaders and political party affiliation of the election cycle, discussed later in this section.

China and Taiwan's Economic Relations

In 1976, Chiang Kai-shek died. His son, Chiang Ching-kuo, took office as the leader of the Republic of China, aiding in Taiwan's transition to democracy. Chiang Ching-kuo was known for being a complex leader with policies drastically different from his father. Chiang Ching-kuo is famous for his 'three waves' of ideology as life experiences shaped his political beliefs and the type of government he supported.[8]

In 1925, when Chiang Ching-kuo was fifteen years old, he was sent to study in the Soviet Union. Indoctrinated into communism during the twelve formative years of his life, Chiang Ching-kuo joined the Communist Party against his father's will.[9] In 1936, Chiang Ching-kuo denounced his father's Nationalist Party policies in favor of the opposition's Chinese Communist Party policies.[10]

At twenty-seven years old, *Taipei Times* records, "he returned to China, where his father ordered him to read the collected works of Wang Yang-ming (王陽 明), a Ming dynasty neo-Confucian scholar; Letters to Home by Tseng Wen-cheng (曾文正 公家書), a 19th-

---

2   Joyce Chepkemoi, "Ethnic Groups of Taiwan," *World Atlas*, June 7, 2018, https://www.worldatlas.com/articles/ethnic-groups-of-taiwan.html

3   Ibid.

4   John C. Copper, "Taiwan," *Encyclopedia Britannica*, September 10, 2020, https://www.britannica.com/place/Taiwan

5   PBS, "Full Report: Taiwan," *PBS*, n.d., https://www.pbs.org/wgbh/commandingheights/lo/countries/tw/tw_full.html

6   Ibid.

7   John C. Copper, "Taiwan," *Encyclopedia Britannica*, September 10, 2020, https://www.britannica.com/place/Taiwan

8   Hsin-Yi Yeh, "A Sacred Bastion? A Nation in Itself? An Economic Partner of Rising China? Three Waves of Nation-Building in Taiwan After 1949," *Studies in Ethnicities and Nationalism*, April 11, 2014, https://onlinelibrary.wiley.com/doi/abs/10.1111/sena.12074

9   Ruan Ming, "Chiang Ching-kuo: Complex Legacy," *Taipei Times*, January 31, 2004, http://www.taipeitimes.com/News/editorials/archives/2004/01/31/2003096930

10 The Editors of Encyclopedia Britannica, "Chiang Ching-kuo," *Encyclopedia Britannica*, n.d., https://www.britannica.com/biography/Chiang-Ching-kuo

Chinese or Taiwanese?
Pew Research Center Data

IN 2020
*66% VIEW THEMSELVES AS TAIWANESE
*28% AS BOTH TAIWANESE AND CHINESE
*4% AS JUST CHINESE
*83% UNDER 30 SAY THEY DO NOT CONSIDER THEMSELVES CHINESE

IN 1994
*20.2% VIEW THEMSELVES AS TAIWANESE
*44.6% VIEW THEMSELVES AS BOTH TAIWANESE AND CHINESE
*26.2% IDENTIFIED AS JUST CHINESE

century administrator; and Chinese history, geography and philosophy."[11] Chiang Kai-shek's ultimate goal was to transform his son's communist ideology into nationalist ones; he succeeded.

Chiang Ching-kuo spent the next twelve years in China as a fervent member of the nationalist party. However, when Mao Zedong initiated the Cultural Revolution in China, Chiang Ching-kuo returned to Taiwan, where he spent the next thirty-nine years of his life.[12] In Taiwan, Chiang Ching-kuo was known to have transformed from a nationalist to a liberal democrat, shaping Taiwan from a military base to a modern liberal democracy.[13]

Though a demanding ruler, Chiang Ching-kuo did not oppose the communist Chinese party. Chiang Ching-kuo had been classmates in the Soviet Union with then-Chinese paramount leader Deng Xiaoping and began forming cross-strait economic relations with mainland China in the late 1970s. As China entered the world stage, led by Deng Xiaoping, Taiwan started to invest in China. Economically, Taiwan has maintained its financial relations ever since.[14]

On September 15, 1971, U.S. Secretary of State, Henry Kissinger, secretly visited China.[15] Taiwan was still a member of the United Nations General Assembly. In a historic turning point internationally, the United Nations passed a resolution on October 25, 1971 recognizing the PRC as, "the only legitimate representative of China to the United Nations, and to expel forth with the representative of Chiang Kai-shek from the place

---

11 Ruan Ming, "Chiang Ching-kuo: Complex Legacy," *Taipei Times*, January 31, 2004, http://www.taipeitimes.com/News/editorials/archives/2004/01/31/2003096930

12 Ibid.

13 Ibid.

14 Eleanor Albert, "China-Taiwan Relations," *Council on Foreign Relations*, January 22, 2020, https://www.cfr.org/backgrounder/china-taiwan-relations

15 The National Security Archive at George Washington University, "The Beijing-Washington Back-Channel and Henry Kissinger's Secret Trip to China," *The National Security Archive Electronic Briefing Book No. 66,* September 1970 – July 1971, https://nsarchive2.gwu.edu/NSAEBB/NSAEBB66/

which they unlawfully occupy at the United Nations…"[16] In 1972, U.S. President Richard Nixon visited China, delivering the Shanghai Communique, severing ties with the ROC (Taiwan).[17]

The United States continued diplomatic ties with the Republic of China after Chiang Kai-shek's death but U.S. President Jimmy Carter broke these in January 1, 1979 toward the end of his presidency when the U.S. Congress and President signed the Taiwan Relations Act in 1979.[18] This act by the Carter administration shifted power and allowed the PRC to gain some leverage with the ROC. However, ROC President Chiang Ching-kuo refused to bridge the relationship with mainland China exclaiming to the Chinese Communist Party his famous three noes - "no contact, no negotiation, and no compromise" (不接觸，不談判，不妥協).[19]

Chiang Ching-kuo is considered a "driving force behind Taiwan's modernization."[20] Taiwan is a member of fifty international organizations, including APEC, OECD committees, the World Trade Organization, and the Asian Development Bank.[21] In addition, China and Taiwan have signed agreements to allow banks, insurers, and other financial service providers to conduct business in each other's markets.

China accounts for nearly thirty percent of Taiwan's total trade, acting as the island's largest trading partner.[22] In 2018, trade between the two nations reached $150.8 billion.[23] In 2020, investments and trade took a sharp decline. China and Taiwan's trade from January to July amidst the COVID-19 pandemic was estimated to be $87 billion.[24]

Former Taiwanese President Ma Ying-jeou (2008-2016), a KMT leader in Taiwan, signed several agreements with the People's Republic of China (PRC) that strengthened Cross-Strait relations and brought Taiwan closer to Beijing.[25] Though supporting the

---

16   United Nations General Assembly, "2758. (XXVI). Restoration of the Lawful Rights of the People's Republic of China in the United Nations," *United Nations General Assembly*, October 25, 1971, https://digitallibrary.un.org/record/192054?ln=en

17   United States Department of State, Office of the Historian, "Foreign Relations of the United States, 1969-1976, Volume XVII, China, 1969-1972, 203. Joint Statement Following Discussions with Leaders of the People's Republic of China," *United States Department of State, Office of the Historian*, February 27, 1972, https://history.state.gov/historicaldocuments/frus1969-76v17/d203

18   Congress.gov, "H.R. 2479 – Taiwan Relations Act," *Congress.gov*, 1979-1980, https://www.congress.gov/bill/96th-congress/house-bill/2479

19   Chen Mao-hsiung, "Democracy Spells the Demise of Colonialism," *Taipei Times*, December 5, 2019, https://www.taipeitimes.com/News/editorials/archives/2019/12/05/2003726981

20   Yang Hengjun, "Chiang Ching-kuo, China's Democratic Pioneer," *The Diplomat*, December 10, 2014, https://thediplomat.com/2014/12/chiang-ching-kuo-chinas-democratic-pioneer

21   Ministry of Foreign Affairs, Republic of China (Taiwan), "Full Member,", *Ministry of Foreign Affairs, Republic of China (Taiwan)*, n.d., https://www.mofa.gov.tw/enigo/Link3enigo.aspx?n=58BD38F4400A7167&sms=A72EC821FB103DD9

22   Ibid.

23   Bureau of Trade – Trade Statistics, "Value of Exports & Imports by Country," *Bureau of Trade – Trade Statistics*, n.d., https://cus93.trade.gov.tw/FSCE040F/FSCE040F

24   Ibid.

25   Yasuhiro Matsuda (2015) Cross-Strait Relations Under the Ma Ying-jeou Administration: From Economic to Political Dependence?", *Journal of Contemporary East Asia Studies*, 4:2, 3-35, DOI: 10.1080/24761028.2015.11869083

concept of independence, the Taiwanese people resented Ma for selling Taiwan short by running to China for help.[26]

Despite the investments in each other's countries, Taiwan and China have begun facing economic strains in recent years. In 2017, Taiwan's investments in China sharply declined as fewer Taiwanese companies executed planned investments.[27] Furthermore, in 2020, Taiwan looked to tighten regulations over Chinese investments in Taiwan-based companies out of fear of data and security breaches.[28]

Conclusion

Seeking to be independent of mainland China, both economically and administratively, Taiwan has begun to build economic relations with many partners. *Bloomberg* records that Taiwanese firms have doubled their foreign direct investments into the six largest Southeast Asian economies between 2011 to 2015.[29] Additionally, Taiwan has signed several free-trade pacts with Panama, New Zealand, Nicaragua, Singapore, Paraguay, and Guatemala.[30]

In December 2020, Taiwan's economic growth is set to outpace mainland China, a feat that has not happened since 1991.[31] At the end of 2020, the U.S. and Taiwan initiated talks regarding a free trade agreement that Wilson Center experts say would benefit both sides. However, China's opposition is a significant obstacle.[32]

What's at Stake?

First, Taiwan's relations with China have fluctuated with olive branches, economic swings, and growing tensions. Though Taiwan's economic outlook improved going into 2021, its future rests in the Taiwanese people's hands.

Second, the Hong Kong National Security Law is a harbinger of Taiwan's fate. Furthermore, the tide of China's all-powerful threats and control is moving east, and military aggression will test the Taiwanese resolve.

Third, Taiwan's strengthening relations with the United States, supported by arms deals, has increased Cross-Strait tensions, discussed in Part 6, Chapter 4.

---

26 Eleanor Albert, "China-Taiwan Relations," *Council on Foreign Relations*, January 22, 2020, https://www.cfr.org/backgrounder/china-taiwan-relations

27 Staff Writer with CNA, "Taiwanese Investment in China in Sharp Decline," *Taipei Times*, January 23, 2017, https://www.taipeitimes.com/News/biz/archives/2017/01/23/2003663607

28 Kathrin Hille, "Taiwan Looks to Tighten Investment Rules for China," *Financial Times*, June 29, 2020, https://www.ft.com/content/3d9bdbae-1aaa-43f9-a5e9-924199dc9464

29 David Roman, "Taiwan's Economy Shifts Towards Southeast Asia," *Bloomberg*, November 21, 2016, https://www.bloomberg.com/news/articles/2016-11-21/amid-friction-with-china-taiwan-s-attention-drifts-south

30 Ministry of Economic Affairs – Bureau of Foreign Trade, "FTAs Signed with Trading Partners," *Ministry of Economic Affairs – Bureau of Foreign Trade*, n.d., https://www.trade.gov.tw/english/Pages/List.aspx?nodeID=672

31 Sidney Leng, "Taiwan's 2020 Economic Growth Looks to Outpace Mainland China's for First Time in Decades," *South China Morning Post*, December 12, 2020, https://www.scmp.com/economy/china-economy/article/3113603/taiwans-2020-economic-growth-looks-outpace-mainland-chinas

32 Tain-Jy Chen, Scott Kastner, & Dick Nanto, "A U.S.-Taiwan Free Trade Agreement: A Win-Win?," *The Wilson Center*, November 8, 2006, https://www.wilsoncenter.org/event/us-taiwan-free-trade-agreement-win-win

Chapter 2
Taiwan's Political Parties
Distinctions between the KMT and DPP

Introduction

In the 1500s, Portuguese sailors traversing past what is now known as Taiwan recorded the island as "Ilha Formosa", translating to 'beautiful island',[1] though some refute this.[2] Han Chinese settlers migrated to Taiwan in waves during the 17th century.[3] Because 95% of today's Taiwan citizenry are of Han Chinese descent and the universal language is Mandarin, many disregard the diversity of the Taiwanese people.[4] Yet, there are sixteen officially recognized Austronesian-speaking tribes and over 510,000 immigrants, many from China.[5]

In the late 1600s, the Qing dynasty annexed Taiwan.[6] On April 17, 1895, China ceded Taiwan to Japan as part of the Treaty of Shimonoseki's settlement after the First Sino-Japanese War.[7] Shortly afterward, Taiwan inaugurated a short-lived government in May 1895, known as the Republic of Formosa.[8] *Taipei News* notes, "The Republic of Formosa was quite a progressive enterprise. It had officials elected by the people of Taiwan,' and a parliament made up of local gentry. It had its own flag — the now-famous yellow tiger flag — issued paper money and postage stamps (today some of the most valuable in the world) and had a functioning cabinet."[9]

When Japan was granted control over Taiwan, the government of the Republic of Formosa continued functioning as long as it could. Due to Japan's southward expansion and invasion, the government recognized that Japan would inevitability take over the Republic of Formosa, and, ultimately, the short-lived administration surrendered.[10]

The Early Emergence of Political Parties

Until 1945, Japan controlled Taiwan as one of its territories but was forced to surrender the island to the Republic of China (ROC) after World War II.[11] In 1945, Chinese nationalist leader Chiang Kai-shek declared that Japan stole Taiwan from China and

---

1 Government Portal of the Republic of China (Taiwan), "History," *Government Portal of the Republic of China (Taiwan)*, n.d., https://www.taiwan.gov.tw/content_3.php

2 Keoni Everington, "Island Named 'Formosa' by Portuguese May Not be Taiwan: Scholar," *Taiwan News*, November 13, 2017, https://www.taiwannews.com.tw/en/news/3296323

3 Government Portal of the Republic of China (Taiwan), "People", *Government Portal of the Republic of China (Taiwan)*, n.d., https://www.taiwan.gov.tw/content_2.php

4 Ibid.

5 Ministry of Foreign Affairs, Republic of China (Taiwan), "2019-2020 Republic of China at a Glance," *Ministry of Foreign Affairs of Republic of China (Taiwan)*, http://multilingual.mofa.gov.tw/web/web_UTF-8/MOFA/glance2019-2020/English.pdf

6 Eleanor Albert, "China-Taiwan Relations," *Council on Foreign Relations*, January 22, 2020, https://www.cfr.org/backgrounder/china-taiwan-relations

7 Ibid.

8 Gerrit van der Wees, "The Rise and Fall of the Republic of Formosa," *Taipei Times*, June 4, 2018, http://www.taipeitimes.com/News/feat/archives/2018/06/04/2003694280

9 Ibid.

10 Ibid.

11 Taiwan Documents Project, "Supreme Commander for the Allied Powers General Order No. One," *Taiwan Documents Project*, September 2, 1945, http://www.taiwandocuments.org/surrender05.htm

demanded its return. With the United States and Britain supporting the ROC-China claim,[12] Japan returned Taiwan to the Republic of China in September of 1945.[13]

In 1949, after years of conflict in China's civil war between the communists and nationalists, the nationalist Republic of China (ROC) lost, led by Chiang Kai-shek.[14] Following Chiang's defeat, the ROC retreated, and his nationalist political group, the Kuomintang (KMT), fled to Taiwan.

From 1949 to 1987, the KMT governed Taiwan under strict martial law. *The Council on Foreign Relations* noted, "Political dissent was harshly repressed and Taiwanese who had long inhabited the island before 1945 faced discrimination. Taiwan held its first free legislative elections in 1992 and presidential elections in 1996."[15]

In 1986, the Democratic Progressive Party (DPP) was founded,[16] directly challenging the philosophies and agenda of the KMT. Though the KMT instituted a ban on establishing opposing political parties, the restriction was released in 1989, and the DPP was legalized.[17] Since its founding, the DPP has firmly supported Taiwan's independence from China.

In 2000, the first DPP leader, Chen Shui-bian, was elected in Taiwan.[18] After his term ended in 2008, a KMT leader, Ma Ying-jeou, took office. However, in 2016, Tsai Ing-wen's election as the Taiwanese president reclaimed the DPP's position as the top elected official in Taiwan's government. In January 2020, President Tsai was re-elected, claiming her second term of office with a national pro-democracy mandate.[19]

The Complexity of the 'China Factor'

In the most objective sense, the KMT and DDP are direct political rivals of one another since, for the most part, the KMT supports close relations with mainland China and the DDP is in opposition to this stance. Political parties in Taiwan, as in most democratic governments, are not always black and white. Complex factors impact the social, economic, and political ideologies of positions and platforms. Taiwan's political system has a growing grey area, and policy reforms and shifting allegiances have impacted its nature, especially in the 2020 elections.

---

12 Britannica, "Taiwan as Part of the Japanese Empire," Britannica, n.d., https://www.britannica.com/place/Taiwan/Taiwan-as-part-of-the-Japanese-empire

13 Taiwan Documents Project, "Supreme Commander for the Allied Powers General Order No. One," *Taiwan Documents Project*, September 2, 1945, http://www.taiwandocuments.org/surrender05.htm

14 Reuters, "Timeline: Taiwan's Road to Democracy," *Reuters*, December 12, 2011 https://www.reuters.com/article/us-taiwan-election-timeline/timeline-taiwans-road-to-democracy-idUSTRE7BC0E320111213

15 Jaushieh Joseph Wu, "Taiwan After the KMT: Interpreting the 2016 Election," *CSIS*, January 19, 2016, https://www.brookings.edu/wp-content/uploads/2016/01/20160119-Wu-at-CSISFINAL.pdf

16 Democratic Progressive Party, "About", *Democratic Progressive Party*, n.d., https://dpptaiwan.wordpress.com/about/

17 John F. Cooper, "Taiwan's Political Party System – Past, Present and Future," *Taiwan Insight*, January 4, 2018, https://taiwaninsight.org/2018/01/04/taiwans-political-party-system-past-present-and-future/

18 Richard C. Bush, "Taiwan Election Results Explained," *Brookings*, January 16, 2016, https://www.brookings.edu/blog/order-from-chaos/2016/01/16/taiwans-election-results-explained/

19 Cedric Sam, "Taiwan 2020 Election Results," *Bloomberg*, January 11, 2020, https://www.bloomberg.com/graphics/2020-taiwan-election-results

One China, Two Systems
Taiwan's Sunflower Movement

Yu Chen-hua, a professor of political science at the National Chengchi University in Taipei, explains, "It now appears voters will have to take sides in next year's presidential elections as there is no more grey area or ambiguity when it comes to cross-strait policy during the polls."[20] This grey area is often noted as the 'China Factor', the issue of how KMT candidates would conduct cross-strait relations with mainland China.

In the 2020 Taiwanese elections, the five KMT candidates hesitated in speaking about their policy stances with China, dodging the question at each opportunity, until even eight months before the election.[21] Wang Yu-min, a former KMT deputy legislative caucus head, explains this phenomenon, noting, "While the KMT supports having conciliatory ties with the mainland to maintain cross-strait peace, it also faces censure and criticism by the

---

20 Lawrence Chung, "Taiwan's DPP and KMT Launch Primaries for 2020 Presidential Elections," *South China Morning Post,* June 10, 2019, https://www.scmp.com/news/china/politics/article/3013924/taiwans-dpp-and-kmt-launch-primaries-2020-presidential

21 Lawrence Chung, "China: The Five-Letter Word Taiwan's Kuomintang 2020 Hopefuls Hesitate to Spell Out," *South China Morning Post,* May 4, 2019, https://www.scmp.com/news/china/politics/article/3008837/china-five-letter-word-taiwans-kuomintang-2020-hopefuls

pro-independence camp here for trying to sell Taiwan to the mainland, thus making both the party and the KMT hopefuls more cautious over the 'China factor' during presidential elections."[22]

Conclusion

The 'China factor' challenges Taiwan. KMT candidates and Taiwan's general population recognize that Taiwan is not the same as when Chiang Kai-shek ruled the island. Potential leaders must strategize and hedge between a pro-unification stance in which Taiwan would benefit from Beijing's economic cooperation and a pro-independence position. There are many grey areas. Yet, an increasing commitment of the Taiwanese toward autonomy ultimately led to President Tsai Ing-wen's victory. Therefore, the 'China factor' and political parties in Taiwan have more layers than a basic internet search of the KMT and DDP political platforms would reveal.

What's at Stake?

First, policies regarding mainland China sway voter opinions during election years, which adds to the ambiguity of the 'China factor'.

Second, Tsai Ing-wen's stance hardened regarding Taiwan's independence as a response to China's aggressive military acts and changes in Beijing's reaction to Hong Kong. Taiwan's 2020 election spoke volumes regarding the Taiwanese position.

Third, the determination of the Taiwanese people foreshadows a growing tension between Beijing and Taipei. This rising conflict is likely to increase with President Tsai's purchase of U.S. military equipment in 2020. President Tsai will need the people's backing for Taiwan to avoid facing the same fate as Hong Kong as China reels in what the *Global Times* calls "separatists".[23]

---

22 Lawrence Chung, "Taiwan's DPP and KMT Launch Primaries for 2020 Presidential Elections," *South China Morning Post*, June 10, 2019, https://www.scmp.com/news/china/politics/article/3013924/taiwans-dpp-and-kmt-launch-primaries-2020-presidential

23 Yang Sheng, "Taiwan Separatists Panic as Mainland Drops 'Peaceful' in Reunification Narrative," *Global Times*, May 23, 2020, https://www.globaltimes.cn/content/1189242.shtml

Chapter 3

'One China' or an Independent Taiwan?

Taipei and Beijing's Clashing Stance on Sovereignty

Introduction

Since 1949, Taiwan, otherwise known as the Republic of China (ROC), has considered itself an independent country. However, China considers Taiwan and all twenty-three million of its citizenry to be Chinese subjects on a China-owned island.[1] Taiwan's internal factions and political parties view its relationship with China differently, particularly as China attempts to influence Taiwanese citizens through propaganda, build economic bridges between the countries, and incentivize emigration from Taiwan.[2]

The "One China" Affirmation and Rebuttal

In 1992, China affirmed that there is only "One China"; Taiwan belongs to China[3] and is China's "inalienable territory".[4] The "One China" viewpoint posits that mainland China and Taiwan are unified and, while they have different leaders, they will reunify.[5] This statement, known as the 1992 Consensus,[6] was challenged by the Taiwanese Democratic Progressive Party (DPP) leader, Tsai Ing-wen, who declared the "One China" system was intolerable. In a 2019 statement, she announced,

> First, I must emphasize that we have never accepted the "1992 Consensus." The fundamental reason is because the Beijing authorities' definition of the "1992 Consensus" is "one China" and "one country, two systems." The speech delivered by China's leader today has confirmed our misgivings. Here, I want to reiterate that Taiwan absolutely will not accept "one country, two systems." The vast majority of Taiwanese also resolutely oppose "one country, two systems," and this opposition is also a "Taiwan consensus."...
>
> The development of cross-strait relations, as I said very clearly in my new year's talk yesterday, requires that: China must face the reality of the existence of the Republic of China (Taiwan), and not deny the democratic system that the people of Taiwan have established together; second, must respect the commitment of the 23 million people of Taiwan to freedom and democracy, and not foster divisions and offer inducements to interfere with the choices made by the people of Taiwan; third, must handle cross-strait differences peacefully, on the basis of equality, instead of using suppression and intimidation to get Taiwanese to submit; fourth, it must be governments or

---

1. Eleanor Albert, "China-Taiwan Relations," *Council on Foreign Relations*, January 22, 2020, https://www.cfr.org/backgrounder/china-taiwan-relations

2. Zhang Yi, "26 Measures to Promote Cross-Straits Cooperation," *China Daily*, November 4, 2019, https://www.chinadaily.com.cn/a/201911/04/WS5dbfbab2a310cf3e35575468.html

3. People's Daily Online, "Backgrounder: "1992 Consensus" on "One-China" Principle," *People's Daily Online*, October 13, 2004, http://en.people.cn/200410/13/eng20041013_160081.html

4. Ministry of Foreign Affairs of the People's Republic of China, "What is the Reason for Saying 'Taiwan is an Inalienable Part of China'?," *Ministry of Foreign Affairs of the People's Republic of China*, n.d., https://www.fmprc.gov.cn/mfa_eng/ljzg_665465/3568_665529/t17798.shtml

5. Fang-Yu Chen, Austin Wang, Charles K.S. Wu, and Yao-Yuan Yeh, "What Do Taiwan's People Think About Their Relationship to China?," *The Diplomat*, May 29, 2020 https://thediplomat.com/2020/05/what-do-taiwans-people-think-about-their-relationship-to-china/

6. People's Daily Online, "Backgrounder: '1992 Consensus' on 'One-China' Principle," *People's Daily Online*, October 13, 2004, http://en.people.cn/200410/13/eng20041013_160081.html

government-authorized agencies that engage in negotiations. Any political consultations that are not authorized and monitored by the people cannot be called "democratic consultations." This is Taiwan's position, a democratic position.[7]

When the KMT ruled Taiwan, they supported the "One China" policy, not the island's independence. This position was bolstered through deeply-rooted relations with Beijing and Chinese business tycoons on the mainland,[8] incentivizing the KMT to side with China's ideologies. Moreover, the KMT held on to the belief that Taipei was only the temporary capital of the ROC. Nevertheless, former leaders of Taiwan have agreed to the message of "One China", but they contended that the "One China" was governed entirely by Taipei, not Beijing.[9]

---

[7]   Office of the President Republic of China (Taiwan), "President Tsai Issues Statement on China's President Xi's 'Message to Compatriots in Taiwan'," *Office of the President Republic of China (Taiwan)*, January 2, 2019, https://english.president.gov.tw/News/5621

[8]   Eleanor Albert, "China-Taiwan Relations," *Council on Foreign Relations*, January 22, 2020, https://www.cfr.org/backgrounder/china-taiwan-relations

[9]   Lawrence Chung, "Taiwan's DPP and KMT Launch Primaries for 2020 Presidential Elections," *South China Morning Post*, June 11, 2019, https://www.scmp.com/news/china/politics/article/3013924/taiwans-dpp-and-kmt-launch-primaries-2020-presidential

Taiwanese Identity and Democracy

Taiwan's DPP has historically sought independence from mainland China, identifying themselves as Taiwanese, not Chinese. An increasing number of Taiwanese citizens want a democratic state, not a communist one.[10] Much of the rising Taiwanese identity is rooted in the 228 incident, a 1947 political uprising against the KMT government that authorities violently suppressed. One record notes, "…Witnesses estimate that 10,000 Formosans were killed by the Chinese armed forces. The killings were described as 'completely unjustified' in view of the nature of the demonstrations."[11]

Furthermore, many surveys indicate that Taiwanese people mainly identify themselves as exclusively Taiwanese. A 2018 survey by the National Chengchi University revealed that fifty-five percent of the population considered themselves as exclusively Taiwanese, thirty-eight percent regarded themselves as both Taiwanese and Chinese, and only four percent identified as fully Chinese.[12] This rising pro-Taiwan sentiment has drastically impacted elections, policies, and the citizens' outlook as the Taiwanese fight to elect leaders who advocate for a democratic state independent from mainland China.

China's Influence on Foreign Companies

China's view of Taiwan as part of mainland China is not one Beijing keeps quiet. China uses its economic might, political alliances, and vast markets as leverage over businesses in China and financial dealings with smaller states. Beijing demands compliance, obedience, and international support. Even further, any business or state that challenges or contradicts China's Taiwan agenda faces serious consequences.

In August 2019, Chinese-state media, *Xinhua*, first reported that twenty-nine Fortune 500 companies were required to replace maps that either excluded Taiwan and Hainan or South China Sea islands from Chinese territory.[13] The Ministry of Natural Resources asked the companies to replace the maps and depict these islands, including Taiwan, as Chinese territory, saying it was "problematic" and "harms state sovereignty, security, and national interests."[14]

Several Fortune 500 companies conducting business operations in Chinese markets faced repercussions. These included hotels, designers, manufacturers, and airlines. Most of these companies kowtowed to China as they demanded their obedience and insisted on public apologies for calling Taiwan and/or Tibet countries and Hong Kong' independent'. China's anger was loud and unforgiving to the companies it shut down until they bowed down in repentance.

---

10   Dennis V. Hickey, "More and More Taiwanese Favor Independence – and Think the US Would Help Fight for It," *The Diplomat*, December 3, 2020, https://thediplomat.com/2020/12/more-and-more-taiwanese-favor-independence-and-think-the-us-would-help-fight-for-it/

11   Tillman Durdin, "Formosa Killings are put at 10,000," *Taiwan's 400 Years of History*, March 29, 1947, http://www.taiwandc.org/hst-1947.htm

12   Hui-Ling Chen, "Taiwanese/Chinese Identity (1992/06~2020/06)," *Election Study Center National Chengchi University*, July 3, 2020, https://esc.nccu.edu.tw/course/news.php?Sn=166

13   Xinhua, "The "Problem Map" on the Official Websites of 29 Fortune 500 Companies Was Rectified," *Xinhua Net*, August 6, 2019, http://www.xinhuanet.com/2019-08/06/c_1124844896.htm

14   Sixth Tone, "29 Fortune 500 Companies Replace 'Problematic' Maps of China," *Sixth Tone*, August 7, 2019, https://www.sixthtone.com/ht_news/1004404/29-fortune-500-companies-replace-problematic-maps-of-china

Conclusion

When most people think of China, they point to mainland China. However, the People's Republic of China (PRC) and the Republic of China (ROC), Taiwan, have distinct cultural and political differences. Nevertheless, the PRC and ROC, both inhabited by predominantly Chinese people with the same language, cooperate on some levels economically. The question, then, essentially comes down to freedom and liberty. This push and pull of unity and separation is a matter of willingness to preserve Taiwan's cultures and customs versus allowing Beijing to silence adversity, similar to the events that unfolded in Hong Kong.

Questions arise. How much freedom and liberty are the Taiwanese willing to give up if Taiwan yields to China's pressure to become 'One Country'? Are the Taiwanese willing to go to war with China, a formidable adversary that is 267 times larger in geographic size,[15] with a GDP 22 times larger and a population size 59 times larger?[16] The waters in the Taiwan Strait and the skies overhead have become heated to the brink of boiling. Meanwhile, in the fall of 2020, Tsai Ing-wen purchased massive amounts of sophisticated weaponry, signaling Taiwan's intentions.

As Hong Kong reeled from censorship in January 2021, phone seizures, internet blockades, and digital sweeps,[17] the writing is scrawled all over the wall that there will not be Two Systems if the 'two countries' come together. Surrounding countries have taken notice and emphatically urged the United States to support Taiwan. The Japanese State Minister of Defense forcefully suggested that President Joe Biden "be strong" in protecting the "red line", suggesting that the U.S. present a clear policy statement so Japan can prepare a response to the turbulent situation in the East China Sea.[18]

What's at Stake?

First, Taiwan has an elected government and is independent of China. The governments are separate and, while each formally claims the other for historical reasons, they act independently rather than codependent. Thus, unless the will of the people changes in 2024, Taiwan's 2020 election was a rebuke of China's "One China" vision.[19]

---

15 My Life Elsewhere, "Country Size Comparison," *My Life Elsewhere*, n.d., https://www.mylifeelsewhere.com/country-size-comparison/china/taiwan

16 Country Economy, "Country Comparison China vs. Taiwan," *Countryeconomy.com*, n.d., https://countryeconomy.com/countries/compare/china/taiwan

17 Shibani Mahtani, "First Came Political Crimes. Now, A Digital Crackdown Descends on Hong Kong," *The Washington Post*, January 12, 2021, https://www.washingtonpost.com/world/asia_pacific/hong-kong-national-security-law-internet/2021/01/12/01738064-53b6-11eb-acc5-92d2819a1ccb_story.html

18 Ju-min Park, "Japan Official, Calling Taiwan 'Red Line,' Urges Biden to 'Be Strong'," *Reuters*, December 25, 2020, https://www.reuters.com/article/japan-usa-taiwan-china/japan-official-calling-taiwan-red-line-urges-biden-to-be-strong-idUSL4N2J50JX

19 Steven Lee Myers and Chris Horton, "In Blow to Beijing, Taiwan Re-elects Tsai Ing-wen as President," *The New York Times*, January 11, 2020, https://www.nytimes.com/2020/01/11/world/asia/taiwan-election-china.html

Second, a China-Taiwan reunification would demolish the pillars of democracy and free-thinking that Tsai Ing-wen and the Taiwanese democratic government are fighting to protect. The citizens of Taiwan will be forced to pledge to Xi Jinping, undertake Beijing's censored media and propaganda, and accept China's demands to act and think as subjects of the CCP.

Third, if Taiwan falls, other countries in the region may be next.

Chapter 4
Taiwan Strait Crises
Historical Firestorms in Sino-Taiwanese Relations

Introduction

Until 10,000 years ago, there was a land bridge of ice connecting the Neolithic people residing in Taiwan and mainland China. However, as glaciers melted and sea levels rose, a strait bounded by the modern-day South China Sea (SCS) and East China Sea (ECS) emerged.[1] This waterway became known as the Taiwan Strait. Additionally, the region between the body of water to the south (SCS) and the body of water to the north (ECS) is home to several island groupings, including the Penghu Islands. Most importantly, the strait connects mainland China with Taiwan, which is 180 km off China's southeastern coast.[2] The Taiwan Strait, centered between Taiwan and China, has been the focal point of armed crises between the two contesting nations since the 1950s.

The First and Second Taiwan Strait Crises

In June 1950, at the beginning of the Korean War, then-U.S. president, Harry Truman, declared Taiwan a neutral territory and began supplying the nation with economic aid and deploying the U.S. Seventh Fleet through the Taiwan Strait.[3] In 1954, China and Taiwan disputed the offshore Quemoy (Kinmen) and Matsu Islands, instigating the "First Taiwan Strait Crisis" and prompting the U.S. and Taiwan to sign a mutual defense treaty.[4]

In August of 1954, the Chinese People's Liberation Army (PLA) launched attacks on the island of Quemoy after the U.S. lifted a restriction on Taiwan that made it possible for the Nationalists in Taiwan to attack mainland China.[5] This led to months of conflict with dangerous consequences:[6]

1. Chiang Kai-shek deployed 58,000 troops to Quemoy and 15,000 to Matsu
2. The U.S. recommended using nuclear weapons against China
3. China sentenced thirteen U.S. airmen to be shot
4. China seized Ichiang Island
5. The U.S. seriously considered the use of atomic weapons in the Quemoy-Matsu area

Ultimately, China stated in April 1955 that it was ready to negotiate with Taiwan and end the conflict.[7] In August 1955, China released the captured U.S. airmen.[8]

---

1 CIMSEC, "Navigating the Black Ditch: Risks in the Taiwan Strait," *CIMSEC*, December 25, 2014, http://cimsec.org/navigating-black-ditch-risks-taiwan-strait/14052

2 Stratfor, "Taiwan," *Stratfor*, n.d., https://worldview.stratfor.com/region/asia-pacific/taiwan

3 Frontline, "Chronology," *PBS*, n.d., https://www.pbs.org/wgbh/pages/frontline/shows/china/etc/cron.html

4 Ibid.

5 Global Security, "First Taiwan Strait Crisis," *Global Security*, n.d., https://www.globalsecurity.org/military/ops/quemoy_matsu.htm

6 Ibid.

7 Jordan E. Shremshock, "China-Taiwan Relations: The Persistent Deadlock Amid Cycles of Stability and Change," T*he College of Wooster Libraries, Open Works*, 2016, https://openworks.wooster.edu/cgi/viewcontent.cgi?article=8373&context=independentstudy

8 Global Security, "First Taiwan Strait Crisis," *Global Security*, n.d., https://www.globalsecurity.org/military/ops/quemoy_matsu.htm

Democracy's Crossroads: Fear of the Dragon Across the Strait | Part 6

Four years after the First Taiwan Strait Crisis, the second one began. On August 23, 1958, China once again shelled the Quemoy and Matsu Islands, firing over 40,000 rounds of artillery at the Chiang Kai-shek-led Quemoy Islands and prompting the U.S. to deploy forces into the Taiwan Strait.[9] Heavy conflict ensued, and the U.S. conveyed a serious message to China that continued attacks on the strategic Taiwan Strait would lead to a war with the United States.[10]

Wanting to avoid this high-risk conflict, then-leader Mao Zedong engaged in high-level meetings with President Dwight Eisenhower to de-escalate. Ultimately, Mao allowed Taiwan to keep the Kinmen Islands with the short-lived promise of maintaining sovereignty.[11]

China Threatens Taiwan
Is Another Taiwan Strait Crisis Coming?

---

9   M.H. Halperin, "The 1958 Taiwan Straits Crisis: A Documented History (U)," *The RAND Corporation*, December, 1966, https://www.rand.org/content/dam/rand/pubs/research_memoranda/2006/RM4900.pdf

10 Thomas Shattuck, "The Second Taiwan Strait Crisis, Mao and the Middle East," *Majalla*, August 24, 2018, https://eng.majalla.com/node/45916/the-second-taiwan-strait-crisis-mao-and-the-middle-east

11 Ibid.

A Possible Third Taiwan Strait Crisis

Emerging as a global superpower, China has magnified its rhetoric that it will not relinquish control over Taiwan, despite previous pronouncements. Though the first and second Taiwan Strait crises sparked over island control, Beijing has demonstrated their incremental but determined persistence and commitment to use forceful methods in overtaking Taiwan and to 'reunify' by the end of 2021. China's resolve has led to the Taiwan Strait's re-emergence as a heated flashpoint of conflict, particularly as China declared that reunification is inevitable and Tsai Ing-wen strongly rejected China's sovereignty claims.[12]

Even more shockingly, China thoroughly prepared a plan in 2017 to invade and attack Taiwan by the end of 2020, even amid the COVID-19 pandemic.[13] As *Foreign Policy* noted in May 2020, the only possible protection Taiwan has from Chinese attacks is incredibly strained and dangerous U.S.-China relations that, if threatened, have high risks of a full-scale regional conflict.[14] Nevertheless, China continued flexing its muscles and holding military exercises, simulating an invasion of Taiwan,[15] acts that have made Taiwanese officials fearful.

In July 2020, the Taiwanese foreign minister, Joseph Wu, stated that China has been conducting an "unprecedented"[16] number of exercises around the Taiwan Strait. As such, Wu noted that, "The threat is on the rise,"[17] adding, "Other than having full military preparedness, we need to also be very careful to avoid letting Taiwan become an excuse for China to declare war or engage militarily."[18]

Taiwan's wariness was justified. In August 2020, China sent fighter jets that crossed over the median line of the Taiwan Strait, an informal line dividing China and Taiwan.[19] The act of crossing over the median line was one done intentionally only three times since 1999.[20] Taiwan's Defense Ministry reported that its warplanes turned the Chinese fighter jets away. This incident occurred in the fall of 2020 after U.S. and Taiwanese officials met to discuss the COVID-19 pandemic and their future relationship. Chinese state-media reported, "The PLA

---

12 Yimou Lee & Ben Blanchard, "Taiwan President Rejects Beijing Rule; China Says 'Reunification' Inevitable," *Reuters*, May 19, 2020, https://www.reuters.com/article/us-taiwan-president-inauguration/taiwan-president-rejects-beijing-rule-china-says-reunification-inevitable-idUSKBN22W08X

13 Bill Gertz, "China's Secret Military Plan: Invade Taiwan by 2020," *The Washington Free Beacon*, October 3, 2017, https://freebeacon.com/national-security/chinas-secret-military-plan-invade-taiwan-2020/

14 Drew Thompson, "China Is Still Wary of Invading Taiwan," *Foreign Policy*, May 11, 2020, https://foreignpolicy.com/2020/05/11/china-taiwan-reunification-invasion-coronavirus-pandemic/

15 Gerry Shih, "Taiwan Says Threat of Military Clash with China is 'On the Rise'," *The Washington Post*, July 22, 2020, https://www.washingtonpost.com/world/asia_pacific/taiwan-says-threat-of-military-clash-with-china-is-on-the-rise/2020/07/22/6f6da4c8-cc0c-11ea-99b0-8426e26d203b_story.html

16 Ibid.

17 Sammy Westfall, "'The Threat is On the Rise': Taiwan Is Increasingly Worried About China. They're Not Wrong," *Vice*, July 24, 2020, https://www.vice.com/en_us/article/y3z5yv/taiwan-increasingly-worried-about-china-theyre-not-wrong

18 Joel Gehrke, "Taiwan Fears Growing Threat of Attack by China," *The Washington Examiner*, July 22, 2020, https://www.washingtonexaminer.com/policy/defense-national-security/taiwan-fears-growing-threat-of-attack-by-china

19 Brad Lendon, "China Increases Military Drills as Tensions With US Heat Up," *CNN*, August 11, 2020, https://www.cnn.com/2020/08/11/asia/china-taiwan-guam-military-exercises-intl-hnk-scli/index.html

20 Ibid.

Taiwan's Dilemma
Raging Waters Across the Taiwan Strait

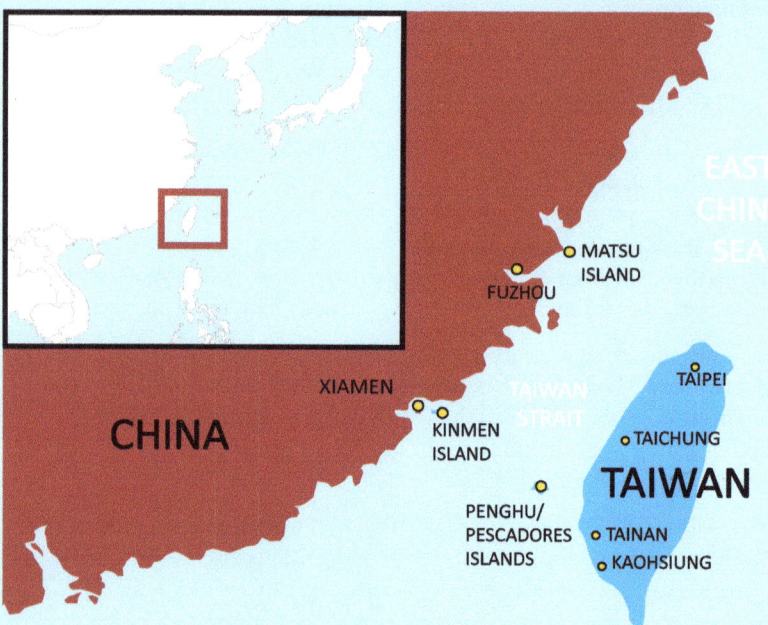

operation is considered a strong response to the US move, which broke a diplomatic bottom line of China-US relations."[21]

Conclusion

Xi Jinping's promise to uphold his 'any means necessary' strategy to achieve his goal of overtaking and forcefully reunifying Taiwan is dangerous, serious, and a genuine threat to Taiwan's democracy. Xi Jinping said Taiwan "must and will be" reunited, even if it means by force.[22]

The Taiwan Strait is riddled with instability and high-level conflicts. Now that Hong Kong's protestors have been silenced, book publishers have been imprisoned, and challengers to the CCP have been kidnapped, the international community must recognize Taiwan's fight for independence and act with the utmost sense of urgency and importance. Without

---

21　Liu Xuanzun, "PLA Fighter Jets Cross 'Middle Line' of Taiwan Straits an Hour Before US Official's Meeting with Tsai Ing-wen," *Global Times,* August 10, 2020, https://www.globaltimes.cn/content/1197280.shtml

22　BBC News, "Xi Jinping says Taiwan 'Must and Will Be' Reunited with China," *BBC News*, January 2, 2019, https://www.bbc.com/news/world-asia-china-46733174

this commitment, China will successfully reunify Taiwan, and democratic governance will be overthrown. However, what is more consequential is the domino effect of salami slicing that will continue until all countries are under China's domination.

What's at Stake?

First, the Taiwan Strait is a hotspot of miscommunication, high-stakes conflict, Chinese aggressiveness, and the potential for the use of nuclear weapons. If another Taiwan Strait Crisis develops, the implications may be riskier than in the past, particularly with sophisticated technologies. Many predict this next event may become a large-scale "international crisis".[23]

Second, China's reunification would eradicate Taiwan's democracy, leaving the citizenry subject to Chinese rule and restrictions.

Third, the U.S. may be drawn into a war to support Taiwan militarily.

Fourth, Donald Trump has been dubbed "the most pro-Taiwan president in U.S. history."[24] Many worry about Biden's commitment to Taiwan during his presidency.

---

23 Keoni Everington, "China Could Create Crisis over Taiwan Strait In 2021: Australian Analyst," *Taiwan News*, May 20, 2020, https://www.taiwannews.com.tw/en/news/3937225

24 Marc A. Thiessen, "Donald Trump is the Most Pro-Taiwan President in U.S. History," *The Washington Post*, January 14, 2020, https://www.washingtonpost.com/opinions/2020/01/14/donald-trump-is-most-pro-taiwan-president-us-history/

Democracy's Crossroads: Fear of the Dragon Across the Strait | Part 6

Chapter 5
U.S.-Taiwan Relations
The Billion Dollar Arms Deal... With Consequences

Introduction

The billion-dollar question is whether or not the United States will engage in another Asia-centered war. However, the present policies in place allow for the sale of military equipment for Taiwan to defend itself. Nevertheless, Beijing is preparing for a showdown and has already started with its gray zone activities, constantly testing Taiwan's military in the sea and overhead and harassing Taiwanese boats or planes on a nearly daily basis. Pressure is mounting both within the People's Liberation Army (PLA) and among Chinese citizenry to 'unify'.

The United States has a history of cautious support for Taiwan, reversing its commitment at times with new administrations. However, in 2020, President Trump underscored the United States' stance, demonstrating a hardened commitment to support Taiwan. Uncertainty looms for 2021 and beyond with President Biden's lack of policy clarity and actual resolve to defend Taiwan.

In 1979, the U.S. issued a joint communiqué with China, stating, "The United States of America recognizes the Government of the People's Republic of China as the sole legal Government of China. Within this context, the people of the United States will maintain cultural, commercial, and other unofficial relations with the people of Taiwan."[1] Though the United States vowed to cut official diplomatic relations with the ROC, months later, with the passing of the Taiwan Relations Act (TRA), the U.S. established unofficial ties with Taiwan.

The Taiwan Relations Act, became effective on January 1, 1979.[2]

It is the policy of the United States–

1. to preserve and promote extensive, close, and friendly commercial, cultural, and other relations between the people of the United States and the people on Taiwan, as well as the people on the China mainland and all other peoples of the Western Pacific area;
2. to declare that peace and stability in the area are in the political, security, and economic interests of the United States, and are matters of international concern;
3. to make clear that the United States' decision to establish diplomatic relations with the People's Republic of China rests upon the expectation that the future of Taiwan will be determined by peaceful means;
4. to consider any effort to determine the future of Taiwan by other than peaceful means, including by boycotts or embargoes, a threat to the peace and security of the Western Pacific area and of grave concern to the United States;
5. to provide Taiwan with arms of a defensive character; and
6. to maintain the capacity of the United States to resist any resort to force or other forms of coercion that would jeopardize the security, or the social or economic

---

1 "Joint Communique on The Establishment of Diplomatic Relations Between the United States of America and The People's Republic of China," January 1, 1979, https://photos.state.gov/libraries/ait-taiwan/171414/ait-pages/prc_e.pdf

2 Congress.gov, "H.R.2479 - Taiwan Relations Act," *Congress.gov*, April 10, 1979, https://www.congress.gov/bill/96th-congress/house-bill/2479

system, of the people on Taiwan.³

The Taiwan Relations Act (TRA), a guide to U.S. policy regarding Taiwan, offers insight into options the U.S. might use for economic, cultural, and military support. However, the TRA does not commit to defending Taiwan. Diplomacy continues to be the preferred route of forward progress in ameliorating the situation between the U.S. and China. Even so, most Taiwanese believe the U.S. will support Taiwan militarily, though U.S. polls show that most Americans do not support military intervention.⁴

A significant part of the TRA was that it established an arms sales relationship between the U.S. and Taiwan. Between 2007 to 2018, U.S. arms sales to Taiwan surpassed $25 billion.⁵ Before President Donald Trump's inauguration, Taiwanese President Tsai Ing-wen spoke with President Trump, the first high-level contact between the U.S. and Taiwan since

U.S.-Taiwan Arms Deal
Billions of Dollars in Arms Sold to Taiwan in 2020

---

3   American Institute in Taiwan, "Taiwan Relations Act (Public Law 96-8, 22 U.S.C. 3301 et seq.)," *American Institute in Taiwan*, January 1, 1979, https://www.ait.org.tw/our-relationship/policy-history/key-u-s-foreign-policy-documents-region/taiwan-relations-act/

4   Dennis V. Hickey, "More and More Taiwanese Favor Independence – and Think the US Would Help Fight for It," *The Diplomat*, December 3, 2020, https://thediplomat.com/2020/12/more-and-more-taiwanese-favor-independence-and-think-the-us-would-help-fight-for-it/

5   Susan V. Lawrence & Wayne M. Morrison, "*Taiwan: Issues for Congress*," *Congressional Research Service*, October 30, 2017, https://fas.org/sgp/crs/row/R44996.pdf

1979.[6] Also, President Trump proposed further arms deals with Taiwan and announced the construction of a $256 million complex, the American Institute in Taiwan, in 2018.[7] At the announcement of the new complex, President Tsai remarked, "The friendship between Taiwan and the U.S. has never been more promising," adding that, "The great story of Taiwan-U.S. relations remains to be filled with the efforts of those that will one day occupy this building."[8]

Though the United States' does not have 'formal' ties with Taiwan, their unofficial alliance has imposed severe strains on U.S.-China relations. The U.S. has directly funded Taiwan's defense system to counter attempts by Beijing to reunify China and Taiwan. In 2018, Taiwan became the world's ninth-largest recipient of weapons between 1979 and 2018[9] while the U.S. supplied over three-quarters of Taiwan's firearms.[10]

In a 2019 speech, at the Great Hall of the People, President Xi Jinping stated that China is fully prepared to use forceful methods in Taiwan to prevent "intervention by external forces," adding, "We make no promise to abandon the use of force, and retain the option of taking all necessary measures."[11] Xi made China's commitment clear. "The country is growing strong, the nation is rejuvenating and unification between the two sides of the strait is the great trend of history."[12]

The Impact of U.S. Intervention

U.S. intervention and arms sales, including the December 2020 approval of a $280 million Field Communication System, threatens and provokes China, but Washington has yet to disengage.[13] In August 2020, top U.S. officials traveled to Taiwan to meet with their Taiwanese counterparts.[14] U.S. Secretary of Health and Human Services Alex Azar met with Taiwan President Tsai Ing-wen, discussing the global response to the COVID-19 pandemic

---

6   Anne Gearan, "Trump Speaks with Taiwanese President, a Major Break With Decades of U.S. Policy on China," *The Washington Post*, December 2, 2016, https://www.washingtonpost.com/world/national-security/trump-spoke-with-taiwanese-president-a-major-break-with-decades-of-us-policy-on-china/2016/12/02/b98d3a22-b8ca-11e6-959c-172c82123976_story.html?utm_term=.be269507dc07

7   Colin Dwyer, "De Facto U.S. Embassy in Taiwan Dedicates New Complex — Over Chinese Objections," *NPR*, June 12, 2018, https://www.npr.org/2018/06/12/619197199/de-facto-u-s-embassy-in-taiwan-dedicates-new-complex-over-chinese-objections

8   Ibid.

9   Eleanor Albert, "China-Taiwan Relations," *Council on Foreign Relations*, January 22, 2020, https://www.cfr.org/backgrounder/china-taiwan-relations

10 Stockholm International Peace Research Institute, "SIPRI Arms Transfers Database," *Stockholm International Peace Research Institute*, n.d., https://www.sipri.org/databases/armstransfers

11 Chris Buckley & Chris Horton, "Xi Jinping Warns Taiwan That Unification Is the Goal and Force Is an Option," *The New York Times*, January 1, 2019, https://www.nytimes.com/2019/01/01/world/asia/xi-jinping-taiwan-china.html

12 Ibid.

13 Lawrence Chung, "Washington Approves US$280 Million Arms Sale to Taiwan," *South China Morning Post*, December 8, 2020, https://www.scmp.com/news/china/diplomacy/article/3113018/washington-approves-us280-million-arms-sale-taiwan

14 Dan Haverty, "U.S. Officials to Hold High-Level Talks With Taiwan as Tensions With China Worsen," *Foreign Policy*, August 7, 2020, https://foreignpolicy.com/2020/08/07/u-s-officials-to-hold-high-level-talks-with-taiwan-as-tensions-with-china-worsen/

and the future of U.S.-Taiwanese relations.[15] The Taiwanese Foreign Ministry commented that the visit was a "testament to the solid mutual trust and smooth communication between Taiwan and the U.S."[16] Beijing warned that China would take "strong countermeasures in response to the U.S. behavior" in response to information surfacing about U.S.-Taiwan discussions.[17]

Conclusion

United States security commitments are not enough to protect states. Although the United States did not have a similar agreement with Hong Kong, many U.S. companies and journalists did conduct business in the city and were threatened. Nonetheless, the U.S. did not protect Hong Kong when China passed a National Security Law that imprisoned numerous individuals in 2020.

As the U.S. relationship with China eroded, and the PRC took over Hong Kong, the global financial hub lost its 'special relationship' status that exempted the city from tariffs.[18] Meanwhile, the United States' consistent arms sales to Taiwan demonstrated a more substantial commitment from the U.S. to protect Taiwan than the strong rhetoric and limited intervention in Hong Kong. However, tensions between China and Taiwan are rising, and China's goal to reunify appears to be intensifying as Beijing drops the word 'peaceful' when speaking about 'reunification'.[19]

The world has watched as China has eradicated freedom of speech, freedom of expression, privacy, and autonomy in Hong Kong, a territory promised to be 'semi-autonomous'. After seeing the liberties taken away from Hong Kong residents, Taiwan, a bastion of democracy, is destined for a similar fate. Free-thinking and autonomy – the very cornerstones of U.S. democratic values – are threatened, although some question whether U.S. intervention is helping or hurting regional disputes.

---

15 HHS Press Office, "HHS Secretary Azar Meets with President Tsai of Taiwan and Praises Taiwan's Transparent COVID-19 Response," *U.S. Department of Health & Human Services*, August 10, 2020, https://www.hhs.gov/about/news/2020/08/10/hhs-secretary-azar-meets-with-president-tsai-of-taiwan-and-praises-taiwans-transparent-covid-19-response.html

16 Dan Haverty, "U.S. Officials to Hold High-Level Talks With Taiwan as Tensions With China Worsen," *Foreign Policy*, August 7, 2020, https://foreignpolicy.com/2020/08/07/u-s-officials-to-hold-high-level-talks-with-taiwan-as-tensions-with-china-worsen/

17 Cate Cadell & Ben Blanchard, "China Threatens Countermeasures as Taiwan Prepares for U.S. Visit," *Reuters*, August 5, 2020, https://www.reuters.com/article/us-taiwan-usa/china-threatens-countermeasures-as-taiwan-prepares-for-us-visit-idUSKCN2520FL

18 Michelle Toh & Laura He, "The United States is Treating Hong Kong as Mainland China. Business is Starting to do the Same," *CNN Business*, July 16, 2020, https://www.cnn.com/2020/07/15/business/hong-kong-special-trade-status-us-intl-hnk/index.html

19 Yew Lun Tian & Yimou Lee, "China Drops Word 'Peaceful' in Latest Push for Taiwan 'Reunification'," *Reuters*, May 21, 2020, https://uk.reuters.com/article/uk-china-parliament-taiwan-idUKKBN22Y06Q

What's at Stake?

First, 'peaceful' reunification is less likely.

Second, the Taiwan Relations Act offers support to Taiwan, but it does not include a military commitment. Meanwhile, the Japanese have requested clarity from the U.S. in order to make decisions regarding China's growing threat.

Third, the U.S. provided support in arms sales to Taiwan, though increased U.S. involvement angers China, which may provoke further aggression from Beijing. Nevertheless, without strong pushback, Taiwan risks being subjected to China's laws, surveillance, and communist principles, despite its citizens' desire to remain democratic.

Part 7

Risk and Uncertainty for Sovereign Islands, Sea, and Air

Staking Claims and Asserting Sovereignty in the East China Sea

Japan's longest-serving Prime Minister, Abe Shinzō, submitted his resignation in August 2020 and Yoshihide Suga began as its Prime Minister in September. Xi Jinping started building rapport with Yoshihide Suga shortly afterward. Xi hopes that China and Japan will establish a cooperative, compatible relationship and find common ground on historical issues. This "cooperative partnership" includes potential economic, social, and political relationships and reciprocal supply interchanges along Beijing's win-win goals based upon "China's Peaceful Rise" declaration. With the Summer Olympic Games slated for July 23, 2021 – August 8, 2021 in Tokyo and the Winter Olympic Games held shortly afterward in Beijing from February 4, 2022 to February 20, 2022, Xi and Suga had much to discuss.

China's shared vision for humanity is very different than that of Japan's, South Korea, or even North Korea. Yet, Chinese President Xi Jinping committed to Regional Comprehensive Economic Partnership (RCEP). Fifteen of the sixteen countries in the Asia-Pacific region signed.

Australia	Indonesia	Myanmar	South Korea
Brunei	Japan	New Zealand	Thailand
Cambodia	Laos	Philippines	Vietnam
China	Malaysia	Singapore	

Though negotiations for the RCEP began in August 2011, this agreement was finally signed on November 15, 2020, without India, though India is invited to return. The signing of the RCEP was seen as an economic victory over the U.S., demonstrating that Beijing is Asia's partner and regional hegemon. The RCEP signing happened amidst China's continued aggression in the South China Sea and the coronavirus pandemic.

Nevertheless, in October 2020, the Pew Research Center published ratings - 86% of Japanese citizens viewed China unfavorably while 75% of South Koreans viewed China unfavorably. During the pandemic, half a million South Koreans petitioned to ban Chinese citizens from entering their country. East Asia also worries about China's Air Defense Identification Zone (ADIZ) and islands that China claims as theirs. The waters are not calm in East Asia as China attempts to use diplomacy and money to pacify its neighbors.

Chapter 1

Conflict in the East China Sea

Overview of Japan and China's Disputed Senkaku/Diaoyu Islands

Introduction

In 2013, China declared an Air Defense Identification Zone (ADIZ) over the entire East China Sea, overlapping the borders of Japan's established ADIZ. This act was part of a long series of recent Sino-Japanese regional conflicts, though sovereignty over the Senkaku (Diaoyu) Islands has been contested by the two nations for centuries.

The Senkaku Islands are a now-uninhabited archipelago in the East China Sea consisting of eight islands: the Uotsuri, Kuba, Taisho (Kumeakashima), Kitakojima, Minamikojima, Tobise, Okinokitaiwa, and Okinominamiiwa.[1] The surrounding waters of the islands, rich in biodiversity, are vital fishing grounds and energy sources.[2] In 1994, the Japanese government approximated there are 500 million kiloliters of oil and gas deposits in the leftward Japanese side of the East China Sea.[3]

Thus, in this natural resource and fishing hotspot, China and Japan dispute the ownership of the Senkaku Islands; both countries recognize that natural resources are the reason for conflict. In the first-ever Japan-China Summit Meeting in September 1972, the then-Japanese Prime Minister, Kukuei Tanaka, asked the then-Chinese Premier Zhou Enlai how the nations should settle the disputed claims over the Senkaku Islands. Zhou Enlai responded, "I don't want to talk about the Senkaku Islands, this time. It is not good to discuss this now. It became an issue because of the oil out there. If there wasn't oil, neither Taiwan nor the United States would make this an issue."[4]

U.S. Relationship with Japan and Ownership of the Senkaku Islands

January 14, 1895:[5] The government of Japan erected a marker on the Senkaku Islands, originating Japan's 'historical claims' to the islands.

1951 San Francisco Peace Treaty:[6] U.S. obtained ownership of the Senkaku Islands after WWII.

---

1. Review of Island Studies, "The Senkaku Islands: Location, Area, and Other Geographical Data," *Review of Island Studies*, February 17, 2015, https://www.spf.org/islandstudies/info_library/senkaku-islands-02-geography--02_geo001.html

2. Ministry of Foreign Affairs of Japan, "Information about the Senkaku Islands" *Ministry of Foreign Affairs of Japan*, n.d., https://www.mofa.go.jp/a_o/c_m1/senkaku/page1we_000009.html

3. Japanese Parliament, "Minutes of the House of Councilors, 164th Diet Committee for Administrative surveillance, No. 4 [Japanese]", *Japanese Parliament*, n.d., http://kokkai.ndl.go.jp/SENTAKU/sangiin/164/0016/16404240016004c.html. A Japanese specialist told that this is a thirtieth of the estimation in 1970 based on ECAFE report in 1969

4. Ministry of Foreign Affairs of Japan, "Senkaku Islands Q&A," *Ministry of Foreign Affairs of Japan*, n.d., https://www.mofa.go.jp/region/asia-paci/senkaku/qa_1010.html

5. Ministry of Foreign Affairs of Japan, "Three Truths about the Senkaku Islands," *Ministry of Foreign Affairs of Japan*, n.d., https://www.mofa.go.jp/region/asia-paci/senkaku/three_truths_1.html

6. Ministry of Foreign Affairs of Japan, "Senkaku Islands Q&A," *Ministry of Foreign Affairs of Japan*, n.d., https://www.mofa.go.jp/region/asia-pacisenkaku/qa_1010.html

1971 Agreement Between Japan and the United States of America Concerning the Ryukyu Islands and the Daito Islands (Okinawa Reversion Agreement):[7] U.S. returns ownership of the Senkaku Islands to Japan; the U.S. makes it clear that the Japan-U.S. Security Treaty applies to the Senkaku Islands

Alongside the signing of the San Francisco Peace Treaty, the agreement that ended World War II and returned Japanese sovereignty,[8] the United States and Japan co-signed the 1951 Japan-U.S. Security Treaty.[9] The Japan-U.S. Security Treaty guarantees U.S. commitment to protecting Japan's sovereignty in exchange for the right to establish military bases and deploy troops on Japanese territory.[10] The treaty states,

> Each Party recognizes that an armed attack against either Party in the territories under the administration of Japan would be dangerous to its own peace and safety and declares that it would act to meet the common danger in accordance with its constitutional provisions and processes. Any such armed attack and all measures taken as a result thereof shall be immediately reported to the Security Council of the United Nations in accordance with the provisions of Article 51 of the Charter. Such measures shall be terminated when the Security Council has taken the measures necessary to restore and maintain international peace and security.[11]

When the Treaty of San Francisco, also known as the Treaty of Peace with Japan, was signed in 1951, its provisions granted the United States administration over the Senkaku Islands. The *Council on Foreign Relations* notes,

> Article 3 [of the Treaty of San Francisco gave the United States sole powers of administration of "Nansei Shoto south of 29 north latitude (including the Ryukyu and the Daito Islands)...." In 1953, the U.S. Civil Administration of the Ryukyus issued U.S. Civil Administration of the Ryukyus Proclamation 27 (USCAR 27), which defined the boundaries of "Nansei Shoto [the southwestern islands] south of 29 degrees north latitude' to include the Senkakus (Diaoyu/Diaoyutai islands)."[12]

The United States returned ownership of the Senkaku Islands to Japan on June 17, 1971, with the Okinawa Reversion Agreement, also known as the Agreement Between Japan and the United States of America Concerning the Ryukyu and Daito Islands.[13] The Okinawa Reversion Agreement specified the return of "all and any powers of administration,

---

7   Ministry of Foreign Affairs of Japan, "Three Truths about the Senkaku Islands," *Ministry of Foreign Affairs of Japan*, n.d., https://www.mofa.go.jp/region/asia-paci/senkaku/three_truths_1.html

8   Review of Island Studies, "The Treaty of Peace with Japan and Takeshima's Legal Status," *Review of Island Studies*, June 10, 2013, https://www.spf.org/islandstudies/research/a00002.html

9   Lindsay Maizland & Beina Xu, "The U.S.-Japan Security Alliance," *Council on Foreign Relations*, August 22, 2019, https://www.cfr.org/backgrounder/us-japan-security-alliance

10 Mark E. Manyin, "The Senkakus (Diaoyu/Diaoyutai) Dispute: U.S. Treaty Obligations," *Congressional Research Service*, October 14, 2016, https://fas.org/sgp/crs/row/R42761.pdf

11 Ministry of Foreign Affairs of Japan, "Japan-U.S. Security Treaty," *Ministry of Foreign Affairs of Japan*, n.d., https://www.mofa.go.jp/region/n-america/us/q&a/ref/1.html

12 Mark E. Manyin, "The Senkakus (Diaoyu/Diaoyutai) Dispute: U.S. Treaty Obligations," *Congressional Research Service*, October 14, 2016, https://fas.org/sgp/crs/row/R42761.pdf

13 Treaty on Reversion to Japan of the Ryukyu and Daito Islands, signed Jun. 17, 1971, 23 U.S.T. 446.

legislation, and jurisdiction"[14] over the Ryuku and Daito Islands. Furthermore, Article I of the Okinawa Reversion Agreement defined the islands to be returned to Japan as "all territories with their territorial waters with respect to which the right to exercise all and any powers of administration, legislation and jurisdiction was accorded to the United States of America under Article 3 of the Treaty of Peace with Japan..."[15]

Nevertheless, China described the "backroom deals between the United States and Japan concerning Diaoyu Dao," using the Chinese name for the Senkaku Islands, as "illegal and invalid".[16] The United States has continued identifying the Senkakus as Japanese territory and, in 1971, reported: "the Japanese claim to sovereignty over the Senkakus is strong, and the burden of proof of ownership would seem to fall on the Chinese."[17]

Competing Historic Claims

China claims that Taiwan, an island territory whose government identifies itself as an autonomous, democratic state, is part of mainland China. Additionally, China cites two 'historical' reasons for its claim over the Senkaku Islands:[18] the archipelago was once Taiwanese territory, and the Senkakus were once Chinese territory.

---

14   Treaty on Reversion to Japan of the Ryukyu and Daito Islands, signed Jun. 17, 1971, 23 U.S.T. 446.

15   Ibid.

16   State Council Information Office, The People's Republic of China, "White Paper on Diaoyu Dao, Full Text: Diaoyu Dao, an Inherent Territory of China," *State Council Information Office, The People's Republic of* China, September 25, 2012, http://en.people.cn/90785/7960320.html

17   Ministry of Foreign Affairs of Japan, "Senkaku Islands Q&A" *Ministry of Foreign Affairs of Japan*, n.d., https://www.mofa.go.jp/region/asia-paci/senkaku/qa_1010.html

18   Koichi Sato, "The Senkaku Islands Dispute: Four Reasons of the Chinese Offensive - A Japanese View," *Taylor & Francis Online,* June 23, 2019, https://www.tandfonline.com/doi/full/10.1080/24761028.2019.1626567

Meanwhile, Taiwan, considering itself independent, also claims the Senkaku Islands. Taiwan submitted claims for the Senkaku Islands, which it calls the Diaoyotai Lieyu, on April 20, 1971, after the United Nations analyzed the rich oil deposits in the East China Sea.[19] Shortly after, China officially submitted claims for the Diaoyu Islands on December 30, 1971.[20]

China cites 'historic' ownership over the Senkakus. During the Ming dynasty (1368-1644), Chinese maps and documents record the Senkakus as Chinese territory.[21] Furthermore, Beijing asserts that during the Qing dynasty (1644-1911), the Chinese government annexed the Senkaku Islands under the jurisdiction of Formosa (Taiwan).[22]

Meanwhile, Japan claims to have discovered the Senkaku Islands, uninhabited, in 1884.[23] Japan annexed the five islets in 1895.[24] The Japanese foreign ministry states,

> From 1885, surveys of the Senkaku Islands had been thoroughly conducted by the Government of Japan through the agencies of Okinawa Prefecture and by way of other methods. Through these surveys, it was confirmed that the Senkaku Islands had been not only uninhabited but showed no trace of having been under the control of the Qing dynasty of China...
>
> A United Nations agency conducted an academic survey in 1968 which indicated the possibility of the existence of petroleum resources in the East China Sea, which urged the Government of China and Taiwan authorities to begin to make their own assertions about territorial sovereignty of the Senkaku Islands since 1970. Prior to this, there had been no objection expressed by any country or region to Japan's sovereignty over the islands.[25]

China and Taiwan reject Japan's claim to have discovered the island uninhabited in 1884.[26] Nevertheless, they claim that Japan regained control of the Senkakus through an unequal treaty. Japan and the Qing dynasty signed the Treaty of Shimonoseki in April 1895, signaling the end of the First Sino-Japanese War. In the treaty, China ceded Formosa (Taiwan) along "with all the islands appertaining or belonging to the said island of

---

19 Ministry of Foreign Affairs, Japan, "The Senkaku Islands," *Ministry of Foreign Affairs,* Japan, March 2013, https://www.mofa.go.jp/region/asia-paci/senkaku/pdfs/senkaku_en.pdf

20 Koichi Sato, "The Senkaku Islands Dispute: Four Reasons of the Chinese Offensive - A Japanese View," *Taylor & Francis Online,* June 23, 2019, https://www.tandfonline.com/doi/full/10.1080/24761028.2019.1626567

21 State Council Information Office, The People's Republic of China, "White Paper on Diaoyu Dao, Full Text: Diaoyu Dao, an Inherent Territory of China," *State Council Information Office, The People's Republic of* China, September 25, 2012, http://en.people.cn/90785/7960320.html

22 Ibid.

23 Ministry of Foreign Affairs of Japan, "Recent Developments in Japan-China Relations. Basic Facts on the Senkaku Islands and the Recent Incident," *Ministry of Foreign Affairs of Japan,* October, 2010, https://www.mofa.go.jp/%20region/asia-paci/china/pdfs/facts1010.pdf

24 D.Z., "Who Really Owns the Senkaku Islands?," *The Economist,* December 3, 2013, https://www.economist.com/the-economist-explains/2013/12/03/who-really-owns-the-senkaku-islands

25 Ministry of Foreign Affairs of Japan, "Three Truths about the Senkaku Islands," *Ministry of Foreign Affairs of Japan,* n.d., https://www.mofa.go.jp/region/asia-paci/senkaku/three_truths_1.html

26 Ministry of Foreign Affairs of the People's Republic of China, "Diaoyu Dao, An Inherent Territory of China," *Ministry of Foreign Affairs of the People's Republic of* China, September 26, 2012, https://www.fmprc.gov.cn/mfa_eng/topics_665678/diaodao_665718/t973774.shtml

Formosa."[27] China asserts that during the negotiations for this treaty, the Senkaku Islands were not discussed transparently.[28] Furthermore, China and Taiwan assert that Japan took advantage of its victory in the Sino-Japanese War to overtake the Senkaku Islands.[29]

Meanwhile, Japan holds the position that its claims to the islands are separate from the Sino-Japanese War settlements. Japan's foreign ministry comments, "[T]hese islands were neither part of Taiwan nor part of the Pescadores Islands which were ceded to Japan from the Qing dynasty in accordance with the Treaty of Shimonoseki signed in April of 1895. Therefore, Japan did not seize the islands as a result of the Sino-Japanese War."[30]

Conclusion

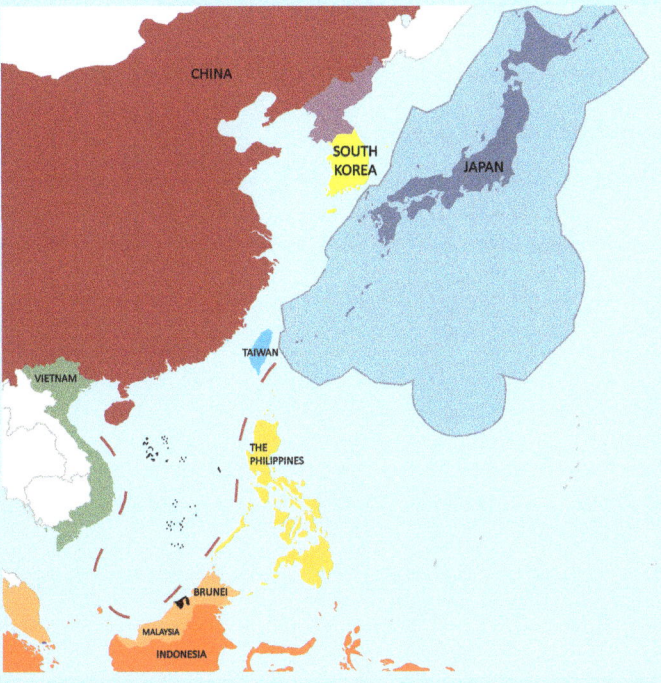

Japan's Exclusive Economic Zone (EEZ)

---

27 Mark E. Manyin, "The Senkakus (Diaoyu/Diaoyutai) Dispute: U.S. Treaty Obligations," *Congressional Research Service*, October 14, 2016, https://fas.org/sgp/crs/row/R42761.pdf

28 Xinhua, "Full Text: Diaoyu Dao, an Inherent Territory of China," *People Daily*, September 25, 2012, http://en.people.cn/102774/7960445.html

29 Mark E. Manyin, "The Senkakus (Diaoyu/Diaoyutai) Dispute: U.S. Treaty Obligations," *Congressional Research Service*, October 14, 2016, https://fas.org/sgp/crs/row/R42761.pdf

30 Ministry of Foreign Affairs of Japan, "Three Truths about the Senkaku Islands," *Ministry of Foreign Affairs of Japan*, n.d., https://www.mofa.go.jp/region/asia-paci/senkaku/three_truths_1.html

Nevertheless, China and Japan recognized their disputes would conflict with their fishing interests as both nations disagreed on the rights to fish in the East China Sea. On November 11, 1997, both parties signed the Japan-China Fisheries Agreement[31] The pact divided the East China Sea into five sections. Japan and China can regulate fishing within their respective Exclusive Economic Zone (EEZ) and cooperate on fishing in certain areas of the East China Sea. Still, the agreement did not determine any regulations on fishing around the Senkaku Islands.[32]

What's at Stake?

First, the persistent claims from both Japan and China that the Senkaku Islands are within their sovereign rights means that any activity in the East China Sea, such as China's Air Defense Identification Zone (ADIZ) over the region, will only escalate the conflict.

Second, the local fisheries dependent on the catch in the waters around the Senkaku's will be forced to find alternative waters to fish. Seeing that most fishing rights in the South China Sea and the East China Sea are contested by China and overfishing is rampant, there may not be sufficient replacements. Furthermore, fish stocks are being depleted at a rapid rate. The Sea of Japan alone lost 34.7% of its fishery size.[33]

Third, toothless laws that lack enforcement, such as the negotiations between China and Japan, undermine the validity of such agreements and diplomatic methods of reaching settlements. China and Taiwan's claims to the archipelago threaten Japanese sovereignty and the legitimacy of international agreements that returned the islands to Japan's authority after World War II.

---

31 *Nicchu Gyogyou Kyotei no Gaiyoto* [Summary of the Japan-China Fisheries Agreement], *Ministry of Agriculture, Forestry, and Fisheries, Japan*. Accessed March 16, 2018. http://www.jfa.maff.go.jp/j/press/kokusai/161118_26.html

32 Ibid.

33 Arthur Nelsen, "East China Sea Fish Stocks Hit Hard by Global Warming," *China Dialogue Ocean*, March 5, 2019, https://chinadialogueocean.net/6923-east-china-sea-global-warming/

Chapter 2

Conflict over the Senkaku Islands

Unresolved Disputes that Spilled into 2020

Introduction

The ambiguity of the 1997 Japan-China Fisheries Agreement created an air of conflict as Chinese and Japanese vessels confronted one another. One major incident flared diplomatic tensions. This event, recorded as the 2010 Boat Collision Incident, ensued on September 7, 2010, when a Chinese fishing trawler inched toward the Senkaku Islands.[1] The Japanese Coast Guard approached the Chinese vessel, and the confrontation soon turned into a collision as the Chinese fishing trawler rammed into the Japan Coast Guard vessel.[2] The Japanese officials accused the Chinese fishing trawler captain, Zhan Qixiong, of intentionally colliding with two Japanese ships, resulting in his arrest for two weeks.[3]

Upon his return to China, Zhan Qixiong remained adamant that he was unlawfully arrested. He avowed, "The Diaoyutai Islands are a part of China. I went there to fish. That's legal," furthering, "Those people grabbed me - that was illegal."[4] Beijing retaliated economically, cutting off the exports of rare earth metals to Japan.[5] The Chinese foreign ministry stated, "The Japanese side must make an apology and compensation for this incident."[6]

The issue was not put to bed in 2010. In fact, in 2014, Japan filed a lawsuit in the Naga District Court in Okinawa seeking retribution of USD $140,000 to pay for damages of the Japanese vessels.[7] In response, Chinese spokesperson Hua Chunyung told reporters that the 2010 incident "was a severe incident when the Japanese side grossly infringed upon China's territorial sovereignty and damaged Chinese fishermen's legitimate rights and interests."[8] He reaffirmed that "any judicial measures adopted by the Japanese side against Chinese fishermen and fishing boats, including detention and investigation are illegal and invalid."[9]

Unresolved disputes over the claims to the Senkaku Islands continued throughout the 2010 decade and into the 2020 pandemic. For months, beginning in April of 2020, China

---

1 Council on Foreign Relations, "China's Maritime Disputes," *Council on Foreign Relations*, n.d., https://www.cfr.org/timeline/chinas-maritime-disputes

2 Shannon Tiezzi, "Japan Seeks Chinese Compensation Over 2010 Boat Collision Incident," *The Diplomat*, February 14, 2014, https://thediplomat.com/2014/02/japan-seeks-chinese-compensation-over-2010-boat-collision-incident/

3 Ibid.

4 BBC News, "Japan Rejects China's Demand for Formal Apology," *BBC News*, September 25, 2010, https://www.bbc.com/news/world-11410568

5 Keith Bradsher, "Amid Tension, China Blocks Vital Exports to Japan," *The New York Times*, September 22, 2010, https://www.nytimes.com/2010/09/23/business/global/23rare.html?pagewanted=all&_r=0

6 BBC News, "Japan Rejects China's Demand for Formal Apology," *BBC News*, September 25, 2010, https://www.bbc.com/news/world-11410568

7 The Japan Times, "Japan Files Damages Suit Against Chinese Captain Over 2010 Collision," *The Japan Times*, February 13, 2014, https://www.japantimes.co.jp/news/2014/02/13/national/crime-legal/japan-files-damages-suit-against-chinese-captain-over-2010-collision/

8 Shannon Tiezzi, "Japan Seeks Chinese Compensation Over 2010 Boat Collision Incident," *The Diplomat*, February 14, 2014, https://thediplomat.com/2014/02/japan-seeks-chinese-compensation-over-2010-boat-collision-incident/

9 Ibid.

deployed sixty-seven ships near the Senkaku Islands.[10] Chinese vessels remained near the islands for what became known as the '100-Day Push'.[11] On June 17, 2020, Japan's chief cabinet secretary, Yoshihide Suga, stated, "The Senkaku Islands are under our control and are unquestionably our territory historically and under international law. It is extremely serious that these activities continue. We will respond to the Chinese side firmly and calmly."[12] Tokyo stated China's campaign to overtake the islands had become "relentless".[13]

Furthermore, in June 2020, Japan passed a bill that would change the status of the Senkaku Islands, despite China's claims. The legislation changes the islands' administrative status, prompting protest from China, who shortly afterward deployed coast guard vessels to the Senkakus.[14] This incident became worrisome.

In another dramatic episode, Japan nationalized the then-private islands to prevent an expected sale to Tokyo's former governor seeking to develop the features. In 2012, Chinese protests turned violent.[15] Citizens ransacked the Japanese embassy, screaming anti-Japanese rhetoric, and destroying Japanese cars, restaurants, and businesses.[16]

In June 2020, Taiwanese President Tsai reiterated that the Senkaku Islands belong to Taiwan and pledged to protect the rights of its fishermen in those waters.[17] Neither party involved seems willing to relinquish their claims anytime soon. On the contrary, minor actions, diplomatic communiqués, and press releases have escalated as the current tinderbox in the East China Sea is ready to ignite. One incident could provoke the tense region, transforming sparks into flames, and the Senkaku Islands conflict into a regional catastrophe.

Conclusion

Diplomacy and multilateral approaches to peace become far more difficult when the temperatures continue to rise a few degrees with each territorial conflict. Another fishing boat

---

10 Murukesh Krishan, "China Teases Japan in East China Sea, Sends 67 Ships Near Tokyo-Controlled Senkaku Islands Since April: Report," *Times Now News*, June 23, 2020, https://www.timesnownews.com/international/article/china-teases-japan-in-east-china-sea-sends-67-ships-near-tokyo-controlled-senkaku-islands-since-april-report/610438

11 Jesse Johnson, "China's 100-Day Push Near Senkaku Islands Comes at Unsettling Time for Sino-Japanese Ties," *The Japan Times*, July 27, 2020, https://www.japantimes.co.jp/news/2020/07/27/national/china-japan-senkaku-islands/#.XzgovRNKhZ0

12 Murukesh Krishan, "China Teases Japan in East China Sea, Sends 67 Ships Near Tokyo-Controlled Senkaku Islands Since April: Report," *Times Now News*, June 23, 2020, https://www.timesnownews.com/international/article/china-teases-japan-in-east-china-sea-sends-67-ships-near-tokyo-controlled-senkaku-islands-since-april-report/610438

13 Keita Nakamura, "Japan's Defense White Paper Takes Aim at China's Actions During Pandemic," *The Japan Times*, July 14, 2020, https://www.japantimes.co.jp/news/2020/07/14/national/japan-defense-white-paper-china-coronavirus/

14 Brad Lendon, "Why This Japan-China Island Dispute Could Be Asia's Next Military Flashpoint," *CNN*, June 22, 2020, https://edition.cnn.com/2020/06/20/asia/china-japan-islands-dispute-hnk-intl/index.html

15 Council on Foreign Relations, "China's Maritime Disputes," *Council on Foreign Relations*, n.d., https://www.cfr.org/timeline/chinas-maritime-disputes

16 Brad Lendon, "Why This Japan-China Island Dispute Could Be Asia's Next Military Flashpoint," *CNN*, June 22, 2020, https://edition.cnn.com/2020/06/20/asia/china-japan-islands-dispute-hnk-intl/index.html

17 George Liao, "President Tsai Reiterates Taiwan's Sovereignty over Diaoyutai Islands," *Taiwan News*, June 24, 2020, https://www.taiwannews.com.tw/en/news/3953552

Exclusive Economic Zone (EEZ) of Japan and China
The Senkaku/Diaoyu Island Dispute

clash, arrest, or miscommunication could trigger a miscalculation. Each time this occurs, the risk heightens, and the possibility of a devastating regional conflict could involve the entire international community. With sparks flying in the Taiwan Strait and uncertainty about the U.S. resolve, concerns grow.

What's at Stake?

First, the Senkaku Islands are another stop in China's 'Salami Slicing' world tour. Navigation, tourism, trade, fishing, and resources are essential to states' economies surrounding the East China Sea.

Second, provocative incidents with Japan could lead the U.S. into a war. Thus, it is in the best interests of the U.S. to simmer the tensions.

Third, U.S.-China conflicts in East Asia may spill over into the South China Sea, where the United States has increased its activity and engagement in regional disputes.

Chapter 3

Air Defense Identification Zones

East Asian State's Quest to Control Overflight

Introduction

Black clouds are filling the skies. Seeking primacy and oversight, China controls much of the airspace over the East China Sea. China covered a large swath of the East China Sea with its Air Defense Identification Zone (ADIZ) and is threatening to create another one over the South China Sea to defend its claim to the region.[1]

Air Defense Identification Zones were created as a buffer to identify aircraft before entering the airspace. The goal is to take defensive measures and defend land territory, though some states also use these over nearby waters. The United States established the first ADIZ in 1950, which created ADIZs over Japan, the Philippines, South Korea, and Taiwan as protection and later transferred these to their respective countries.[2] Nonetheless, China's ADIZ in East Asia is extensive, partly covering the Senkaku Islands, legally owned and controlled by Japan. If China extends its authority, flight plans and locations would require reporting to China's national air control unit for all planes in its airspace.

The United States is a treaty ally with Japan, South Korea, and the Philippines.[3] Additionally, the U.S. has a security agreement through the Taiwan Relations Act of 1979, which assures Taiwan defensive support.[4] The 1960 "U.S.-Japan Treaty on Mutual Cooperation and Security,"[5] stated explicitly and reaffirmed that the Senkaku Islands, administered by Japan, are included in the agreement.

In 1953, after the Korean War, the U.S. and South Korea signed the "Mutual Defense Treaty Between the United States and the Republic of Korea". Under Article III, neither party is obligated "to come to the aid of the other except in case of an external armed attack against such party."[6] Nevertheless, in June 2020, the U.S. had 28,500 troops in South Korea.[7]

ADIZ by the Numbers

To understand the numbers, according to a Federation of American Scientists report, in 2019, there were more than 700 unauthorized Chinese ADIZ intrusions, including 675 in

---

1 Minnie Chan, "Beijing Plans for South China Sea Air Defence Identification Zone Cover Pratas, Paracel, and Spratly Islands, PLA Source Says," *South China Morning Post*, May 31, 2020, https://www.scmp.com/news/china/military/article/3086679/beijings-plans-south-china-sea-air-defence-identification-zone

2 Shin Nakayama, "US Reluctant to Slam China's ADIZ," *NIKKEI Asian Review*, January 8, 2014, https://asia.nikkei.com/Politics/Washington-Reacts-Less-Strongly-To-Chinas-ADIZ

3 Congressional Research Service, "U.S.-China Strategic Competition in South and East China Seas: Background and Issues for Congress," *Congressional Research Service*, Updated August 28, 2020, https://crsreports.congress.gov/product/pdf/R/R42784

4 Congress, "H.R.2479 Taiwan Relations Act," *Congress.gov*, 1979-1980, https://www.congress.gov/bill/96th-congress/house-bill/2479

5 Treaty of Mutual Cooperation and Security, signed January 19, 1960, entered into force on June 23, 1960, 11 UST 1632; TIAS 4509; 373 UNTS.

6 American Foreign Policy, "Mutual Defense Treaty Between the United States and the Republic of Korea; October 1, 1953," *Department of State Publication 6446, General Foreign Policy Series 117*, October 1, 1953, https://www.usfk.mil/Portals/105/Documents/SOFA/H_Mutual%20Defense%20Treaty_1953.pdf

7 Congressional Research Service, "U.S.-South Korea Alliance: Issues for Congress," *Congressional Research Service*, Updated June 23, 2020, https://crsreports.congress.gov/product/pdf/IF/IF11388

Japan alone - an increase from 96 in 2010.[8] Most of these missions were considered a threat with no deterrence signal. These People's Liberation Army Air Force (PLAAF) flights could have resulted in a miscalculation.

The number is likely to increase given China's intensified assertiveness in its surrounding seas. Chinese fighter jets have established a growing presence as a warning to regional states. In July 2020, Japan's aircraft engaged in daily flights to protect its ADIZ.[9] Concerned, Japan committed billions of dollars to air disruption strategies to thwart Chinese air sorties.[10]

---

8   Federation of American Scientists, "Over the Line: The Implications of China's ADIZ Intrusions in Northeast Asia," *Federation of American Scientists*, August, 2020, https://fas.org/wp-content/uploads/2020/08/ADIZ-Report.pdf

9   Kyodo News, "Japan Now Instantly Scrambles Jets Against China's from Fujian," *Kyodo News*, July 18, 2020, https://english.kyodonews.net/news/2020/07/c0f33e803562-japan-now-instantly-scrambles-jets-against-chinas-from-fujian.html

10 Kyodo News, "Japan SDF to Set Up Electronic Warfare Capability Unit Next Spring," *Kyodo News*, August 15, 2020, https://english.kyodonews.net/news/2020/08/c5a5502a3e4f-japan-sdf-to-set-up-electronic-warfare-capability-unit-next-spring.html?phrase=Kagoshima&words

Japan is not the only country facing China's provocations. In 2020, Taiwan was increasingly faced with China's overflight forays. In February 2020, China crossed the median line toward Taiwan. Tsai Ing-wen rapidly responded, condemning China. In September 2020, during continued Chinese incursions into Taiwan's territory, "the defence ministry once again urged the Chinese Communist Party not to repeatedly destroy regional peace and stability."[11] By October 2020, China crossed the median line 49 times, which is greater than at any time since 1990.[12] Furthermore, as China attempts to entice Taiwan into a fight, concerns abound that war could be imminent.

In 2020, more than a dozen countries had an official or unofficial ADIZ, including:

- Bangladesh
- Canada
- China
- Iceland
- India
- Japan
- North Korea
- Norway
- Pakistan
- Russia
- South Korea
- Sweden
- Taiwan
- United Kingdom
- United States

China continues to take small steps as it seeks greater control of the East China Sea region. By making its ADIZ claim and laying low, China takes another step in its long march as it effectively uses 'salami-slicing' to place a stake in the skies overhead.[13] A January 2015 *Congressional Research Service* report explains how China's incremental 'salami-slicing' progress could work effectively. China

> ...would acquire strategic advantage by asserting a maximalist position, then seeming to back down while preserving some incremental gain—akin to a "ratchet" effect. According to this theory, [China] would project a calm image and justify the East China Sea ADIZ as a 'reasonable' step to which foreign nations should not object. If there is an accident, crisis, or loss of life, Beijing could then blame Tokyo, Seoul, Taipei, or Washington.[14]

Conclusion

There are no treaties or international rules that regulate ADIZ areas, and few ADIZs venture past their own Exclusive Economic Zone (EEZ). China, though, has extended its reach over other states' EEZs. Beijing's military violates overflight allowances over

---

11   Reuters staff, "Chinese Su-30 Fighters and Y-8 Aircrafts Buzz Taiwan for a Second Day as Tensions Rise," *The Economic Times*, September 10, 2020, https://economictimes.indiatimes.com/news/defence/chinese-su-30-fighters-and-y-8-aircrafts-buzz-taiwan-for-a-second-day-as-tensions-rise/articleshow/78035137.cms?from=mdr

12   Ralph Jennings, "Taiwan Says Chinese Warplanes Are Crossing a Median Line, But Is There a Median Line?," *VOA News*, October 26, 2020, https://www.voanews.com/east-asia-pacific/taiwan-says-chinese-warplanes-are-crossing-median-line-there-median-line

13   Robert Haddick, "America Has No Answer to China's Salami-Slicing," *War on the Rocks*, February 6, 2014, http://warontherocks.com/2014/02/america-has-no-answer-to-chinas-salami-slicing

14   Ian E. Rinehart and Bart Elias, "China's Air Defense Identification Zone," *Congressional Research Service*, January 30, 2015, https://fas.org/sgp/crs/row/R43894.pdf

international waters provided for by the United Nations Convention on the Law of the Sea (UNCLOS).

China calls its flights "defensive measures", even when they appear threatening. People's Liberation Army Air Force (PLAAF) pilots repeatedly encroach on other states' territories as they fly over land that is administered by other countries. Thus, there is great concern about China's incursions. Miscommunication regarding provocative military flights continues to heat the skies.

In September 2020, China's PLAAF fighter jets encroached on Taiwan's ADIZ, threatening the area.[15] Taiwan's Ministry of Foreign Affairs denounced China's offensive actions, stating the "Taiwan government strongly condemns provocations on consecutive days by China's military aircraft; calls on the international community to squarely face China's threat to the region."[16]

Russia has also explored weaknesses in other countries' ADIZ regions. In August 2020, Russian military aircraft flew over South Korea's airspace forcing Seoul to scramble its jets.[17] In June 2020[18] and August 2020, Russia flew its bombers over the U.S. ADIZ around Alaska's waters.[19]

What's at Stake?

First, an ADIZ that stretches over another state's territory is likely to cause an 'unintended consequence'.

Second, the ADIZ regions in the East China Sea are either very close to one another or overlap, which is dangerous and could result in collisions or miscalculations.

Third, some treaties with other countries necessitate U.S. action. Thus, frictionless overflight must be strategically considered. What is at stake is the threat of war and possibly war itself.

---

15 Steven Stashwick, "Chinese Jets Intrude Taiwan Air Defense Zone for Second Day," *The Diplomat,* September 11, 2020, https://thediplomat.com/2020/09/chinese-jets-intrude-taiwan-air-defense-zone-for-second-day/

16 Ministry of Foreign Affairs, Republic of China (Taiwan), "Taiwan Government Strongly Condemns Provocations on Consecutive Days by China's Military Aircraft; Calls on International Community to Squarely Face China's Threat to the Region," *Ministry of Foreign Affairs, Republic of China (Taiwan),* September 10, 2020, https://www.mofa.gov.tw/en/News_Content.aspx?n=1EADDCFD4C6EC567&sms=5B9044CF1188EE23&s=3A8756A37F5B4464

17 China Military Online, "Russian Bombers Enter US's Alaskan ADIZ, Why?," *China Military Online,* June 16, 2020, http://eng.chinamil.com.cn/view/2020-06/16/content_9836193.htm

18 Ibid.

19 NORAD HQ Public Affairs, "NORAD Conducts Three Intercepts of Russian Aircraft Entering Air Defense Identification Zone," *North American Aerospace Defense Command (NORAD),* August 28, 2020, https://www.norad.mil/Newsroom/Article/2328902/norad-conducts-three-intercepts-of-russian-aircraft-entering-air-defense-identi

Chapter 4
The North Korea Question
Nuclear Powered, Unstable, and Demonstrated Willingness to Act on Impulse

Introduction

China and North Korea have an unusual relationship. North Korea's nuclear capabilities and China's 'salami-slicing' ambitions have made the dynamic between the two states volatile and uneasy at times. China is capable of overthrowing the North Korean regime at any time[1] but fears its nuclear capabilities.[2] On the other hand, North Korea is dependent on China for trade, and its ability to keep the United States at arm's length has been of strategic importance for Beijing.[3] There is much ambiguity between the two states' relations, but their relationship is essential to understand Asia's regional power dynamic.

The Power Balance of China and North Korea

During the Korean War, CCP leaders launched the "War to Resist U.S. Aggression and Aid Korea," saving North Korea from its loss in the war, though clashes ensued between the Chinese and North Korean leaderships.[4] To the rest of the world, Beijing's interference saved North Korea, as Chinese troops intervened and later provided free labor to North Korea's post-war reconstruction that stimulated North Korea's economic and political recovery.[5] However, North Korea's propaganda machine spun a narrative that undermined China's role in the war. Soviet diplomats in 1955 noted that "the Korean comrades underrate the role and importance of Chinese aid to Korea and, in particular, downplay the role of the Chinese volunteers in the fight against the American intervention."[6]

North Korea's perspective of China's generosity after the Korean War caused strains on Sino-North Korean relations. Even so, China still donated 230,000 tons of food aid, as estimated by the National Committee on North Korea, and resolved border demarcation disputes in favor of Pyongyang during the Cold War. Seeking to pursue a hedging strategy, North Korea signed a mutual defense treaty with China and the Soviet Union, rivals of the Cold War, just five days apart in 1961.[7]

Relations between North Korea and China plummeted during the Cultural Revolution as North Korea severely distrusted the CCP. The Chinese Red Guards persecuted North

---

1 Nick Bisley, "What's China's Relationship with North Korea Really Like?," *La Trobe University,* n.d., https://www.latrobe.edu.au/nest/whats-chinas-relationship-north-korea-really-like/

2 BBC News, "China Fears North Korea-Us Conflict 'At Any Moment'," *BBC News,* April 14, 2017, https://www.bbc.com/news/world-asia-39600426

3 Daniel Wertz, "China-North Korea Relations," *The National Committee on North Korea,* November, 2019, https://www.ncnk.org/resources/briefing-papers/all-briefing-papers/china-north-korea-relations

4 Ibid.

5 Zhihua Shen and Yafeng Xia, "China and the Post-War Reconstruction of North Korea, 1953-1961," *Woodrow Wilson Center for International Scholars, North Korea Documentation Project, Working Paper #4,* May, 2012, Available at: https://www.wilsoncenter.org/publication/china-and-the-post-war-reconstruction-north-korea-1953-1961

6 Boris Nikolaevich Ponomarev and Nikolai Trofimovich Fedorenko, "Information on the Situation in the DPRK," *Woodrow Wilson Center, History and Public Policy Program Digital Archive, RGANI, Fond 5, Opis 28, Delo 314, listi 34-59,* April, 1955, Obtained for NKIDP by James Person and translated for NKIDP by Gary Goldberg, Available at: https://digitalarchive.wilsoncenter.org/document/114590

7 Ankit Panda, "China and North Korea Have a Mutual Defense Treaty, But When Would It Apply?," *The Diplomat,* August 14, 2017, https://thediplomat.com/2017/08/china-and-north-korea-have-a-mutual-defense-treaty-but-when-would-it-apply/

Koreans and attempted to coerce North Korea to replicate its own Cultural Revolution.[8] These heightened tensions led to an armed clash along the China–North Korea border in 1969.[9] It was not until the early 1970s that relations between the two states began to recover, though the establishment of trust was unlikely.[10] Nevertheless, policy stances with the United States, nuclear threats, and modern geopolitical conflict continued rocking the boat between China and North Korea.

Kim Jong-un Executes Five Officials in North Korea
Firing Squad Guns Down Economic Ministry Officials After Criticizing the Regime

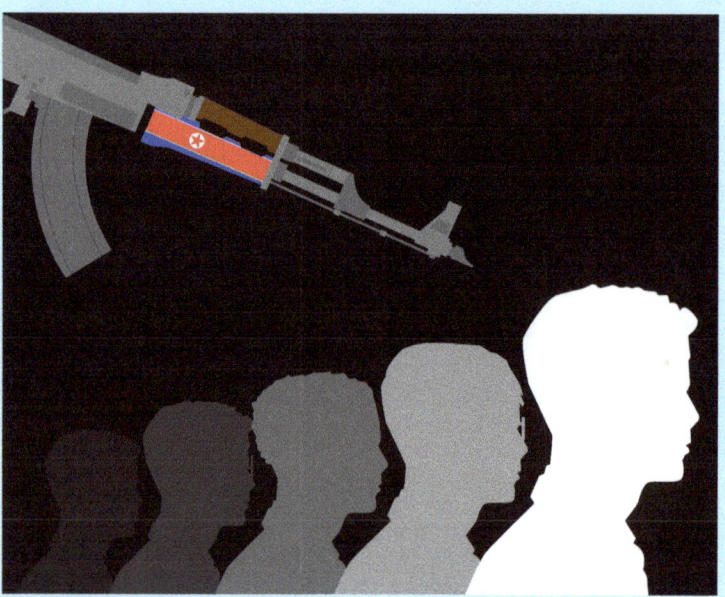

Key Strategic Interests

China and North Korea have a turbulent history of betrayal and conflict with one another. The two nations' shared strategic interests, politically and economically, keep the power players linked. China has bolstered Kim Jong-un's leadership as Kim's regime creates

---

8   Wilson Center, "North Korean Attitudes Toward China: A Historical View of Contemporary Difficulties," *Wilson Center*, April 2, 2009, https://www.wilsoncenter.org/event/north-korean-attitudes-toward-china-historical-view-contemporary-difficulties

9   Wilson Center Digital Archive, "Sino-Soviet Border Conflict, 1969," *Wilson Center Digital Archive*, n.d., https://digitalarchive.wilsoncenter.org/collection/192/sino-soviet-border-conflict-1969

10 James Person, "Chinese-North Korean Relations: Drawing the Right Historical Lessons," *Wilson Center*, October 19, 2017, https://www.wilsoncenter.org/article/chinese-north-korean-relations-drawing-the-right-historical-lessons

a buffer between China and South Korea. Jennifer Lind, Dartmouth College professor and *CNN* author, writes, "while the Chinese certainly would prefer that North Korea not have nuclear weapons, their greatest fear is regime collapse."[11]

Furthermore, North Korea benefits from its trade relations with China economically, while the same dynamic provides leverage to China for its own geopolitical strategies in the Korean Peninsula. Between 2016 to 2017, China accounted for 95 percent of North Korea's reported merchandise trade.[12] In 2017, Chinese food exports to North Korea sharply increased.[13] In 2019, China continued increasing food aid to North Korea when a severe drought reduced crop production and agricultural shortages, forcing ten million North Koreans to be desperate for food.[14] China's assistance to North Korea has been welcomed and needed. Moreover, access to the Korean Peninsula has greatly aided Beijing's strategic push in East Asia.

U.S. Policy Stance

The U.S. has played a significant role in shaping the dynamic between China and North Korea in recent years. It is no secret that U.S.-North Korean relations are turbulent, threatening, and fragile at best. U.S. President Donald Trump did not ease this dynamic. President Trump called Kim Jong-un the 'rocket man',[15] firing his Twitter fingers away to jab at the legitimacy of Kim Jong-un's authority. Still, North Korea and the United States made diplomatic progress during Trump's administration after the President attempted to ease tension over a potential war in 2017.[16] Trump met with Kim Jong-un in Singapore in 2018 in a historic meeting for U.S.-North Korea relations.[17]

Though these negotiations had strategic implications for Washington, strengthening U.S.-North-Korea diplomatic relations, simultaneously straining those between China and North Korea,[18] especially amidst lowered trade rates between North Korea and China. Still, in 2020, Trump's initiative to pacify relations with North Korea took a turn as sources reported that

---

11   Jennifer Lind, "Will Trump's hardball tactics work on China and North Korea?," *CNN*, August 7, 2017, https://www.cnn.com/2017/08/07/opinions/china-north-korea-opinion-lind/index.html

12   Daniel Wertz, "China-North Korea Trade: Parsing the Data," *38 North*, February 25, 2020, https://www.38north.org/2020/02/dwertz022520/

13   Kristin Huang, "Sharp Rise in Chinese Food Exports to North Korea as Starving Nation Leans Heavily on its Only Ally," *South China Morning Post*, August 16, 2017, https://www.scmp.com/news/china/diplomacy-defence/article/2107075/sharp-rise-chinese-food-exports-north-korea-starving

14   Elizabeth Shim, "Report: China Boosts Food Aid to North Korea," *UPI*, August 20, 2019, https://www.upi.com/Top_News/World-News/2019/08/20/Report-China-boosts-food-aid-to-North-Korea/7541566299449/

15   Jessica Campisi, "Trump Resurrects 'Rocket Man' Nickname for North Korean Leader," *The Hill*, December 3, 2019, https://thehill.com/homenews/administration/472734-trump-resurrects-rocket-man-nickname-for-north-korean-leader

16   Jacob Heilbrunn, "Trump's Fire and Fury Foreign Policy," *National Interest*, August 10, 2017, https://nationalinterest.org/feature/trumps-fire-fury-foreign-policy-21854

17   Everett Rosenfeld, "Trump Says He and Kim are 'Going Right Now for a Signing'," *CNBC*, June 11, 2018, https://www.cnbc.com/2018/06/11/donald-trump-and-kim-jong-un-meet-at-historic-summit-in-singapore.html

18   Eleanor Albert, "The China–North Korea Relationship," *Council on Foreign Relations*, June 25, 2019, https://www.cfr.org/backgrounder/china-north-korea-relationship

U.S. relations with North Korea worsened during the Trump presidency, while North Korea became more connected and developed new weapons.[19]

North Korean Sailors Shot a South Korean Official, Doused Him with Oil, & Burned His Body in September 2020

COVID-19 Trade Troubles

Though North Korea prides itself on its economic self-reliance, China is North Korea's biggest donor.[20] However, during the COVID-19 pandemic, North Korea closed its sea and land ports to China, concerned with the potential coronavirus spread.[21] Furthermore, the United Nations Security Council had already sanctioned trade into North Korea over its

---

19 Noah Bierman, "North Korea was Trump's Chief Foreign Policy Boast, but Things Got Worse on His Watch," *Los Angeles Times*, August 24, 2020, https://www.latimes.com/politics/story/2020-08-24/north-korea-trump-foreign-policy

20 Reality Check Team, "North Korea: Who is Sending Aid?," *BBC News*, June 20, 2019, https://www.bbc.com/news/world-asia-48637518

21 Hyemin Son, "North Korea Traders Chafe as Reopening of China Border Put Off on New COVID-19 Fears," *Radio Free Asia*, July 2, 2020, https://www.rfa.org/english/news/korea/postpone-07022020175016.html

nuclear activity.[22] Both of these factors combined resulted in a sharp decline in imports and exports between the two nations.

Between January and May of 2020, trade between the two nations plummeted nearly 70 percent.[23] Chinese customs indicated that between January and February, trade fell 24 percent.[24] Compared to the same period in 2019, Chinese exports declined $198 million, and Chinese imports from North Korea drastically declined 74 percent.[25] North Korea's economy faced a crisis during the pandemic. In September 2020, the *Financial Times* explained that Kim Jong-un would become increasingly dependent on China's business markets and aid.[26]

Conclusion

During the COVID-19 pandemic, much of the world's activities slowed. However, North Korea took this time to develop and introduce new nuclear weapons, plutonium production abilities, intercontinental ballistic missiles, and submarine-launched ballistic missiles.[27] While North Korea has not been particularly confrontational in 2020, with new and better missiles, 2021 may be a different story. The Biden administration's diplomatic policies toward North Korea will determine which of many scenarios may come next from closer ties with the U.S., partnership with China, reunification with South Korea, or some other scenario.

What's at Stake?

First, the threat of North Korea's nuclear capability frightens even China. Without stability between the two power players, conflict may quickly heighten as it did during the Cultural Revolution.

Second, China's economic and material aid offers Beijing leverage over North Korea and a vital link between the two nations. Diminishing trade between China and North Korea amidst the COVID-19 pandemic may not be worth worrying over, but it may be alarming if trade rates do not recover. Only time will tell how North Korea recovers from the pandemic's economic strains and how it may alter China's and North Korea's future relations.

---

22 Kelsey Davenport, "UN Security Council Resolutions on North Korea," *Arms Control Association*, April, 2018, https://www.armscontrol.org/factsheets/UN-Security-Council-Resolutions-on-North-Korea

23 Shin Watanabe, "North Korea Loses Access to Foreign Cash as China Trade Drops 70%," *NIKKEI Asian Review*, July 22, 2020, https://asia.nikkei.com/Spotlight/N-Korea-at-crossroads/North-Korea-loses-access-to-foreign-cash-as-China-trade-drops-70

24 William Brown, "North Korea's China Trade Suffers Coronavirus Shock," *38 North*, April 8, 2020, https://www.38north.org/2020/04/wbrown040820/

25 Ibid.

26 Edward White, "Kim Jong Un's Dependence on China Grows as Virus Hits Economy," *Financial Times*, September 8, 2020, https://www.ft.com/content/34574764-b2fc-44cf-a195-f73281039f75

27 Khang Vu, "North Korea's Very Odd Year," *The Lowy Institute*, December 4, 2020, https://www.lowyinstitute.org/the-interpreter/north-korea-s-very-odd-year

Chapter 5

South Korean Relations with Allies and Unfriendlies

The Conflux of Coalitions and Instability in East Asia

Introduction

China and South Korea's relations are impacted by an array of external factors: North Korea's nuclear capabilities, U.S. foreign policy, issues on the Korean Peninsula, and regional trade conditions. Nevertheless, the two nations have held rocky relations with one another for decades, despite establishing diplomatic relations after the Cold War.[1]

For context, during the Korean War, the U.S. backed the south while China supported the north.[2] Throughout much of recent history, these relationships have fluctuated significantly. This phenomenon continued to exist in 2021, though in February 2020, at the beginning of the pandemic, Chinese President Xi Jinping and South Korean President Moon Jae-in discussed a strategy to handle the pandemic. Xi expressed "deep gratitude" for Moon.[3] This chapter focuses on recent China and South Korean relations that became increasingly strained in 2016 when South Korea deployed its nuclear defense system.

Map of The East China Sea

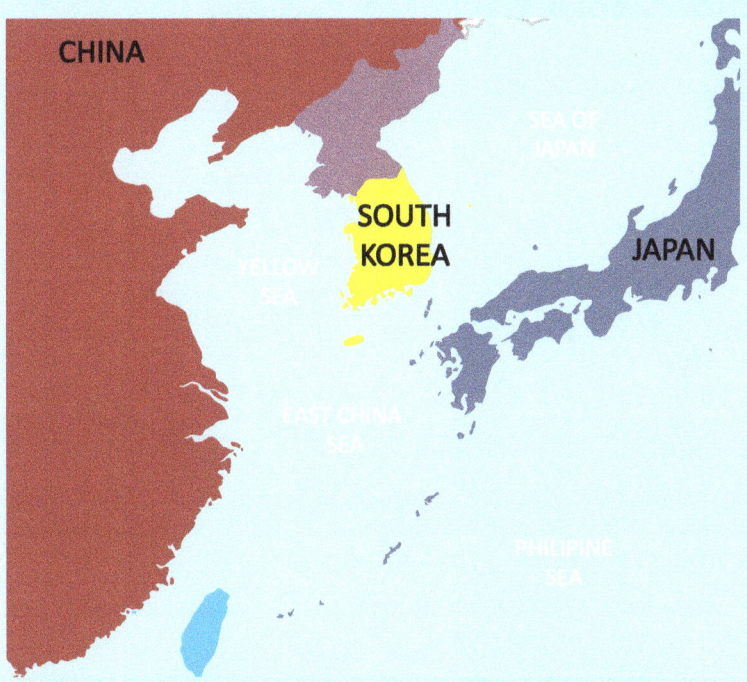

---

1 Doug Bandow, "South Korea is Charting an Independent Course on China," *CATO Institute*, July 27, 2020, https://www.cato.org/publications/commentary/south-korea-charting-independent-course-china

2 Chinasage, "Relations Between China and Korea," *Chinasage*, n.d., https://www.chinasage.info/korea.htm

3 SCMP's Asia Desk, "Xi Jinping and Moon Jae-in Discuss Coronavirus and Chinese Leader's Planned Visit to South Korea," *South China Morning Post*, February 20, 2020, https://www.scmp.com/news/asia/south-asia/article/3051665/xi-jinping-and-moon-jae-discuss-coronavirus-and-chinese

With Tensions Rising, Pyongyang Blows Up Inter-Korean Building in North Korea Border Town of Kaesong – June 2020

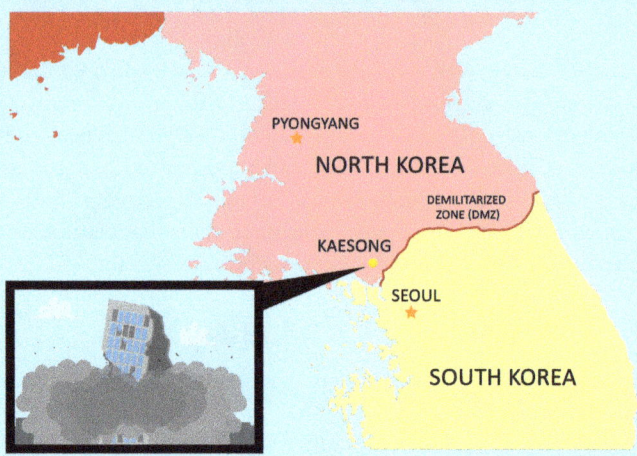

THAAD Causes Problems

In 2016, the U.S. deployed Terminal High Altitude Area Defense (THAAD) anti-missile defense system in South Korea.[4] THAAD can shoot down ballistic missiles in their flight paths on a range of 200 km and an altitude of 150 km.[5] South Korea accepted this system from their U.S. ally to counter the very real threat of nuclear attacks from their North Korean neighbors. Though THAAD deployments impacted strategies and relations in the entire Eastern Asian region, the anti-missile defense system was most fervently protested by Beijing. Russia also challenged the THAAD deployment.[6]

China's Foreign Ministry posted a statement on its website, saying, "China expresses strong dissatisfaction and resolute objection to this," and cautioning, "Refrain from taking actions that complicate the region's situation and do not do things that harm China's strategic

---

4   DOD News, "US to Deploy THAAD Missile Battery to South Korea," *U.S. Army,* September 16, 2016, https://www.army.mil/article/171316/us_to_deploy_thaad_missile_battery_to_south_korea

5   BBC News, "US and South Korea Agree THAAD Missile Defence Deployment," *BBC News,* July 8, 2016, https://www.bbc.com/news/world-asia-36742751

6   Reuters Staff, "China, Russia Share Opposition to U.S. THAAD in South Korea: Xi," *Reuters,* July 3, 2017, https://www.reuters.com/article/us-china-thaad-russia/china-russia-share-opposition-to-u-s-thaad-in-south-korea-xi-idUSKBN19O0N8

security interests."⁷ THAAD's deployment worried China, providing the possibility for South Korea to interfere with China's strategic interests in the region.⁸

Before the deployment of U.S.-supported THAAD, China and South Korea's bilateral relationship strengthened.⁹ However, after Beijing's intense and persistent protests to THAAD were ignored, China imposed economic sanctions. China boycotted South Korea's tourism industry, costing Seoul $6.8 bn.¹⁰

Nevertheless, in October of 2017, Seoul and Beijing both agreed to resolve their disputes over THAAD after South Korean businesses were harshly impacted by China's economic sanctions.¹¹ South Korea's foreign ministry stated, "Both sides shared the view that the strengthening of exchange and cooperation between Korea and China serves their common interests and agreed to expeditiously bring exchange and cooperation in all areas back on a normal development track."¹²

Insecurity Amid COVID-19 Pandemic

In June 2020, North Korea bombed a joint liaison office with South Korea, threatened to move troops into the demilitarized zone, and drastically escalated tension between the North and South.¹³ *The Washington Post* explains, "The uptick in aggressive behavior from Pyongyang is also unfolding at a time of heightened insecurity in Asia, where China has been forcefully asserting its influence amid concern about the Trump administration's commitments to longstanding U.S. alliances."¹⁴

Furthermore, this instability, fostered by U.S.-South Korean relations, challenges China's anti-U.S. intervention stance. In July 2020, the *U.S. Army War College's Strategic Studies Institute* published a report that *The Diplomat* pragmatically analyzed. The source explains,

> It questioned U.S. preparedness in the Indo-Pacific vis-à-vis China and argued that U.S. forces in South Korea (and Japan) are too concentrated and, though sufficient for a large-scale clash with North Korea, are "grossly inadequate for either hypercompetition or armed hostilities" with China.

---

7   DW, "Despite Chinese, Russian Objections, US Deploys Missile Shield to South Korea," *DW*, August 7, 2016, https://www.dw.com/en/despite-chinese-russian-objections-us-deploys-missile-shield-to-south-korea/a-19387468

8   Choe-San Hung, "South Korea and China End Dispute Over Missile Defense System," *The New York Times*, October 30, 2017, https://www.nytimes.com/2017/10/30/world/asia/north-korea-nuclear-test-radiation.html

9   Doug Bandow, "South Korea is Charting an Independent Course on China," *CATO Institute*, July 27, 2020, https://www.cato.org/publications/commentary/south-korea-charting-independent-course-china

10 Echo Huang, "China Inflicted a World of Pain on South Korea in 2017," *Quartz*, December 20, 2017, https://qz.com/1149663/china-south-korea-relations-in-2017-thaad-backlash-and-the-effect-on-tourism/

11 Christine Kim and Ben Blanchard, "China, South Korea Agree to Mend Ties After THAAD Standoff," *Reuters*, October 30, 2017, https://www.reuters.com/article/us-northkorea-missiles/china-south-korea-agree-to-mend-ties-after-thaad-standoff-idUSKBN1D003G

12 Choe-San Hung, "South Korea and China End Dispute Over Missile Defense System," *The New York Times*, October 30, 2017, https://www.nytimes.com/2017/10/30/world/asia/north-korea-nuclear-test-radiation.html

13 Min Joo Kim, "North Korea Blows Up Joint Liaison Office, Dramatically, Raising Tensions with South," *The Washington Post*, June 16, 2020, https://www.washingtonpost.com/world/asia_pacific/north-korea-liaison-office-kaesong-explosion-demolish-dmz/2020/06/16/7c7a2dc0-af9d-11ea-98b5-279a6479a1e4_story.html

14 Ibid.

Despite being the product of a U.S. Army think tank and not official U.S. government policy, the report apparently caused significant consternation among South Korean officials as a sign of things to come: either U.S. troop reductions or U.S. forces becoming entangled in wider regional contingencies.[15]

Conclusion

A wide range of potentialities exists for the 2020s. Emerging from the pandemic, countries will forge a new path forward as they seek to regain their economic steam and put their labor force back to work. Many, like South Korea, will seek partners that can bring their country to new heights. China furnishes countries with cheap manpower. Furthermore, with a population of 1.4 billion people, China offers an expansive avenue for purchasing power of citizenry who can buy company's products and energize nations' manufacturing industries.

In December 2020, South Korean President Moon Jae In expressed an interest in joining the Trans-Pacific Partnership (TPP) trade agreement.[16] In November 2020, South Korea signed on to the Regional Comprehensive Economic Partnership Agreement (RCEP), the world's largest free trade agreement with fourteen other signatories.[17] Countries are eager to get back on track. Yet, the United States remains a wildcard with a change in its presidency, new policies, and uncertainties regarding the global balance of power.

What's at Stake?

First, whether South Korea will increase or decrease its U.S. military presence in the region is critical to how North Korea, China, and even Russia will respond.

Second, growing insecurity in Asia only leads to the risk of nuclear weapons being launched. Further miscalculation will exacerbate any destructive outcome.

Third, China-South-Korea relations fluctuate periodically, but genuine diplomacy necessitates open communication, transparency, and cooperation, a leadership dynamic yet to be created.

---

15 Clint Work, "The US-South Korea Alliance and the China Factor," *The Diplomat*, August 26, 2020, https://thediplomat.com/2020/08/the-us-south-korea-alliance-and-the-china-factor/

16 Sotaro Suzuki, "Moon Raises Prospect of South Korea Joining TPP Trade Pact," *NIKKEI Asia*, December 9, 2020, https://asia.nikkei.com/Economy/Trade/Moon-raises-prospect-of-South-Korea-joining-TPP-trade-pact

17 Lee Sun-young, "S. Korea Signs World's Largest Free Trading Deal," *The Korea Herald*, November 15, 2020, http://www.koreaherald.com/view.php?ud=20201115000235

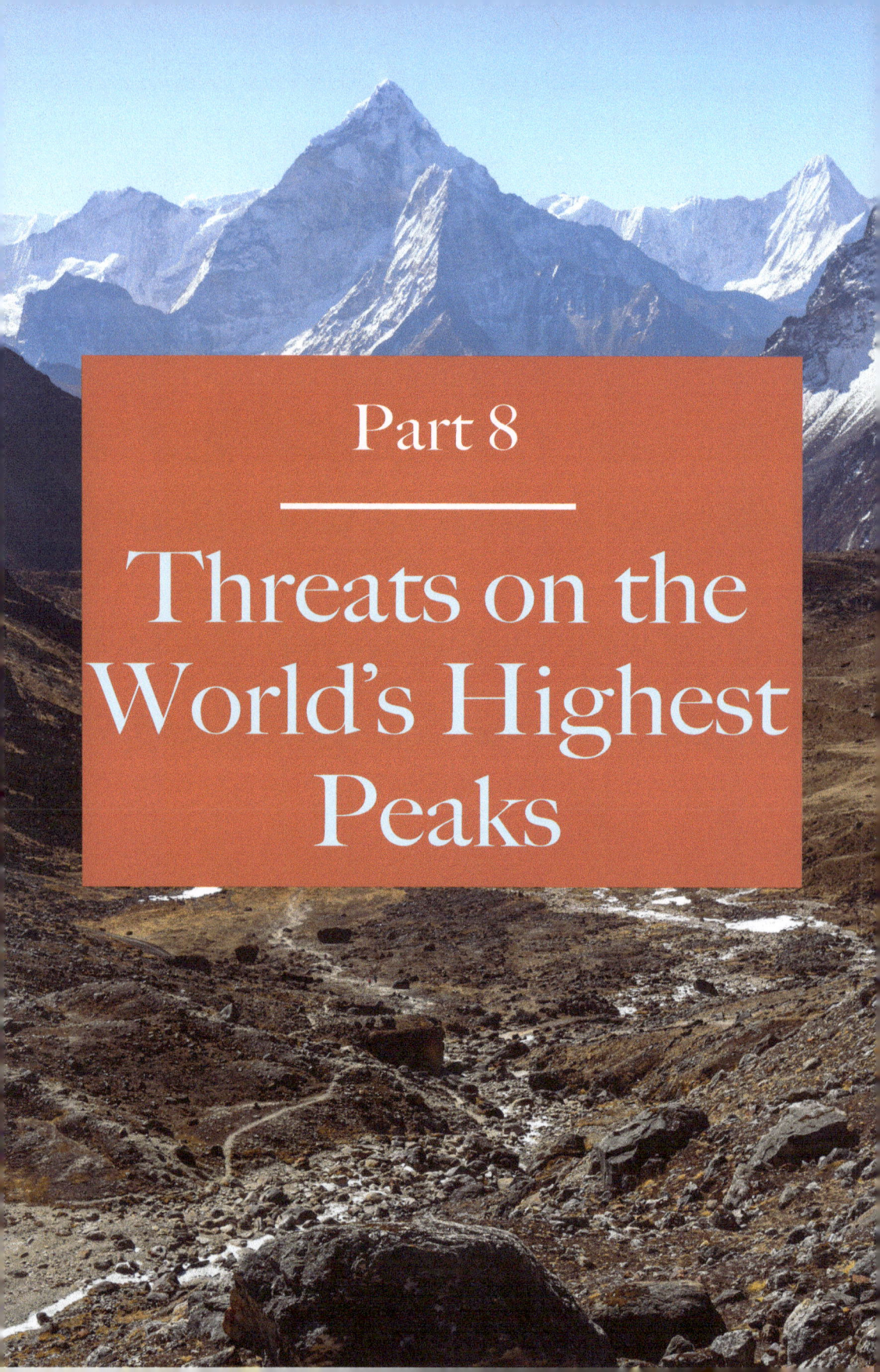

Part 8

Threats on the World's Highest Peaks

Peril and Intimidation in Himalayan Territories

Tensions have been running high in the Himalayas. China is waging war with countries worldwide, overtaking their territory, water, information, and even a wildlife sanctuary. However, the altercations have not always been diplomatic, they have occasionally been deadly. For forty-five years, from October 1975 to June 2020, there were no deaths on the India-China border between the two nuclear powers. This period of relative calm changed when the Chinese military killed twenty Indian troops while the world grappled with the coronavirus pandemic. Tensions and distrust increased. In the fall of 2020, 100,000 Chinese and Indian soldiers amassed on the border in a standoff that became increasingly heated. Negotiations have not mollified this battle for sovereignty and water.

China is gaining ground, literally. Earlier, China engaged in a diplomatic attempt to take territory in Bhutan's Sakteng Wildlife Preserve. This dispute was one of China's most recent territorial claims. Beijing continues to slice off bigger chunks of territory that it insists is its 'historic right', which, over time, could encompass much of South Asia.

Nepal is also concerned about its land that China claims. Meanwhile, China purchased Himalayan land from Pakistan. All in all, Beijing's economic power could demand ever-increasing slices of other countries' sovereignty. Grants and loans provided valuable relief during the pandemic as countries struggled financially. However, Beijing's loans result in a debt that must be paid or pledged assets seized.

Meanwhile, Tibet has suffered endlessly. Tibetans were silenced through surveillance, security, imprisonment, and the demolishing of temples. Many were forced into slave labor camps. South Asia's story is not finished, but hope dims as states attempt to retain their sovereignty.

Chapter 1

Strained Sino-Indian Relations

How Border and Resource Conflicts Escalated Through COVID-19

Introduction

China and India are the two most populous countries on the planet, with the potential to globally impact trade and economics. Yet, aside from their influence and importance, the countries are also the center of a dangerous conflict, butting heads with one another in disputes that threaten the world.

The McMahon Line
India-Tibet Border

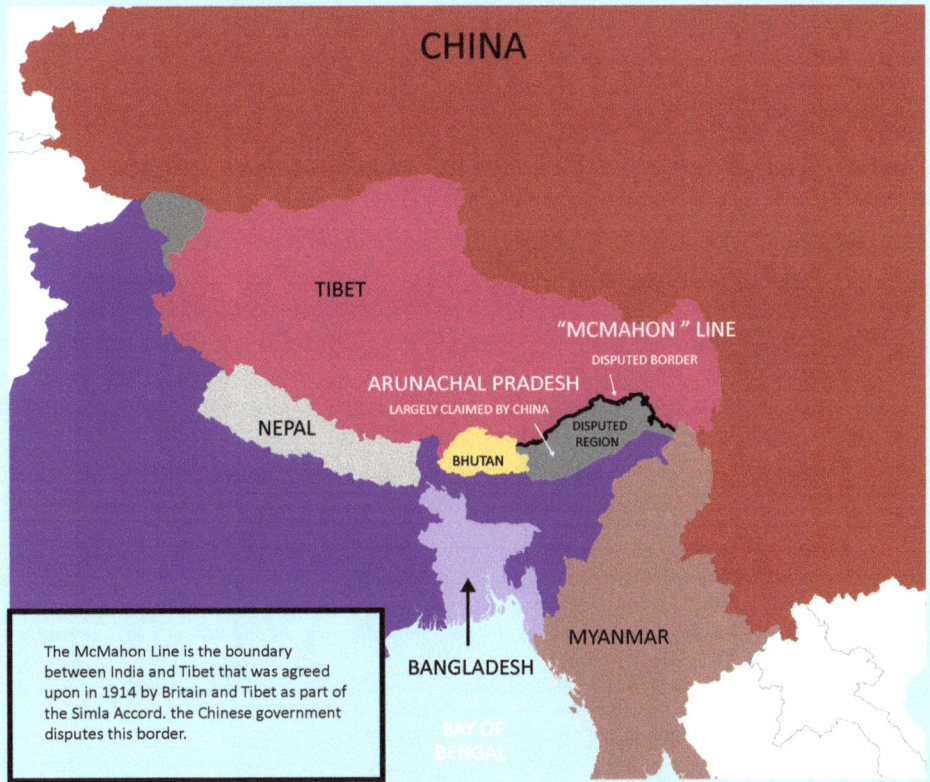

The McMahon Line is the boundary between India and Tibet that was agreed upon in 1914 by Britain and Tibet as part of the Simla Accord. the Chinese government disputes this border.

Historical Relationships

India's 2,000-year-old relationship with China was redefined with the 1949 founding of the People's Republic of China (PRC). China and India formed diplomatic ties in 1950,[1] entering a 'honeymoon phase' where both countries highly regarded each other due to their similar struggles in overcoming imperial control.[2] This 'honeymoon phase' was short-lived.

---

1 South Asian Voices, "India-China: 70 Years of Diplomatic Relations," *South Asian Voices*, n.d., https://southasianvoices.org/india-china-70-years-of-diplomatic-relations/

2 Srinath Raghavan, "A Brief History of India's Relationship with the People's Republic of China," *Carnegie India*, September 25, 2019, https://carnegieindia.org/2019/09/25/brief-history-of-india-s-relationship-with-people-s-republic-of-china-pub-79914

In 1959, Tibet was submerged in escalating tensions and violence as an ongoing guerilla war ensued between Tibetan rebels and Chinese soldiers over a border conflict.[3] The Dalai Lama, Tibetan's spiritual and political leader, quietly escaped from Tibet and sought asylum in India, sparking tension between the PRC and India.[4] The then-Chinese leader Mao Zedong became angered by India's acceptance of the Dalai Lama.[5]

For the following three years, tensions intensified as China perceived India as a threat to Tibetan rule.[6] In the summer of 1962, Sino-Indian relations strained to the brink with a border standoff at Chushul, a disputed region in Indian territory that China claims near its Kashmir territory.[7] On July 10, 1962, roughly 350 Chinese troops surrounded an Indian post at Chushul and used microphones to yell at the Gurkhas not to fight for India. The Gurkhas are Nepalese soldiers, some of whom are part of the Indian army.[8]

After years of flaring hostilities, the tinderbox finally ignited in October 1962, with the Sino-Indian War. On October 20, 1962, China's People's Liberation Army (PLA) invaded India's Ladakh region, crossing the McMahon Line into Indian territory.[9] India was wholly unprepared for the attack, believing that war was avoidable, and that China would not fire first.

China utilized India's vulnerability, cutting Indian telephone lines, preventing soldiers from contacting their bases, lighting bushfires, and deploying hundreds of attacking troops, leading some Indian soldiers to flee to Bhutan.[10] In response, India opened fire with machine guns and mortars, killing roughly 200 Chinese soldiers.[11] The war continued until November 21, 1962, when India accepted defeat and was forced to give China control over the Aksai Chin, a region the size of Switzerland.[12] Around 3,250 Indian soldiers died in the three

---

3   CNN Wire Staff, "Timeline of Tibetan protests in China," *CNN*, January 31, 2012, https://www.cnn.com/2012/01/31/world/asia/tibet-protests-timeline/index.html

4   Jennifer Latson, "How and Why the Dalai Lama Left Tibet," *Time Magazine*, Updated: March 5, 2019, https://time.com/3742242/dalai-lama-1959/

5   PTI, "Mao launched 1962 war for internal control; saw India as soft target: Book," *The Economic Times*, December 24, 2017, https://economictimes.indiatimes.com/news/defence/mao-launched-1962-war-for-internal-control-saw-india-as-soft-target-book/articleshow/62230646.cms?from=mdr

6   Alastair Iain Johnston & Robert S. Ross, "New Directions in the Study of China's Foreign Policy," *Stanford University*, April 2006, https://www.chinacenter.net/wp-content/uploads/2016/04/china-decision-for-war-with-india-1962.pdf

7   Ivan Lidarev, "History's Hostage: China, India and the War of 1962," *The Diplomat*, August 21, 2012, https://thediplomat.com/2012/08/historys-hostage-china-india-and-the-war-of-1962/

8   Alexis Moran, "Who are the Gurkhas? Here's What You Need to Know About The 'Bravest of the Brave'," *Australia Broadcasting Corporation (ABC) News*, June 5, 2018, https://www.abc.net.au/news/2018-06-06/bravest-of-the-brave-who-are-the-fierce-gurkhas/9839746

9   Larry M. Wortzel, "Chapter 9: Concentrating Forces and Audacious Action: PLA Lessons from the Sino-Indian War," in *The Lessons of History: The Chinese People's Liberation Army at 75*, ed. Laurie Burkitt, Andrew Scobell, & Larry M. Wortzel (Strategic Studies Institute, 2003) 327-352. Accessed by https://web.stanford.edu/group/tomzgroup/pmwiki/uploads/0199-2003-Burkitt-a-IEM.pdf

10 India Today, "India-China War of 1962: How It Started and What Happened Later," *India Today*, Updated: November 21, 2018, https://www.indiatoday.in/education-today/gk-current-affairs/story/india-china-war-of-1962-839077-2016-11-21

11 Ibid.

12 The Economist, "Thunder out of China," *The Economist*, May 4, 2013, https://www.economist.com/china/2013/05/04/thunder-out-of-china

weeks.[13]

Sino-Indian relations did not pacify for almost three decades after the end of the 1962 war.[14] In 1989, Prime Minister Rajiv Gandhi visited Beijing to meet with Deng Xiaoping, marking the revitalization of Sino-Indian diplomatic ties and hope for a new beginning.[15]

With this new beginning for China and India, economic ties took center stage. Bilateral

2017 Sino-Indian Doklam Border Dispute

---

13 Prabhash K. Dutta, "This Day in 1962: China-India War Started with Synchronised Attack on Ladakh, Arunachal," *India Today,* October 2-, 2017, https://www.indiatoday.in/india/story/india-china-war-1962-20-october-aksai-chin-nefa-arunchal-pradesh-1067703-2017-10-20

14 Will Green, "Conflict on the Sino-Indian Border: Background for Congress," *U.S.-China Economic and Security Review Commission*, July 2, 2020, https://www.uscc.gov/sites/default/files/2020-07/Conflict_on_Sino-Indian_Border.pdf

15 Srinath Raghavan, "A Brief History of India's Relationship with the People's Republic of China," *Carnegie India,* September 25, 2019, https://carnegieindia.org/2019/09/25/brief-history-of-india-s-relationship-with-people-s-republic-of-china-pub-79914

trade between China and India neared $100 billion in 2018, even amidst conflict.[16] Nevertheless, economic relations were not strong enough to mitigate the high stakes border conflicts that continued as China insisted on further claims to Indian territory.

The 2017 Doklam Standoff

In the summer of 2017, China and India engaged in a 73-day standoff atop of the eastern Himalayan mountain region at the tri-junction where China, India, and Bhutan's borders meet.[17] In mid-June, Bhutan noticed that Chinese crewmembers were paving a road on the Doklam Plateau,[18] a region the Chinese call Donglang. Bhutan alerted India, whose soldiers were immediately deployed to the border to halt China's construction.[19]

Doklam is a critical territory, and its borders were delineated between British India and the Chinese Qing dynasty in an 1890 agreement.[20] However, by constructing a road along the border, India and Bhutan feared China was extending its control over the greater Doklam Plateau, surrounding the Doklam territory. India sent hundreds of troops who unlawfully crossed into China's part of the Doklam region.

India's acts angered China, who claimed that the road construction did not impact any other country and should be considered an internal affair.[21] China's foreign minister, Wang Yi, said, "The solution to this issue is also very simple," admonishing, "That is, behave yourself and humbly retreat."[22]

By crossing into Chinese territory, India triggered a standoff that ended abruptly with Indian troops retreating from the region as any further tension could have risked an all-out war between the two nations.[23] India released a Ministry of External Affairs (MEA) press statement, saying "expeditious disengagement of border personnel at the face-off site at

---

16 South Asian Voices, "India-China: 70 Years of Diplomatic Relations," *South Asian Voices*, n.d., https://southasianvoices.org/india-china-70-years-of-diplomatic-relations/

17 Christopher Woody, "Tensions Are Still Simmering a Year After the World's 2 Biggest Countries Almost Clashed over a Border at the Top of the World," *Business Insider*, August 22, 2018, https://www.businessinsider.com/tensions-between-china-and-india-continue-year-after-doklam-standoff-2018-8

18 Jonah Blank, "What Were China's Objectives in the Doklam Dispute?," *RAND Corporation*, September 8, 2017, https://www.rand.org/blog/2017/09/what-were-chinas-objectives-in-the-doklam-dispute.html

19 Christopher Woody, "Tensions Are Still Simmering a Year After the World's 2 Biggest Countries Almost Clashed over a Border at the Top of the World," *Business Insider*, August 22, 2018, https://www.businessinsider.com/tensions-between-china-and-india-continue-year-after-doklam-standoff-2018-8

20 Prabhash K. Dutta, "How India and China Can Defuse Doklam Tension by Blaming Colonial Britain," *India Today*, October 6, 2017, https://www.indiatoday.in/india/story/india-china-doklam-sikkim-bhutan-britain-1890-calcutta-convention-1024307-2017-07-14

21 Steven Lee Myers, Ellen Barry, & Max Fisher, "How India and China Have Come to the Brink Over a Remote Mountain Pass," *The New York Times*, July 26, 2017, https://www.nytimes.com/2017/07/26/world/asia/dolam-plateau-china-india-bhutan.html

22 Ibid.

23 Ankit Panda, "Disengagement at Doklam: Why and How Did the India-China Standoff End?," *The Diplomat*, August 29, 2017, https://thediplomat.com/2017/08/disengagement-at-doklam-why-and-how-did-the-india-china-standoff-end/

Doklam has been agreed to and is on-going".[24]

In a press conference, Chinese Foreign Ministry spokesperson, Hua Chunying, confirmed that India withdrew "all of its border personnel and equipment that were illegally on Chinese territory to the Indian side", furthering that, despite this, "Chinese border troops continue with their patrols in the Dong Lang area."[25]

China's foreign minister, Wang Yi, released an additional statement saying, "We of course hope that India could learn some lessons from this, and [hope] events similar to this one would not happen again."[26] Nevertheless, with such a fiery tinderbox, and no actual diplomacy resulted, and sparks were bound to ignite again.

The 2020 COVID-19 Standoffs

While China and India 'celebrated' 70 years of diplomatic relations in 2020,[27] they also engaged in life-threatening border disputes that took the pandemic-struck world by storm. For the first time in forty years, a Sino-Indian border clash became deadly.[28]

In the disputed Himalayan Ladakh region, along an established Line of Actual Control (LAC) between China and India, Chinese and Indian troops engaged in a standoff beginning in May 2020 that lasted several weeks before escalating to a risky conflict.[29] The LAC divides the China-controlled but India-claimed Aksai Chin and the Ladakh region. Though a standoff had been ongoing, on June 15, 2020, tension erupted into a full out skirmish and death.

China placed two tents as well as observation towers in the Ladakh region's Galwan Valley that Indian officials stated was established on India's side of the LAC.[30] Chinese troops crossed into Indian territories, prompting Indian patrol crewmembers to confront the troops. The Chinese troops left the area, leaving behind their tents and observation posts. Once the Chinese left, Indian troops demolished their "structures".[31]

---

24 Ankit Panda, "Disengagement at Doklam: Why and How Did the India-China Standoff End?," *The Diplomat*, August 29, 2017, https://thediplomat.com/2017/08/disengagement-at-doklam-why-and-how-did-the-india-china-standoff-end/

25 Ministry of Foreign Affairs of the People's Republic of China, "Foreign Ministry Spokesperson Hua Chunying's Regular Press Conference on August 28, 2017," *Ministry of Foreign Affairs of the People's Republic of China*, August 28, 2017, https://www.fmprc.gov.cn/mfa_eng/xwfw_665399/s2510_665401/t1487932.shtml

26 Simon Denyer & Annie Gowen, The Washington Post, "Who Blinked in the China-India Military Standoff?," *The Washington Post*, August 30, 2017, https://www.washingtonpost.com/news/worldviews/wp/2017/08/30/who-blinked-in-china-india-military-standoff/

27 South Asian Voices, "India-China: 70 Years of Diplomatic Relations," *South Asian Voices*, n.d., https://southasianvoices.org/india-china-70-years-of-diplomatic-relations/

28 Al Jazeera, "Five Things to Know About the India-China Border Standoff," *Al Jazeera*, June 22, 2020, https://www.aljazeera.com/news/2020/06/india-china-border-standoff-200621111215771.html

29 James Palmer & Ravi Agrawal, "Why Are India and China Fighting?," *Foreign Policy*, June 16, 2020, https://foreignpolicy.com/2020/06/16/why-are-india-china-fighting-ladakh-skirmish/

30 Al Jazeera, "Five Things to Know About the India-China Border Standoff," *Al Jazeera*, June 22, 2020, https://www.aljazeera.com/news/2020/06/india-china-border-standoff-200621111215771.html

31 Australian Broadcasting Corporation (ABC) News, "Satellite Images Suggest Chinese Activity in Indian Territory Before Violent Himalayan Border Clash," *Australian Broadcasting Corporation (ABC) News*, June 18, 2020, https://www.abc.net.au/news/2020-06-19/satellite-images-suggest-chinese-activity-at-himalayan-border/12374094

In response, a large group of Chinese soldiers confronted the Indian troops. Heavy and heated conflict ensued, resulting in fighting, including hand-to-hand combat, where the Chinese reportedly used iron rods and spiked batons to kill twenty Indian soldiers.[32] It is unclear how many, or if any, Chinese soldiers had died. This standoff was the first deadly attack in decades, escalating the conflict drastically as India sought ways to counterattack and China continued pressing on with their continued claims to Indian LAC territory.

Prime Minister Modi faced immense pressure to dismantle economic relations with China and fuel a self-reliant economy after the incident. Modi initially responded to the disputes by blocking several Chinese apps from being used in India,[33] a symbol of India's potentially nearing independence from China's technology, markets, and developments. However, both nations have engaged in several rounds of discussions where they have both agreed to use diplomatic talks to handle the disputes. China and India stated they settled on "complete disengagement" of troops from the region for the "full restoration" of peace.[34]

After the fifth round of military-level talks to negotiate the Ladakh border dispute in August 2020, Chinese officials stated they were prepared to "avoid differences escalating into disputes."[35] In Beijing, Chinese Foreign Ministry spokesperson Wang stated,

> We also believe that stronger solidarity and cooperation between China and India…will not only inject strong impetus into our respective development, but also add stability and positive energy to world peace and prosperity. The two sides should always place the boundary issue in an appropriate position in bilateral relations and avoid differences escalating into disputes. It is hoped that India will work with China in the same direction and jointly safeguard bilateral relations.[36]

Conclusion

China and India may 'talk the talk', but they do not 'walk the walk'. Since their agreement to mediate the border conflict diplomatically, Chinese and Indian troops began flocking the Line of Actual Control (LAC), weeks after the standoff, despite pledges to "disengage". China deployed heavy machinery to the LAC, including a "blizzard of new

---

32 BBC News, "Galwan Valley: Image Appears to Show Nail-Studded Rods Used on India-China Brawl," *BBC News*, June 18, 2020, https://www.bbc.com/news/world-asia-india-53089037

33 Eric Bellman & Rajesh Roy, "India's Retaliation Against China Carries Economic Costs," *The Wall Street Journal*, July 4, 2020, https://www.wsj.com/articles/indias-retaliation-against-china-carries-economic-costs-11593869295

34 PTI, "India, China Agree on "Complete Disengagement" of Troops from Eastern Ladakh in Timely Manner," *The Economic Times*, July 10, 2020, https://economictimes.indiatimes.com/news/defence/india-china-agree-on-complete-disengagement-of-troops-from-eastern-ladakh/articleshow/76897215.cms?from=mdr

35 Shubhajit Roy, "LAC Standoff: China Says Avoid Differences Escalating Into Disputes," *The Indian Express*, August 5, 2020, https://indianexpress.com/article/india/lac-standoff-china-says-avoid-differences-escalating-into-disputes-6539694/

36 Consulate General of the People's Republic of China in Mumbai, "Excerpt of Foreign Ministry Regular Press Conference on August 4, 2020," *Consulate General of the People's Republic of China in Mumbai*, August 4, 2020, http://mumbai.china-consulate.org/eng/zxhd/t1804172.htm

tents, new storage sheds, artillery pieces and even tanks".[37] Indian troops remained at the LAC, armed and unwavering, even after both nations agreed to avoid conflict.[38]

It has become increasingly clear that China and India will both fight for what they want. India wants to reclaim the Aksai Chin region it was forced to turn over to China in the 1962 Sino-Indian War. China is on its conquest to acquire more territory to control and will not give up the Aksai Chin anytime soon. Furthermore, China continues to encroach, pushing further into Indian territory. As both nations fervently defend territories and claims, high-stakes disputes like the fatal 2020 standoff are, unfortunately, inevitable.

What's at Stake?

First, territorial claims are at stake. The champion of the standoff sets the tone for who owns much of the ambiguous territory along the South Asian borders. China has been the winner, with its powerful military, just about every time. In this case, both nations are unwilling to relinquish their claim as China seeks to advance its regional control, and India strives to maintain its sovereignty.

Second, miscalculation is quickly becoming a real threat. Twenty Indian soldiers are dead from just one standoff due to China's illegal movement into Indian territory and setting up a camp. However, even more threatening and dangerous events are likely to follow that would drastically affect and involve regional and extra-regional states.

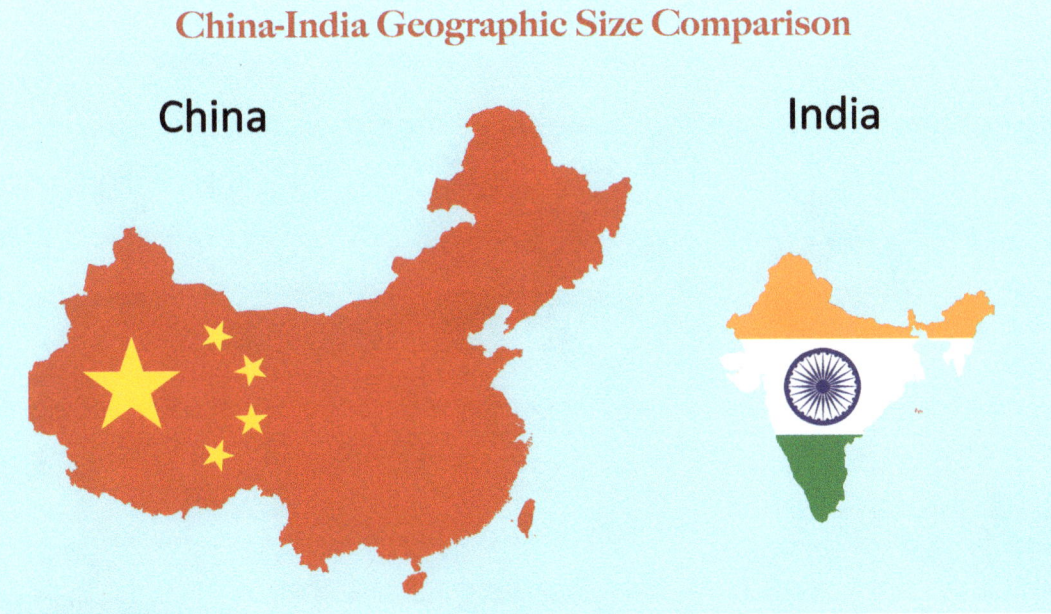

---

37 Jeffrey Gettleman, "Caught Between Indian and Chinese Troops, at 15,000 Feet," *The New York Times,* July 11, 2020, https://www.nytimes.com/2020/07/11/world/asia/india-china-border-ladakh.html

38 Alyssa Ayres, "The China-India Border Dispute: What to Know," *Council on Foreign Relations*, June 18, 2020, https://www.cfr.org/in-brief/china-india-border-dispute-what-know

Chapter 2

Waging a War Over Water

Introduction to China's Dam Construction and Hydrological Data Sharing

Introduction

High atop the Himalayas are more than 50,000 glaciers packed with ice, and they are melting. Of these, more than 30,000 glaciers sit around the Tibetan Plateau now controlled by China. As the snow melts in the Himalayas, water pours down Nepal and Tibet's northern side, flowing toward China's Yangtze and Yellow Rivers. As the rivers stream southward, they drain into the Brahmaputra, Ganges, and Mekong Rivers toward those who live in countries to the south. Freshwater drainage from this high elevation water reserve is the lifeblood for hundreds of millions of people in multiple countries. In these extreme highlands, considered the "roof of the world", water is being redirected in dozens of China's elaborate dam and tunneling projects. Moreover, Beijing has proposed engineering specialized tunneling operations underneath the mountains to reroute tens of billions of gallons more per year.

Limited Water Resources

Although 70% of the Earth is covered in water,[1] only 2.5% of that water is fresh. With snow-capped glaciers and ice fields trapping most of the freshwater, only 1% of the Earth provides accessible and potable water.[2] That said, and with a global population that has surpassed 7.3 billion, only 1% of the world's water can provide sustenance.

---

1 National Geographic, "Freshwater Crisis," National Geographic, n.d., https://www.nationalgeographic.com/environment/freshwater/freshwater-crisis/

2 Ibid.

Yet, water is the most essential life-giving, life-supporting, and life-sustaining element. Rivers, many that are now polluted, provide much of the remaining available water source, and they are critical to every nation's survival. Furthermore, each country has a vested interest in ensuring that its population has enough. Competition for water is fierce in some areas, mainly where populations are burgeoning; a water fight is underway.

Beyond partisanship, every human being understands the importance of water. Since this valuable resource is necessary, shortages have created regional catastrophic water crises.

The United Nations University's Institute of Water, Environment, and Health estimates that by 2035, 40% of the global population will be living in "seriously water-stressed areas."[3] The World Wildlife Organization approximates that by 2025, two-thirds of the world's population will face water shortages.[4] Since 2016, the Center for Disease Control and Prevention estimates that 760 million global citizens lack access to safe water sources.[5]

Mother nature has dealt a difficult hand to nations who now face an array of water-related issues. Rivers, lakes, and aquifers are drying up and being contaminated. The World Wide Fund for Nature (formerly the World Wildlife Fund) estimates that over half of the

---

3   Lisa Guppy & Kelsey Anderson, "Global Water Crisis: The Facts," *United Nations University*, 2017, https://inweh.unu.edu/wp-content/uploads/2017/11/Global-Water-Crisis-The-Facts.pdf

4   WWF, "Water Scarcity," *WWF*, n.d., https://www.worldwildlife.org/threats/water-scarcity

5   CDC, "Global WASH Fast Facts," *CDC*, n.d., https://www.cdc.gov/healthywater/global/wash_statistics.html

world's wetlands have vanished.[6] Wetlands are crucial, as they are nature's sponges to recycle freshwater and groundwater and mitigate the impacts of flooding.[7]

Production and manufacturing industries over-consume water. Agriculture utilizes more water than any other industry; related farming practices require and waste a tremendous amount of water.[8] Additionally, climate change and its associated increase in global temperatures pose rising threats of water shortages and droughts.[9]

Together, water challenges not only create humanitarian crises but also pave the way for geopolitical clashes. With limited water availability, neighboring geographic territories dispute access. As nations seek water supplies large enough for their population, 'water wars' have become an inevitable fresh ground for instability.

In Asia, with an estimated population of 4.6 billion,[10] a whopping thirteen times that of the United States, water wars have become a raging battle zone of 'survival of the fittest' as governments strategically seek to sustain their populations. With enlarged populations, leaders face high stakes decisions.

Conclusion

Water, economic, and military challenges have tested South and Southeast Asia. China, desperate to support its 1.4 billion citizens, continues to redefine its boundaries to include additional water sources. In an innovative shift of natural resources, China has redirected water to its territory through the construction of dams. For example, China has built eleven dams to block water and nutrient-rich sediment from traveling down the Mekong River and has announced plans to build eighteen more.[11] These additional dams will reroute water that previously flowed into Vietnam, Cambodia, Thailand, Laos, and Myanmar. The same water diversion strategy is being planned along the Brahmaputra River in Tibet to reroute water away from India, Bangladesh, Nepal, and Bhutan.

Meanwhile, as climates change and environmental conditions link to both flooding and water shortages, China has used data as a weapon. China's advanced technology is capable of predicting flood patterns. India needs this data to mitigate the impact of flooding, discussed in another chapter. Although China and India have an agreement vis-à-vis water and associated flood data, recently, China has leveraged this pact due to their intensifying border conflicts. Though water is life-giving, life-supporting, and life-sustaining, water becomes a weapon capable of devastating destruction when it flows through geopolitical conflict.

---

6   WWF, "Water Scarcity," *WWF*, n.d., https://www.worldwildlife.org/threats/water-scarcity
7   United States Environmental Protection Agency, "Why are Wetlands Important?," *United States Environmental Protection Agency,* n.d., https://www.epa.gov/wetlands/why-are-wetlands-important
8   WWF, "Water Scarcity," *WWF*, n.d., https://www.worldwildlife.org/threats/water-scarcity
9   Ibid.
10 Worldometers, "Asia Population (Live)," *Worldometers*, n.d., https://www.worldometers.info/world-population/asia-population/
11 Brian Eyler, "Science Shows Chinese Dams Are Devastating the Mekong," *Foreign Policy,* April 22, 2020, https://foreignpolicy.com/2020/04/22/science-shows-chinese-dams-devastating-mekong-river/

What's at Stake?

First, statistics estimate that 40% of the global population will be living in "seriously water-stressed areas" by 2035. This prognosis may occur sooner if water supplies to South and Southeast Asian states are threatened.

Second, the current manufacturing and production rates pave the path to an unsustainable future with the associated need for natural resources required to satisfy consumer demand.

Third, the weaponization of water, a global necessity, and China's dam construction have proven that Beijing can and will utilize anything and everything to achieve its status as Asia's hegemon regardless of the toll on its neighbors' populations.

Gangotri, India at the Himalayan Origin of the Ganges River

Chapter 3

Weaponizing Himalayan Water Information
China and India's 'Hydrological Data Sharing'

Introduction

China and India are prone to monsoons, droughts, and water shortages. To mitigate this threat, in 2006, China and India arranged to implement a plan to reduce the impact of these weather-related water shocks to their respective countries. In this agreement, they committed to monitoring and reporting potential flooding during monsoon seasons through early detection. This agreement was signed and renewed by both parties in 2013 and 2015.[1]

Hydrological Data Sharing Agreement

On May 20, 2013, China and India renewed a plan, called 'hydrological data sharing'. This agreement required China to warn India of incoming flooding from its high elevation perch when identification systems indicated dangerous levels. India depends on China for hydrological data sharing to prepare for a deluge of water.

In the joint hydrological data-sharing agreement, China is obligated to send New Delhi information regarding the Brahmaputra and Sutlej Rivers,[2] two major water sources that flow through South Asia. The Brahmaputra River is a vital source of water for Indians, flowing from the Himalayas to the Ganges River and emptying into the Bay of Bengal.

Brahmaputra River Flow

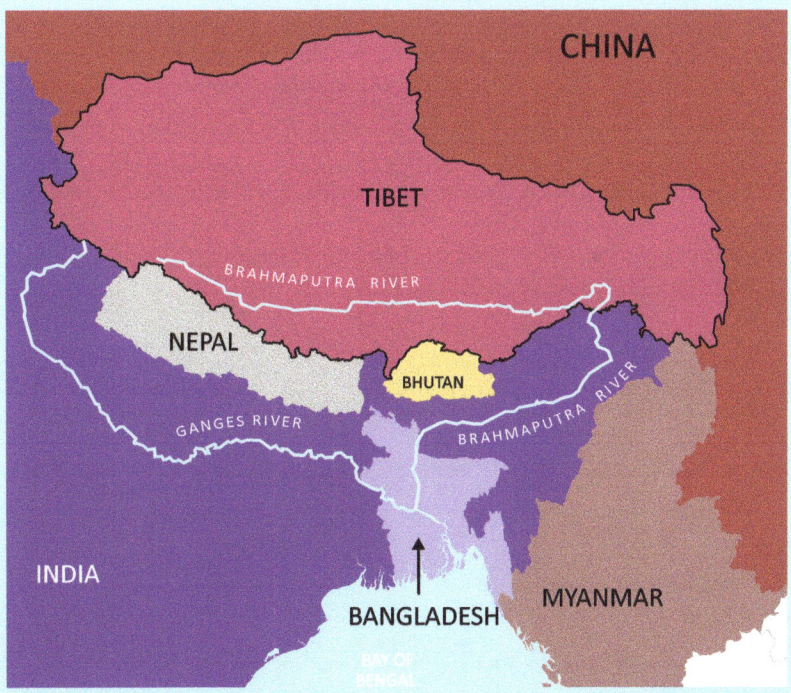

---

1. Chandan Kumar Duarah, "South Asia Journal: India-China Water Sharing Data," *Yale University,* September 29, 2018, https://yaleglobal.yale.edu/content/south-asia-journal-india-china-water-sharing-data
2. Ritesth K. Srivastava, "China Starts Sharing Hydrological Data for Brahmaputra River," *Zee News*, May 16, 2020, https://zeenews.india.com/india/china-starts-sharing-hydrological-data-for-brahmaputra-river-2283902.html

Accordingly, China agreed to send hydrological data recorded from the two rivers during the annual monsoon season that runs from May 15 to October 15. The sharing of hydrological information, particularly high-water levels, is crucial in alerting India to prepare for possible flooding.[3] Though this agreement began as a collaborative effort to protect regional citizens, China quickly weaponized the treaty in a political battle.

Weaponizing the Agreement

In 2017, China and India entered a standoff atop the Himalayan mountains that left the rest of the world holding their breath. On June 16, 2017, China began constructing a road along the border of Dong Lang, also known as Doklam.[4] This territory impinges upon a tri-junction intersection between China, India, and Bhutan, India's ally. Threatened by China's proximity and wanting to stop China's road construction, Indian border troops illegally crossed into Chinese territory on June 18, 2017, instigating a high-stakes standoff between the two nations that lasted for 73 days,[5] involving over 3,000 soldiers.[6]

Afterward, India initiated troop removal and stepped down from the Doklam region; China followed. Though the Doklam border conflict de-escalated, China's anger was still present. This time, frustrations were evidenced in a new form of dispute: hydrological data sharing.

In September 2017, Delhi announced that it had not received its annual hydrological data report from China, agreed upon by both nations in 2006 and renewed in 2013 and 2015. In an August 2017 press briefing, Raveesh Kumar, a spokesperson from India's Ministry of External Affairs (MEA), stated, "For this year...we have not received the hydrological data from the Chinese side beginning 15 May until now."[7]

China responded to India's statement and dire condition, scapegoating a technical problem for the 'delay' in data sharing. In a September 2017 press briefing, China's Foreign Ministry Spokesperson Geng Shuang affirmed, "Last year, due to the needs for reconstruction after being damaged by the flood and out of such technological reasons as upgrading and renovation, the relevant hydrological stations in China do not have the conditions to collect relevant hydrological data now."[8]

---

3   Navin Singh Khadka, "China and India Water 'Dispute' After Border Stand-Off," *BBC News,* September 18, 2017, https://www.bbc.com/news/world-asia-41303082

4   Christopher Woody, "Tensions are Still Simmering a Year After The World's 2 Biggest Countries Almost Clashed Over a Border At The Top Of The World," *Business Insider,* August 22, 2018, https://www.businessinsider.com/tensions-between-china-and-india-continue-year-after-doklam-standoff-2018-8

5   PTI, "Amid Border Tensions with India, China Starts Sharing Hydrological Data for Brahmaputra River," *The New Indian Express,* May 16, 2020, https://www.newindianexpress.com/nation/2020/may/16/amid-border-tensions-with-india-china-starts-sharing-hydrological-data-for-brahmaputra-river-2143909.html

6   Christopher Woody, "Tensions are Still Simmering a Year After The World's 2 Biggest Countries Almost Clashed Over a Border At The Top Of The World," *Business Insider*, August 22, 2018, https://www.businessinsider.com/tensions-between-china-and-india-continue-year-after-doklam-standoff-2018-8

7   PTI, "Can't Share Hydrological Data of Brahmaputra River With India For Now: China", *The Economic Times,* July 13, 2018, https://economictimes.indiatimes.com/news/defence/cant-share-hydrological-data-of-brahmaputra-river-with-india-for-now-china/articleshow/60478124.cms?from=mdr

8   Embassy of the People's Republic of China in the Socialist Republic of Vietnam, "Foreign Ministry Spokesperson Geng Shuang's Regular Press Conference on September 12, 2017," *Embassy of the People's Republic of China in the Socialist Republic of Vietnam,* September 12, 2017, http://vn.china-embassy.org/eng/fyrth/t1492339.htm

However, Bangladesh squashed any validity to Beijing's statement. Mofazzal Hossain, a member of the joint rivers commission of Bangladesh, told *BBC News* that Bangladesh "received data of water level of the Brahmaputra from China" when India did not, adding that they "have been receiving such data from three hydrological stations in Tibet since 2002 and [China has] continued to share the figure with us even during this monsoon season."[9] The water resources minister of Bangladesh, Anisul Islam Mohammad, confirmed Hossain's claim to *BBC News*.[10]

Conclusion

China withheld hydrological data from New Delhi from 2017 until 2018. Despite ongoing border disputes with India, Beijing shared the data of the Brahmaputra River with India in the monsoon season of May 2020.[11] Although now complying, China's acts of retaliation against India after the Doklam border standoff sent a message to the rest of the world that China will use its power to monopolize resources and information, as evidenced in its hydropolitical leverage. There is no limit to Beijing's geopolitical capability; China has and will go to any extent to exert its influence, though its rhetoric cautiously deflects and denies culpability.

What's at Stake?

First, India vitally needs the hydrological data from China to protect against flooding. Without this information, India could face large-scale natural disasters that risk displacement, infrastructure damage, casualties, economic distress, and detriment to the citizenry.

Second, by using hydrological data as a geopolitical weapon, China believes it can coerce India to comply with any demands it chooses. Furthermore, as long as India remains dependent on China, Beijing can pull any strings it wants in regional disputes. Hydrological data sharing is just one of many strings China can pull.

Third, according to the United Nations, 31 million people were adversely affected by flooding during those same months, including 12.33 million children, 15,455 schools, and 805,183 houses.[12]

---

9   Navin Singh Khadka, "China and India Water 'Dispute' After Border Stand-Off," *BBC News*, September 18, 2017, https://www.bbc.com/news/world-asia-41303082

10 Ibid.

11 PTI, "Amid Border Tensions with India, China Starts Sharing Hydrological Data for Brahmaputra River," *The New Indian Express*, May 16, 2020, https://www.newindianexpress.com/nation/2020/may/16/amid-border-tensions-with-india-china-starts-sharing-hydrological-data-for-brahmaputra-river-2143909.html

12 UNICEF, "16 Million Children Affected by Massive Flooding in South Asia, with Millions More at Risk," *UNICEF*, September 2, 2017, https://www.unicef.org/media/media_100719.html

Chapter 4
China's Investments in Pakistan
A Pawn in the Broader South Asian Conflict

Introduction

In 2015, before landing in Islamabad, **Xi Jinping wrote**, "This will be my first trip to Pakistan, but I feel as if I am going to visit the home of my own brother."[1] Announcing this segment of Beijing's Belt and Road Initiative, the China-Pakistan Economic Corridor (CPEC), headed full steam ahead. Meanwhile, Beijing and Pakistan battled their ongoing border disputes with their mutual rival, India. With their increasing economic ties, China-Pakistan relations have flourished in the 21st century.

Though China and Pakistan have engaged in separate conflicts with India over the decades, recent disputes in the Kashmir region have intertwined three nations in diplomatic and militaristic disputes. China and India's 2020 border dispute on the Line of Actual Control (LAC) occurred where the LAC separates the Pakistan-administered territories of Azad Kashmir and Gilgit-Baltistan from the India-administered territories of Jammu, Kashmir, and Ladakh.[2] Nevertheless, China's cozied relation with its "iron brother"[3] and

China-Pakistan Economic Corridor (CPEC)
China's Route to the Arabian Sea

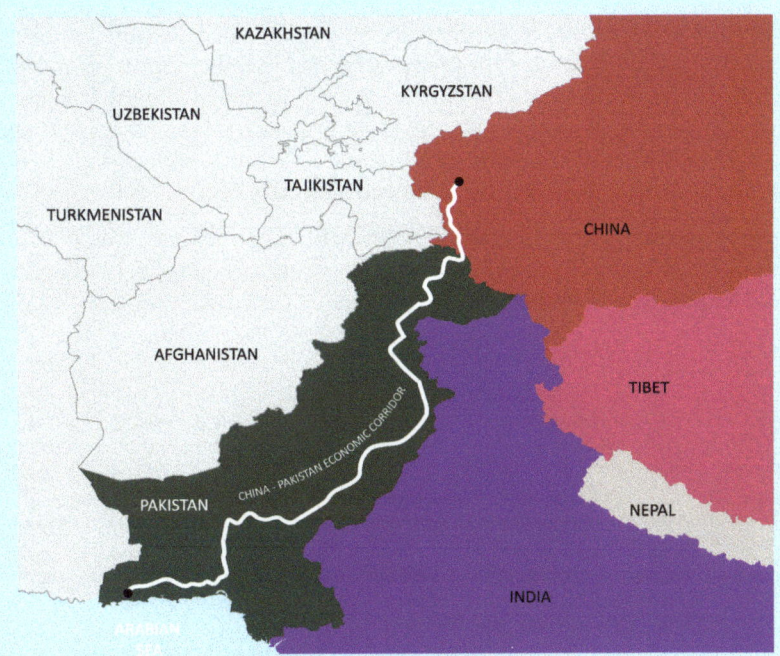

---

1. Ankit Panda, "Xi Jinping on Pakistan: 'I Feel As If I Am Going to Visit the Home of My Own Brother,'" *The Diplomat*, April 20, 2015, https://thediplomat.com/2015/04/xi-jinping-on-pakistan-i-feel-as-if-i-am-going-to-visit-the-home-of-my-own-brother/

2. Eduardo Baptista, "Why Pakistan is a Big Factor in China's Border Clashes with India," *South China Morning Post*, June 27, 2020, https://www.scmp.com/news/china/diplomacy/article/3090758/why-pakistan-big-factor-chinas-border-clashes-india

3. SAMAA, "Pakistan is China's 'Iron Brother', Says Chinese Foreign Minister Wang Yi," *SAMAA*, March 10, 2019, https://www.samaa.tv/news/2019/03/pakistan-is-chinas-iron-brother-says-chinese-foreign-minister-wang-yi/

India's ongoing rivalry with Pakistan has fostered a unique geopolitical climate. Accordingly, China and Pakistan have strengthened their economic and political relations while impeding India.

Investments and Loans in Pakistan

With its strengthening alliance with Pakistan, China has offered its economic might to develop Pakistani infrastructure, energy, and transportation projects. Despite protests from India, China has invested over $8 billion into the Pakistani Diamer Bhasha multipurpose dam, expected to generate 4,500 megawatts of inexpensive, clean energy and slated to be completed in 2028.[4] Furthermore, in 2018, Pakistan reportedly planned to construct a city, especially for Chinese nationals living in the port city of Gwadar to be completed by 2022.[5] This city would be a financial district for China, giving Beijing a colony in Pakistan exclusively for China's access.[6]

The largest collaboration between the two nations remains the China-Pakistan Economic Corridor, with $62 billion invested for infrastructure projects.[7] China pledged a $46 billion superhighway from Xinjiang Province to Gwadar to give China direct access to the Indian Ocean.[8]

The United States criticized Pakistan for its trust in China in the CPEC investment. *Reuters* explains, "Washington says the project is not sufficiently transparent and will saddle Pakistan with the burden of expensive Chinese loans."[9] In response to the U.S. comments, Aisha Farooqui, a Pakistani foreign office spokeswoman, defended China, asserting, "To claim that CPEC is always in the form of loans and other forms of financing often non-concessional with sovereign guarantees is not based on facts."[10]

However, the International Monetary Fund (IMF) has similar concerns with China-Pakistan financial relations. In IMF's findings, Pakistan owes China $6.7 billion in commercial loans.[11] This payment is more than double what Pakistan owes the IMF.[12]

---

4   Ayaz Gul, "China's Investments in Pakistan-Administered Kashmir Seen as 'Blow' to India," *VOA News,* July 15, 2020, https://www.voanews.com/east-asia-pacific/voa-news-china/chinas-investments-pakistan-administered-kashmir-seen-blow-india

5   Business Today, "'Chinese-Only Colony' in Pakistan to House 5 Lakh Workers," *Business Today*, August 21, 2018, https://www.businesstoday.in/current/world/chinese-colony-in-pakistan-international-port-city-cpec-gwadar/story/281497.html

6   Dipanjan Roy Chaudhury, "As part of CPEC, 'Chinese only' colony coming up in Pakistan," *The Economic Times*, August 21, 2018, https://economictimes.indiatimes.com/news/defence/as-part-of-cpec-chinese-only-colony-coming-up-in-pakistan/articleshow/65481132.cms

7   Hussain Haqqani, "Pakistan Discovers the High Cost of Chinese Investment," *The Diplomat*, May 18, 2020, https://thediplomat.com/2020/05/pakistan-discovers-the-high-cost-of-chinese-investment/

8   BBC News, "China's Xi Jinping Agrees $46bn Superhighway to Pakistan," *BBC News*, April 20, 2015, https://www.bbc.com/news/world-asia-32377088

9   Gibran Peshimam, "Pakistan Defends Chinese Investment After U.S. Official's Criticism," *Reuters*, January 23, 2020, https://www.reuters.com/article/us-pakistan-cpec-criticism/pakistan-defends-chinese-investment-after-u-s-officials-criticism-idUSKBN1ZM23W

10   Ibid.

11   Faseeh Mangi, "Pakistan Owes China More Money Than It Owes the IMF," *Bloomberg,* October 2, 2019, https://www.bloomberg.com/news/articles/2019-10-03/pakistan-owes-china-more-money-than-it-does-imf-as-loans-mature

12   Ibid.

Kashmir Region Boundary Conflict: India, Pakistan, China
CPEC and Water Rights Controversy

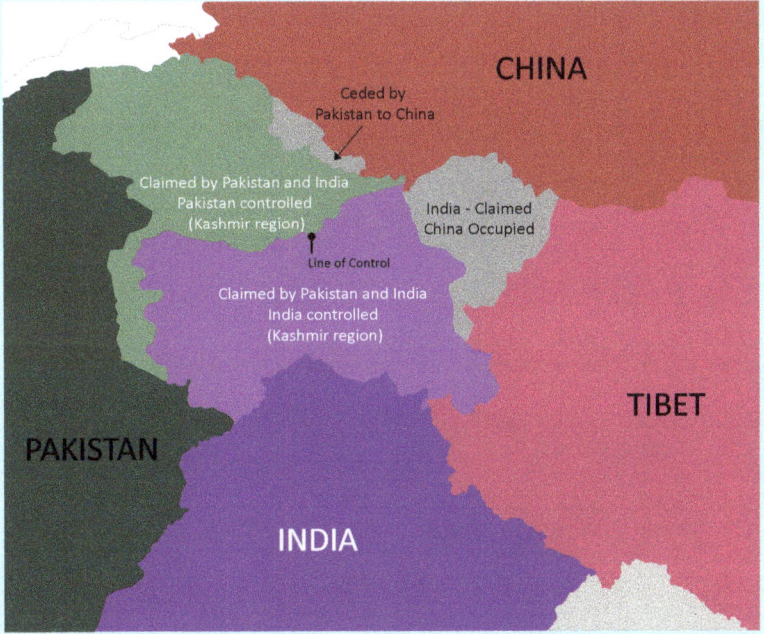

'Gifted' Land and Conflict with India

The China-Pakistan alliance has mutually benefitted both states, but has also escalated tension with their common 'disputant', India. Much of this conflict has occurred over the sovereignty and status of the Kashmir region. In the 1950s, China began its construction of a road (NH 219) through the Aksai Chin in northeast Ladakh.[13] This road gave China access to control Tibet and linked Ladakh to Xinjiang Province.[14] With China's ongoing and expanding presence, in 1963, Pakistan gifted thousands of square miles of its land in Jammu and Kashmir to China.[15] This gift became part of the China-Pakistan Boundary Agreement,

---

13 Dipanjan Roy Chaudhury, "China's Plan in Ladakh Dates Back to 1950s: Exiled Kashmiri Leader," *The Economic Times*, June 11, 2020, https://economictimes.indiatimes.com/news/defence/chinas-plan-in-ladakh-dates-back-to-1950s-exiled-kashmiri-leader/articleshow/76314497.cms

14 Adrija Roychowdhury, "Why Ladakh Matters to India, China: History, Geography, and Strategy," *The Indian Express*, June 19, 2020, https://indianexpress.com/article/explained/why-ladakh-matters-to-india-and-china-lac-galwan-faceoff-6465198/

15 Dipanjan Roy Chaudhury, "China's Plan in Ladakh Dates Back to 1950s: Exiled Kashmiri Leader," *The Economic Times*, June 11, 2020, https://economictimes.indiatimes.com/news/defence/chinas-plan-in-ladakh-dates-back-to-1950s-exiled-kashmiri-leader/articleshow/76314497.cms

signed in Peking on March 2, 1963.[16]

However, Pakistan's grant of land, also claimed by India, sparked a protest from Indian officials. The Indian government questioned how Pakistan could 'gift' the Jammu and Kashmir region to China when the territory was not theirs in the first place. India delivered a complaint to the U.N. Security Council, calling the agreement illegal on several grounds.[17] In 2019, India stated, "Jammu and Kashmir are an integral part of India and the issue is strictly internal to the country."[18]

To further assert its claim, in 2019, without consultation from Pakistan or China, India revoked special status over Kashmir, splitting the region into two federal territories to integrate the area into Indian sovereign land.[19] Geng Shuang, a Chinese foreign ministry spokesman, publicly responded to India's action, stating,

---

16 Dr. Ahmad Rashid Malik, "Who Ceded the Land?," *Pakistan Today*, June 26, 2016, https://www.pakistantoday.com.pk/2016/06/26/who-ceded-the-land/

17 Ibid.

18 Press Trust of India, "Jammu and Kashmir an Internal Matter and Integral Part of Country, Says India on OIC Resolution," *Firstpost,* March 3, 2019, https://www.firstpost.com/world/jammu-and-kashmir-an-internal-matter-and-integral-part-of-country-says-india-on-oic-resolution-6185431.html

19 Zeba Siddiqui & Fayaz Bukhari, "India, China Clash Over Kashmir as it Loses Special Status and is Divided," *Reuters*, October 30, 2019, https://www.reuters.com/article/us-india-kashmir/india-china-clash-over-kashmir-as-it-loses-special-status-and-is-divided-idUSKBN1XA0M9

The Indian government officially announced the establishment of so called Jammu Kashmir territory and Ladakh Union territory which included some of China's territory into its administrative jurisdiction. China deplores and firmly opposed that. India unilaterally changes its domestic law and administrative divisions, challenging China's sovereignty and interests. This is awful and void, and this is not effective in any way and will not change the fact that the area is under China's actual control.[20]

Furthermore, India's MEA responded to Geng's assertations, stating,

> China is well aware of India's consistent position on this issue. The Union Territory of Jammu & Kashmir has been, is and shall continue to be an integral part of India. Issues related to J&K are internal matter to India. It is, therefore, our expectation that other countries, including China, would refrain from commenting on matters that are internal affairs of India and respect India's sovereignty and territorial integrity. We also expect China to recognise and condemn the scourge of cross-border terrorism that affect the lives of the people of India, including in J&K.[21]

Conclusion

International bodies and the United States warned Pakistan that its alliance with China, though appealing for national interests, may come at a hefty price. Pakistan has such significant debt that the nation may need to give up more than just one port city to the Chinese, possibly the Port of Gwadar itself, like Sri Lanka did with its 99-year lease for the Port of Hambantota. Furthermore, India has shown that it is willing to defend its territory despite China's growing military strength. Jammu and Kashmir may become the next hotspots on the world stage if Pakistan attempts to relinquish additional northern territory to the Chinese.

What's at Stake?

First, the CPEC grants China entree to India's South Asian backyard and waterways, where its access to Kashmir and the port city of Gwadar extends Beijing's influence.

Second, India's protest of the growing alliance heightens the tension between Pakistan and India, two nations who have been in conflict for decades and are struggling to make peace without China's added pressure.

Third, Pakistan's substantial debt to China could give Beijing leverage over the South Asian nation, making Pakistan China's puppet in the region if it cannot make ends meet or force the negotiation of loan extensions.

---

20 Tamil Guardian, "China Condemns India's Division of Kashmir," *Tamil Guardian*, October 31, 2019, https://www.tamilguardian.com/content/china-condemns-india%E2%80%99s-division-kashmir

21 India.com News Desk, "'China Must Refrain From Commenting on India's Internal Matters,' MEA on Kashmir Issue," *India.com*, April 9, 2020, https://www.india.com/news/india/china-must-refrain-from-commenting-on-indias-internal-matters-mea-on-kashmir-issue-3995457/

Chapter 5

China-Bhutan Territorial Conflict Over an Ecological Preserve

Dispute Over the Sakteng Wildlife Sanctuary

Introduction

Bhutan submitted a request to the Global Environmental Facility (GEF) to create the Sakteng Wildlife Sanctuary in eastern Bhutan during the 58th GEF Council meeting in June 2020.[1] Aparna Subramani, the Executive Director of the World Bank, responsible for Bangladesh, Bhutan, India, and Sri Lanka, represented Bhutan.

United Nations Development Program (UNDP) Proposal

Bhutan requested $5.4 million in UNDP biodiversity funding, stating, "If approved, the proposal will be prepared and implemented by the Gross National Happiness Commission (GNHC), Tourism Council of Bhutan, and Department of Forests & Park Services."[2]

Bhutan-China Territorial Dispute
Sakteng Wildlife Sanctuary

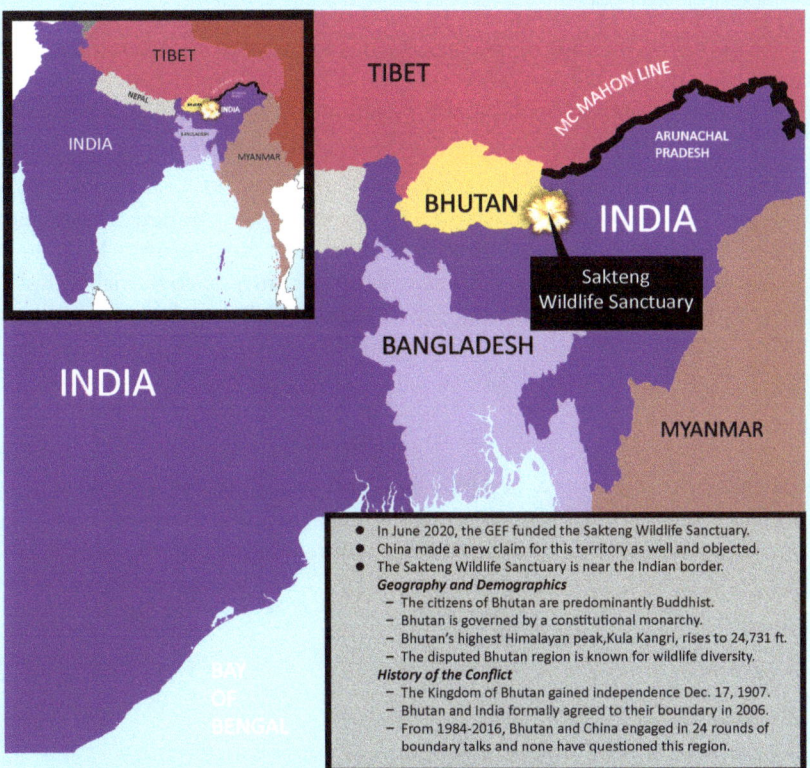

- In June 2020, the GEF funded the Sakteng Wildlife Sanctuary.
- China made a new claim for this territory as well and objected.
- The Sakteng Wildlife Sanctuary is near the Indian border.

Geography and Demographics
- The citizens of Bhutan are predominantly Buddhist.
- Bhutan is governed by a constitutional monarchy.
- Bhutan's highest Himalayan peak, Kula Kangri, rises to 24,731 ft.
- The disputed Bhutan region is known for wildlife diversity.

History of the Conflict
- The Kingdom of Bhutan gained independence Dec. 17, 1907.
- Bhutan and India formally agreed to their boundary in 2006.
- From 1984-2016, Bhutan and China engaged in 24 rounds of boundary talks and none have questioned this region.

---

1   Sha Hua & Rajesh Roy, "China Pulls Back From One Disputed Border, Makes New Claims on Another," *The Wall Street Journal*, July 7, 2020, https://www.wsj.com/articles/china-pulls-back-from-one-disputed-border-makes-new-claims-on-another-11594052370

2   Rinchen Wangdi, "Endorsement for the Mainstreaming Biodiversity Conservation into the Tourism Sector in Bhutan Project," *Royal Government of Bhutan, Gross National Happiness Commission*, March 10, 2020, https://www.thegef.org/sites/default/files/project_documents/OFPsLetterofEndorsementCountryname_Bhutan-LoE-GWP-UNDP-March102020_0.pdf

Bhutan and China do not have embassies in the other's country. Thus, they conduct diplomatic relations through Delhi, India. The GEF Council member representing Beijing stated that the Sakteng Wildlife Sanctuary project is located in the China-Bhutan disputed area,[3] adding, "China opposes and does not join the Council decision on this project." The GEF Council member representing Bhutan retorted, "Bhutan totally rejects the claim made by the Council Member of China. Sakteng Wildlife Sanctuary is an integral and sovereign territory of Bhutan and at no point during the boundary discussions between Bhutan and China has it featured as a disputed area."[4]

In June 2020, Bhutan suggested the creation of a 650 sq km sanctuary in eastern Bhutan. China eyed Bhutan's territory and sought to take a salami slice or two. However, until 2020, Bhutan and China had two disputed areas. In June 2020, China added territory further into Bhutan. None of the written documents during the two countries' 24 rounds of negotiations between China and Bhutan have included this region. However, the Chinese foreign ministry issued a statement saying, "China always stands for a negotiated package solution to the China-Bhutan boundary issue."[5]

There is a precedent for China's "package" offer. In this way, China can take control of those regions and "settle" the boundary issues. The divide and conquer method, settling disputes with money, trade, or land, country-by-country, provides China with greater leverage to sway the country's decision-making in their favor.

Former Indian ambassador to China, Ashok K. Kantha, stated, "China is expanding its territorial claims against Bhutan. Sakteng was not previously in a disputed area identified and jointly surveyed by Bhutan and China in western and central sectors." He went on to say that this dynamic is a "pattern of China pursuing its contested territorial claims, old and new, against its neighbours, land and maritime."[6] Former Indian ambassador to Bhutan, V. P. Haran, said, "Sakteng or any other part of eastern Bhutan was not disputed. Sakteng is quite some distance from the border with China."[7]

Conclusion

This new regional dispute may be a ploy for China to use the area as a "bargaining chip for Beijing when negotiating this round of disengagement with Indian troops and to signal to its home audience that China will defend its territorial claims even though it is pulling

---

3   Sha Hua & Rajesh Roy, "China Pulls Back From One Disputed Border, Makes New Claims on Another," *The Wall Street Journal*, July 7, 2020, https://www.wsj.com/articles/china-pulls-back-from-one-disputed-border-makes-new-claims-on-another-11594052370

4   Geeta Mohan, "Bhutan Demarches China on its Claim to Sakteng Sanctuary, Beijing Reiterates Position," *India Today*, July 6, 2020, https://www.indiatoday.in/world/story/china-bhutan-territory-dispute-demarche-chinese-embassy-new-delhi-sakteng-sanctuary-1697392-2020-07-06

5   Rosy Huong, "China's New Claim on Bhutan Land and 'Third Party'," *Vietnam Times*, June 7, 2020, https://vietnamtimes.org.vn/chinas-new-claim-on-bhutan-land-and-third-party-22034.html

6   Ibid.

7   Shubhajit Roy, "China Makes New Claim in Eastern Border with Bhutan," *The Indian Express*, July 6, 2020, https://indianexpress.com/article/world/china-makes-new-claim-in-eastern-border-with-bhutan-6491875/

back troops from one of the disputed areas."[8] In June 2020, China pressed forward into the Indian corridor of Siliguri, attempting to build a road on disputed territory, which resulted in the killing of 20 Indian soldiers. India's Prime Minister, Narendra Modi, exclaimed China's aggression is part of its wide-ranging "expansionism". In 2017, India and China were engaged in another deadlock that led to a 73-day standoff.

What's at Stake?

First, if China can claim new territory that they have not claimed before, they can claim territory anywhere. This pattern of engagement in "China's Power Grab" is a salami-slicing model, taking one small salami slice at a time.

Second, Bhutan serves as today's pawn in a chess match with other countries to gain leverage China believes it needs to have if Beijing intends to win the battle for global supremacy.

Third, this disagreement is not about wildlife, but it shows that even projects as benign as a wildlife preserve are not off limits to China.

---

8   Sha Hua and Rajesh Roy, "China Pulls Back From One Disputed Border, Makes New Claims on Another," *The Wall Street Journal,* July 7, 2020, https://www.wsj.com/articles/china-pulls-back-from-one-disputed-border-makes-new-claims-on-another-11594052370

Chapter 6

The Destruction of Tibetan Land and Culture

Borders, Minerals, Water, and Genocide

Introduction

How far will China go to take over land, minerals, and water to satisfy its growing population? The Central Tibetan Administration explains, "Tibetans were not only shot, but also were beaten to death, crucified, burned alive, drowned, mutilated, starved, strangled, hanged, boiled alive, buried alive, drawn and quartered, and beheaded."[1] As Tibetan monks attempted to honor their culture, language, religion, and spiritual relationship to their land, they were being massacred. In protest, more than a hundred and fifty Tibetans have self-immolated, setting themselves on fire in public squares in an attempt to gain the world's attention.[2]

Most of the world has forgotten about Tibet's plea for help. After all, there are too many other concerns, and most global citizens are resigned to China's occupation of Tibet. China now has complete control of the citizenry and has engaged in environmental destruction, though unheard of by many global citizens. COVID-19 distracted the masses as the world

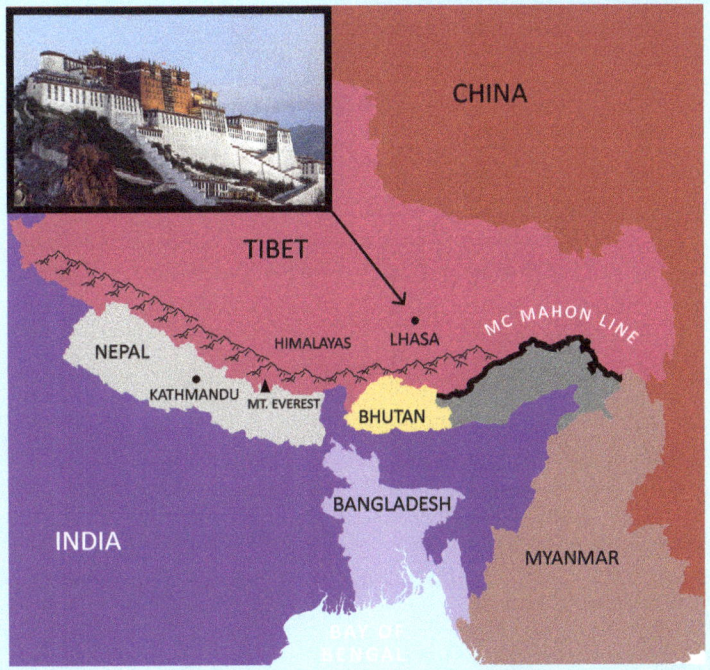

Tibetan Autonomous Region
6,000 Buddhist Monasteries Destroyed by China's Red Guards

---

1 Yeshe Choesang, "China is Guilty of Mass Genocide Against 1.2 Million People of Tibet," *Tibet Post International*, June 12, 2019, http://www.thetibetpost.com/en/outlook/opinions-and-columns/4643-china-is-guilty-of-mass-genocide-against-12-million-people-of-tibet

2 Central Tibetan Administration, "Fact Sheet on Tibetan Self-Immolation Protests in Tibet Since February 2009," *Central Tibetan Administration*, Retrieved on July 30, 2020, https://tibet.net/important-issues/factsheet-immolation-2011-2012/

became legitimately concerned with the health and future of themselves and their families. Meanwhile, though, there is a contradiction in what Beijing's spokespeople say and what China does. Australia-based Tibet analyst Bawa Kalsang Gyaltsen noted, "On the one hand, the Chinese Communist Party says that Tibetans in Tibet live freely and comfortably, but in reality, Tibetans are constantly living under scrutiny and threat from the Chinese government."[3]

Buddhist Monks – Threat?

If you take someone's land, rights, and freedoms, and then destroy their temples and persecute them through torture, they could become a threat - even pacifist Buddhist monks. Tibet was a prayerful, peaceful, and humble country where Buddhists meditated and sought a spiritual road toward goodness and happiness by practicing the 8 Noble Paths:[4]

1. Correct Thoughts
2. Correct Speech
3. Correct Actions
4. Correct Livelihood
5. Correct Understanding
6. Correct Effort
7. Correct Mindfulness
8. Correct Concentration

Even today, Beijing sees Tibetan Buddhism as a threat.[5] Without an automatic right to a passport, Tibetans are restricted in where they can travel. Those who attempt to escape are beaten, tortured, or imprisoned.[6] Yet, these acts seem to contradict China's constitution, which states, "Discrimination against and oppression of any nationality are prohibited; any act which undermines the unity of the nationalities or instigates division is prohibited."[7]

---

3   Central Tibetan Administration, "China Calls Tibet's Stability into Question with 'Show of Force' in Lhasa," *Radio Free Asia*, March 9, 2020, Accessed on July 30, 2020, https://tibet.net/china-calls-tibets-stability-into-question-with-show-of-force-in-lhasa/

4   Tibetan Buddhism Conference, "Tenets of Tibetan Buddhism," *Tibetan Buddhism Conference*, n.d. https://www.tibetanbuddhismconference.com/the-tenets-of-tibetan-buddhism/

5   Peter Ford, "For Beijing, Tibet Threat is 'Life and Death'," *The Christian Science Monitor*, March 20, 2008, https://www.csmonitor.com/World/Asia-South-Central/2008/0320/p01s03-wosc.html

6   Free Tibet, "Human Rights in Tibet," *Free Tibet*, n.d., https://www.freetibet.org/about/human-rights

7   National People's Congress of the People's Republic of China, "Constitution of the People's Republic of China," *National People's Congress of the People's Republic of China*, Accessed on July 30, 2020, http://www.npc.gov.cn/zgrdw/englishnpc/Constitution/2007-11/15/content_1372963.htm

To date, China has killed between 500,000[8] and 1.2 million[9] Tibetans, taking away their rights, freedoms, language, and expression of culture, not to mention their very lives.[10] The fate of Tibet, an independent country during the period between 1912 to 1951,[11] is worrisome. Today, Tibetans are required to pledge their allegiance to the Chinese Communist Party (CCP), or else they will face imprisonment or severe punishment. Unlawful acts include having an image of His Holiness the Dalai Lama or praising his birthday,[12] celebrating Tibetan anniversaries or festivals, or possessing the Tibetan flag.[13]

Brief Introduction to Tibetan History

China invaded Tibet in 1950 and took control in 1959 after a short but confrontational revolt; the Dalai Lama fled to India soon after China's takeover. China insists that they once controlled Tibet long ago, though Tibetan people have vastly different beliefs, language, and culture. Since that time, Tibet and its culture have struggled for survival; its people have fought for safety and freedom from China's authoritarian domination, surveillance, and violence. Although China claims the contrary, Dr. Hon-Shiang Lau states, "Tibet was never a part of China since antiquity."[14]

Importance of Tibet to China

China' needs Tibet as a buffer with countries to its south, minerals contained in its territory, and control of the water that flows from the Himalayas down into the Yellow River, Yangtze River, and Brahmaputra River. "The Chinese government has already removed most Tibetan nomads," which "allows the Chinese to use the land for their own purposes, whether it is to preserve water sources for China or make all of Tibet available for mining."[15]

The Himalayas make a perfect line of demarcation between China and India, Nepal, and Bangladesh. The disputed territory on those mountaintops was the site of an aggressive lethal confrontation between China and India that started on May 5, 2020, on the India-Tibet border. Twenty Indian soldiers died, and dozens were wounded. The confrontation continued throughout June with an increased military presence and Chinese construction projects to

---

8   Patrick French, *Tibet, Tibet: A Personal History of a Lost Land* (New York: Vintage Books, 2003), 292.

9   Yeshe Choesang, "China is Guilty of Mass Genocide Against 1.2 Million People of Tibet," *Tibet Post International*, June 12, 2019, http://www.thetibetpost.com/en/outlook/opinions-and-columns/4643-china-is-guilty-of-mass-genocide-against-12-million-people-of-tibet

10 Edward Wong, "Tibetans Fight to Salvage Fading Culture in China," *The New York Times*, November 28, 2015, https://www.nytimes.com/2015/11/29/world/asia/china-tibet-language-education.html

11 Ian Ransom, "FACTBOX: Historical Ties Between China and Tibet," *Reuters*, Accessed July 30, 2020 from https://www.reuters.com/article/us-china-tibet-history-factbox-idUSTRE52Q0CR20090327

12 International Campaign for Tibet, "Thousands Celebrate Dalai Lama's Birthday in Dharamsala," *International Campaign for Tibet*, July 6, 2005, https://savetibet.org/thousands-celebrate-dalai-lamas-birthday-in-dharamsala/

13 Yeshe Choesang, "China is Guilty of Mass Genocide Against 1.2 Million People of Tibet," *Tibet Post International*, June 12, 2019, http://www.thetibetpost.com/en/outlook/opinions-and-columns/4643-china-is-guilty-of-mass-genocide-against-12-million-people-of-tibet

14 Lobsang Tenchoe, "Tibet Was Never a Part of China Since Antiquity: Dr. Hon-Shiang Lau," *The Tibet Express*, April 23, 2018, https://tibetexpress.net/8126/tibet-was-never-a-part-of-china-since-antiquity-dr-hon-shiang-lau/

15 Warren Smith, "China's Exploitation of Tibet's Mineral Resources," *Radio Free Asia*, n.d., https://www.rfa.org/english/news/tibet/warrensmithbooks/Warren1.pdf

fortify their positions. This conflict is just one incident in China's "salami-slicing", designed to increase its territory inch by inch over a long period of time.

Minerals are another major reason for China's push into Tibet.[16] Research data show that Tibet contains copper, iron, lead, chromium, molybdenum, silver, and gold, along with numerous rare earth minerals that China had previously purchased from Africa and South America.[17] To mitigate against the high costs of mining in the Tibetan Plateau, miners are given incentives, including allowing them permission to disregard the local Tibetans and their environmental regulations.[18] Tibetans have protested these destructive activities, which have polluted their air, land, and water.

Tibet is usually discussed in tandem with human rights arguments about the loss of free speech, practice of religion, and genocide. However, Gabriel Lafitte's book, *Spoiling Tibet*, focuses his argument on environmental devastation.[19] He suggests, "Tibetan communities see mining as a central issue, a core concern. In many remote areas of a plateau the size of Western Europe, the only presence of Chinese power is the miners, an intrusive, transgressive presence backed by the repressive apparatus of party-state coercion when Tibetans make it clear mining is unwelcome." Furthermore, the removal of other natural resources has also destroyed the environment in Tibet. Since 1959, over 80% of Tibetan forests have been destroyed by the Chinese,[20] as they removed over $54 billion worth of timber.[21] In total disregard of the environment and people, large amounts of toxic nuclear waste have been disposed of in Tibet.[22]

Water may be the most important reason, though, China's ability to control the direction and flow of water from the Himalayas is a life and death proposition for 1.4 billion Chinese citizens.[23] Dams are being built to direct the water away from several southern countries, including Pakistan, Bangladesh, and India.[24] Additionally, China has plans to build a tunnel to channel and redirect water that would flow into Tibet toward Xinjiang Province.[25]

---

16 Warren Smith, "China's Exploitation of Tibet's Mineral Resources," *Radio Free Asia*, n.d., https://www.rfa.org/english/news/tibet/warrensmithbooks/Warren1.pdf

17 Gabriel Lafitte, *Spoiling Tibet: China and Resource Nationalism on the Roof of the World* (New York: Zed Books, 2013).

18 Rukor, "Mining Tibet," *Rukor*, April 23, 2016, https://rukor.org/mining-tibet/

19 Gabriel Lafitte, *Spoiling Tibet: China and Resource Nationalism on the Roof of the World* (New York: Zed Books, 2013).

20 Tarja Ketola, "Developing Tibet Into a Special Sustainability Zone Of China?," *University of Turku, Finland*, 2015, https://case.edu/affil/tibet/tibetanNomads/documents/DevelopingTibetintoaspecialsustainabilityzoneofchina.pdf

21 Students for a Free Tibet, "Some Startling Facts," *Students for a Free Tibet*, n.d., http://www.umass.edu/rso/fretibet/education.html

22 Van Praag and Michael C. Walt, *The Status of Tibet: History, Rights, And Prospects In International Law* (Westview Press, 1987).

23 Worldometers, "China Population," *Worldometers*, n.d., https://www.worldometers.info/world-population/china-population/

24 Ameya Pratap Singh and Urvi Tembey, "India-China Relations and the Geopolitics of Water," *The Interpreter*, July 23, 2020, https://www.lowyinstitute.org/the-interpreter/india-china-relations-and-geopolitics-water

25 Stephen Chen, "Chinese Engineers Plan 1,000km Tunnel to Make Xinjiang Desert Bloom," *South China Morning Post*, October 29, 2017, https://www.scmp.com/news/china/society/article/2116750/chinese-engineers-plan-1000km-tunnel-make-xinjiang-desert-bloom

Conclusion

Tibetans are predominantly Buddhist, peaceful, and compassionate. These tranquil characteristics have been threatened, though some did protest and attempt to fight back. The surveillance state and complete intrusion in all aspects of Tibetans' lives has silenced those who have tried to rebel or speak out. Tashi Wangchuk attempted to use Chinese law to allow Tibetans' people the right to speak their own language. China's Constitution of the People's Republic of China Article 4 states that "All nationalities have the freedom to use and develop their own spoken and written languages and to preserve or reform their own folkways and customs."[26]

Strangely, in China's narrative, "If China cannot submerge Tibet with Chinese colonists, then it seems they will try to do so with Chinese tourists. Chinese tourism will further the assimilation of Tibet by turning Tibet into a huge theme park where Chinese can go to indulge their fantasies about the poor Tibetan barbarians graciously liberated by China and now content to sing and dance to express their gratitude to their Chinese liberators."[27]

Patrick French, former Director of the Free Tibet Campaign, resigned himself to the loss of Tibetan land and culture. He explains in his book, *Tibet, Tibet: A Personal History of a Lost Land*, "After all I had seen and heard in the Tibet Autonomous Region and its borderlands, I could no longer view things with the necessary simplicity to be part of a political campaign. I doubted whether a free Tibet had any meaning without a free China . . . Caught by circumstance and history, the old Tibet had been undone, and would never be recovered."[28]

In December 2020, President Trump signed into law the Tibetan Policy and Support Act of 2020.[29] This law supports Tibet through providing $20 million in support of initiatives for Tibet, such as a U.S. consulate in the capital of Lhasa and allowing Tibet to select its own successor.[30]

Chinese Foreign Ministry spokesperson Zhao Lijian firmly admonished the U.S., stating that Beijing opposes Washington's move explaining, "We urge the U.S. side to stop exploiting relevant issues to interfere in China's internal affairs, and take no actions to implement articles in the Act that target China and hurt China's interests, so as to avoid further damaging China-U.S. cooperation and long-term development of bilateral relationship."[31]

---

26 People's Republic of China, "The National People's Congress of the People's Republic of China," *People's Republic of China*, Accessed on July 30, 2020, http://www.npc.gov.cn/zgrdw/englishnpc/Constitution/2007-11/15/content_1372963.htm

27 Warren Smith, "China's Exploitation of Tibet's Mineral Resources," *Radio Free Asia*, n.d., https://www.rfa.org/english/news/tibet/warrensmithbooks/Warren1.pdf

28 Patrick French, *Tibet, Tibet: A Personal History of a Lost Land* (New York: Vintage Books, 2003).

29 Radio Free Asia, "Trump Signs Tibetan Policy and Support Act into Law, Prompting Warnings from Beijing," *Radio Free Asia*, December 28, 2020, https://www.rfa.org/english/news/tibet/law-12282020181154.html

30 WION Web Team, "Donald Trump Signs Laws to Further US's Support to Taiwan, Tibet; Drawing China's Criticism," *World Is One News (WION)*, December 28, 2020, https://www.wionews.com/world/donald-trump-signs-laws-to-further-uss-support-to-taiwan-tibet-drawing-chinas-criticism-352951

31 Reuters, "China Foreign Ministry Says Firmly Rejects New U.S. Law on Tibet Policy," *Reuters*, December 27, 2020, https://www.reuters.com/article/us-china-tibet-usa/china-foreign-ministry-says-firmly-rejects-new-u-s-law-on-tibet-policy-idUSKBN2920IR

What's at Stake?

First, China's persecution of religious practitioners and open hatred toward the Dalai Lama threatens the belief system rooted in Tibet. Furthermore, history, culture, and religion are at risk as Beijing exerts its power and influence.

Second, Tibetan autonomy and independence are incomprehensible to Beijing. China's control over Tibet's citizenry, government, resources, water distribution, privacy, and rivers is inevitable. Internal and external protests have taken place for decades. However, without forceable action, which no country has been willing to do, China will continue to push its boundary line across every sovereign border.

Third, China's takeover of Tibetan land has led to a loss of culture and has set a precedent for Beijing to control the future of all states it seeks to overwhelm.

Fourth, the Tibetan Policy and Support Act of 2020 is likely to ruffle more than just a few feathers in Beijing, and China's response may be greater than its initial rhetoric from Chinese spokesperson Zhao Lijian.

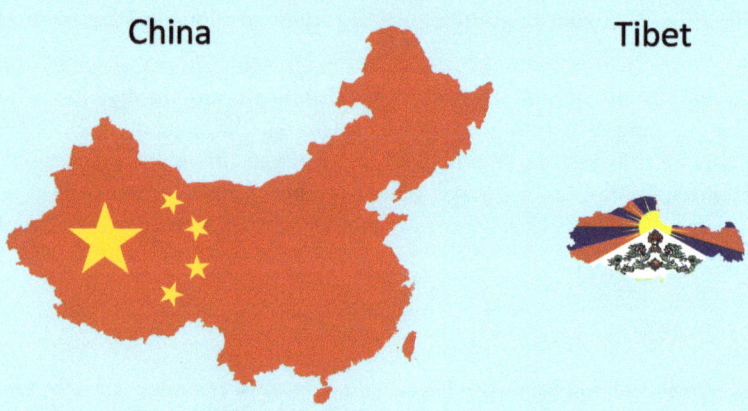

Part 9
China Encroaches on All Sides: Slowly Taking Regional Control

Money and Power: China's Coercion and Crackdown

Countries to the north, south, east, and west are part of China's massive plan to move into territories around the world through its Belt and Road Initiative (BRI). Governments pay for development and transportation projects that enhance their infrastructure and bring access and business to China. In the form of loans that many of these countries cannot pay back, states are trapped in debt. Government leaders worldwide are now socially, politically, and militarily beholden to China as it hands out more money.

The consequences of the Belt and Road Initiative are particularly apparent around Asia. China has cracked down on Mongolian culture in its attempt to wipe out the Mongolian language, rewrite history, and incorporate Chinese customs. The conversion to the Chinese language in books was just the beginning. Kazakhs to the west are being imprisoned in Xinjiang Province concentration camps, though Kazakhstan leaders are not speaking out. The Chinese even published an article saying that the Kazakhs pledge allegiance to China and are eager to return to China where they "belonged".

Money and power have also been extended to Tajikistan, Kyrgyzstan, Cambodia, Laos, Thailand, Pakistan, Nepal, and other states discussed in this part. Along with encroaching on countries surrounding China, Beijing's ambitions have furthered into military oversight and cultural modifications. However, these aspirations began by taking other states' land, inch-by-inch, costing lives, livelihoods, or culture. This part of the book is a brief introduction - a primer for further research.

Chapter 1

States Caught in the Crossfires of Sino-Indian Disputes

Nepal, Bangladesh, and Myanmar

Introduction

As China extends its 'salami-slicing' tactics to obtain control over more states, hostile contests have enflamed South Asia over Beijing-contested territories. However, the greater regional issue at stake remains the disputed territories between China and India, two globally powerful states engaged in diplomatic and militaristic disputes that project onto surrounding states. Three nations in particular – Nepal, Bangladesh, and Myanmar – have been caught in the crossfire of China and India's battles, each with their own national interests on the line.

China-Nepal Geographic Size Comparison

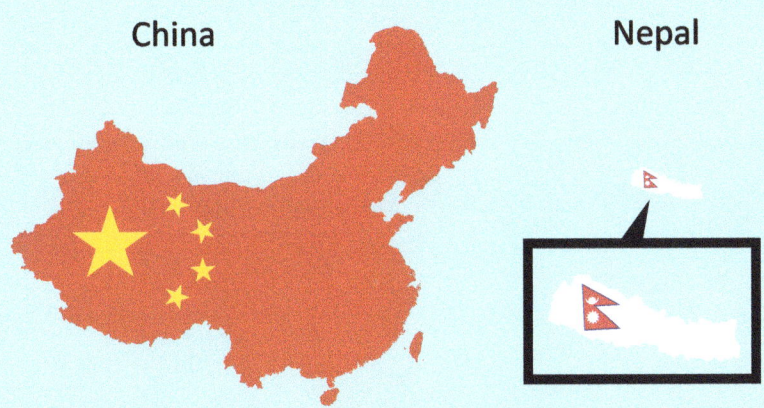

Nepal

The Himalayan mountain region of Nepal has been the center of militarized conflicts between China and India in recent years. These turned fatal in 2020 amidst the COVID-19 pandemic. In May 2020, India began constructing a road on a three-way trijunction between India, China, and Nepal. The India Ministry of Defense stated,

> The other two road ways via Sikkim and Nepal are along. They entailed approximately 20 per cent land journeys on Indian roads and 80 per cent land journeys in China. With the opening of Ghatiabgarh-Lipulekh road, this ratio has been reversed. Now Pilgrims to Manasarovar will traverse 84 per cent land journeys on Indian Roads and only 16 per cent land Journeys in China. This is truly historic...[1]

The construction strained trijunction relations. Nepal's Prime Minister, KP Sharma Oli, was outraged by India's road construction along the trijunction. India's road would connect the Himalayan border of China and the Lipulekh pass in territory claimed by Nepal, though

---

1   PIB Delphi, "Raksha Mantri Shri Rajnath Singh Inaugurates 80 km Long Road Curtailing Kailash-Mansarovar Pilgrimage Time," *PIB Delhi,* May 8, 2020, https://pib.gov.in/PressReleasePage.aspx?PRID=1622091

India has been in possession of the territory for sixty years.[2]

China often uses other countries as a proxy. Beijing's surrogate approach may be the case regarding India's road to the Hindu's sacred Mount Kailash. However, Nepal used this incident to lash out against India. This route construction was seen by Prime Minister Oli as an attack on Nepal's sovereignty. Oli released an official map outlining the disputed region inside of Nepalese borders.[3] Furthermore, Oli went one step further to prove his point to India. He pushed through an amendment that requires foreign women, many of whom are Indian marrying Nepali men, to wait seven years before obtaining naturalization.[4]

Al Jazeera explains, "Commentators and officials both in India and Nepal accused him of cynically using the border dispute to stir nationalist sentiment and outmanoeuvre his rivals in the NCP, or acting at China's behest."[5] In response to such allegations, Oli affirmed that they were "neither politically correct nor diplomatically appropriate."[6]

Nevertheless, China has been seen as a highly strategic neighbor to Nepal, gaining more and more political clout over the years. In 2005, China provided military assistance to Nepal during its internal conflict with King Gyanendra's military coup.[7] Ever since, the Nepal Communist Party (NCP) and CCP have regularly held high-level meetings with each other. In addition, China continues to invest in the nation. Nepal joined China's Belt and Road initiative in 2017. This included twenty-five reconstruction projects, USD 483m USD to

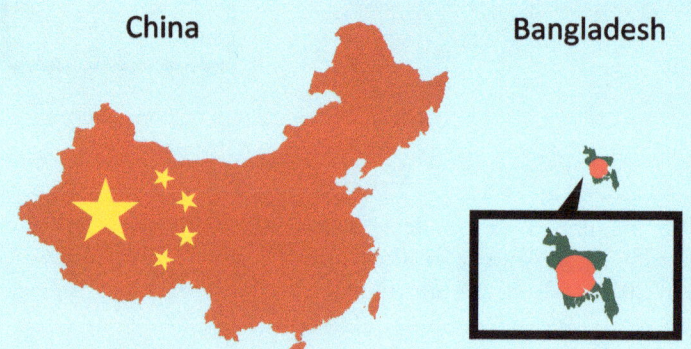

China-Bangladesh Geographic Size Comparison

---

2   Constantino Xavier, "Interpreting the India-Nepal Border Dispute," *Brookings*, June 11, 2020, https://www.brookings.edu/blog/up-front/2020/06/11/interpreting-the-india-nepal-border-dispute

3   Anbarasan Ethirajan, "India and China: How Nepal's New Map is Stirring Old Rivalries," *BBC News*, June 10, 2020, https://www.bbc.com/news/world-asia-52967452

4   PTI, "Nepal Proposes Giving Citizenship to Foreign Woman Married to Nepali Man After 7 Years of Union," *Indian Express*, June 22, 2020, https://indianexpress.com/article/world/nepal-proposes-giving-citizenship-to-foreign-woman-married-to-nepali-man-after-7-years-of-union-6470406

5   Arif Rafiq, "Nepal is Walking a Tightrope between India and China," *Al Jazeera*, July 29, 2020, https://www.aljazeera.com/indepth/opinion/nepal-walking-tightrope-india-china-200728102536128.html

6   PTI, "Nepal's Ruling Communist Party's Standing Committee to Meet on Saturday to Decide Oli's Fate," *Financial Express*, July 3, 2020, https://www.financialexpress.com/world-news/nepals-ruling-communist-partys-standing-committee-to-meet-on-saturday-to-decide-olis-fate/2012489/

7   Kamal Dev Bhattarai, "China's Growing Political Clout in Nepal," *The Diplomat*, May 22, 2020, https://thediplomat.com/2020/05/chinas-growing-political-clout-in-nepal

post-earthquake development, and has invested USD 130m in a powerplant.[8] Furthermore, China has given Nepal access to seven seaports (Tianjin, Shenzhen, Lianyungang and Zhanjiang) and dry ports (Lanzhou, Lhasa and Xigatse).[9]

In March 2016, Nepal signed the Agreement on Transit Transport that included bilateral cooperation and ten separate Memorandums of Understanding for construction projects, which put China center-stage in Nepali politics.[10] China continues to pledge foreign direct investment (FDI) into Nepal, opening border points for the Chinese to cross as visitors. Nepali cities now boast 100 Chinese restaurants. Mandarin is now required mastery in many Nepali schools. A hundred Chinese teachers have been brought into Nepal, and China has granted Nepalese students scholarships to study Mandarin in China to popularize Chinese.[11] In considering the great power rivalry, Indiana University professor, Sumit Ganguly, explained,

"The United States is no longer an important global player. The U.S. even in the past didn't have much stake in Nepal, and now it seems even [other] developed countries are [too busy] with their own problems." China is taking advantage of this vacuum.[12]

On February 1, 2020, the Nepal-China Transit protocol came into effect that brought China and Nepal closer together as partners and ended Nepal's reliance on India for international trade.[13]

Bangladesh

With China and India's border skirmishes escalating, China's debt-trap diplomacy with Bangladesh has been seen as a 'charity' case.[14] China has invested in and established a dependent trade relationship with Bangladesh. In July 2020, China declared that it would increase its duty-free exports to Bangladesh from 60 percent to 97 percent.[15] However, *The Economic Times* reports,

> China's decision to offer duty-free access to Bangladesh is merely a promise on paper as Beijing has very stringent Rules of Origin criteria and a lot of concessions remain on paper. This so-called "diplomatic victory" by China involving duty-free access taking

---

8 The Record, "How Much is China Investing in Nepal, Where, and How?," *The Record*, September 13, 2019, https://www.recordnepal.com/category-explainers/how-much-is-china-investing-in-nepal-where-and-how

9 Ibid.

10 Ministry of Foreign Affairs, Government of Nepal, "Nepal-China Relations," *Ministry of Foreign Affairs, Government of Nepal*, February 2019, https://mofa.gov.np/nepal-china-relations/

11 Yeshi Dorje, "Some Nepalis Uneasy Over Influx of Chinese Language Teachers," *VOA News*, October 17, 2019, https://www.voanews.com/east-asia-pacific/some-nepalis-uneasy-over-influx-chinese-language-teachers

12 Ibid.

13 Megha Gupta, "Should India be Concerned About Nepal China Transit Protocol," *Observer Research Foundation*, January 29, 2020, https://www.orfonline.org/expert-speak/should-india-be-concerned-about-nepal-china-transit-protocol-60863/

14 Kallol Bhattacherjee, "Bangladesh Rejects Criticism of China Deal," *The Hindu*, June 22, 2020, https://www.thehindu.com/news/national/bangladesh-rejects-criticism-of-china-deal/article31893183.ec

15 Shafiqul Islam, "Is Duty-Free Facility Enough to Boost Export to China?," *The Daily Star*, July 12, 2020, https://www.thedailystar.net/business/news/duty-free-facility-enough-boost-export-china-192895

China-Myanmar Geographic Size Comparison

advantage of the pandemic can only push a promising economy into distress and despair.[16]

Furthermore, in 2016, China and Bangladesh signed twenty-seven Memoranda of Understandings (MOU) worth $24.45 billion for development projects.[17] However, only five of these MOUs were implemented by the end of 2019, three years later.[18] China has reached a sum of $38.05 billion of investments in Bangladesh, the largest any single nation has contributed before.[19] After President Xi visited Bangladesh in 2016 and signed 40 deals worth $20 billion with Bangladesh, Xi stated, "China-Bangladesh relationship is now at a new historical starting point and heading towards a promising future."[20] However, this 'starting point' is dangerously beginning to inch upon the debt-trap scenario that China has established with dozens of other countries as it gains political and regional traction in its battle with India.

Myanmar

Though Myanmar has had uneven relations with the United States,[21] a January 2020 visit from Xi Jinping to the nation has alarmed western nations that this dynamic is officially

---

16 Dipanjan Roy Chaudhury, "ET Analysis: China's Trade Concessions to Bangladesh a 'Dual-Deficit and Debt Trap'," *The Economic Times*, July 11, 2020, https://economictimes.indiatimes.com/news/international/world-news/et-analysis-chinas-trade-concessions-to-bangladesh-a-dual-deficit-and-debt-trap/articleshow/76907291.cms

17 Rezaul Karim & Shakhawat Liton, "Strategic Partners," *The Daily Star*, October 15, 2016, https://www.thedailystar.net/frontpage/strategic-partners-1298923

18 Adam Pitman, "China's Stake in Bangladesh is Overplayed," *The Diplomat*, August 8, 2020, https://thediplomat.com/2020/08/chinas-stake-in-bangladesh-is-overplayed

19 Rezaul Karim & Shakhawat Liton, "Strategic Partners," *The Daily Star*, October 15, 2016, https://www.thedailystar.net/frontpage/strategic-partners-1298923

20 PTI Dhaka, "China, Bangladesh Ink 40 Deals Worth $20 bn During Xi Visit," *The Hindu BusinessLine*, October 14, 2016, https://www.thehindubusinessline.com/news/world/china-bangladesh-ink-40-deals-worth-20-bn-during-xi-visit/article9220678.ece?homepage=tru

21 Udai Bhanu Singh, "Myanmar's Relations with the United States," *Indian Journal of Asian Affairs*, June, 2006, https://www.jstor.org/stable/41950465

shifting.[22] On the 70th anniversary of diplomatic relations, China and Myanmar celebrated China's infrastructure development, trade and shipping, and special economic zone (SEZ) investments.[23]

Xi Jinping and the Myanmar leader, Aung San Suu Kyi, signed thirty-three agreements as part of China's Belt and Road Initiative. This pact included the China Myanmar Economic Corridor, which *Reuters* notes is a "giant infrastructure scheme worth billions of dollars, with agreements on railways linking southwestern China to the Indian Ocean, a deep seaport in conflict-riven Rakhine state, a special economic zone on the border, and a new city project in the commercial capital of Yangon."[24]

Though Myanmar sees Xi's investments as an infrastructure and economic boost that brings necessary capital inflow, China seeks entry to the Indian Ocean, which it views as vital to its Indo-Pacific strategy.[25] Having access to the Indian Ocean would allow Beijing to contain India.

Still, with this dynamic, Myanmar is inching upon the fate of a debt trap hostage as it holds an international debt of U.S. $10 billion, forty percent of which is owed to China.[26] China and Myanmar minimized previous deals as Myanmar feared it was falling into a debt trap.[27] At this current rate though, Myanmar's debts are too large and too entrapping for minor economic trims to save it.

In 2020, China began constructing a 2,200 km border wall with its southern neighbor, Myanmar.[28] The code name for the reinforced steel wall is the "Southern Great Wall", intended to keep Chinese dissidents from fleeing the country.[29] The expected completion of this barbed wire-topped wall is October 2022. Meanwhile, in 2020, China began constructing a concrete border wall on its 1,300 km Sino-Vietnamese border to prevent Chinese citizens from leaving.[30]

---

22 Hunter Marston, "Has the US Lost Myanmar to China?," *The Diplomat*, January 20, 2020, https://thediplomat.com/2020/01/has-the-us-lost-myanmar-to-china

23 Ibid.

24 Thu Thu Aung & Poppy McPherson, "Myanmar, China Ink Deals to Accelerate Belt and Road as Xi Courts an Isolated Suu Kyi," *Reuters*, January 17, 2020, https://www.reuters.com/article/us-myanmar-china/myanmar-china-ink-deals-to-accelerate-belt-and-road-as-xi-courts-an-isolated-suu-kyi-idUSKBN1ZH054

25 Amara Thiha, "Xi's Upcoming Visit to Myanmar Could Reshape the Indian Ocean Region," *The Diplomat*, January 4, 2020, https://thediplomat.com/2020/01/xis-upcoming-visit-to-myanmar-could-reshape-the-indian-ocean-region

26 Current Affairs Correspondent East Asia, "Myanmar Fears Chinese Debt Trap," *Belt & Road News*, February 28, 2020, https://www.beltandroad.news/2020/02/28/myanmar-fears-chinese-debt-trap

27 Dipanjan Roy Chaudhury, "Myanmar to Trim Chinese Loans to Avoid Debt Trap," *The Economic Times*, August 31, 2018, https://economictimes.indiatimes.com/news/politics-and-nation/myanmar-to-trim-chinese-loans-to-avoid-debt-trap/articleshow/65628957.cms?from=md

28 Sebastian Strangio, "China Building Massive Myanmar Border Wall: Reports," *The Diplomat*, December 17, 2020, https://thediplomat.com/2020/12/china-building-massive-myanmar-border-wall-reports/

29 John Feng, "China Building 1,200-Mile Southern Great Wall Along Myanmar Border: Reports," *Newsweek*, December 15, 2020, https://www.newsweek.com/china-building-1200-mile-southern-great-wall-along-myanmar-border-reports-1554793

30 Qiao Long, "Vietnam Cracks Down on Growing Wave of Migrant Workers from China," *Radio Free Asia*, October 29, 2020, https://www.rfa.org/english/news/china/workers-10292020111656.html

Barbed Wire Topped Wall – "China's Southern Great Wall"

Conclusion

China's push to control its people and prevent them from leaving through porous southern borders is matched by its determination to control other countries. The coronavirus pandemic, rather than slowing the signing of infrastructure loan agreements, has, on the contrary, intensified Beijing's push to help and indebt countries. As indebtedness grows in the states to China's south, concern builds regarding ties that will put Nepal, Bangladesh, and Myanmar under Beijing's thumb.

What's at Stake?

First, Nepal, Bangladesh, and Myanmar engaged in asymmetric relations with Beijing, giving China access and leverage to their economic, political, and diplomatic relations with regional states.

Second, CCP values may inevitably be instilled in Nepal, Bangladesh, and Myanmar as China demands that these countries pursue Beijing's wishes using its economic leverage.

Third, China has begun to strategically engage with South Asian states, creating a chessboard to checkmate countries.

Fourth, as China controls more of these political economies, nations formerly friendly with India could succumb to political wrangling as a proxy for Beijing. Involving and leveraging regional states, China meddles with diplomacy and stability in the region as Beijing widens its control and forcefully applies its strategic containment with New Delhi.

Chapter 2

More Money Down South

China's Financial and Political Relations with Cambodia, Laos, and Thailand

Introduction

China's vast reach in Asia extended southward in the past decade to Cambodia, Laos, and Thailand. These countries have each engaged with Beijing in economic, diplomatic, and political relations. Like other nations that have entered asymmetric ties to Beijing, these three states have teetered toward debt-trap diplomacy while cozying up to the dragon nation.

China-Cambodia Geographic Size Comparison

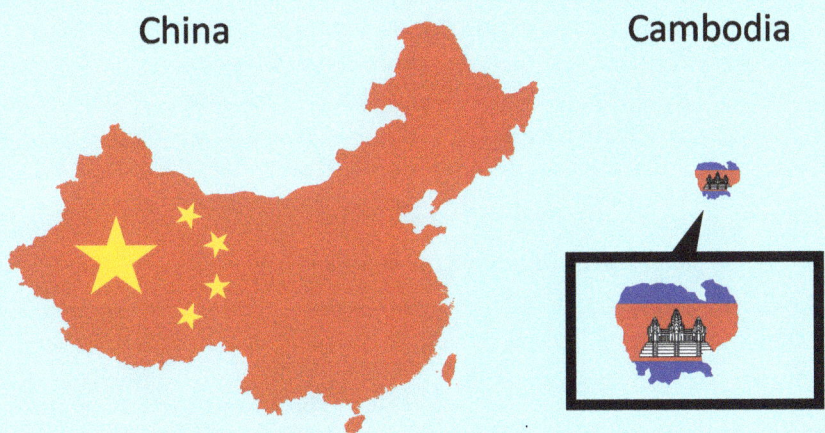

Cambodia

Cambodia and China have a long-standing relationship, beginning with Cambodia's bold decision to terminate its diplomatic relations with the United States in 1965.[1] When then-Prince Norodom Sihanouk ended its ties to the U.S., Cambodia shifted its former neutral stance with the People's Republic of China (PRC) to form an alliance.

However, Sihanouk's decision resulted in several unforeseen consequences that affected Cambodia's national security.[2] *The Diplomat* explains,

> For one thing, Cambodia's alignment with China allowed Beijing to take advantage of Sihanouk's unbalanced foreign policy. Chinese officials pressured the prince to allow Viet Cong supply lines to run through Kompong Som port up to the Ho Chi Minh trail. That turned out to be an unofficial invitation for American B-52 Stratofortress bomber runs, and Cambodia is still feeling the effects of this today.

---

1 Kenton J. Clymer, "The Perils of Neutrality: The Break in U.S.-Cambodian Relations, 1965," *Diplomatic History*, October, 1999, https://academic.oup.com/dh/article-abstract/23/4/609/390981?redirectedFrom=fulltext

2 Chansambath Bong, "Cambodia's Disastrous Dependence on China: A History Lesson," *The Diplomat*, December 4, 2019, https://thediplomat.com/2019/12/cambodias-disastrous-dependence-on-china-a-history-lesson

In the short term, Sihanouk's choice also pushed Cambodia into deeper diplomatic isolation with no friend to rely on as the decision to break off ties with the United States in 1965 came just as the Great Proletariat Cultural Revolution was about to sweep across China...Prince Sihanouk became increasingly suspicious of China's intentions after rumors that Beijing was secretly exporting its revolutionary ideas through the Cambodian-Chinese Friendship Association spread across the country.

The last straw came when Chinese Premier Zhou Enlai, who was a target of the Red Guards at this point, openly asked Cambodia to allow the ethnic Chinese community to pledge their allegiance to Communism and Chairman Mao, a move that broke with Beijing's long-held tradition of *Pancha Shila*. These developments greatly unnerved Sihanouk, who had previously expected that China would stand behind him through thick and thin without trying to impose its ideology on Cambodia.

The alliance between China and Cambodia grew closer once again in 2018. China pledged over $100 million in military aid to Cambodia to be used at Cambodia's discretion.[3] While these investments dangerously mirror debt-trap tactics, the Cambodian Prime Minister Hun Sen remarked, "I've heard so many people saying that Cambodia may fall into China's debt trap," adding, "we maintain our sovereignty in borrowing, we borrowed according to the projects we need, and China respects our decision."[4]

Over the past decade, Cambodia increased its domestic budget and focused on infrastructure development. This policy shift was primarily responsible for Phnom Penh's reported 2018 debt of $7 billion.[5] Furthermore, Cambodia joined China's Belt and Road Initiative (BRI) early as China pledged to invest in "Cambodian agriculture, finance, special economic zone development, capacity building, culture and tourism, and environmental protection—though the lion's share of funding will be set aside for infrastructure projects that include highways, bridges, ports, airports, and high-speed rail."[6]

In China and Cambodia's asymmetric economic relations, Beijing is the country's largest investor.[7] Meanwhile, the China-Cambodia relationship has been criticized by many, including the U.S. embassy which stated,

> China is Cambodia's largest trade partner, but this relationship is heavily skewed in China's favor. About 87% of trade are Chinese imports, which do not support jobs or

---

3   Reuters Staff, "China Pledges Over $100 Million Military Aid to Cambodia," *Reuters*, June 18, 2018, https://fr.reuters.com/article/us-cambodia-china-idUSKBN1JF0KQ

4   Reuters Staff, "Cambodia PM Dismisses Fears of Chinese Debt Trap," *Reuters*, May 30, 2019, https://www.reuters.com/article/us-cambodia-china/cambodia-pm-dismisses-fears-of-chinese-debt-trap-idUSKCN1T00U8?il

5   Cambodia Constructors Association, "Will Cambodia Fall into the Chinese Infrastructure Debt Trap?," *Cambodia Constructors Association*, September 6, 2019, https://www.construction-property.com/will-cambodia-fall-into-chinese-infrastructure-debt-trap

6   RFA's Khmer Service, "Expert Warns of 'Debt-Trap' Ahead of Cambodian PM Visit to China Belt and Road Forum," *Radio Free Asia*, April 23, 2019, https://www.rfa.org/english/news/cambodia/trap-04232019163513.html

7   Sim Vireak, "Dynamism of Chinese Investment in Cambodia," *Asia Times*, November 8, 2019, https://asiatimes.com/2019/11/dynamism-of-chinese-investment-in-cambodia/

industry in the same way Cambodia's trade relationship with the United States or E.U. does. This is just one more way Cambodia has shifted from a more balanced and diverse economic approach to one more dependent on China.[8]

In response, the Chinese embassy in Phnom Penh posted on Facebook, stating, "Cambodian friends beware! The U.S. is trying to stir things up again with the so-called trade deficit issue. It is common sense that in a globalized world, trade goes far beyond bilateral."[9] Since the time when China supported the Khmer Rouge in the 1970-1975 Cambodian war, the U.S. and China have disputed Cambodia's domestic affairs.[10]

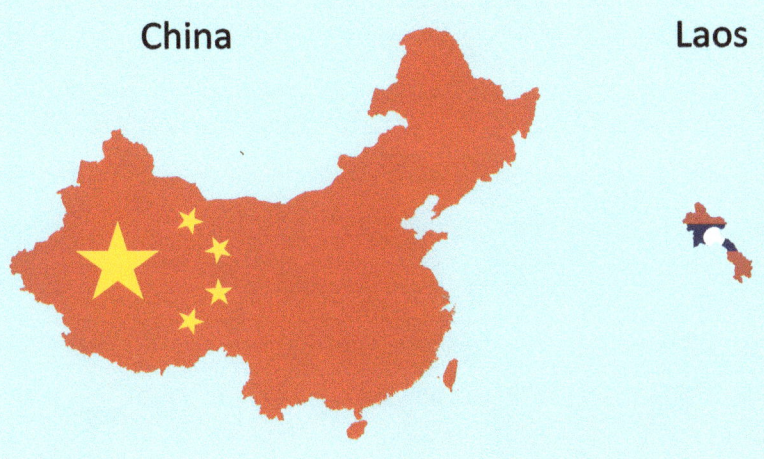

Laos

Despite Laos' land-locked geography, the nation is a vital strategic location on China's southward expansion. Laos is a central point along the Mekong River,[11] and is also a natural resource hotspot. As such, Beijing has sought out infrastructure and investment projects that would create a mutually-beneficial symbiotic relationship between the two states.

In November 2015, China underwrote and launched a $259 million satellite for Laos.[12] Also, in 2015, the two states agreed to build a $40 billion Yuan railway from Kunming to

---

8   Ben Sokhean, "Chinese, US Embassies Trade Barbs Over Trade Relationship With Cambodia," *Khmer Times*, April 21, 2019, https://www.khmertimeskh.com/50596469/chinese-us-embassies-trade-barbs-over-trade-relationship-with-cambodia/

9   Ibid.

10 Sun Narin, "US, China Face Off Over Legacy in Cambodia," *VOA*, February 9, 2019, https://www.voanews.com/east-asia-pacific/us-china-face-over-legacy-cambodia

11 Tae-jun Kang, "Laos: New Hydropower Dams, Old Mekong Worries," *The Diplomat*, April 20, 2018, https://thediplomat.com/2018/04/laos-new-hydropower-dams-old-mekong-worries/

12 Peter B. de Selding, "Laos, with China's Aid, Enters Crowded Satellite Telecom Field," *Space News*, November 30, 2015, https://spacenews.com/laos-with-chinese-aid-is-latest-arrival-to-crowded-satellite-telecom-field/

Vientiane, two capital regions of the countries.¹³ China agreed to contribute 70 percent of the funding for the project with its completion in 2020.¹⁴ In April 2019, Chinese-state media reported that two tunnels were completed and railway construction continued.¹⁵

On November 28, 2020, *Xinhua* announced that the longest tunnel of the China-Laos railway was completed with the railway expected to open in 2021, despite the unfavorable geological features.¹⁶ The railway will stretch 1,000 km; the total Belt and Road Initiative investment for this project by 2020 was $47.35 billion Yuan.¹⁷

China became Laos' largest foreign investor with over 745 projects in the nation.¹⁸ Consequentially, Laos continues to accept loans from Chinese banks while its public debt has grown past 65 percent of its GDP.¹⁹ Laos is estimated to owe 45 percent of its GDP to China.²⁰ Nevertheless, China's hydropower projects, Belt and Road Initiative, and continued infrastructure development only increase the dept-trapped nation's liability.

---

13 Prashanth Parameswaran, "China, Laos to Build $6 Billion Railway by 2020," *The Diplomat*, November 16, 2015, https://thediplomat.com/2015/11/china-laos-to-build-6-billion-railway-by-2020/

14 Ibid.

15 Xinhua, "2 Tunnels Dug Through in China-Laos Railway Construction," *Xinhua*, April 15, 2019, http://www.xinhuanet.com/english/2019-04/15/c_137979085.htm

16 Xinhua, "Longest Tunnel on China-Laos Railway Drilled Through," *Xinhua*, November 28, 2020, http://www.xinhuanet.com/english/asiapacific/2020-11/28/c_139549710.htm

17 Ibid.

18 The Economist, "China Becomes Largest Investor in Laos," *The Economist*, November 15, 2013, http://country.eiu.com/article.aspx?articleid=1171209901&Country=Laos&topic=Politics&subtopic=For_5

19 International Monetary Fund, "IMF Executive Board Completes the 2017 Article IV Consultation with Lao People's Democratic Republic," *International Monetary Fund*, March 12, 2018, https://www.imf.org/en/News/Articles/2018/03/12/pr1883-lao-peoples-democratic-republic-imf-executive-board-completes-the-2017-article-iv

20 VOA News, "Analysts: Rising Debt Burden Could Make Laos More Reliant on China," *VOA News*, June 8, 2020, https://www.voanews.com/east-asia-pacific/analysts-rising-debt-burden-could-make-laos-more-reliant-china

During the pandemic, Laos, on the verge of default,[21] looked again to China. This time, Chinese news media, Xinhua, announced Beijing's win-win cooperation with Laos in celebration of the China Southern Power Grid (CSG) joint venture to manage Laos' electrical grid.[22] The implications are grave. Beijing could impose its will on Laos, control its power supply, and put its government decision-making control in jeopardy. The agreement's financial transaction, though not publicly stated, may have been a "debt-equity swap" or cash, though the structural problem of Laos' 50.5 percent public sector debt to China is disproportionate and troubling.[23] Though Laos could seek financial support from the International Monetary Fund (IMF), the IMF would require financial transparency whereas China would not. The Economist reports that China has a vested interest in gaining access to Laos' natural resources, influence in the South China Sea (SCS), power exports, international support for its Belt and Road Initiative (BRI), and leverage over the country's economy and politics.[24]

Thailand

Thailand uniquely hedges between the United States and China, holding centuries of commercial and military ties with China[25] and celebrating over 200 years of diplomatic ties with the United States.[26] China invested $262 billion baht (USD $8.6 billion) in Thailand in 2019.[27] In 2020, China surpassed Japan, who held the title for five decades, as the lead investor in Thailand.[28]

Much of this investment, $101 billion baht, was set aside for a high-speed railway linking three airports in Thailand.[29] Furthermore, China and Thailand set aside plans of their own to build a China-Thailand railway along the greater Belt and Road Initiative. The engineering design of the railway's first phase was completed in July 2019.[30] *The Diplomat* explains,

---

21   Keith Zhai and Kay Johnson, "Exclusive: Taking Power - Chinese Firm to Run Laos Electric Grid Amid Default Warnings," *Reuters*, September 15, 2020, https://www.reuters.com/article/china-laos/exclusive-taking-power-chinese-firm-to-run-laos-electric-grid-amid-default-warnings-idUSKBN25V15G

22   Xinhua, "Chinese, Lao Firms Sign Shareholders' Pact for Grid Joint Venture," *Xinhua*, September 2, 2020, http://www.xinhuanet.com/english/2020-09/02/c_139338047.htm

23   Scott Wingo, "China and the Lao Electrical Grid: Implications for Future Borrowers and China," *Center for Advanced China Research*, n.d., https://www.ccpwatch.org/single-post/china-and-the-lao-electrical-grid-implications-for-future-borrowers-and-china

24   The Economist, "China to Take a Share in the Lao National Grid," The Economist, September 7, 2020,

25   Jitsiree Thongnoi, "Is Thailand Pivoting Away from the US with Chinese Arms Deals?," *South China Morning Post,* January 27, 2019, https://www.scmp.com/week-asia/politics/article/2183707/thailand-pivoting-away-us-chinese-arms-deals

26   Issara Sereewatthanawut, "Thailand Must Not Make the Mistake of Choosing Between China and the US," *South China Morning Post*, May 6, 2019, https://www.scmp.com/comment/insight-opinion/article/3008886/thailand-must-not-make-mistake-choosing-between-china-and

27   Apornrath Phoonphongphiphat, "Spurred by Trade War, Chinese Investment in Thailand Skyrockets," *NIKKEI Asian Review,* January 24, 2020, https://asia.nikkei.com/Business/Business-trends/Spurred-by-trade-war-Chinese-investment-in-Thailand-skyrockets

28   Jitsiree Thongnoi, "China Becomes Thailand's Top Source of Foreign Investment for First Time," *South China Morning Post,* January 24, 2020, https://www.scmp.com/week-asia/economics/article/3047489/china-becomes-thailands-top-source-foreign-investment-first

29   Lamonphet Apisitniran, "Boi: Chinese in the Lead," *Bangkok Post*, January 14, 2020, https://www.bangkokpost.com/business/1835084/boi-chinese-in-the-lead

30   CGTN, "China-Thailand Railway Project: The Route and Key Events," *CGTN*, August 13, 2019, https://news.cgtn.com/news/2019-08-01/China-Thailand-Railway-INqEbn7Suc/index.html

Notably, the Thai-Chinese high speed rail project is likely to have a moderate, albeit significant, impact on Thailand's overall debt position. The Thai government budgets 179 billion baht (around $5.8 billion) for Phase 1 of the project, which covers roughly half of the entire Bangkok-Nong Khai route. Scaling this budget up for the full route, suggests that the overall cost will be upwards of 300 billion baht (U.S. $9.9 billion). This is equivalent to 2 percent of the size of Thailand's economy in 2017. Of course, major infrastructure projects are often under-budgeted, and can end up costing multiple times more than their original budgets.[31]

Conclusion

With Thailand's increasing dependence on China to finance its growing domestic agenda, many caution that Thailand should be wary of its potential debt-trap.[32] With its current financial relationship with Beijing, Thailand has become a strategic location for Beijing to exert its influence, just as it is doing with its neighbors Cambodia and Laos.

Cambodia, Laos, and Thailand are becoming steadily indebted to China. With the Belt and Road Initiative's infrastructure projects as a lure, these countries are willing to commit their government to ever-increasing debt for the chance that these hundreds of projects can increase their efficiency and economic position. There are likely to be positive outcomes for each of these countries, but with many projects ending up at double or triple the cost, the question remains – are these countries ultimately willing to give up their sovereignty in exchange?

What's at Stake?

First, Cambodia's hydropower and resources open doors to an unrealized sector that Beijing seeks to monopolize. China would have regional control over each country's vital energy, mineral, rubber, and resource deposits, which would leave surrounding states to adhere to Beijing's demands.

Second, as with all of China's debt-trapped states, there is a thin line between investments and influence.

Third, when states do not take necessary precautions, they give China control of their markets, operations, customs, resource exploration projects, and ultimately the citizenry of their Southeast Asian states.

---

31 Pechnipa Dominique Lam, "Will Thailand's Chinese High-Speed Railway Be Worth It?," *The Diplomat,* March 6, 2019, https://thediplomat.com/2019/03/will-thailands-china-built-railway-be-worth-it/

32 Bangkok Post Editorial Column, "Beware of BRI Debt Trap," *Bangkok Post,* April 27, 2019, https://www.bangkokpost.com/opinion/opinion/1667904/beware-of-bri-debt-trap

Chapter 3
China and Mongolia
Outer Mongolia's Independence and Inner Mongolia's Subjugation

Introduction

China's early history with Mongolia is one that is characterized by raids, invasions, and conflict. In the 13th century, the infamous revolutionary conqueror Chinggis (Genghis) Khan established the Mongolian Empire, exerting his vast rule that stretched across Asia. In 1279, Genghis Khan's grandson, Kublai Khan, defeated the last of the Chinese Song dynasty and its leaders to the south, leaving all of China under foreign rule for the first time.[1]

Expansion of the Mongol Empire in China

Although 13th-century conquests partly shaped relations between Mongolia and China, there is much more context to the era in which the Mongol Empire united to conquer China. Prior to Genghis Khan's rise, many Mongols and Turkic pastoral nomads led by the Khans lived in tents on the East Asian Steppes where they herded sheep and cattle and were classified by their nomadic lifestyles.[2] Many of the men rode horses in the conquest of land and peoples across Asia. Thus, since women remained behind on the family land, nomadic women were often in positions of authority.

In 1162, Temujin, later known as Chinggis (Genghis) Khan, was born into an aristocratic Mongol family. He rose to power, forming alliances with leaders, and strategically building relations. Genghis promoted soldiers on a merit system, integrated the nomads he conquered, eliminated diversity, and distributed both land and resources. Genghis Khan employed Turkic Uyghurs to create a unifying written language for the Mongolian Empire based upon Uyghur script.[3]

Genghis Khan was a shamanist whose folk religion maintained that spirits retained a physical presence after death. The Mongolian and Turkic nomads "believed in one God (Tenggeri), who is considered to be the creator of all visible and invisible beings, and He is also considered to be the creator of happiness and sufferings in the world."[4] Genghis believed that those who challenged Tenggeri's wishes deserved to die.

Persian and Turkmenistan histories are replete with Genghis Khan's brutality. When the head of Genghis Khan's ambassador was delivered in a sack, Genghis sent an army of 200,000 men back to viciously slaughter a half million people; during the Mongol campaigns, more than 30 million people were massacred.[5] Beijing fell in 1215, as did the Jin

---

1   Jean Johnson, "The Mongol Dynasty," *Asia Society*, n.d., https://asiasociety.org/education/mongol-dynasty

2   Anna F. Broadbridge, "The Rise and Fall of the Mongol Empire," filmed August 2019 by TED-Ed, TED Video, 4:49, https://www.ted.com/talks/anne_f_broadbridge_the_rise_and_fall_of_the_mongol_empire/transcript?language=en#t-288497

3   Asia for Educators, Columbia University, "Key Figures in Mongol History," *Asia for Educators, Columbia University*, n.d., http://afe.easia.columbia.edu/mongols/figures/figu_geng_legacy.htm

4   Translated by Peter Jackson, Introduction, Notes, and Appendices by Peter Jackson and David Morgan, *The Mission of Friar William of Rubruck: His Journey to the Court of the Great Khan Möngke,* 1253 – 1255 (Hackett Publishing Company, 2009).

5   Spencer Day, "Genghis Khan: The Mongol Warlord Who Almost Conquered the World," *History Extra,* November 2018, https://www.historyextra.com/period/medieval/genghis-khan-mongol-warlord-conquered-world-china-medieval/

Outer and Inner Mongolia

empire, Chinese Song empire, east Turkestan, Tibetan Buddhists, and lands as far as today's Europe.[6] Genghis Khan, one of the top three global leaders in history (with Alexander the Great and Napoleon), was known for lifelong learning, adaptability, and striking alliances with rival tribes.[7]

After Genghis's death in 1227, his third son, Ögedei Khan, succeeded his father to expand the Khan empire, before his grandson Kublai Khan's rise to conquer even more territory.[8] The Mongol Empire eventually extended from the East China Sea to Poland.[9] All conquered lands maintained local administrations while silk road and maritime trade flourished.

Mongol Downfall

When Genghis Khan's grandsons disputed control over the dynasty, the Mongol Empire split with Kublai Khan governing the Yuan (meaning "origin of the universe") dynasty in China.[10] During the Yuan dynasty, ethnic Chinese citizens formed the Ming dynasty, led by

---

6 The Editors of Encyclopaedia Britannica, "Mongol Empire," *Britannica*, November 9, 2020, https://www.britannica.com/place/Mongol-empire

7 John Man, T*he Mongol Empire: Genghis Khan, His Heirs and the Founding of Modern China* (Transworld Publishers, 2016).

8 Timeline Index, "Ögedei Khan, Son of Genghis Khan," *Timeline Index*, n.d., https://www.timelineindex.com/content/view/2651

9 Peter Jackson, *The Mongols and the West*, (Routledge, 2005).

10 Jean Johnson, "The Mongol Dynasty," *Center for Global Education*, n.d., https://asiasociety.org/education/mongol-dynasty

the peasant, Zhu Yuanzhang, who fought with the Mongols. The Ming dynasty remained in control from the 14th to 17th centuries.[11]

Yuan China was defeated while riddled with famine, plagues, flooding, cold weather, inflation, and uprisings.[12] It was then when Zhu Yuangzhang led the infamous Red Turban Movement to reinstate traditional Song dynasty customs. Zhu led several successful coups to gain traction of his Ming dynasty, beginning with overtaking Nanjing in 1356 CE.[13] After Zhu took control of Beijing, the last Yuan emperor, Toghon Temur, fled to Mongolia where the Yuan continued to rule under the name Northern Yuan dynasty (1368-1635 CE).[14] Nevertheless, in 1635, the last Mongol leader submitted to the Manchu-led Qing dynasty that replaced the Ming dynasty and all of what was then known as China.[15]

China's history is long and complicated. However, to understand current China-Mongol relations, it is important to note that Northern China suffered during numerous famines in the 18th century, primarily affecting what is now known as Inner Mongolia. Many Han Chinese settlers immigrated into Inner Mongolia during the famines, displacing Mongol citizens and populating the region with Han Chinese.

Mongolia's Independence

As the Qing dynasty weakened, losing two opium wars, social conflict and fighting ensued. In 1911, a full-scale rebellion in China ousted the last emperor of dynastic China, creating the Chinese republic and transforming the century-old form of leadership. Meanwhile, Mongolia sought and achieved independence in 1911 with the Bogd Khanate government ruling over the autonomous region.

Inner Mongolia also supported the Bogd Khanate's independence movement and wanted the same for the Mongol citizenry. However, since many Han Chinese moved into Inner Mongolia during the famines, the Mongols living in Inner Mongolia were outnumbered and not powerful enough to achieve independence. Thus, Inner Mongolia was re-incorporated into the Republic of China (ROC).

Although the Bogd Khanate obtained independence for Mongolia, they underwent cycles of freedom between, Russian rule and Chinese rule for a decade. The Soviet Union, dissatisfied with the Bogd Khanate rule, launched a successful rebellion over the Mongolian order and formed the Mongolian People's Republic in 1924. Mongolia became a communist state, continuing close ties with the USSR throughout World War II, while Inner Mongolia

---

11   Mark Cartwright, "Hongwu Emperor," *Ancient History Encyclopedia*, February 13, 2019, https://www.ancient.eu/Hongwu_Emperor/

12   Mark Cartwright, "Yuan Dynasty," *Ancient History Encyclopedia*, October 29, 2019, https://www.ancient.eu/Yuan_Dynasty/

13   Mark Cartwright, "Hongwu Emperor," *Ancient History Encyclopedia*, February 13, 2019, https://www.ancient.eu/Hongwu_Emperor/

14   Mark Cartwright, "Yuan Dynasty," *Ancient History Encyclopedia*, October 29, 2019, https://www.ancient.eu/Yuan_Dynasty/

15   Peter Perdue, "The Expansion of the Qing Dynasty of China and the Zunghar Mongol State," *Oxford Research Encyclopedias*, June, 2017, https://oxfordre.com/asianhistory/view/10.1093/acrefore/9780190277727.001.0001/acrefore-9780190277727-e-7

formed a collaborationist state within China's rule. In 1945, the Republic of China agreed to leave Mongolia to exist as a separate nation, and in 1947, Chinese communist leaders established governance over what is now known as the Inner Mongolia Autonomous Region (Inner Mongolia).[16]

Conclusion

Mongolia has a long and complex history. Much of the written evidence was destroyed during the battles from nearly a thousand years ago. Yet, piecing together information, it is clear that Mongolia governed the largest territory in world history with both an iron fist for those who rejected Genghis Khan's rule and welcoming acceptance for those who acquiesced. Thus, Genghis Khan is painted by some as either a ruthless warlord or a brilliant hero.[17]

What's at Stake?

First, Mongolia today is challenged by political struggles and the infiltration of Beijing's propaganda machine, 'wolf warriors', and the influx of Han Chinese.

Second, although Mongolia has achieved a status of independence, the nation remains subject to CCP influence.

Third, Inner Mongolia, which remained part of Chinese rule, has not achieved 'autonomous' status and was subjected to a crackdown to eradicate Mongolian culture.

---

16   Ben Blanchard, "China Marks 70 Years of Inner Mongolia's Founding, Activist Complains of Curbs," *Reuters*, August 8, 2017, https://www.reuters.com/article/us-china-innermongolia/china-marks-70-years-of-inner-mongolias-founding-activist-complains-of-curbs-idUSKBN1AO0YH

17   Horseback Mongolia, "Genghis Khan: Barbarian or Hero?," *Horseback Mongolia*, January 5, 2016, https://www.mongolia-trips.com/genghis-khan-barbarian-or-hero

Chapter 4

Mongolia's Knight in Shining Armor

China's Economic Aid to Outer Mongolia

Introduction

Mongolia's territory lies between China and Russia. Its Gobi Desert makes part of the country largely uninhabited. However, Mongolia also contains valuable mineral assets, including gold, uranium, and copper, much of which is unexploited. According to the International Monetary Fund (IMF), "Overall, current proven reserves are estimated at around $1 trillion and much of the country has yet to be prospected—the ultimate value could be much higher."[1] Though conquests, incursions, and raids characterize historic China-Mongolia interactions, modern relations are less 'invasive' in a militaristic sense. Instead, China and Mongolia have built relations on strengthened economic ties that have coincidentally and subtly infused Chinese Communist Party (CCP) principles within Mongolia.

China-Mongolia Geographic Size Comparison

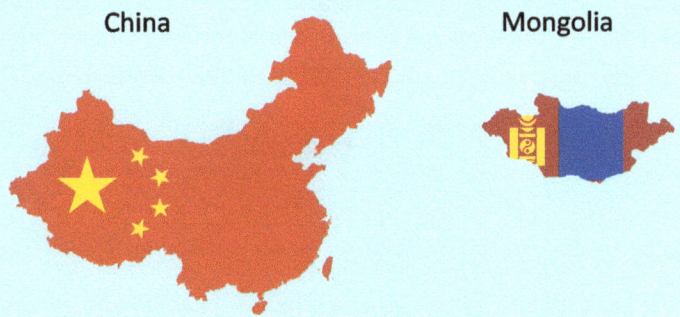

Mongolia's Economic Troubles

Over the 2010-2020 decade, Mongolia's economy has been under duress. This reality comes as a shock, as between 2011 to 2012, Mongolia was crowned as one of the world's fastest-growing economies with a GDP of 17.3 percent.[2] Mongolia earned the title of 'Minegolia'. Its rich natural resources enabled the nation to be a noteworthy market investor in 2011, which excited other nations.[3] 'Minegolia' attracted international investors

---

1   International Monetary Fund. Asia and Pacific Department, "Mongolia : 2017 Article IV Consultation and Request for an Extended Arrangement Under the Extended Fund Facility-Press Release: Staff Report; and Statement by the Executive Director for Mongolia," *International Monetary Fund,* May 31, 2017, https://www.imf.org/en/Publications/CR/Issues/2017/05/31/Mongolia-2017-Article-IV-Consultation-and-Request-for-an-Extended-Arrangement-Under-the-44954

2   Ibid.

3   Clement Huaweilang Dai & David Tyler Gibson, "MINEGOLIA PART 1 – China and Mongolia's Mining Bloom," *China Environment Forum,* n.d., https://www.wilsoncenter.org/sites/default/files/media/documents/publication/Dai%20and%20Gibson_Minegolia.pdf

who boosted the nation's foreign direct investment to 44 percent in 2011.[4] However, that investment rate declined to around 0.8 percent just four years later.[5]

China Briefing explains,

Mongolia's economic difficulties can be attributed to various causes. First of all, a steady dip in global prices for commodities has dealt a major blow to Mongolia's export volumes. The price index for all types of coal supplied by Mongolia, its biggest export by volume, decreased by 15 percent from 2014 to 2015. Secondly, a less experienced government, led by the Democratic Party, took a series of protectionist steps to try and increase domestic control over expected riches, but ended up severely eroding FDI rates. In particular, government attempts to renegotiate a deal with mining company Rio Tinto over the terms of the large Oyu Tolgoi copper and gold mining site took a toll on investor confidence.

Furthermore, in 2012, the Mongolian government-issued "Chinggis Bonds", raising USD $1.5 billion that was to be spent on infrastructure investment, salary improvement, and subsidized mortgages.[6] Yet, due to "the commodities glut, decrease in FDI and slowdown

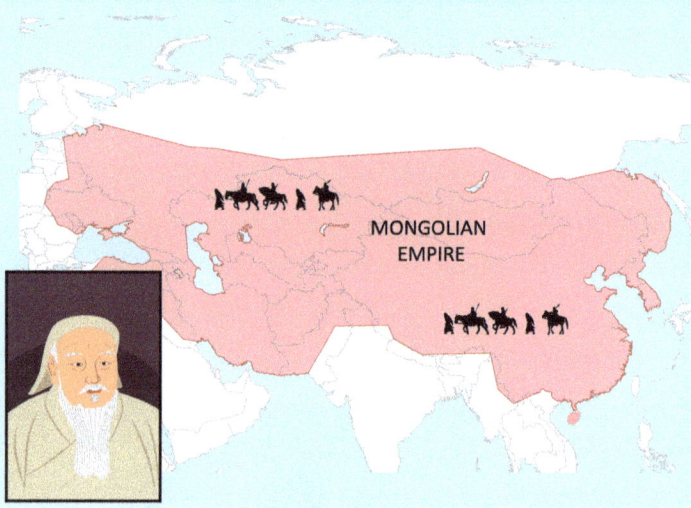

The Mongolian Empire 13th and 14th Centuries
Genghis Khan (1162 - 1227)
The Largest Land Empire in History

---

4 Zolzaya Erdenebileg, "China-Mongolia Relations: Challenges and Opportunities," *China Briefing*, January 6, 2017, https://www.china-briefing.com/news/china-mongolia-relations/

5 Ibid.

6 World Bank Group, "Mongolia Economic Update", *World Bank Group*, November 2015, http://pubdocs.worldbank.org/en/920971447119845335/meu-nov2015-en.pdf

in demand from China, Mongolia faced about USD $2 billion in public and private debt payments, due as early as March 2017. The budget deficit rose to 20 percent of GDP in 2016, and total external debt is estimated to be USD $23.5 billion, USD $8.4 billion of which is government debt. In short, Mongolia needs money."[7]

These conditions have not improved in recent years. Economic growth declined from 7.2 percent in 2018 to 5.1 percent in 2019, attributed to declining mining sector profits.[8]

Chinese Investments

With severely strained financial conditions due to drastically declining export rates, Mongolia turned toward China, hoping to form a relationship that would salvage their economy – it did. By November 2016, eighty percent of Mongolia's exports were shipped to China. At the same time, China became Mongolia's largest importer, equating to thirty percent of Mongolia's imports.[9]

China's aid went beyond a trade relationship. Mongolia united with Beijing, providing China with a stop along its extensive Belt and Road Initiative (BRI), a vast shipping and trading network connecting 138 countries.[10] Mongolia allied with Russia and China in June 2016 to create the critical passageway, known as the China-Mongolia Russia Economic Corridor (CMREC) along the Belt and Road Initiative transit route.[11] In 2016, Russia, China, and Mongolia traded 24.6 trillion kilos of freight with one another.[12] This trade relationship and shipping passageway development proved to be in the best interests of each of the countries. The three states' partnership serves to facilitate trade routes, invest in infrastructure, and strengthen economic cooperation between the three nations.[13]

Chinese state media explains, "The CMREC has two key traffic arteries: One extends from China's Beijing-Tianjin-Hebei region via Hohhot in the Inner Mongolia Autonomous Region to Mongolia and Russia; the other extends from China's northeastern cities Dalian, Shenyang, Changchun, Harbin and Manzhouli to Russia's Chita."[14] Regarding the China-

---

7   Zolzaya Erdenebileg, "China-Mongolia Relations: Challenges and Opportunities," *China Briefing*, January 6, 2017, https://www.china-briefing.com/news/china-mongolia-relations/

8   The World Bank, "The World Bank in Mongolia," *The World Bank*, n.d., https://www.worldbank.org/en/country/mongolia/overview

9   Zolzaya Erdenebileg, "China-Mongolia Relations: Challenges and Opportunities," *China Briefing*, January 6, 2017, https://www.china-briefing.com/news/china-mongolia-relations/

10 Green Belt and Road Initiative Center, "Countries of the Belt and Road Initiative (BRI)," *Green Belt and Road Initiative Center*, n.d., https://green-bri.org/countries-of-the-belt-and-road-initiative-bri

11 Engen Tham, "China, Russia, Mongolia ink Economic Corridor Plan – Xinhua," *Reuters*, June 23, 2016, https://www.reuters.com/article/uk-china-trade-corridor/china-russia-mongolia-ink-economic-corridor-plan-xinhua-idUKKCN0ZA03G

12 Wade Shepard, "How China's Belt And Road Economic Corridors Are Enhanced By The UN's TIR Convention," *Forbes*, August 22, 2016, https://www.forbes.com/sites/wadeshepard/2016/08/22/how-the-emerging-china-mongolia-russia-economic-corridor-is-enhanced-by-the-uns-tir-convention/#53be3b7c1c13

13 Engen Tham, "China, Russia, Mongolia Ink Economic Corridor Plan – Xinhua," *Reuters*, June 23, 2016, https://www.reuters.com/article/uk-china-trade-corridor/china-russia-mongolia-ink-economic-corridor-plan-xinhua-idUKKCN0ZA03G

14 Zhang Hui, "Large Number of Joint Projects Materialized Via Cooperation Scheme," *Global Times*, May 7, 2019, http://en.people.cn/n3/2019/0507/c90000-9575634.html

Mongolia-Russia Economic Corridor (CMREC), President Xi remarked, "We three sides should actively engage in the discussion of building cross-border economic cooperation zones, enhance industrial tie-in, boost sub-regional cooperation in our adjacent areas, and promote the common development of our adjacent areas."[15]

Mongolia sees great potential for economic growth in the CMREC. As a landlocked nation with 3.3 million citizens, Mongolia hopes that the CMREC will overcome its blocked-in nature as it can incorporate the CMREC's blueprints into its own infrastructure development.[16]

Before the pandemic, Mongolia's economy recovered from its downturn. In 2019, Mongolia's economic growth accelerated to 8.6 percent, and gross international reserves increased by $2.5 billion since 2016.[17]

The Promise of Autonomy with Some Strings Attached

Mongolia's modern independent state dates back to August 14, 1945, when China signed the Treaty of Friendship and Alliance, promising to recognize Mongolia's autonomy.[18] Before this agreement, Mongolia had been ruled by Soviet Union officials and troops.[19] *The Diplomat* explains,

> The Chinese had by then lost all effective control of what they then called "Outer Mongolia." The last Chinese forces in Mongolia were chased out by the anti-Bolshevik general Roman von Ungern-Stenberg in 1921 (who was in turn defeated by the Bolsheviks later that year). Mongolia soon became the "People's Republic of Mongolia" – the first Soviet satellite, even as it remained, de jure, a part of China. In February 1945, at Yalta, the Soviet leader Joseph Stalin asked his wartime allies, the United States and the United Kingdom, to consent to Mongolia maintaining its "status quo" after the war, and obtained their agreement to this innocuous proposition.[20]

Inner Mongolia, or the southernmost territory, remains as an autonomous territory in China where the Han Chinese currently outnumber the Mongolians five to one.[21] Inner Mongolia's population is approximately 24 million people, in which 17.1% are Chinese

---

15 Engen Tham, "China, Russia, Mongolia Ink Economic Corridor Plan – Xinhua," *Reuters*, June 23, 2016, https://www.reuters.com/article/uk-china-trade-corridor/china-russia-mongolia-ink-economic-corridor-plan-xinhua-idUKKCN0ZA03G

16 Antonio Graceffo, "Mongolia and the Belt and Road Initiative: The Prospects for the China-Mongolia-Russia Economic Corridor," *The Jamestown Foundation*, July 15, 2020, https://jamestown.org/program/mongolia-and-the-belt-and-road-initiative-the-prospects-for-the-china-mongolia-russia-economic-corridor/

17 International Monetary Fund. Asia and Pacific Department, "Mongolia : 2019 Article IV Consultation-Press Release; Staff Report; and Statement by the Executive Director for Mongolia," *International Monetary Fund*, September 17, 2019, https://www.imf.org/en/Publications/CR/Issues/2019/09/17/Mongolia-2019-Article-IV-Consultation-Press-Release-Staff-Report-and-Statement-by-the-48680

18 Sergey Radchenko, "The Truth About Mongolia's Independence 70 Years Ago," *The Diplomat*, October 22, 2015, https://thediplomat.com/2015/10/the-truth-about-mongolias-independence-70-years-ago/

19 Country Studies, "Modern Mongolia, 1911-84," *Country Studies*, n.d., http://countrystudies.us/mongolia/26.htm

20 Sergey Radchenko, "The Truth About Mongolia's Independence 70 Years Ago," *The Diplomat*, October 22, 2015, https://thediplomat.com/2015/10/the-truth-about-mongolias-independence-70-years-ago/

21 Andrew Jacobs, "Ethnic Protests in China Have Lengthy Roots," *The New York Times*, June 11, 20111, https://www.nytimes.com/2011/06/11/world/asia/11mongolia.html

Mongolian, and 79.5% are Han-Chinese, according to the sixth population census.[22]

However, China only signed the Treaty of Friendship and Alliance out of obligation, not genuine commitment. Joseph Stalin remarked, "If this [China's recognition] does not happen Outer Mongolia will be a rallying point for all Mongolians. It's to the detriment of China and us."[23] Stalin sent his soviet troops to corner northern and northeast China, prepare to invade, and threaten the Chinese leadership. Then-leader Chiang Kai-shek, recognizing the validity of Stalin's threats, caved and signed the treaty, recognizing Mongolia as an independent nation. However, this 'recognition' only came when the Chinese were under pressure and forced to oblige. China considered the 1945 referendum as a pretense for diplomacy since they believed they were manipulated by the Soviets into signing.[24]

In entering Mongolia in the 21st century, China has used similar façade-like tactics to 'recognize Mongolia's independence' and 'uphold its autonomy' while having different intentions. This phenomenon was reflected in 2017 when China condemned Mongolia over their invitation to the Dalai Lama to visit their nation.

The Dalai Lama is a Tibetan spiritual leader who Beijing views as a 'dangerous separatist'.[25] Many Buddhist Mongolians follow the Dalai Lama as their leader. In November 2016, Mongolia invited the Dalai Lama on an official visit to the nation. China warned Mongolia that this act would come with great repercussions. Wang Yi, China's Foreign Minister, warned the Mongolian Minister of Foreign Affairs, "The Dalai Lama's furtive visit to Mongolia brought a negative impact to China-Mongolia relations."[26] Wang further commented, "We hope that Mongolia has taken this lesson to heart," adding he hoped Mongolia would "scrupulously abide by its promise" not to extend this invitation to the spiritual leader again.

To ensure that Mongolia would uphold this asymmetric "promise", China imposed financial strains on the Inner Mongolia region. The following week after the Dalai Lama's visit, "China imposed fees on commodity imports from Mongolia, charging additional transit costs on goods passing through a border crossing into China's northern region of Inner Mongolia."[27]

Conclusion

There is no doubt that China holds all of the cards in its asymmetric relationships with countries worldwide, which is why Beijing can tell countries who they can invite, how they

---

22 Ivana Stojcic, Qingwang Wei, and Xiaopeng Ren, "Historical Sustenance Style and Social Orientations in China: Chinese Mongolians Are More Independent Than Han Chinese," *Frontiers in Psychology* 11, (2020): 864, https://www.ncbi.nlm.nih.gov/pmc/articles/PMC7225263/

23 Sergey Radchenko, "The Truth About Mongolia's Independence 70 Years Ago," *The Diplomat*, October 22, 2015, https://thediplomat.com/2015/10/the-truth-about-mongolias-independence-70-years-ago/

24 Ibid.

25 Christian Shepherd, "China Says Hopes Mongolia Learned Lesson After Dalai Lama Visit," *Reuters*, January 24, 2017, https://www.reuters.com/article/us-china-mongolia-dalailama-idUSKBN158197

26 Reuters Staff, "China Says Hopes Mongolia Learned Lesson after Dalai Lama Visit," *Reuters*, January 24, 2017, https://www.reuters.com/article/us-china-mongolia-dalailama-idUSKBN158197

27 Christian Shepherd, "China Says Hopes Mongolia Learned Lesson After Dalai Lama Visit," *Reuters*, January 24, 2017, https://www.reuters.com/article/us-china-mongolia-dalailama-idUSKBN158197

should vote at the U.N., and with what countries they can create partnerships. Mongolia is no exception to this reality. There is no surprise that China dictates whether the Dalai Lama can enter another sovereign country when they punish other non-cooperating countries with painful economic surcharges.

China may have ridden into Mongolia as a knight in shining armor to 'save' Mongolia's economy. However, the ulterior motive may actually be a trillion or more in minerals and control over Mongolia's geopolitical activities.

What's at Stake?

First, though China's economic might aids Mongolia, the nation unwittingly became subject to Beijing's CCP principles.

Second, Mongolia's yield to Beijing should be a wake-up call for the rest of the world as states who accept China's economic aid must abide by CCP ideologies and give up some of their sovereignty. The Dalai Lama incident in which China exerted its own beliefs onto Mongolia is repeated with nations globally when they engage in economic ties with China.

Third, a large influx of foreign direct investment from China could be extremely detrimental to Mongolians. With Chinese workers and contractual restrictions, small industries may be pushed out.

Fourth, states that seek autonomy, independence, and democracy should be cautious of Beijing's primary intention to extend its long arms and take control.

Chapter 5
China's Crackdown on Inner Mongolia
Beijing's Policies to Remove Mongolian Culture

Introduction

In 2017, China celebrated 70 years of its founding of the Inner Mongolian region. However, China and Inner Mongolia have not peacefully co-existed since the great Cultural Revolution (1966-1976) in China when China launched full-scale persecutions on minority groups, including the Mongols. Southern Mongolia suffered tremendously; 100,000 Southern Mongolians died and half a million were persecuted.[1]

Thus, while China claimed they were "purging the members of Southern Mongolian People's Revolutionary Party," *Bitter Winter* reports its government launched its version of ethnic cleansing on one-third of the Mongolian population.[2] Though China and the Mongolian nation, also known as 'Outer Mongolia' have their own conflict, China has continued its persecution of Mongols in Inner Mongolia throughout 2020.

Education in Inner Mongolia - Lesson 1 - "We Are Chinese"
School Will Now be Taught in the "Native Language" – Mandarin

The Inner Mongolia Autonomous Region (IMAR)

- Established with Soviet support in 1947, then absorbed by the People Republic of China (PRC).

- In October 2020, the population of Inner Mongolia is 3.278 million, while the population of Mongolia is 3.292 million.

- Activists consider Inner Mongolia "Southern Mongolia."

Mongolia

- Achieved independence from the Republic of China in 1921.

- A 1990 democratic revolution replaced the Soviet-controlled state in 1924.

"Our language is Mongolian; our homeland is Mongolia forever!
Our mother tongue is Mongolian; we will die for our mother tongue!"

BBC News. "Rare Rallies in China Over Mongolian Language Curb." *BBC News*, September 1, 2020, https://www.bbc.com/news/world-asia-china-53981100

---

1 Massimo Introvigne, "Southern Mongolia, the Unknown Cultural Genocide," *Bitter Winter*, July 22, 2020, https://bitterwinter.org/southern-mongolia-the-unknown-cultural-genocide/

2 Ibid.

Education and Language Crackdown

China's crackdown on Inner Mongolia has primarily targeted the Mongolian language and culture. *Radio Free Asia* reported that the CCP "will end" the Mongolian form of education.[3] Inner Mongolia is outnumbered by Han Chinese, with a 6 to 1 ratio of Han Chinese to Mongolians.[4] Furthermore, seats in bilingual public schools in Inner Mongolia have decreased from 190,000 to 17,000, where Han Chinese students are also filling seats.[5] Not only is Beijing replacing space in classrooms with Han Chinese students, they also require that four subjects – language and literature, politics, and history – be taught in Mandarin.[6]

***The Southern Mongolian Human Rights Information Center* explains,**

> At midnight for the past three days, hundreds of Mongolian teachers across eastern Southern Mongolia, particularly in the Tongliao and Ulaanhad municipalities, were called to urgent closed-door meetings at their respective schools. The school authorities notified them of the Chinese Central Government's decision to use Chinese as the language of instruction in all elementary and middle schools across Southern Mongolia starting September 1, 2020.[7]

One anonymous Mongolian teacher said, "We are forced to sign a paper not to discuss anything about this program. All teachers were warned not to raise any questions or opinions of opposition," while another confirmed, "Yes, there is a secret official document from the Central Government. The school authorities and the personnel from the Bureau of Education showed us the red letterhead of the official document but declined to show us the contents."[8]

September 2020 Protests

With Beijing's new policy to implement Mandarin-taught classes, ethnic Mongolians in northern China have protested the new policy.[9] The student community has been active in protesting, with students at rallies chanting, "Our language is Mongolian and our homeland is Mongolia forever! Our mother tongue is Mongolian, and we will die for our mother tongue!"[10]

---

3   Radio Free Asia, "China 'Will End' Mongolian-Language Education Starting This Semester: Reports," *Radio Free Asia,* August 24, 2020, https://www.rfa.org/english/news/china/language-08242020101614.html

4   Antonio Graceffo, "China's Crackdown on Mongolian Culture," *The Diplomat*, September 4, 2020, https://thediplomat.com/2020/09/chinas-crackdown-on-mongolian-culture/

5   Ibid.

6   Gerry Shis, "Chinese Authorities Face Widespread Anger in Inner Mongolia After Requiring Mandarin-Language Classes," *The Washington Post,* August 31, 2020, https://www.washingtonpost.com/world/asia_pacific/chinese-authorities-face-widespread-anger-in-inner-mongolia-after-requiring-mandarin-language-classes/2020/08/31/3ba5a938-eb5b-11ea-bd08-1b10132b458f_story.html

7   SMHRIC, "China's Finishing Touch on Cultural Genocide in Southern Mongolia," *Southern Mongolian Human Rights Information Center,* August 20, 2020, http://www.smhric.org/news_671.htm

8   Ibid.

9   BBC News, "Rare Rallies in China over Mongolian Language Curb," *BBC News*, September 1, 2020, https://www.bbc.com/news/world-asia-china-53981100

10 Andrés Vacca, "CCP Restricts Mongolian Language in China and Student Community Protests," *The BL*, September 3, 2020, https://thebl.com/world-news/ccp-restricts-mongolian-language-in-china-and-student-community-protests.html

Reports reveal that protests have escalated, with tanks seen on the streets and state-run media reporting Mongolian workers joining the fight.[11] Videos have surfaced of middle-schoolers trampling through police barricades at their school entrance to escape the forced participation in the "bilingual" language program.[12]

In response to the backlash, one Mongolian shared that police had been entering the Mongols' homes to make them sign pledges to remain silent against the bilingual program or else risk becoming "key individuals" in police databases, requiring surveillance and control.[13] The six million Mongols in China constitute just 18% of the Inner Mongolian population.[14] Though protests have continued despite CCP threats, they may soon find themselves outnumbered and forced to cave in to Beijing's pressure.

Conclusion

The change in policy means that schools once taught in Mongolian with language classes in Mandarin are now classes taught in Mandarin with a language class in Mongolian. The shift in Chinese influence and control of Inner Mongolia has not been widely accepted by Mongolians. Parents were arrested. Teachers were silenced. Mongolian citizens were threatened. This event mirrors what happened in Tibet and what is happening in Xinjiang Province as China tightens its control over its people along with their beliefs, culture, and language.

What's at Stake?

First, China's language re-education initiative is part of a greater ethnic cleansing of the Mongols. The Mongol people's entire culture is at stake with Beijing's severe crackdown and guise of a "bilingual" future.

Second, as Beijing exerts its CCP principles onto Outer Mongolia, including its anti-Dalai-Lama stance, its greater control of Inner Mongolia is a prelude to what is to come for the independent Mongolian nation.

Third, with threats of surveillance and severe police brutality against protesters, Mongolians' rights and liberties are dangerously dissipating at the behest of the CCP.

---

11 NTD Television, "China in Focus (Sept. 4): Resistance Rising in Inner Mongolia," *The Epoch Times*, September 4, 2020, https://www.theepochtimes.com/china-in-focus-chinese-netizens-refute-xi-jinpings-claims_3488935.html

12 Alice Su, "China Cracks Down on Inner Mongolian Minority Fighting for its Mother Tongue," *Los Angeles Times*, September 3, 2020, https://www.latimes.com/world-nation/story/2020-09-03/china-inner-mongolia-bilingual-education-assimilation-xinjiang-resistance-crackdown

13 Ibid.

14 Minority Rights Group International, "World Directory of Minorities and Indigenous Peoples - China : Mongols," *Refworld*, November, 2017, https://www.refworld.org/docid/49749d3d3c.html

Chapter 6
China's BRI Connection in Central Asia
Kazakhstan, Kyrgyzstan, & Tajikistan

Introduction

Central Asia is a key region for the global community.[1] Its strategic location between China and Russia makes these states vital for trade. Furthermore, vast oil and natural gas deposits offer a treasure chest of energy resources. The potential to develop ports and railways has attracted flocks of international companies looking to invest and finance infrastructure projects. Thus, it is no surprise that China has been particularly interested in the region.

China's investment in Central Asia is magnified by its Belt and Road Initiative (BRI) advanced in 2013. Kazakhstan, Kyrgyzstan, and Tajikistan provide valuable access routes to port cities for shipping and trade. Foreign direct investment (FDI) has increased over the decades as the region's vital natural resource markets have boomed. As nations worldwide jump at Central Asia's financial opportunities, China has emerged as a prominent investor and partner with the three states - Kazakhstan, Kyrgyzstan, and Tajikistan. Furthermore, "China intends to realize the Silk Road Economic Belt (SREB) of its global Belt and Road Initiative (BRI)."[2]

China-Kazakhstan Geographic Size Comparison

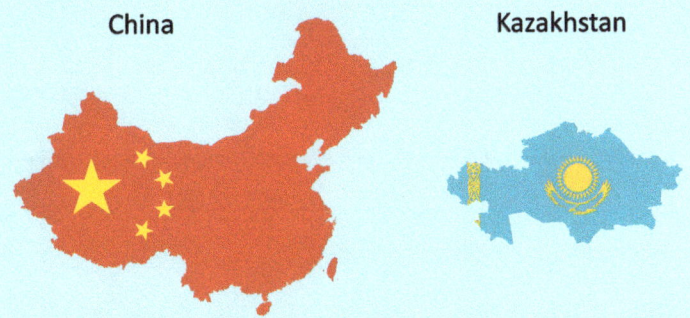

Kazakhstan

Kazakhstan accounted for approximately 75 percent of inflow in Central Asia in 2018.[3] China was recorded as the fourth largest investor in Kazakhstan for five years, following the Netherlands ($33.8 billion), the U.S. ($19.4 billion), and Switzerland ($12.5 billion).[4] Kazakhstan welcomes this foreign direct investment, seeking to increase FDI inflow 26

---

1 Amorith Tan, "China and Russia: Competition in Kyrgyzstan," *Future Directions International*, January 30, 2020 https://www.futuredirections.org.au/publication/china-and-russia-competition-in-kyrgyzstan/

2 Farkhod Tolipov, "New Strategy, Old Game: The Realigning Geopolitics of Central Asia," *The Central Asia-Caucasus Analyst*, March 26, 2020, https://www.cacianalyst.org/publications/analytical-articles/item/13610-new-strategy-old-game-the-realigning-geopolitics-of-central-asia.html

3 Baurzhan Sartbayev, "Kazakhstan Aims to Become a Destination for Global Investment," *Foreign Policy*, n.d., https://foreignpolicy.com/sponsored/kazakhstan-aims-to-become-a-destination-for-global-investment/

4 Ibid.

Kazakhs Imprisoned and Tortured in Xinjiang Province
Seek Asylum but Fear Deportation Back to China

1   Claire Press, "The Kazakh Muslims detained in China's camps," *BBC News*, January 15, 2020, https://www.bbc.com/news/av/world-asia-51097159

---

percent by the year 2022.[5]

In 2019, FDI stock in Kazakhstan reached $150 bn.[6] That same year, Kazakhstan officially released a list of China's fifty-five investment projects in the nation, which accounted for a total of $27.6 bn.[7] Roughly half of the investments were for oil and natural gas projects.[8] With such vast investments by China, Kazakhstan faces challenges in its other industries.

Nordea Trade explains,

Kazakhstan's main challenge remains attracting investment in sectors and activities other than oil extraction, natural resources, which account for more than 70% of total FDI

---

5   Baurzhan Sartbayev, "Kazakhstan Aims to Become a Destination for Global Investment," *Foreign Policy*, n.d., https://foreignpolicy.com/sponsored/kazakhstan-aims-to-become-a-destination-for-global-investment/

6   Nordea Trade, "Foreign Direct Investment (FDI) in Kazakhstan," *Nordea Trade*, n.d., https://www.nordeatrade.com/en/explore-new-market/kazakhstan/investment

7   Eugene Simonov, "Half China's Investment in Kazakhstan is in Oil and Gas," *China Dialogue*, October 29, 2019, https://chinadialogue.net/en/energy/11613-half-china-s-investment-in-kazakhstan-is-in-oil-and-gas-2/

8   Ibid.

stock, and to retain investors already in the economy. US-based energy firm Chevron's Tengiz oil field expansion project, one of the largest foreign investments in the country, is expected to be completed by 2022.[9]

The COVID-19 pandemic slowed the demand for oil and natural gas while also plunging the price per barrel down. Although expected to rise, China's gas consumption has dropped by 17 percent from February 2019 to February 2020, and PetroChina even suspended some natural gas imports.[10] This decrease has made it even more difficult for the Kazak government to repay its loans.

Furthermore, Kazakhstan is known as the "buckle" in China's Belt and Road Initiative (BRI).[11] Its location between China, Russia, and Europe makes the newly expanded railway network highly strategic.[12] China's roughly 7,000 km Western Europe-Western China Highway has a 2,700 km portion through Kazakhstan.[13] *Bloomberg* explains,

> ...[E]xpanding northern and southern rail routes have already dramatically increased shipping volume and capacity. The southern rail route goes across Kazakhstan to Aktau, on the Caspian Sea, then across the water and into Georgia, Turkey and the EU through Bulgaria. The northern route goes from southwest China through Kazakhstan en route to Russia, Belarus, Poland and Germany, ending in Duisberg, the largest dry port in Europe.
>
> This game-changing rail network saw 200,000 containers shipped from China to Europe, via Kazakhstan, last year. According to Roman Vassilenko, Kazakhstan's Deputy Minister of Foreign Affairs, that number is expected to double to 400,000 in 2018, and reach 1.5 million containers by 2020. Although shipping by rail is more costly than shipping via sea, these new rail links enable freight to travel from China through Kazakhstan to Europe in just 15 days, and on to London in 18 days— considerably faster than the 30—45 days it takes by sea.[14]

As China ramps up its regional investment strategy, Beijing has also sought ways to amplify its influence in Kazakhstan.

One controversial moment, in particular, sets the tone for China's future vision of its involvement in Kazakhstan. In April 2020, a private-owned Chinese website, sohu.com,

---

9   Nordea Trade, "Foreign Direct Investment (FDI) in Kazakhstan," *Nordea Trade*, n.d., https://www.nordeatrade.com/en/explore-new-market/kazakhstan/investment

10 Azad Garibov, "Central Asia Caught in Economic Perfect Storm amid Oil Price Collapse and COVID-19 Pandemic," *The Central Asia-Caucasus Analyst*, May 12, 2020, https://www.cacianalyst.org/publications/analytical-articles/item/13617-central-asia-caught-in-economic-perfect-storm-amid-oil-price-collapse-and-covid-19-pandemic.html

11 Bradley Jardine, "Why Are There Anti-China Protests in Central Asia?," *The Washington Post*, October 16, 2019, https://www.washingtonpost.com/politics/2019/10/16/why-are-there-anti-china-protests-central-asia/

12 Arif Durrani & Gabe Kirchheimer, "Why Invest in Kazakhstan?," *Bloomberg*, November 20, 2018, https://sponsored.bloomberg.com/news/sponsors/aifc/why-invest-in-kazakhstan/?adv=19268&prx_t=hSIEAAAAAAFEANA

13 Alexander Kruglov, "New Silk Road Money is Paving the Old Silk Roads," *Asia Times*, November 6, 2019, https://asiatimes.com/2019/11/new-silk-road-money-is-paving-the-old-silk-roads/

14 Arif Durrani & Gabe Kirchheimer, "Why Invest in Kazakhstan?," *Bloomberg*, November 20, 2018, https://sponsored.bloomberg.com/news/sponsors/aifc/why-invest-in-kazakhstan/?adv=19268&prx_t=hSIEAAAAAAFEANA

published an article entitled, "Why Kazakhstan is eager to return to China."[15] The article briefly explained the history of Kazakh trips to China that pledged allegiance to the Chinese emperor. The Kazakh ministry stated this article "runs counter to the spirit of permanent comprehensive strategic partnership."[16]

"The article does not reflect the position of China's government, and the two countries' friendship shall not be shaken by any matter, said China's foreign ministry in a statement sent to *Reuters*."[17] Though China clarified its intentions, the optics of the situation remain. Even further, Tuotiao.com, a Beijing news source, published an article entitled, "Why didn't Kyrgyzstan return to China after gaining Independence?"[18] Thus, it will be unsurprising if China's ambitious initiative to 'salami slice' nations expands to Kazakhstan.

Kyrgyzstan

While Kazakhstan is nearing a debt-trap sentence with China, Kyrgyzstan has already received theirs. The nation is a highly strategic piece of land in Central Asia.[19] Kyrgyzstan's geography is an essential part of its attractiveness. Kyrgyzstan surrounds and controls the Tien Shan mountain region, which is a wide-ranging geographic feature, extending through a significant portion of Central Asia. Because of its vast size, the mountain region grants a weight of geopolitical and economic leverage that both Russia and China seek to obtain.[20]

---

15 Olzhas Auyezov, Judy Hua, & Gabriel Crossley, "Kazakhstan Summons Chinese Ambassador in Protest Over Article," *Reuters*, April 14, 2020, https://www.reuters.com/article/us-kazakhstan-china/kazakhstan-summons-chinese-ambassador-in-protest-over-article-idUSKCN21W1AH

16 Ibid.

17 Ibid.

18 Siddhant Sibbal, "Chinese Websites Claim Kyrgyzstan, Kazakhstan Part of China; Draws Ire of Central Asia," *Zee News*, May 11, 2020, https://zeenews.india.com/world/chinese-websites-claim-kyrgyzstan-kazakhstan-part-of-china-draws-ire-of-central-asia-2282791.html

19 Amorith Tan, "China and Russia: Competition in Kyrgyzstan," *Future Directions International*, January 30, 2020 https://www.futuredirections.org.au/publication/china-and-russia-competition-in-kyrgyzstan/

20 Ibid.

The University of Central Asia determined that "for 2006-2017, the cumulative gross of Chinese FDI inflow was equal to USD $2.3 billion. For this period, Chinese FDI constituted 25-50% of total FDI to Kyrgyzstan, which is equivalent to 2-7% of the country's GDP."[21] Kyrgyzstan's highly lucrative oil industry has attracted an abundance of Chinese investments. Chinese-state media reports that China's largest investment project in the country is the Zhondga China Petrol Company refinery.[22] This project cost USD $500 million and created a refinery for oil imported from Russia, Kazakhstan, and Kyrgyzstan.[23]

In addition, China has funded Belt and Road Initiative (BRI) infrastructure projects in Kyrgyzstan. In 2019, China built a highway from Bishkek to Naryn, a 350km road for transport.[24] However, these developments have begun to lead to financial repercussions as experts fear Kyrgyzstan has fallen into China's debt trap. The Center for Global Development notes,

> By the end of March 2017, public and publicly guaranteed debt amounted to roughly 65 percent of GDP, of which external debt represented about 90 percent of the total. China's Exim Bank is the largest single creditor, with reported loans by the end of 2016 totaling $1.5 billion, or roughly 40 percent of the country's total external debt. Kyrgyz and Chinese authorities are reportedly discussing the construction of a chain of hydropower plants, a China-Kyrgyzstan-Uzbekistan railway, additional highway construction, and completion of the Central Asia-China gas pipeline.[25]

It is especially important to note that China's Exim Bank holds two percent interest rates, making it far cheaper for Kyrgyzstan to borrow from China than its local banks that hold interest rates roughly five times higher.[26]

---

21 Roman Mogilevskii, "Kyrgyzstan and the Belt and Road Initiative," *University of Central Asia*, 2019, https://www.ucentralasia.org/Content/downloads/UCA-IPPA-Wp50%20-%20ENG.pdf

22 Wu Guoxiu, "Chinese Refinery Becomes Kyrgyzstan's Second Largest Taxpayer," *CGTN*, June 11, 2019, https://news.cgtn.com/news/3d3d514f7a496a4d35457a6333566d54/index.html

23 Ibid.

24 Belt & Road News, "China's BRI Extends to Kyrgyzstan, But Are New Transport Links Worth All That Debt?," *Belt & Road News,* April 28, 2019, https://www.beltandroad.news/2019/04/28/chinas-bri-extends-to-kyrgyzstan-but-are-new-transport-links-worth-all-that-debt/

25 John Hurley, Scott Morris, & Gailyn Portelance, "Examining the Debt Implications of the Belt and Road Initiative from a Policy Perspective," *Center for Global Development,* March, 2018, https://www.cgdev.org/sites/default/files/examining-debt-implications-belt-and-road-initiative-policy-perspective.pdf

26 Belt & Road News, "China's BRI Extends to Kyrgyzstan, But Are New Transport Links Worth All That Debt?," *Belt & Road News,* April 28, 2019, https://www.beltandroad.news/2019/04/28/chinas-bri-extends-to-kyrgyzstan-but-are-new-transport-links-worth-all-that-debt/

China-Tajikistan Geographic Size Comparison

Tajikistan

Tajikistan is moving closer to China's orbit. In addition to its indebtedness, militarization, and security, China has begun intelligence sharing through the Quadrilateral Cooperation and Coordination Mechanism, which allows them to coordinate efforts between China, Tajikistan, Pakistan, and Afghanistan.[27]

Tajikistan has also received investments from China in its Belt and Road Initiative (BRI). Tajikistan is deemed the "first leg"[28] of land-based routes of transportation along the BRI. Tajikistan's companies are spending money coming from China despite not making money with the promise that they will bring jobs in the future. However, Chinese citizens have entered Tajikistan during the pandemic to work on mineral and natural resource projects.[29]

China has become Tajikistan's single largest creditor in the country, accounting for "almost 80 percent of the total increase in Tajikistan's external debt over the 2007-2016 period."[30] The IMF and World Bank have declared Tajikistan as a "high risk" state to have debt distress.[31] However, Tajikistan will continue to raise its debt to repay China's BRI and other investments, including a $3bn loan to finance Tajikistan's Central Asia-China gas pipeline.[32]

---

27 Stephen Blank, "China's Military Base in Tajikistan: What Does it Mean?," *The Central Asia-Caucasus Analyst*, April 18, 2019, https://www.cacianalyst.org/publications/analytical-articles/item/13569-chinas-military-base-in-tajikistan-what-does-it-mean?.html

28 John Hurley, Scott Morris, & Gailyn Portelance, "Examining the Debt Implications of the Belt and Road Initiative from a Policy Perspective," *Center for Global Development*, March, 2018, https://www.cgdev.org/sites/default/files/examining-debt-implications-belt-and-road-initiative-policy-perspective.pdf

29 Niva Yau, "China Business Briefing: Whose Belt and Road is it Anyway?," *Eurasianet*, September 9, 2020, https://eurasianet.org/china-business-briefing-whose-belt-and-road-is-it-anyway

30 John Hurley, Scott Morris, & Gailyn Portelance, "Examining the Debt Implications of the Belt and Road Initiative from a Policy Perspective," *Center for Global Development*, March, 2018, https://www.cgdev.org/sites/default/files/examining-debt-implications-belt-and-road-initiative-policy-perspective.pdf

31 Ibid.

32 Ibid.

Because China has significant financial leverage over Tajikistan, Beijing has stepped its foot into regional geopolitical issues. In the long view, China may be seeking to supplant Russian interests in the region.[33] Backing that assertion, *The Wall Street Journal* reported that China and Tajikistan signed secret agreements in 2015 or 2016 that "gave Beijing rights to refurbish or build up to 30 to 40 guard posts on the Tajik side of the country's border with Afghanistan."[34] The *WSJ* sources stated,

> Under the accords, Chinese border guards have replaced their Tajik counterparts along large swathes of the territory along the Tajikistan-Afghanistan border, where Beijing deems the Tajiks incapable of stopping militants potentially infiltrating Tajik territory, the official said. "There are parts of the country where the Chinese have taken over border control completely," the official said. "They patrol on their own, in their own vehicles."

China's Not-So-Secret Military Base
Tajikistan Gives China Room to Increase its Claim Across the Border

---

33 Stephen Blank, "China's Military Base in Tajikistan: What Does it Mean?," *The Central Asia-Caucasus Analyst*, April 18, 2019, https://www.cacianalyst.org/publications/analytical-articles/item/13569-chinas-military-base-in-tajikistan-what-does-it-mean?.html

34 Craig Nelson & Thomas Grove, "Russia, China Vie for Influence in Central Asia as U.S. Plans Afghan Exit," *The Wall Street Journal*, June 18, 2019, https://www.wsj.com/articles/russia-china-vie-for-influence-in-central-asia-as-u-s-plans-afghan-exit-11560850203

The Diplomat explains the importance of China's patrolling, noting "that China was assisting Tajikistan in border security was not a secret, but the scale and depth of that cooperation was not known."[35]

Recently, images and reports show that China constructed a 'secret' military base in Tajikistan, which has prompted leaders in other countries to take notice.[36] Tajikistan had little power to stop China, given the debt it owes. However, this is one step closer to Tajikistan losing its territorial control and sovereignty.

Conclusion

Kazakhstan's citizenry has openly spoken up, challenging Beijing's 55 projects in the country to protest China's influence.[37] Though China promises jobs and investment, hidden strings attached to contracts may result in similar 'debt-trap' uncertainties, as is occurring in other nations. Kazakhstan may be subjected to China's surveillance and human rights abuses faced by the Uyghur people, a fate which also created tension for Kazakhstani citizens.[38]

Kyrgyzstan and Tajikistan's large sum of debt are startling. Continued dependence on Beijing's investments indicates China will significantly benefit from the debt-traps it created, such as its increased patrol in the Tajik border. Lower interest rates from Chinese banks will continue to attract borrowers and entrap them. Debt-trap states will be dominated and controlled by Beijing. Nevertheless, citizenry who depend on local economies will suffer.

China's land grab techniques expand its territorial conflicts with a handful of countries beyond Kazakhstan, Kyrgyzstan, and Tajikistan, making the risk of Beijing's exerted influence alarming.[39]

What's at Stake?

First, Kazakhstan, Kyrgyzstan, and Tajikistan are slowly but surely consumed by debt to China.

Second, sources in China say that Beijing seeks to claim territory in Kazakhstan, Kyrgyzstan, and Tajikistan. China has already placed a 'secret' military base on Tajikistan's land.[40]

---

35   Catherine Putz, "China in Tajikistan: New Report Claims Chinese Troops Patrol Large Swaths of the Afghan-Tajik Border," *The Diplomat*, June 18, 2019, https://thediplomat.com/2019/06/china-in-tajikistan-new-report-claims-chinese-troops-patrol-large-swaths-of-the-afghan-tajik-border/

36   Stephen Blank, "China's Military Base in Tajikistan: What Does it Mean?," *The Central Asia-Caucasus Analyst*, April 18, 2019, https://www.cacianalyst.org/publications/analytical-articles/item/13569-chinas-military-base-in-tajikistan-what-does-it-mean?.html

37   Pavel Mikheyev & Tamara Vaal, "Dozens Protest Against Chinese Influence in Kazakhstan," *Reuters*, September 4, 2019, https://www.reuters.com/article/us-kazakhstan-china-protests/dozens-protest-against-chinese-influence-in-kazakhstan-idUSKCN1VP1B0

38   Ibid.

39   Pia Krishnankutty, "Not Just India, Tibet — China Has 17 Territorial Disputes With Its Neighbours, On Land & Sea," *The Print*, July 15, 2020, https://theprint.in/theprint-essential/not-just-india-tibet-china-has-17-territorial-disputes-with-its-neighbours-on-land-sea/461115/

40   Eurasianet, "Tajikistan: Secret Chinese Base Becomes Slightly Less Secret," *Eurasianet*, September 23, 2020, https://eurasianet.org/tajikistan-secret-chinese-base-becomes-slightly-less-secret

Third, since Kazakhstan, Kyrgyzstan, and Tajikistan are part of China's 'Belt and Road grand plan', they are likely to lose sovereignty, territory, and resources.

Fourth, the drop in oil revenues caused by both the decrease in oil prices and the lowered demand is debilitating to Kazakhstan since much of its revenue comes from oil income.[41]

Fifth, Kazakhstan's currency, the tenge, has dropped.[42] From January 2009 to August 2020, the tenge decreased 250 percent compared to the dollar. From July 2015 to August 2020, the tenge's drop was 121 percent, which has limited Kazakhstan's ability to pay.

Growing Indebtedness to China

---

41 Azad Garibov, "Central Asia Caught in Economic Perfect Storm amid Oil Price Collapse and COVID-19 Pandemic," *The Central Asia-Caucasus Analyst*, May 12, 2020, https://www.cacianalyst.org/publications/analytical-articles/item/13617-central-asia-caught-in-economic-perfect-storm-amid-oil-price-collapse-and-covid-19-pandemic.html

42 Mariya Gordeyeva Dmitry Solovyov, "Kazakhstan Floats Tenge, Currency Tumbles," *Reuters*, August 20, 2015, https://www.reuters.com/article/us-kazakhstan-tenge/kazakhstan-floats-tenge-currency-tumbles-idUSKCN0QP0PN20150820

Chapter 7
Beijing Eyes Russian Territory
21st Century Claims on Qing Dynasty Land

Russia's port city of Vladivostok has been on China's radar ever since Moscow celebrated the city's 160th anniversary of its founding.[1] Vladivostok, loosely translated as "master of the East"[2] was annexed by Russia in 1860 after the British and French defeated China in the Second Opium War.[3] However, prior to Russia's ownership, the Qing dynasty owned Vladivostok, a city previously named Haishenwai.[4]

China Claims Part of Russia
Including Vladivostok

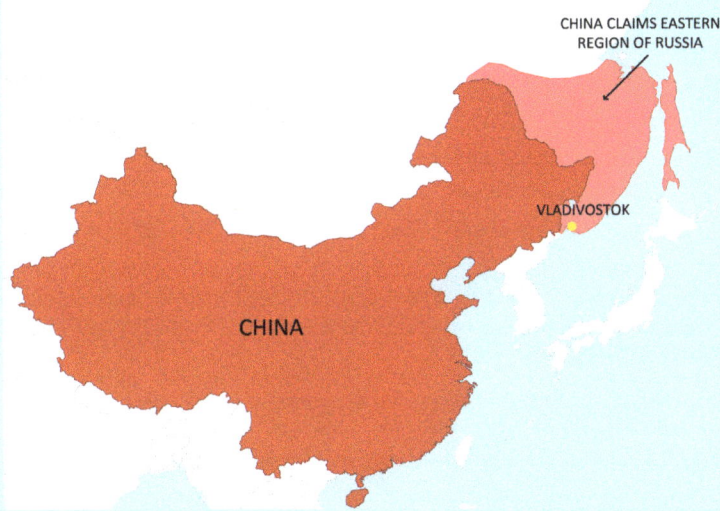

Vladivostok's Value

After Russia annexed Vladivostok, it was considered a military fortification for two years and became a port in 1862.[5] In 1882, it became a town.[6] Since its signing over to Russia, the city transformed from a trading center to a Soviet military base. During World War II, Russia used the city as a citadel for the Red Army's offensive strategies against attack. In 1948, the

---

1. EurAsian Times Desk, "FACT CHECK: Has China Really Claimed Russian Port City of Vladivostok?," *EurAsian Times*, July 4, 2020, https://eurasiantimes.com/fact-check-has-china-really-claimed-russian-port-city-of-vladivostok/
2. Andrew Higgins, "Vladivostok Lures Chinese Tourists (Many Think It's Theirs)," *The New York Times*, July 23, 2016, https://www.nytimes.com/2016/07/24/world/asia/vladivostok-china-haishenwai-tourists.html
3. Somoy News, "'This is Our Land,' China Now Claims Russia's Vladivostok as Part of its Territory," *Somoy News*, July 4, 2020, https://en.somoynews.tv/9451/news/This-is-our-land%E2%80%99-China-now-claims-Russia%E2%80%99s-Vladivostok-as-part-of-its-territory
4. Sidharth Shekhar, "'This is Our Land,' China Now Claims Russia's Vladivostok as Part of its Territory," *Times Now News*, July 3, 2020, https://www.timesnownews.com/international/article/after-galwan-valley-china-lays-claim-on-russia-s-vladivostok-calling-it-haishenwai/615563
5. Vladivostok City Info, "History," *Vladivostok City Info*, n.d., https://vladivostok-city.com/info?history
6. Ibid.

Soviets secretly transformed Vladivostok into a military base, stocking the city with troops, warships, and tanks.[7]

Beyond serving as a periodic military base, the port city became a strategic economic hub for Moscow. *The Diplomat* explains,

> ...Vladivostok has experienced a renaissance for the past several years. The Far Eastern region encompasses more than a third of Russia's vast landmass and some of the country's largest deposits of natural resources. In contrast, it is home to only 7.2 million people, with almost 110 million Chinese living in the three neighboring provinces of Manchuria. As the Kremlin feels the threat of Sinification, it has started pouring money into regional development with the unofficial capital at Vladivostok becoming a stage for displaying Moscow's ambitions.

China's Outrage at Russia's Anniversary Celebration

In July 2020, the Russian Embassy hosted a celebration on Weibo for its 160th anniversary of Vladivostok, prompting Chinese officials to backlash. Specifically, Shen Shiwei, a Chinese-state media journalist, tweeted,

> This "tweet" of #Russian embassy to #China isn't so welcome on Weibo[.] "The history of Vladivostok (literally 'Ruler of the East') is from 1860 when Russia built a military harbor." But the city was Haishenwai as Chinese land, before Russia annexed it via unequal Treaty of Beijing.[8]

Furthermore, Chinese diplomat Zhang Heqing commented on the tweet, "Isn't this what in the past was our Haishenwai?"[9] In China's eyes, the city of Vladivostok was taken from them during their 'Century of Humiliation' and as a result of several unequal treaties with international bodies and states. Now, with Beijing's economic, geopolitical, and influential might, China seeks to reclaim and regain ownership over its city of Haishenwai.

Conclusion

China and Russia's stability in the region is of the utmost importance for surrounding states. Recognizing this reality, in 1991, Moscow and Beijing began negotiations to resolve their ongoing territorial disputes from historic conflicts that were settled years later in 2008.[10] In this agreement, Russia obliged to cede islands in the Ussuri and Amur rivers to China, but Vladivostok's ownership was never discussed in meetings.[11]

---

7   Dmitriy Frolovskiy, "Vladivostok: The Many Lives of Russia's Far Eastern Capital," *The Diplomat*, September 3, 2016, https://thediplomat.com/2016/09/vladivostok-the-many-lives-of-russias-far-eastern-capital/

8   Akshay Narang, "'This is Our Land,' China Now Claims Russia's Vladivostok as Part of its Territory," *TFI Post*, July 4, 2020, https://tfipost.com/2020/07/this-is-our-land-china-now-claims-russias-vladivostok-as-part-of-its-territory/

9   James Patterson, "Russia's Vladivostok Celebration Prompted An Online Backlash In China: Another Dispute From The Past," *International Business Times*, July 3, 2020, https://www.ibtimes.com/russias-vladivostok-celebration-prompted-online-backlash-china-another-dispute-past-3005050

10 Eduardo Baptista, "Why Russia's Vladivostok Celebration Prompted a Nationalist Backlash in China," *South China Morning Post*, July 2, 2020, https://www.scmp.com/news/china/diplomacy/article/3091611/why-russias-vladivostok-celebration-prompted-nationalist

11 Ibid.

What's at Stake?

First, Vladivostok is Russian territory, though it is a constant and nearby reminder of the unequal treaties.

Second, Vladivostok symbolizes China's 21st-century hopes for expansion through the Belt and Road Initiative, 5G network, infrastructure loans, and vast alliances that Beijing is creating.

Third, Beijing seeks to erase its losses during the Century of Humiliation.

Fourth, there is no conflict yet over Vladivostok, just a rejection of Russia's celebration, which was seen as both historically incorrect and humiliating. Nothing escalated beyond aggressive tweets and statements. Yet, history shows that the tipping point in these scenarios is very fragile. If any dispute were to occur between Russia and China, it could be devastating, despite the presently friendly relationship between Putin and Xi.

Vladimir Putin and Xi Jinping
Friend or Foe as China Eyes Russia's Vladivostok

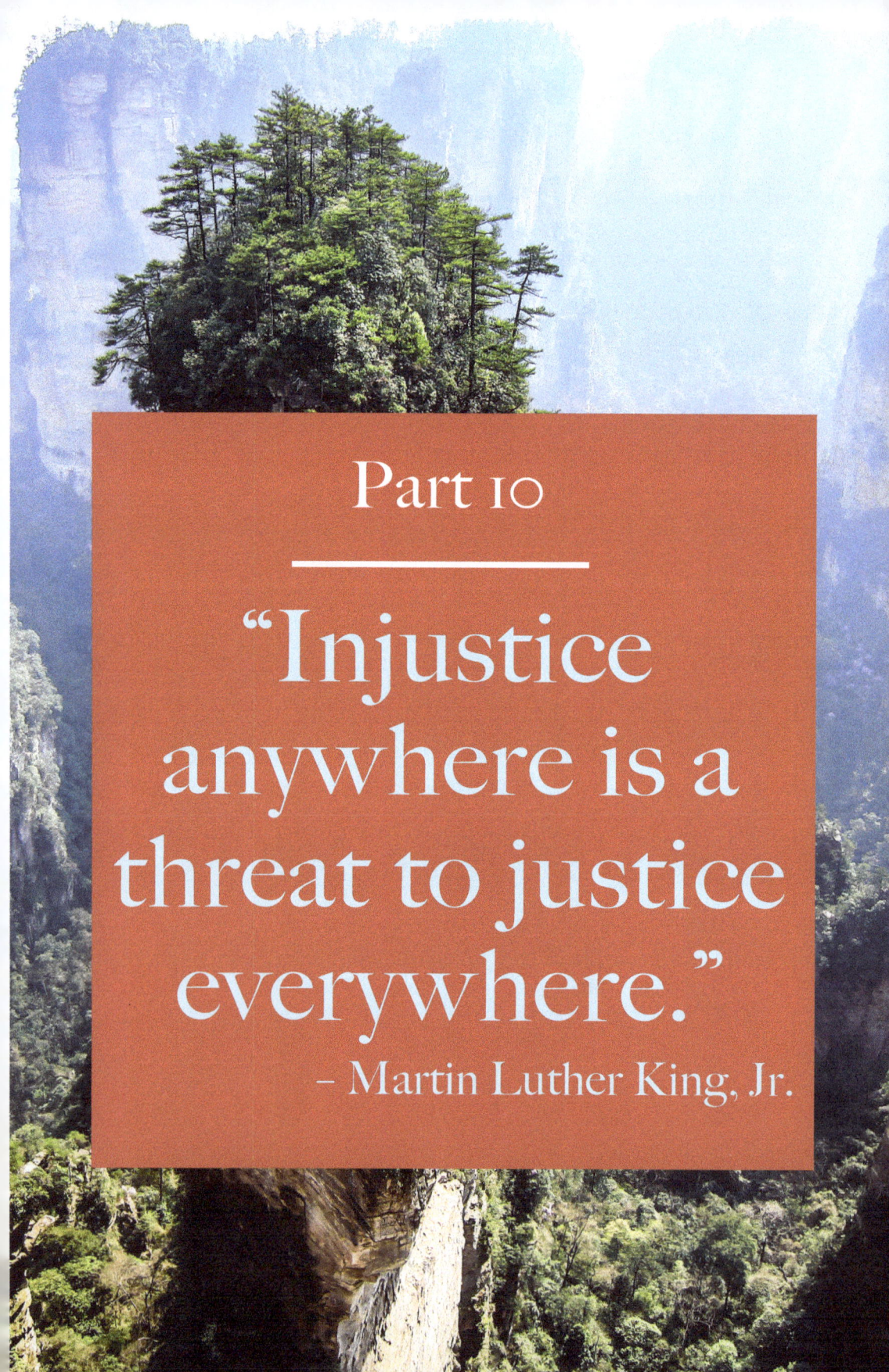

Part 10

"Injustice anywhere is a threat to justice everywhere."

– Martin Luther King, Jr.

For to be free is not merely to cast off one's chains, but to live in a way that respects and enhances the freedom of others." – Nelson Mandela

What does it mean to be free?

Is it okay to buy clothes and technology from Uyghurs enslaved in forced labor?

Now that we know that literally tons of human hair were cut from the heads of Chinese prisoners and delivered to New York ports, do we wear those extensions and wigs?

Should we feel bad if we need an organ and it is removed from a Chinese prisoner while they were alive?

Is the indiscriminate rounding up and 're-education' of Uyghurs acceptable?

And, do we believe our current world order upholds freedom?

"China's Power Grab" is predominantly about Beijing's salami-slicing of power and authority, stripped from countries in Asia, as China uses economic coercion to subjugate nations. However, the bigger picture goes beyond territorial, social, and religious control to create a population of "unyielding Marxist Atheists".

This book is ultimately about freedom. "China's Power Grab and Expanding Claims" is about the seductiveness of money and the power Beijing wields over individuals, corporations, and companies through the temptation of capital. This is a story about humanity, and how far we are willing to go to defend freedom. Though many questions remain and the future is uncertain, in the end, we must decide whether the allure of cheap prices and shortcuts is worth the cost in the long run.

As we remain vigilant to learn, understand, and become more aware, remember this,

"Freedom is not free!"

- U.S. Air Force Colonel Walter Hitchcock

Chapter 1

"Freedom is the last, best hope of earth."

– Abraham Lincoln

Asia is in the center of a great power competition with sparks igniting fires throughout the region. While the South China Sea is a hotbed of action, the tinderbox could just as easily explode in the East China Sea, Himalayas, Western China, North of China, or another locale. Strategic competition and great power-balancing fan the flames as the Wolf Warriors howl about how the U.S. does not respect China's sovereignty. Meanwhile, China has increasingly staked its claim to sovereignty to ever-expanding areas throughout Asia in China's great power grab. Although the U.S. and other Asian states are committed to a peaceful resolution of disagreements, Beijing's "might makes right" arm-twisting and salami-slicing tactics allow China to gain ground as it rewrites history and exerts its economic and military force.

With China's swift shutdown of Hong Kong, shifting economic power to Shenzhen,[1] the events unfolding take little imagination to read the tea leaves that foretell Taiwan's future. Without military support from countries afar, Taiwan's sovereignty may not last through the 2020s. Yet, this 'eventuality' does not need to result in China's 'give up or be blown up' dichotomy. China does not have to threaten Taiwan or Japan, India, Nepal, Bhutan, Mongolia, or other neighbors.

China is not threatening Russia. On the contrary, the two countries have formed an alliance. Thus, Beijing could leave states alone to have their own culture, language, and political system without arm-twisting. This course of action is simplistic, though complications can always arise. China knows not to instigate a fight with Russia as China needs Russia to gain access through the Arctic.

Meanwhile, within China, the CCP's oppressive acts have intensified as Xi's leadership cut off freedoms, even brutally within his own ranks. Beijing's totalitarian regime is primarily concerned with social control and coercion. With the coronavirus pandemic, the CCP proudly points to its all-seeing surveillance system with hundreds of millions of cameras to ensure compliance and prevent the spread. This domineering and positioning leaves people silenced, as is happening in Hong Kong, creating uncertainty for Taiwan and imprisoning millions in Xinjiang Province.

The CCP's threat to humanity includes indoctrination, re-education, and forced labor of the Uyghurs and Tibetans. Beijing's overarching goal is for China's ethnic populations to speak their new language of Mandarin and retrain or 're-educate' them for their new role as the unpaid or nearly unpaid labor of the world's global manufacturing of cheap products. Policies at work in both Xinjiang and Tibet have been implemented to develop 'vocational training', including the installation of a disciplined work ethic overseen by drill sergeants to extinguish what is seen as 'negative influence of religion'. Thus, Tibetans turn over their land and animals, give up their religion, learn Mandarin, and work for firms to produce clothes, shoes, phones, and other technologies, much like the Uyghurs who are imprisoned in concentration camps.

---

1   Josephine Ma, Catherine Wong, and Echo Xie, "Why China is Looking to Shenzhen – And Not Hong Kong – To Reinvent its Economic Future," *South China Morning Post*, July 31, 2019, https://www.scmp.com/news/china/politics/article/3020710/why-china-looking-shenzhen-and-not-hong-kong-reinvent-its

Methods perfected by Chen Quanguo in Tibet and imported to the Xinjiang Uyghur Autonomous Region (XUAR) have been newly reestablished and expanded in Tibet. Chen's extra-judicial imprisonment efforts in the XUAR have been extraordinary and harsh. Cross-pollination of effective methods of control between Xinjiang and Tibet allow both areas to be 'successful' in suppressing the people, extinguishing their culture, taking their land, teaching Chinese patriotism, and allowing them to produce goods for China's growing markets. Social control via extreme surveillance methods keeps China's citizenry in line. Removing faith, religion, and hope are essential to indoctrination and subjugation.

Karl Marx believed religion had no place in society. Thus, he famously stated, "Religion is the sigh of the oppressed creature, the heart of a heartless world, and the soul of soulless conditions. It is the opium of the people."[2] He believed that a state could be transformed through Socialism.[3] China relies, in part, on Marxist theory. However, the world denounces China's level of religious intolerance whereby citizens are ordered to be "unyielding Marxist Atheists" if they want to be accepted as a patriot, offered well-paying positions, or members of the Chinese Communist Party.

However, not everyone in the world desires to live in these extreme versions of Socialism and social control, continually feeding off Marx-infused 'opium'. As China reshapes the world in its image, it is essential to remember what that vision means. It means a draconian social credit system that forces all free expressions into socially-acceptable Group Think. For many, it means fear, repression, uncertainty, and the threat of constant surveillance.

Imprisonment is not an outcome for just the Uyghurs, Tibetan Buddhists, or people of other religions. Anyone who speaks out against the CCP has reason to worry, like booksellers, Falun Gong practitioners, and VPN users. There is essentially no freedom of speech or freedom of thought since the control of ideas is pumped through propaganda and excised out of social media. The Great Firewall also falsely 'protects' Chinese citizens. If other states do not want to succumb to this fate, they should heed the warning.

The United States' regional security commitments must be sacrosanct. Irrespective of presidential administrations, the U.S. must keep promises with treaty allies designed to protect states from China's takeover. If not, history affirms that the U.S. loses respect, abolishes trust, and risks irrelevance. Beijing's economic coercion, subtly driven home on a country-by-country basis, has proven to be extremely effective. Thus, China's 'carrot and stick' dual approach offers both appeasement and intimidation. China's buildup of reinforcements in the South China Sea, East China Sea, and the Line of Actual Control bordering India strengthen China's perception as a powerhouse and encourages China's investment into regional states. Through nationalism, socialism, propaganda, and Wolf Warrior Diplomacy, Beijing rallies its people in a fight to regain its global supremacy. New border walls with Vietnam and Myanmar add another nail to the coffin of those in China who seek to leave Beijing's tightening grip.

---

2   Joseph Cronin, "Still an Opium? Contemporary Marxists Versus Karl Marx on the Question of Religion," *The London School of Economics and Political Science*, May 14, 2018, https://blogs.lse.ac.uk/religionglobalsociety/2018/05/still-an-opium-contemporary-marxists-versus-karl-marx-on-the-question-of-religion/

3   Bertell Ollman, "Marx's Vision of Communism," *Dielectical Marxism*, n.d., https://www.nyu.edu/projects/ollman/docs/vision_of_communism.php

Beijing's approach is effectively nibbling away around the edges by salami slicing. Nibble by nibble, China's boundaries are being pushed out as it annexes territory and water, declaring that part of Asia is its 'historic right'. How much China will purchase, co-opt, or take over is yet to be seen, but its efforts have been successful thus far. Furthermore, China is effectively testing and pushing the U.S. to move past the first island chain, beyond the Philippines and Japan, with the hopes of increasing that distance to the second island chain out into the Pacific Ocean.

China's periphery is expanding slice by slice with its growing strategic interests. With an increasing power base, bolstered by financial control worldwide, China's ambitious vision of "globalization" takes on new meaning. China is expanding into international diplomatic channels with the help of its 'friends'. These coercive efforts offer corresponding influence in United Nations' institutions and thereby change the balance of power. China's ascendency is less than a decade away from surpassing the United States on all levels. Beijing's investment into technology, military, and economic development is unlikely to slow as China continues to be the world's chief manufacturer, particularly with the retraining of millions to mass-manufacturing, mining, forestry, and other globally marketable products and services.

Taking control of land, water, sky, and space, China is rapidly expanding its reach in a power grab that encircles the globe. Xi Jinping is determined to reshape the world and fulfill its vision of 'rejuvenation'. Since political leaders worldwide have been enticingly lured with Beijing's financial enticements, the slow march toward domination is climbing upward toward a totalitarian apex.

A buzzing of excitement is growing among the Chinese people. Yet, this moment is a terrifying wake-up call for everyone else. As the new world order is slowly being realized, an 'out-of-sight, out-of-mind' mentality is no longer feasible. The alarm clock has been placed on snooze for years. The time is now to open our eyes and wake up to this new red dawn and act before the sun sets, and there are no longer any good options.

Earlier in this book, we posed the idea that if freedom is a value the West still holds, then this rising world order is problematic. With enough context, perspective, and information, we hope that you consider the hopes and dreams of your future in this new world order and the values you want to define for the next generation. Your children and grandchildren will face pressures unlike anything imaginable as freedoms are stripped away one-by-one, and individuals in democratic countries are placed under house arrest.

This book puts into perspective a world where surveillance, scrutiny, and imprisonment challenge the virtues of freedom often taken for granted. Without action steps now, the loss of freedom will be a fait accompli. If you treasure freedom, we hope you spread the word about this book, take a stand, and support freedom everywhere.

As you remember those who are imprisoned today in China's concentration camps, reflect on Martin Luther King, Jr.'s unforgettable statement, "Injustice anywhere is a threat to justice everywhere."

Index

Symbols

5G viii, xii, 27, 43, 50, 51, 52, 53, 54, 55, 57, 65, 71, 325
99-Year Lease 143, 263

A

Rushan Abbas 126
Abbasid Dynasty 112
Afghanistan 16, 122, 318, 319
Africa 24, 26, 31, 54, 109, 145, 272
Agrarian 3, 83
Air Defense Identification Zone (ADIZ) 165, 165, 207, 207, 209, 209, 214, 214, 221, 221
Aksai Chin 242, 245, 247, 261, 262
Hami Aksoy 134, 135
Alibaba 29, 60
Apple 21, 64, 65, 124, 157, 162
Apple Daily 157, 162
Arabian Empire 112
Arunchal-Pradesh 243
Aung San Suu Kyi 283
Australia xii, xiii, 11, 26, 31, 33, 45, 115, 117, 133, 207, 242, 270

B

Bangladesh x, 109, 223, 251, 257, 265, 271, 272, 278, 279, 280, 281, 282, 284
Belt and Road Initiative (BRI) 122, 277, 288, 291, 303, 313, 315, 317, 318
Bhutan x, 26, 42, 43, 46, 100, 239, 242, 244, 251, 256, 264, 265, 266, 267, 329
Big Brother 53, 55
Bitter Winter 85, 86, 95, 103, 125, 309
Black Sheep 99
BMW 124
Bogd Khanate 297
Book Burnings 147

Brahmaputra River 251, 255, 256, 257, 271

Sergey Brin 53

Britain xii, 35, 53, 95, 133, 142, 143, 147, 152, 156, 164, 184, 244

British Airways 38

Brunei xii, 26, 45, 207

Buddhism 85, 87, 270

Buddhist 75, 77, 85, 87, 91, 92, 269, 270, 273, 305

C

Cambodia x, xii, 207, 251, 277, 286, 287, 288, 289, 292

Canton 141, 142

Cantonese ix, 156, 168, 169, 170, 171, 172

Cao Kefan 20

Catholicism 87

Catholics 83

Causeway Bay Books 148

CCTV 12, 25, 57, 67, 92

Central Tibetan Administration 269, 270

Cheng Lei 163

Chen Quanguo 61, 121, 122, 132, 330

Chen Yixin 100

Chiang Ching-kuo 178, 179, 180

Chiang Kai-shek 170, 171, 177, 178, 179, 180, 183, 184, 186, 195, 196, 305

China-Mongolia Russia Economic Corridor (CMREC) 303, 304

China-Pakistan Economic Corridor (CPEC) xiii, 259, 260

Chinese Communist Party (CCP) vii, 11, 29, 31, 67, 75, 80, 84, 107, 147, 149, 161, 271, 301

Chinggis Bonds 302

Chinggis (Genghis) Khan 295

Agnes Chow 156, 158, 159

Christian Dior 36

Christianity 83, 86

Church 79, 85, 87

Chushul 242

Citizen Lab 64

Coach 36, 37

Cold War 227, 233

Communist Manifesto 100

Concentration Camps ix, 107, 113, 120, 123, 129

Confucian 53, 77, 114, 171, 178

Corruption vii, 29, 30, 31, 33, 71, 142

COVID-19 x, xiii, 16, 17, 20, 26, 46, 57, 60, 139, 158, 180, 197, 203, 204, 230, 231, 235, 240, 245, 269, 279, 315, 321

Ted Cruz 132

Cultural Revolution 7, 80, 83, 115, 171, 179, 227, 228, 231, 288, 309

Customs and Border Protection xiii, 119, 127

D

Dalai Lama 77, 147, 242, 271, 274, 305, 306

Daoist 77

Delta 38

Democratic Progressive Party (DPP) 184, 189

Deng Xiaoping 179

Development Program xvi, 265

Diaoyu Islands x, 208, 212

Doklam Standoff 244

E

East China Sea x, 46, 100, 177, 192, 195, 207, 208, 209, 212, 214, 218, 219, 221, 222, 223, 224, 233, 296, 329, 330

Emirates Airline 38

Ericsson 51, 54

Extradition Bill ix, 146, 149, 151, 152

F

Facebook 37, 59, 63, 163, 289

Falun Gong ix, 65, 75, 77, 78, 90, 91, 92, 93, 94, 95, 96, 147, 330

Haze Fan 162, 163

Fang Fenhui 31

First Island Chain 331

First Opium War 142, 143

Fisheries 214, 217

Five Demands 151

Five Eyes Alliance xiii

Foreign Direct Investment (FDI) 23, 281

Formosa 177, 183, 191, 212, 213

Fortune 500 viii, 34, 191

Foxes viii, 28, 31, 32

Fox Hunt 31, 33

Patrick French 271, 273

G

Ganges River 252, 255

Gap 8, 124

Genghis Khan 295, 296, 298, 302

Geng Shuang 256, 262

Germany 4, 5, 6, 51, 57, 124, 133, 315

GitHub 64

Gobi Desert 301

Google vi, 53, 59, 63, 64, 163

Great Britain xii, 35, 95, 143

Great Cannon viii, 62, 63, 64, 65

GreatFire 64, 65

Great Firewall viii, 19, 20, 59, 62, 63, 64, 65, 330

Great Leap Forward 83

Guangzhou 112, 141, 142

H

Haishenwai 323, 324

Hakka 169, 170, 178

Halal 85, 128

Han Chinese 113, 114, 115, 117, 118, 123, 126, 169, 178, 183, 297, 298, 304, 305, 310

Himalayas 43, 239, 249, 255, 271, 272, 329

Hong Kong ix, xii, 6, 15, 16, 19, 26, 32, 33, 36, 38, 39, 41, 46, 63, 65, 70, 78, 102, 139, 140, 141, 142, 143, 144, 145, 146, 147, 148, 149, 150, 151, 152, 154, 155, 156, 157, 158, 159, 160, 161, 162, 163, 164, 165, 166, 167, 169, 170, 171, 172, 175, 181, 186, 191, 192, 198, 204, 329

Mofazzal Hossain 257

Hua Chunying 16, 19, 132, 245

Huawei 43, 52, 53, 54, 55, 124

Hui 112, 113, 114, 191, 303

Human Rights ix, 29, 30, 79, 109, 115, 124, 130, 131, 132, 133, 134, 135, 161, 167, 270, 310

Human Rights Watch 29, 30

Hungarian Communist Party 24

Hun Sen 288

Hydrological Data x, 248, 254, 255, 256, 257

I

India x, xii, 3, 14, 16, 20, 26, 31, 42, 43, 44, 46, 60, 100, 122, 207, 223, 239, 241, 242, 243, 244, 245, 246, 247, 251, 252, 254, 255, 256, 257, 259, 260, 261, 262, 263, 265, 266, 267, 271, 272, 279, 280, 281, 282, 283, 284, 320, 329, 330

Inner Mongolia x, xi, 46, 85, 294, 296, 297, 298, 303, 304, 305, 308, 309, 310, 311

Instagram 36

Intellectual Property ii, 5, 6, 8, 39, 65

International Court of Justice xiv, 26, 45

International Monetary Fund (IMF) 260, 291, 301

Internment Camps ix, 120, 125, 126

Islam 84, 85, 87, 111, 112, 113, 114, 115, 117, 119, 123, 124, 134, 257, 281

Islamophobia 84, 114, 117

J

Lebron James 38

Japan x, xii, xiii, xiv, 6, 26, 45, 46, 51, 133, 156, 178, 183, 184, 192, 207, 208, 209, 210, 211, 212, 213, 214, 217, 218, 219, 221, 222, 223, 235, 291, 329, 331

Japan-China Fisheries Agreement 214, 217

Japanese xiv, 45, 46, 156, 171, 177, 178, 183, 184, 192, 205, 207, 209, 210, 211, 212, 213, 214, 217, 218

Jiang Zemin 91, 93

K

Ashok K. Kantha 266

Kashmir 242, 259, 260, 261, 262, 263

Kathmandu 42

Kazakhstan xi, 117, 122, 277, 312, 313, 314, 315, 316, 317, 320, 321

Khmer Rouge 289

Kinmen Islands 196

Korean War 195, 221, 227, 233

Kowtow viii, xiv, 34

KP Sharma Oli 279

Kublai Khan 295, 296

Kukuei Tanaka 209

Raveesh Kumar 256

Kuomintang (KMT) 184

Kyrgyzstan xi, 122, 277, 312, 313, 316, 317, 320, 321

L

Ladakh 44, 242, 243, 245, 246, 259, 261, 262, 263

Gabriel Lafitte 272

Jimmy Lai 156, 157, 158, 159, 162

Carrie Lam 149, 150, 151, 152, 163, 167, 169, 171

Ivan Lam 156, 159

Laos x, xii, 207, 251, 277, 286, 287, 289, 290, 291, 292

Nathan Law 166

Leng Feng 12, 13, 14

Liberalism 6

Li Heping 167

Li Hongzhi 91, 92, 95

Line of Actual Control (LAC) 43, 245, 246, 259

Li Qiang 30

Little Red Book 83

Li Xiaosi 17

Lu Shaye 17

M

Made in China 2025 xv, 7

Maglev xiv, 5

Rukiya Maimati 121

Mandarin ix, 24, 107, 118, 168, 169, 170, 171, 172, 183, 281, 309, 310, 311, 329

Mao Zedong 7, 80, 83, 86, 102, 115, 171, 177, 179, 196, 242

Marriott 36

Martin Luther King, Jr. 49, 326, 331

Matsu Islands 195, 196

Ma Ying-jeou 180, 184

McMahon Line 43, 241, 242

Medtronic 37

Mekong River 251, 289

Memorandum of Understanding xv

Michael McFaul 78

Middle Kingdom 35

Minegolia 301

Ming Dynasty 35, 112, 113, 178, 212, 296, 297

Steven T. Mnuchin 132

Narendra Modi 267

Mongol 295, 296, 297, 311

Mongolia x, xi, xiii, 26, 46, 85, 294, 295, 296, 297, 298, 300, 301, 302, 303, 304, 305, 306, 308, 309, 310, 311, 329

Muhammad 54, 112

Muslim ix, 16, 60, 61, 77, 84, 85, 87, 107, 110, 111, 112, 114, 115, 117, 119, 121, 123, 124, 125, 130, 133, 134, 135, 136

Myanmar x, xii, 207, 251, 278, 279, 282, 283, 284, 330

N

Naga District Court 217

National Security Law ix, 41, 139, 144, 145, 147, 151, 152, 154, 155, 156, 157, 158, 161, 164, 167, 175, 181, 204

NBA xv, 38, 39

Nepal x, 42, 43, 46, 100, 239, 249, 251, 271, 277, 278, 279, 280, 281, 284, 329

Nepalese 42, 43, 242, 280, 281

Martin Niemoller 136

Nike 124

Ningxia 85

Nokia 54

North Korea x, 207, 223, 226, 227, 228, 229, 230, 231, 233, 234, 235, 236

O

Okinawa Reversion Agreement 210, 211

Shaquille "Shaq" O'Neal 39

"One China" policy 190–193

One Country, Two Systems 189

Organ Harvesting 77

Ottoman Empire 79

Outer Mongolia x, xi, 294, 300, 304, 305, 309, 311

P

Pakistan x, xiii, 17, 122, 134, 223, 239, 258, 259, 260, 261, 262, 263, 272, 277, 318

Pandemic viii, 60, 62, 218, 235, 315, 321

Paracel Islands xv, 44

People's Liberation Army Air Force (PLAAF) 222, 224

People's Liberation Army Navy Air Force (PLANAF) xv

People's Liberation Army Navy (PLAN) 14

People's Liberation Army (PLA) 11, 13, 14, 45, 195, 201, 242

People's Republic of China (PRC) 7, 41, 114, 115, 177, 180, 192, 241, 287

Philippines xii, xiii, xiv, xv, xvi, 26, 44, 45, 109, 134, 170, 207, 221, 331

Philippines v. China xv, 26, 45

Phnom Penh 288, 289

Pinterest 65

Mike Pompeo 55, 95, 165

Matthew Pottinger 53

Premier Zhou Enlai 209, 288

Prime Minister Rajiv Gandhi 243

Prince Norodom Sihanouk 287

Propaganda 1, 8, 9, 11, 12, 18, 19, 20, 21, 25, 49, 63, 65, 68, 71, 78, 125, 128, 159, 189, 193, 227, 298, 330

Q

Qantas 38
Qigong 91, 92, 95
Qingdao 49
Qing dynasty 114, 141, 183, 212, 213, 244, 297, 323
Qi Yu 17
Quemoy Islands 196
Qun Jue 91

R

Radio Free Asia 19, 126, 133, 230, 270, 271, 272, 273, 283, 288, 310
Raging Waters vii, 44, 46, 198
Recep Tayyip Erdogan 135
Reddit 65
Religious Persecution 79, 80, 136
Ren Zhiqiang 29
Republic of China xiii, 7, 14, 41, 45, 95, 99, 102, 103, 114, 115, 124, 141, 148, 155, 177, 178, 180, 183, 184, 189, 190, 192, 201, 211, 212, 224, 241, 243, 245, 246, 256, 270, 273, 287, 297, 298
Susan Rice 16, 17
Marco Rubio 132
Rule of law 100
Russia xiii, 6, 78, 122, 223, 224, 234, 236, 301, 303, 304, 313, 315, 316, 317, 319, 323, 324, 325, 329

S

Saad ibn Abi Waqaas 112
Sakteng Wildlife Sanctuary x, 43, 264, 265, 266
Salami Slicing viii, xvi, 22, 23, 26, 145, 219
San Francisco Peace Treaty 209, 210
Scarborough Shoal 44
Second Opium War 143, 323
Self-Immolation 269
Senkaku Islands x, 45, 46, 209, 210, 211, 212, 213, 214, 216, 217, 218, 219, 221
Shen Shiwei 324

Norodom Sihanouk 287

Silicon Valley 64

Simla Accord 43

Sinitic 169

Sino-Indian War 242, 247

Social Credit 8, 9, 49, 53, 55, 59, 61, 67, 69, 71, 72, 330

Song Dynasty 295, 297

Sony 124

George Soros 53, 55

South China Sea vii, xiii, xv, xvi, 25, 26, 27, 44, 45, 46, 100, 141, 145, 177, 191, 195, 207, 214, 219, 221, 291, 329, 330

South Korea xii, 162, 207, 221, 223, 224, 229, 231, 233, 234, 235, 236

Special Administrative Region (SAR) 143

Spoiling Tibet 272

Joseph Stalin 114, 304, 305

State-Owned Enterprises (SOE) 60

Sunflower Movement 185

Surveillance 8, 27, 53, 54, 55, 57, 59, 60, 67, 69, 71, 88, 117, 122, 128, 139, 145, 205, 209, 239, 271, 273, 311, 320, 329, 330, 331

Swarovski 37

T

Taiwan ix, x, xv, 32, 33, 36, 37, 38, 39, 41, 45, 46, 70, 128, 145, 148, 149, 164, 165, 167, 169, 170, 171, 172, 175, 176, 177, 178, 179, 180, 181, 182, 183, 184, 185, 186, 188, 189, 190, 191, 192, 193, 194, 195, 196, 197, 198, 199, 200, 201, 202, 203, 204, 205, 209, 211, 212, 213, 214, 218, 219, 221, 223, 224, 273, 329

Taiwanese ix, x, xiv, 38, 165, 168, 169, 170, 171, 172, 175, 179, 180, 181, 183, 184, 185, 186, 189, 191, 192, 193, 194, 197, 201, 202, 203, 204, 211, 218

Taiwan Relations Act 180, 201, 202, 205, 221

Taiwan Strait Crisis 195, 196, 197, 199

Tajikistan xi, 134, 277, 312, 313, 318, 319, 320, 321

Kukuei Tanaka 209

Tao 91

Tenggeri 295

THAAD xvi, 234, 235

Thailand x, xii, 31, 148, 207, 251, 277, 286, 287, 290, 291, 292

Margaret Thatcher 53, 143

Thousand Talents Program 5

Tiananmen Square Massacre 144, 147

Tibet 26, 33, 36, 37, 43, 46, 61, 69, 102, 121, 122, 132, 147, 191, 239, 241, 242, 249, 251, 257, 261, 269, 270, 271, 272, 273, 274, 311, 320, 329, 330

Tibetan Monks 75, 79, 269

Tibet, Tibet 271, 273

Tigers and Flies viii, 28, 30

TikTok 39, 60

Treaty of Nanjing xiii, 142

Treaty of Shimonoseki 183, 212, 213

Trigger Warning ix, 108, 109

Donald Trump 199, 202, 229, 273

Tsai Ing-wen 41, 175, 184, 186, 189, 190, 192, 193, 197, 198, 202, 203, 223

Turkestan 107, 296

Turkey 134, 135, 315

Twitter viii, xvi, 10, 12, 15, 16, 17, 18, 19, 20, 21, 43, 53, 55, 59, 63, 132, 163, 165, 229

Twitter Fingers 15, 229

U

UIGHUR Act 131, 132

Uighurs 78, 79, 107, 111, 114, 115, 132, 133, 134, 135

Umbrella Movement 157

UNCLOS xiii, xv, xvi, 26, 45, 224

UNESCO 25

United Nations vii, xiii, xvi, 15, 16, 23, 26, 44, 45, 79, 109, 127, 134, 143, 179, 180, 210, 212, 224, 230, 250, 257, 265, 331

United Nations Development Program (UNDP) 265

United States xiii, xvi, 4, 7, 17, 20, 33, 43, 46, 51, 52, 54, 57, 77, 109, 115, 127, 131, 132, 175, 180, 181, 184, 192, 196, 201, 203, 204, 209, 210, 211, 219, 221, 223, 227, 228, 229, 236, 251, 260, 263, 281, 282, 287, 288, 289, 291, 304, 330, 331

Urumqi 60, 84, 117, 122

U.S. Customs and Border Protection (CBP) 127

U.S. Immigration and Customs Enforcement (ICE) 109

Uyghur ix, xvii, 60, 61, 79, 84, 107, 111, 112, 114, 115, 116, 117, 118, 119, 120, 121, 122,

123, 124, 125, 126, 127, 131, 132, 133, 134, 136, 295, 320, 330

Uyghur Massacre ix, 116, 117

V

Donatella Versace 36

Vietnam xii, xiv, xv, 25, 26, 44, 45, 109, 149, 207, 251, 256, 266, 283, 330

Virtual Private Network (VPN) 19

Vladivostok 323, 324, 325

Volkswagen 124

W

Tashi Wangchuk 273

Wang Yi 15, 244, 245, 259, 305

Wang Yu-min 185

David A. Waugh iv

WeChat 60

Weibo 60, 324

WhatsApp 59, 163

Wolf Warrior 1, 11, 16

Wolf Warrior 2 12, 14, 15

Joshua Wong 156, 159, 166

World Bank 3, 7, 265, 302, 303, 318

World Economic Forum 53

World Wide Fund for Nature xvii, 250

World Wildlife Fund xvii, 250

Christopher Wray 32, 33

X

Xi Jinping 1, 9, 11, 14, 15, 17, 20, 30, 31, 33, 35, 36, 41, 42, 53, 61, 63, 71, 75, 77, 78, 79, 80, 83, 85, 86, 87, 88, 99, 100, 102, 103, 104, 107, 111, 122, 125, 136, 144, 155, 166, 193, 198, 203, 207, 233, 259, 260, 282, 283, 325, 331

Xinjiang Province ix, 33, 60, 65, 69, 75, 77, 84, 85, 107, 110, 114, 118, 119, 121, 122, 124, 125, 127, 131, 132, 136, 139, 260, 261, 272, 277, 311, 314, 329

XUAR xvii, 111, 123, 330

Xu Zhiyong 29, 30

Y

Yangtze River 271
Yuan Dynasty 112, 169, 296, 297

Z

Shohrat Zakir 121
Zha Liyou 16
Zhang Yan 31
Zhan Qixiong 217
Zhao Lijian 11, 16, 273, 274
Zhongnanhai government 93
Zhou Enlai 209, 288
Zhu Yuanzhang 297
ZTE xvii, 52